Reconsidering
**Mississippian
Communities** and
**Households**

Archaeology of the American South: New Directions and Perspectives

# Reconsidering
# **Mississippian**
# **Communities** and
# **Households**

Edited by
**Elizabeth Watts Malouchos**
and **Alleen Betzenhauser**

Foreword by **Gregory D. Wilson**

The University of Alabama Press
Tuscaloosa

The University of Alabama Press
Tuscaloosa, Alabama 35487-0380
uapress.ua.edu

A Dan Josselyn Memorial Publication

Typeface: Minion and Helvetica Neue

Cover image: Mississippian community plan at the Pfeffer site; rendering by
Elizabeth Watts Malouchos, with data courtesy of the Illinois State Archaeological
Survey
Cover design: Lori Lynch

Cataloging-in-Publication data is available from the Library of Congress.
ISBN: 978-0-8173-2088-1
E-ISBN: 978-0-8173-9346-5

# CONTENTS

List of Illustrations                                                          vii

Foreword
     Gregory D. Wilson                                                         ix

Acknowledgments                                                               xi

Introduction
     Elizabeth Watts Malouchos and Alleen Betzenhauser                        1

## Part I. Articulating Communities and Households

1  Reconsidering Mississippian Communities and Households in Context
   Elizabeth Watts Malouchos                                                  9

2  Making Mounds, Making Mississippian Communities in
   Southern Illinois
   Tamira K. Brennan                                                          32

3  The Battle Mound Community: Interaction along the Red River and
   throughout the Caddo Homeland
   Duncan P. McKinnon                                                         50

4  Negotiating Community at Parchman Place, a Mississippian Town in
   the Northern Yazoo Basin
   Erin S. Nelson                                                             63

5  Mississippian Communities and Households from a Bird's-Eye View
   Benjamin A. Steere                                                         81

## Part II. Coalescing and Conflicting Communities

6  Variability within a Mississippian Community: Houses, Cemeteries,
   and Corporate Groups at the Town Creek Site in the North Carolina
   Piedmont
   Edmond A. Boudreaux III, Paige A. Ford, and Heidi A. de Gregory           101

7  Mississippian Communities of Conflict
   Meghan E. Buchanan and Melissa R. Baltus                                  120

## Part III. Community and Cosmos

8 Households, Communities, and the Early History of Etowah
  Adam King                                                        135

9 Unpacking Storage: Implications for Community-Making
  during Cahokia's Mississippian Transition
  Elizabeth Watts Malouchos and Alleen Betzenhauser               146

10 The Social Lives and Symbolism of Cherokee Houses and
  Townhouses
  Christopher B. Rodning and Amber R. Thorpe                      164

## Part IV. Movement, Memory, and Histories

11 Moving to Where the River Meets the Sea: Origins of the Mill
  Cove Complex
  Keith Ashley                                                    179

12 Resilience in Late Moundville's Economy
  Jera R. Davis                                                   197

13 Multiscalar Community Histories in the Lower Chattahoochee
  River Valley: Migration and Aggregation at Singer-Moye
  Stefan Brannan and Jennifer Birch                              213

Commentary
The Archaeology of Mississippian Communities and Households:
Looking Back, Looking Forward
  Jason Yaeger                                                    227

References Cited                                                  241

List of Contributors                                             309

Index                                                            313

# ILLUSTRATIONS

Figures

I.1. Mapping a Mississippian structure at the Pfeffer site, 2008 · 2

2.1. Regional map of southern Illinois, showing the locations of Greater Cahokia and the Kincaid site · 33

2.2. Plan map of the East St. Louis Precinct · 37

2.3. Early Lohmann single-set post structures overprinting a late Terminal Late Woodland II courtyard group · 38

2.4. Dense special-use architecture in the Exchange Avenue corridor of the New Mississippi River Bridge Project · 40

2.5. Plan map of the Kincaid Mound center · 41

3.1. Caddo archaeological area and the Trans-Mississippi South · 51

3.2. Distribution of sites within the Battle community · 54

3.3. Distribution of rayed circle · 58

3.4. Distribution of zoomorphic pendants · 60

4.1. Northern Yazoo Basin with locations of Parchman Place and nearby sites · 67

4.2. Magnetic gradiometry results from Parchman Place · 68

4.3. Topographic contour map of Parchman Place · 69

4.4. Ash heap in Neighborhood 1 excavation trench at Parchman Place · 71

4.5. White veneer on summit at Mound E, Parchman Place · 73

5.1. Map of Mississippian period sites · 84

5.2. Model of household clusters for each chronological period · 87

5.3. Bar chart of average and median floor area for domestic structures · 89

6.1. Selected architectural elements at Town Creek · 104

6.2. Histogram of completely excavated circular houses by size · 107

6.3. Clusters of burials in Structures 1, 2, and 7 at Town Creek · 114

7.1. Proportions of serving, cooking, and special-use vessels at Olin, Common Field, and Cahokia · 125

8.1. Plan map of the Etowah site · 136

8.2. Gradiometer map of Etowah neighborhood · 139

8.3. Etowah complicated stamped motifs · 141

9.1. Changing community at Downtown Cahokia · 152

9.2. Percentage of total pits that are inside structures and that have rectangular plan shapes · 155

9.3. Changing community layout at the Range site 157
10.1. Cherokee town areas and the Coweeta Creek site 164
10.2. Settlement layout at the Coweeta Creek site 165
10.3. Sequence of townhouses at Coweeta Creek 173
10.4. Selected domestic structures and sequences at Coweeta Creek 174
11.1. Location of Mill Cove Complex and early Mississippian world 180
11.2. Mill Cove Complex and Mount Royal 183
11.3. Select Colorinda and St. Johns II sites along lower St. Johns River 185
12.1. Black Warrior River Valley with locations of sites mentioned in
     the text 198
12.2. Examples of craft objects and tools recovered from the Pride
     Place, Fitts, and Powers sites 204
12.3. Pride Place site map 205
12.4. Fitts site map 206
12.5. Powers site map 207
13.1. The Lower Chattahoochee River Valley and local sites 215
13.2. Singer-Moye site plan, circa AD 1100–1300 217
13.3. Singer-Moye site plan, circa AD 1300–1400 219
13.4. Singer-Moye site plan, circa AD 1400–1500 224
13.5. Mound summit architecture at Singer-Moye and Rood's Landing 225

## Tables

5.1. List of archaeological sites recorded in the database 85
6.1. Size and rebuilding data for excavated domestic-area structures 107
6.2. Artifacts associated with burials by structure 110
6.3. Burials by gender in excavated, domestic-area structures 113
9.1. Comparative data for Terminal Late Woodland and Early
     Mississippian occupations at Cahokia and Range 153
11.1. Comparison of middle and lower St. Johns region chronologies
     after AD 500 184
12.1. Mississippian phases and sequences for the Black Warrior
     River Valley 198
12.2. Counts, abundance measures, and pooled values for Moundville
     contexts 209

# FOREWORD

Gregory D. Wilson

The authors who have contributed chapters to this book are among the best Mississippian archaeologists of their generation. In returning to the subject matter of the popular 1995 volume *Mississippian Communities and Households*, these scholars have provided us with a collection of compelling, detail-oriented studies informed by contemporary social theory that will be of great interest to archaeologists working elsewhere in the world.

I have engaged in the archaeology of households and communities for most of my scholarly career, and it is heartening to see a new volume on this topic. My interest in this subject stems from an archaeological research background in and around the American Bottom, the region that witnessed the rise and fall of Cahokia, the largest and most complex of all Mississippian societies. Numerous large-scale excavations in and around the Saint Louis metropolitan area have generated some of the world's largest and most detailed regional datasets on residential social and spatial contexts. The availability of such impressive datasets makes it possible to investigate the details of everyday life in a subtle and temporally fine-grained manner.

Many prominent investigations at Cahokia and other associated Mississippian sites have been informed by the processual-era household archaeology of the 1960s and 1970s, a rigorous and often comparative analytical approach that focused on the seemingly mundane aspects of spatial, architectural, and artifactual data to make inferences about group size, occupation span, mobility, mode of abandonment, and status and wealth, among others. Emerging from such investigations has been a nuanced understanding that Cahokia consisted of many different residential precincts and civic/ceremonial cores that were inhabited by a complex assortment of local and immigrant groups. By carefully documenting how these diverse groups constructed and dwelled in thatch-and-pole houses and crafted, used, and disposed of pottery, stone tools, and foodstuffs, archaeologists have been able to shed light on the array of sociopolitical, religious, and economic negotiations that contributed to Cahokia's consolidation and collapse.

The scholars in this volume successfully employ the rigorous analytical techniques of processual-era household archaeology to investigate contemporary theoretical issues related to identity politics, religion, and social memory. In doing so, they elucidate dynamic regional histories of transformation that overturn older theoretical assumptions about organizational redundancy and continuity. There also appears to be an emerging appreciation, if not an outright expectation, that organizational variability defined Mississippian societies and that the best way of investigating their histories is through the detailed analysis of large and diverse datasets.

Most of the authors have also adopted the historical processual investigative procedure of tacking back and forth between different social and spatial scales. This technique has proven to be particularly important for understanding how the connections among individuals, places, objects, times, and even cosmological forces generated the broader social entities archaeologists conceive of as communities. Indeed, relationality and the generative intersectionality of different social and spatial scales are prominent themes running through many of the volume's chapters. Taken as a whole, this volume compellingly demonstrates that Mississippian communities were not stable and enduring social entities. They also were not necessarily always well integrated or comprising culturally and organizationally homogeneous residential groups. When and where unity and uniformity did exist, they were often fleeting states and appear to have been the outcome of frequent and multifaceted interactions among people, places, and things. Indeed, many of the volume's authors emphasize the concept of materiality in their studies, and earthen mounds, temples, domiciles, and cemeteries play key roles in their historical narratives of Mississippian community construction.

I predict that this scholarship will have an important positive impact on the way in which archaeologists conceive of scale, relationality, and causality in the contexts of Mississippian social organization.

# ACKNOWLEDGMENTS

We would like to acknowledge the contributors to *Mississippian Communities and Households*, and in particular the editors, J. Daniel Rogers and Bruce D. Smith, for their rigorous research that laid the foundation for the present volume. Special thanks go to J. Daniel Rogers who kindly agreed to be interviewed and shared his retrospective thoughts. We are also indebted to the scholars and colleagues who participated in the symposium organized for the 81st Annual Meeting of the Society for American Archaeology and shared their original research, most of whom are also contributors to this volume, including Jason Yaeger who served as the discussant for the symposium and contributed a commentary here. Gregory D. Wilson graciously provided the foreword. We were inspired by work we conducted through the Illinois State Archaeological Survey. We also thank the two anonymous reviewers and the editors at the University of Alabama Press for their insightful comments that strengthened this work. Finally, we extend our gratitude to our family and friends (especially CABB) who supported us throughout this process. All royalties from this volume will be donated to the Society for American Archaeology's Native American Scholarships Fund.

# INTRODUCTION

Elizabeth Watts Malouchos and Alleen Betzenhauser

*It is fundamentally more interesting and more informative to start as close to the ground as you can get . . . it's still all about the house.*

—J. Daniel Rogers (personal communication)

You're an archaeologist?!" people say with wonder in their eyes. Every professional archaeologist knows what question is coming next: "What is the coolest thing you've ever found?" It is usually about ten seconds later that the excitement fades and eyes start to glaze over, as we drone on about how the coolest "things" we have ever found were soil stains, the remnants of centuries-old buildings that were constructed by the peoples we now associate with the Mississippian culture (c. AD 1000–1600). These ephemeral remains of ancient structures have left a deep impression on us.

In summer 2008, we were working for what is now the Illinois State Archaeological Survey's American Bottom Field Station at the Pfeffer site, a Mississippian mound site in the uplands east of the American Bottom in southwestern Illinois (Figure I.1). Together, we excavated an atypical Mississippian residence. Its architectural biography was indeed extraordinary. Prior to construction of the building, a large marker post was emplaced and then removed. Next, the special T-shaped wall-trench structure was built with a hearth centered over where the post had been previously emplaced. After the house was abandoned, deconstructed, or decommissioned, another large marker post was placed as the last layer of the post and hearth palimpsest. The excavation of this structure was one of the first times we had a visceral understanding that these architectural elements were clearly more than the sum of their parts.

In a 2017 conversation, J. Daniel Rogers, coeditor of and contributor to *Mississippian Communities and Households* (Rogers and Smith 1995), sympathized with our fascination with architecture, whereby tangible traces of domestic architecture can still be located in the often abstract world of archaeology. Benjamin A. Steere (2017:1) captured this trowel's-edge sentiment when he wrote, "The map of an excavated post pattern can be read like an architect's map." The detectability of archi-

Figure I.1. Elizabeth Watts Malouchos (*left*), Jeff Kruchten (*center*), and Alleen Betzenhauser (*right*) map a Mississippian structure at the Pfeffer site, 2008. (Courtesy of the Illinois State Archaeological Survey, University of Illinois at Urbana-Champaign)

tectural remains of the structures in which families, kin groups, religious specialists, and other social groups dwelled makes household archaeology an attractive and intriguing point of analysis. However, as foundational household scholars Richard R. Wilk and William L. Rathje (1982) point out, finding the architecture of houses can be far more straightforward than interpreting what households *do*.

The 1995 publication of *Mississippian Communities and Households* brought household archaeology to the forefront of Mississippian studies and inspired a new generation of research on small-scale social dynamics, domestic space, and everyday contexts. The volume's publication was a watershed moment for archaeologists grappling with the complexities of Mississippian social organization. Despite Rogers's (1995a:2) apprehension that scaling down to the level of the household would leave archaeologists "hopelessly mired in our own data," the contributions tacked between providing a compendium of household data and exploring the broader contexts of regional models. With contributions spanning the Mississippian world, from Illinois to Florida, the case studies demonstrated the diversity of ways Mississippian societies were socially and spatially configured. That volume continues to inform how Mississippian archaeologists conceptualize Mississippian societies and social organizations (see Barrier and Horsley 2014; Lacquement 2007; O'Brien 2001; Steere 2017; for review see Pluckhahn 2010).

Rogers and Smith (1995) pinpointed their motivations for centering household research in *Mississippian Communities and Households* as taking the "next logical step" after the prior disciplinary focus on settlement systems. Following early household studies from Mesoamerica (see chapter 1 in this volume), researchers saw households as the most basic level of social organization, the foundational building blocks of chiefly society (Ashmore and Wilk 1988; Rogers 1995b; Wilk and Rathje 1982). Highlighting data, often from large-scale excavations, these studies provided important regional comparisons that refined extant models of social organization and culture change and positioned households as dynamic and interactional.

Thomas J. Pluckhahn (2010:336) notes that contributions to the original volume "generally displayed decidedly processualist orientations, with attendant functionalist, behavioralist, and evolutionary leanings." Indeed, despite the title, the volume did not explicitly address or theorize Mississippian social organization at the scale of community. Mississippian communities were considered only indirectly, "by extension" of the household (Rogers 1995b:10). Mississippian communities were synonymous with archaeological sites and the nucleation of residential structures and were understood through constituent household dynamics. Volume contributors operationalized communities as archaeological sites and settlements composed of aggregations of houses, pits, and people.

The "next logical step" for us was to revisit Mississippian households and move Mississippian communities to the center of the discussion. Just as Rogers and Smith's original volume took data and inspiration from large-scale cultural resource management projects in the American Bottom (e.g., FAI-270 [Bareis and Porter 1984] and ICT-II [Collins 1990]) and under the Tennessee Valley Authority, our volume was in part inspired by our experiences participating in large-scale transportation data recovery projects at some of the largest and most complex Mississippian sites in the American Bottom region (e.g., the New Mississippi River Bridge project [Emerson, Koldehoff, and Brennan 2018]; see chapter 2 in this volume). As we approached the twenty-fifth anniversary of the Rogers and Smith volume, our goal was to reevaluate the subjects of Mississippian households and communities to address advances in household archaeology, the archaeology of communities, and the myriad of more recently accumulated data. Also like the original volume, this project was born out of a session presented at the Society for American Archaeology (SAA) Annual Meeting. With the session, we aimed not only to revisit but to challenge notions of Mississippian households and communities that were set forth in or absent from the original volume. The SAA session brought together research spanning the Mississippian world; however, neither in the original session nor in this volume was it possible to achieve comprehensive geographic, temporal, and cultural coverage of Mississippian societies. Logistical limitations aside, the contributions to this volume provide a much-needed update on the theories, methods, and data that frame and inform our current understandings of the social dynamics of Mississippian societies (see chapter 1, this volume).

Building on the Rogers and Smith volume, the contributors here approach the concepts of community and households in Mississippian societies across both regional (northeastern Florida to southwestern Arkansas) and temporal (AD 900s to 1700s) scales. They present results from their original and rigorous research into aspects of community and household construction, maintenance, and dissolution. By tacking back and forth between daily domestic practices and the wider communal landscapes, contributors engage with households and communities as locations of daily social, political, economic, and religious negotiations. Although we encouraged the use of a lens of ontological alterity, wherein communities are dynamic multiscalar assemblages of persons, places, things, and powerful nonhuman actors (see chapter 9, following Harris 2014), we do not intend for our relational approach to be programmatic. Indeed, we believe that the diverse theoretical and methodological perspectives presented in the following chapters represent the multitude of productive approaches to the archaeological study of households and communities.

The volume is divided into four thematic parts, focused on particular aspects of Mississippian communities and households. Part 1, "Articulating Communities and Households," comprises five chapters that deal with how communities and households are connected from methodological, theoretical, and practical perspectives. These chapters examine the relationships between households and communities at multiple scales, importantly bridging gaps between scales of analysis. Elizabeth Watts Malouchos (chapter 1) provides a review of archaeological approaches to the investigation of households and communities and the ways in which they have been utilized in Mississippian research. Tamira K. Brennan (chapter 2) investigates how Mississippian communities at Cahokia and Kincaid in southern Illinois were created and altered as reflected in architectural diversity and the physical and social construction of space. Duncan P. McKinnon (chapter 3) describes his regional spatial analysis of the Caddo presence in the Red River Valley of southwestern Arkansas. Erin S. Nelson (chapter 4) approaches the construction of communities in the Yazoo Basin at multiple scales, paying particular attention to kinship ties. Benjamin A. Steere (chapter 5) compares Mississippian houses from throughout the Southeast and Midwest to investigate how changes in architecture are implicated in changing communities.

The two chapters in Part 2, "Coalescing and Conflicting Communities," explore both the integration and dissolution of communities and the ways in which communal identities and relationships are materially created, negotiated, and challenged within the contexts of socioeconomic instability and conflict and warfare. In chapter 6, Edmond A. Boudreaux III, Paige A. Ford, and Heidi A. de Gregory describe how multiple social groups came together and created and used communal spaces and household cemeteries at Town Creek in North Carolina. Meghan E. Buchanan and Melissa R. Baltus (chapter 7) compare the physical and embodied practices associated with the creation of community identities during times of heightened conflict in the American Bottom and parts of the Central Mississippi River Valley.

Part 3, "Community and Cosmos," focuses on the ways that households and communities were entangled with Mississippian cosmological practices and the recursive relationships between everyday lived experiences, the built landscape, and conceptions of the cosmos. The three chapters within provide insight into how cosmology is implicated in the creation of communities particularly in relation to the construction of space at multiple scales. Adam King (chapter 8) discusses how the physical aspects of community construction that reflect cosmological principles were variously mobilized after abandonment and through reoccupation of Etowah. Elizabeth Watts Malouchos and Alleen Betzenhauser (chapter 9) investigate how community relationships were altered with respect to changes in the physical and spatial creation and use of storage facilities in the American Bottom. In chapter 10, Christopher B. Rodning and Amber R. Thorpe focus on Cherokee townhouses in southern Appalachia and the ways in which community and household identities were entwined with cosmology through the maintenance of the sacred fire and use of shared spaces.

Part 4, "Movement, Memory, and Histories" addresses the roles that migrations of people, trade of objects, and movement of traditions have played in the interactions between disparate communities and consolidation of new communal identities. Keith Ashley (chapter 11) points to historical processes including the permanent relocation of people into northeastern Florida and periodic interaction through reinvigorated long-distance trade networks as part of a complex process that resulted in the creation of new communities. Jera R. Davis (chapter 12) provides an analysis of the production of certain material classes in the hinterlands of Moundville to investigate shifts in authority during its political decline. Finally, Stefan Brannan and Jennifer Birch (chapter 13) trace the movements of people and consider how these movements relate to the physical and social construction of communities. The volume concludes with insightful commentary and thoughts about future directions for the study of Mississippian communities and households from Jason Yaeger.

In *Mississippian Communities and Households*, J. Daniel Rogers (1995a:6) noted that a focus on households and communities cannot be an end in itself. While the studies herein highlight the divergent developmental histories of individual households and communities, they also emphasize how households and communities are inherently entangled in complex relationships of peoples, places, practices, and things, constitutive of broader-scale structures of society. Indeed, it is *still* all about the house.

# I

# ARTICULATING COMMUNITIES AND HOUSEHOLDS

# 1

# RECONSIDERING MISSISSIPPIAN COMMUNITIES AND HOUSEHOLDS IN CONTEXT

Elizabeth Watts Malouchos

In the quarter century since J. Daniel Rogers and Bruce D. Smith's (1995) *Mississippian Communities and Households* was published, the accumulation of new data and advancements in method and theory have pushed archaeologists to reconsider conventional understandings of Mississippian social organization. To contextualize the developments in Mississippian archaeology demonstrated by contributing chapters, this introduction offers a brief historical overview of household archaeology and the archaeology of communities and deeper discussions of attendant Mississippian studies. What follows is an extensive, but not exhaustive, literature review tailored for practitioners that traces the broader theoretical and methodological trajectories of households and communities and articulates Mississippian studies past and present. This chapter is organized into two major sections separately addressing household archaeology and the archaeology of communities, with subsections addressing prevalent themes in Mississippian research.

## HOUSEHOLD ARCHAEOLOGY
### The Household in Culture History and Processual Frameworks
Initially, houses and households were a subsidiary subject of anthropological inquiry and regarded as a byproduct of kinship. Explorations of the family and domestic group emphasized coresidence as integral to small-scale social reproduction (see Murdock 1949; Goody 1958). During this period, archaeologists undertook sweeping settlement surveys (e.g., Willey 1953) to identify different cultures and organized the archaeological record into territorial and chronological units. The incidental beginnings of Mississippian household studies are found in these renderings of culture history, which, in part, tracked the chronological and geographic distributions of different architectural styles. The recognition of pole-and-thatch and wattle-and-daub construction techniques as an architectural type—and the mapping of architectural patterns of structures—was central to defining and interpreting Mississippian sites (Griffin 1952; Lewis and Kneberg 1946).

The simple identification of social groups and architectural variability was not innately interesting; archaeologists became more interested in how these small social units could help explain changes in political and social systems (Kramer 1982). Scholars shifted to activity-based definitions, whereby households were "undeniably . . . about production, exchange, power, inequality, and status" (Yanagisako 1979:199; see also Ashmore and Wilk 1988; Kent 1984). For archaeologists, the architectural remains of house structures and debris from domestic activities were measurable. Kent V. Flannery (1976:16) pursued an explicit household-level analysis by identifying spatial patterns in household activities, and Marcus C. Winter (1976) delineated "household clusters" as the facilities and features part of the activities of the family. Contemporary Mississippian period studies were focused on monumental and elite contexts, creating a paucity of research concerning settlements at a scale smaller than the village (B. Smith 1978b, 1995). To address this gap, Bruce D. Smith (1978a) undertook excavations at the Gypsy Joint site in southeastern Missouri that focused on the analysis of artifact distributions to identify activity areas, seasonality and duration of occupation, and composition of occupants. Smith characterized Gypsy Joint as a "nuclear family homestead" and by doing so initiated house-level analysis emphasizing the social organization at the scale of the domestic group.

As processual theories became the dominant framework in archaeology and concerns shifted to universal models of environmental adaptation, the household became an important point of analysis. Household archaeology emerged as a distinct subfield through Mesoamerican archaeology (e.g., Flannery 1976; Hirth 1993a; see also Robin 2003) and cross-cultural ethnographic studies of domestic organization (Ashmore and Wilk 1988; Hammel 1980; Kent 1984; Kramer 1982; Netting et al. 1984; Rapoport 1969; Wilk 1988; Wilk and Rathje 1982; Yanagisako 1979). Foundational studies positioned the household as the most basic unit of "consumption, production, distribution, transmission, reproduction, and coresidence in human society" (Wilk and Netting 1984:2). Households were considered to be the "building block" of larger-scale social formations, "sensitive indicators of evolutionary change in social organization" (Ashmore and Wilk 1988:1; see also Hirth 1993a). The access to finer resolution allowed for larger-scale interpretations of social organization and culture change and complemented predominant macroscale top-down approaches.

## The New Archaeology of Mississippian Households

Mississippian studies soon followed suit, and production, consumption, and domestic economies emerged as popular themes throughout the 1980s and 1990s (see Pluckhahn 2010; Steere 2017). Studies primarily focused on domestic ceramic assemblages (Hally 1983; Pauketat 1987; Shapiro 1984) and the relationship between Cahokia's complexity, craft specialization, and the microlith tool industry in the wider American Bottom (Milner 1990; Muller 1984, 1997; Pauketat 1987, 1997; Prentice 1983, 1985; Trubitt 1996; Yerkes 1983, 1989). Not entirely or explicitly focused on households, the debates surrounding Cahokia's political economy implicated the household and domestic activities in larger socioeconomic systems (see also Welch 1991; Blitz 1993).

Lynne P. Sullivan (1986, 1987, 1995) introduced a household-based approach in her work on Late Mississippian Mouse Creek phase sites in the Lower Hiwassee Valley in southeastern Tennessee. Sullivan (1986:48) defined the household as minimal coresidence in relation to chiefdom-level organization: "At the bottom of this hierarchy of leaders, land divisions, and ramages was the basic unit of society: the household." The building-block approach was embraced by Mississippian researchers more widely (e.g., Mehrer and Collins 1995; Muller 1997; Peregrine 1992; Smith 1990). For example, Mark W. Mehrer's (1988, 1995) doctoral work focused on rural households at Cahokia's hinterland sites with the expectation that changes in hinterland households reflected larger trends in the development of sociopolitical complexity at Cahokia.

Rogers and Smith's (1995) *Mississippian Communities and Households* brought together a region-wide synthesis of Mississippian household archaeology. Contributions to the volume followed foundational views of the household as the smallest social and economic unit, and thus central issues in the volume included spatial analysis, social dynamics, demography, and subsistence economies (Rogers 1995b:11; Steere 2017:5). Utilizing data from large-scale excavations across the Mississippian world, contributors explained changes in spatial organization along two broad themes: diachronic change in intersite socioeconomic organization, and synchronic shifts in intrahousehold power dynamics and status differentiation. The volume marked the culmination of the first wave of Mississippian household studies and inspired numerous doctoral theses (e.g., Barker 1999; Hargrave 1991; Oetelaar 1987; Polhemus 1998; Stout 1989; see also Pluckhahn 2010).

## Households in the Post-Processual Paradigm

Criticisms of early formulations of the household posited that processual models were reductive and portrayed households as homogeneous and static (Allison 1999:3; Hendon 1996; Tringham 1991). Coterminous with the paradigmatic shift to post-processual tenets, household archaeology was shaped by agency theory and practice theory in anthropological discourse. Drawing from the work of Pierre Bourdieu (1977, 1990) and Anthony Giddens (1979, 1984), archaeologists began to humanize the past by considering people as social agents embedded in and mutually constitutive of larger systems and institutions (Dobres and Robb 2000:5; Hodder 1982; Ortner 1984). Agent-centered approaches emphasized the individual's actions as the locus of cultural reproduction (Hendon 2004). Households and domestic groups were made up of diverse social actors rather than "faceless blobs" (Tringham 1991), integral to social processes rather than a mere byproduct of them (Allison 1999; Hendon 1996). Accordingly, household archaeology moved away from concerns of form and function to explore the social construction of households along themes of gender, identity, memory, agency, power, ritual and symbolism, and the everyday (Allison 1999; Gillespie 2000a, 2000b; Hendon 1996; Joyce 2000a, 2000b; Robin 2002, 2003; Tringham 1991).

Particularly important in the new paradigm was the renewed interest in the symbolic construction of household spaces. Drawing from Bourdieu's (1970, 1973) early ruminations of practice theory in "The Berber House" (see also Cunningham 1973), archaeologists drew connections between the organization of domestic space and cosmological orders, rendering the house as "world view writ small" (Rapoport 1969:2) and "microcosmic model" (Gillespie 2000b, 2007). The construction of household space reflected and reinforced socioreligious structures and recursively "shape[d] the activities, roles, beliefs, memories, and subjectivities of its inhabitants" (Gillespie 2007:27). Dwelling structures and their architectural elements were active in the construction of social relations rather than being simply the context in which these relations were acted out (Wesson 2008:9). The articulation of households within broader physical landscapes emphasized multisensorial construction of place and the formation of identities through architectural and material practices linked to place and social memory (Allison 1999; Gillespie 2000a; Hendon 1996; Robin 2002; Tilley 1994; Tringham 1991; see also Carsten and Hugh-Jones 1995; Hendon 2000a).

There has been renewed interest in Claude Lévi-Strauss's (1982, 1987) concept of *house societies*, an enduring social institution enabled through the succession and transmission of titles and property. While this concept has been influential in some areas of household archaeology (see Carsten and Hugh-Jones 1995; Joyce and Gillespie 2000; Beck 2007), it has garnered little attention in the Mississippian Southeast. In contributions to Robin A. Beck Jr.'s (2007) edited volume *The Durable House: House Society Models in Archaeology*, James A. Brown and Christopher B. Rodning evaluated the house society model. Investigating elite mortuary practices at Etowah, Brown (2007) suggested that the Mound C copper plates were part of sacred bundles, that is, the corporate resources and the estate holdings of Mississippian aristocracies. Brown interpreted the closing of the first period of construction activity at Etowah's Mound C as representative of a "termination of the sacred family line" (242). Evaluating the architecture and spatial organization at the late prehistoric and protohistoric Cherokee Coweeta Creek site, Rodning (2007) suggested that the rebuilding of structures repeatedly in the same location embedded multiple generations within the social and physical landscape. Recent studies of relevance to the enduring social house include: honored and/or founding families interred in Cahokia's Mound 72 (Emerson et al. 2016), potential rival families or factions violently interred in Cahokia's Wilson Mound (Pauketat and Alt 2007), and the intergenerational relationships of powerful descent groups with dwellings and the landscape at sites like Moundville (Wilson 2008, 2010) and Town Creek (Boudreaux 2007, 2013, 2017; chapter 6 in this volume).

## Post-Processual Mississippian Household Studies

Rather than throwing the proverbial household baby out with the theoretical bath water, Charles R. Cobb (2000:188) understood the problems inherent in household archaeology as double edged: the household is effective for comparative studies, but this usage undermines the historicity of households; and vice versa, historicized conceptualizations of the households impede broad cross-cultural comparisons. The second wave of Mississippian household studies reflected this dual edge with a broad range of new theoretical and methodological perspectives combined with classic household themes and theories. For example, several studies continued to build on foundational household tenets like the household as building block (Cook 2008; O'Brien 2001) and the identification and interpretation of activity areas and household clusters (e.g., Gougeon 2002, 2006, 2012; Homsey-Messer and Humkey 2016; Koldehoff and Brennan 2010; Polhemus 1998; Wilson 2008). Thomas J. Pluckhahn (2010:335) has discussed six, often overlapping, themes that emerged from Mississippian household studies in the new paradigm: "production and consumption, status differentiation, agency and power, gender, ritual and symbolism, and identity and ethnicity" (see also Steere 2017:31; chapter 5 in this volume).

### Production, Prestige, and Power

Discussions of production and consumption in more recent research have broadened to include nuanced analysis of the tensions between domestic production, prestige goods and political economies, elite power, and household status (Alt 1999; Cobb 2000, 2003; Marcoux 2007; Mehta et al. 2016; Wilson et al. 2006; see further discussion in Pluckhahn 2010). For example, the Moundville political economy has been traditionally characterized as a highly centralized prestige economy driven through the centripetal movement of tribute in exchange for prestige items or display goods to higher-status hinterland households (Peebles and Kus 1977; Welch 1991, 1996; chapter 12 in this volume). However, Jon B. Marcoux's (2007) reevaluation of the production and exchange of display goods at Moundville and contemporaneous sites in the Black Warrior Valley demonstrated that the production and consumption of both nonlocal and local prestige items were almost entirely restricted to elite households at Moundville. Moreover, Marcoux reported that the majority of prestige goods were locally made rather than originating in far-flung locales. Likewise, Gregory D. Wilson (2001) questioned the division between domestic and political economies by exploring power dynamics of utilitarian household tool production (see also Alt 1999; Cobb 2000). Wilson (2001) asserted that the scarcity of utilitarian greenstone tool production debris at Moundville and outlying sites was *not* indicative of centralized or elite control over production; rather, recycling formal greenstone tools into expedient tools was a common household practice. These studies disputed traditional prestige economy models, throwing into question traditional notions of Mississippian power dynamics (see also chapter 12 in this volume). However, when comparing chipped-stone debitage from household contexts in the American Bottom and confluence regions, Brad H. Koldehoff and Tamira K. Brennan (2010) found that elite households at mound centers had access to both local and nonlocal cherts. In contrast, debitage was restricted to local cherts in a nonelite hinterland household. Koldehoff and Brennan argued that attaining status and power at the household level involved obtaining blocks and cobbles of nonlocal cherts (see also Cobb 2000). These studies underscored the tensions between household production and the political economy, reiterating the need for diversity and flexibility in Mississippian economic models.

## Architecture and Status

The practice of drawing connections between household architecture and rank has figured prominently in Mississippian household studies. Following Hirth (1993b; see also Blanton 1994), several researchers embraced the idea of dwelling size as indicative of status (e.g., Betzenhauser 2018; Gougeon 2002, 2006; Hammerstedt 2005; Payne 2002; Trubitt 1996, 2000). David J. Hally (2008) utilized house size and construction history in conjunction with an analysis of burial goods across six domestic structures at the King site in northwestern Georgia. Discrepancies in size, number of rebuilds, and the presence or absence of grave goods led Hally to posit that some households corresponded to more influential leaders or elite founding families. Similarly, during the late Moundville sequence, Wilson (2008, 2010) interpreted the clustering of burials in former household spaces as staking claim to land, inheritance, or privileges associated with the higher status of certain kin groups (see also Cook 2008; Peebles and Kus 1977).

Investigating the degree to which households of different statuses were integrated at the Little Egypt site in northwestern Georgia, Ramie A. Gougeon (2006) compared a mound-top elite household with two off-mound households. All three structures were similar in architectural form and the spatial division of interior activity areas; however, the elite structure comprised a larger floor area and may have contained important ritual substances (see also Blitz 1993). Despite the discrepancies in size and contents, Gougeon argued, the use of ubiquitous house form was an elite mobilization of power, an intentional masking of difference to promote social cohesion between ranks.

Alleen Betzenhauser (2018) recently reevaluated disparities in structure size at Cahokia and questioned long-standing notions of increasing differentiation through time at Cahokia (see Trubitt 2000). Working within a framework of economic inequality (see Kohler and Smith 2018), Betzenhauser utilized Gini indices to measure the dispersion of structure morphometrics of over one thousand Cahokian structures. She found that Gini coefficients were higher (less equal) during the earlier Lohmann and Stirling phases and lower (more equal) during the later Moorehead/Sand Prairie phase. Her analysis contradicts foundational interpretations (Trubitt 2000) and general models that propose that rank became more pronounced later in the sequence elsewhere in the Mississippian world (e.g., Wilson 2008).

## Gendered Division of Labor and Space

Much of the discussion of gender in the Mississippian world had focused on iconography and broadscale mortuary programs, and few studies have tackled gender at the household level (see also Cobb 2000). Larissa A. Thomas (2001) explored the gendered division of labor in production and exchange at two sites in southern Illinois. Thomas identified seasonal shifts in household subsistence activities at the Great Salt Springs site, indicating that women reorganized domestic food production to compensate for diverting their labor to salt production for exchange. However, she found that annual domestic production at Dillow's Ridge was not interrupted, so local hoe production for exchange was likely the undertaking of men. Similarly, Gougeon (2002, 2012) identified discrete activity areas within three residential structure floors at the Little Egypt site. Utilizing comparative ethnographic analogies, Gougeon concluded that most activities associated with domestic production and consumption (namely, food preparation) rather than extramural economic activities were activity areas utilized mostly by women.

Putting production aside, Sullivan and Rodning (2011; see also Rodning 2001a; Rodning and VanDerwarker 2002; Sullivan 2001a, 2001b, 2018) investigated the relationships between gender, power, and dwelling in Cherokee communities in southern Appalachia, particularly the spatial dimensions of mortuary practices. They explored a dual mortuary program wherein females were often interred within or near residential structures, while males were buried in or near public and community buildings. Sullivan and Rodning suggested that the differential mortuary arrangements demonstrate the persistence of traditional gender ideologies and leadership roles: women held power through matrilineal kin groups and household lineage, while men held power through town governance. This mortuary program both created and reinforced gendered architectural spaces, embedding gendered power dynamics and ancestral status in the domestic landscape.

## Vernacular Architecture and Cosmology

Although the symbolic associations between the ordering of the Mississippian world and the organization of monumental landscapes and architecture have long been recognized (e.g., Brown 1997; Hudson 1976; Knight 1986, 2006), the figuring of domestic or vernacular architecture as symbolic of cosmological and religious principles has not been as pervasive in Mississippian literature (but see Pauketat 2013a; Wesson 2008). However, the research discussed below blurred the lines between domestic and ritual realms, positioning vernacular architecture as entangled with ritual practices, religious principles, and cosmological ideologies (e.g., Watts Malouchos 2020a).

Investigating changes in domestic architecture before and after European contact, Hally (2002:108–109, 2008) combined ethnohistorical and archaeological evidence to identify a series of symbolic cosmological associations in domestic architecture that are widely encountered across the Late Mississippian world. Particularly relevant associations for household studies include the correspondence between square structure floorplans and the shape of the earth, and that between the quadruplet structure walls and roof support posts and the cardinal directions (see also Hudson 1976; Rodning 2015a). The connections between the cardinal quartering of the Mississippian world and repetition of quadrilateral architecture in domestic structures led Cameron B. Wesson (2008:9) to describe Creek households as cosmic representations or "microcosms reflective of society writ large" (see also Rodning 2015a). However, rather than viewing the household as reflective of cosmology, Sullivan (1987, 1995) and Pluckhahn (2010:360) suggested that cosmological principles may instead emerge from the household and be appropriated by elites to legitimize authority. For example, according to Susan M. Alt (2017), vernacular architecture played an important role in establishing an emergent Cahokian religion. Immigrants, pilgrims, and new or potential religious converts arriving in the American Bottom would have been immersed in unfamiliar social and physical landscapes. Those traveling through the upland Emerald site, in contrast, would have experienced Cahokian religious shrine buildings constructed with single-set posts, a vernacular familiarity in a foreign land.

The reiterative interment in household places and persistence of household groups have been interpreted as public acknowledgment of ancestral and cosmological realms across the Mississippian Southeast (Hally 2002, 2008; Hally and Kelly 1998; Rodning 2004, 2007, 2009b, 2015a; Schroedl 1998:86; Wilson 2008). Benjamin A. Steere (2017) discussed the panregional Late Mississippian investment in rebuilding domestic structures as the physical expression of cosmological and religious ideologies tied to ancestor commemoration, continuity in household identities, and intergenerational dwelling (see also Hally and Kelly 1998). Rodning (2015a:139) interpreted burials within and beside households at Coweeta Creek as creating a "point of connection between the land of the living and the world of ancestral spirits." At both Town Creek (Boudreaux 2007, 2013, 2017; chapter 6 in this volume) and Moundville (Wilson 2008, 2010), domestic structures that were repeatedly rebuilt and organized into spatially distinct residential areas were eventually transformed into discrete cemeteries. Both Wilson and Edmond A. Boudreaux III approach this transformation/sequence as ancestor creation and veneration, a process of embedding both new group identities and enduring social groups in the landscape.

*Authority, Agency, and Resistance in Mississippian Household Architecture*
Households have played a central role in the study of Mississippian power dynamics, particularly in explorations of the tensions between mound centers and

hinterland sites (see also Wesson 2001, 2008). Cahokia's authority and control over the surrounding countryside has been a point of debate, with the concept of nodal households (i.e., rural residences with evidence of suprafamily activities) figuring prominently into both sides of the argument. Mehrer (1995) argued that dispersed hinterland households and communities retained a degree of autonomy by abstaining from Cahokia-centric socio-spatial organization and maintaining relationships with hinterland nodal households rather than Cahokia. Thomas E. Emerson (1997a, 1997b), however, envisioned a Cahokian countryside not only integrated with but controlled by a centralized Cahokian hegemony. Emerson maintained that these power dynamics were manifest at nodal sites through material culture (e.g., access to prestige goods, magico-ritual objects, and differential mortuary practices) and the construction of an "architecture of power" that included large or specialized Cahokian-style structures with greater storage facilities.

At Cahokia and beyond, discussions of agency and authority have focused on the role of architecture as a physical expression of resistance (see also chapter 10 in this volume; Scarry 1995, 2001; Scarry and McEwan 1995). Emerson and Timothy R. Pauketat (2002) reimagined the Cahokian debate and explored power and agency in terms of embodied practices of resistance; rural residents in the uplands resisted Cahokian domination with sustained traditional architectural and material practices (see also Mehrer 2000; Pauketat 2001; Pauketat and Alt 2005). For Alt (2001, 2002), the persistence of traditional architecture (i.e., single-post house construction) and experimentations with Cahokian architecture (i.e., wall-trench house construction) can be interpreted as the negotiation or contestation of new Cahokian political and religious identities. James M. Collins (1997) and Wesson (1999) interpreted household resistance through shifts in the spatial practice of storage at Cahokia: the movement of storage pits to the interior of structures was a form of resistance to centralized control of surplus (see chapter 9 in this volume; Barrier 2011).

## Households and Mississippian Identities

The multiplicity of Mississippian identities has been addressed in the studies discussed in previous sections, in which identity construction intersects with material expressions and experiences of power, agency, labor, gender, kinship, ancestry, tradition, and religion. Indeed, the complex nature of identity-making transcends scales of analysis, and the above research blurs the line between households, communities, and other social formations (Waselkov and Smith 2017; Wilson and Sullivan 2017). The studies discussed here focus on the interplay between identity politics and households in culture contact situations, emphasizing the roles of vernacular architecture, organization of domestic space, and everyday practices in mitigating tensions of tradition and change between competing social identities (see also Hally 2002, 2008; Wesson 2008).

Pauketat and Alt (2005) reconsidered the construction of vernacular architecture, specifically the ubiquitous act of setting posts in the construction of domestic structures as integral to formation of social identities during Cahokia's foundation. By reframing the physical act of setting posts as an act of culture-making, Pauketat and Alt attributed powerful agential qualities to the quotidian practice. Their approach is particularly salient in the context of Cahokia's rapid foundation and transformation circa AD 1050, whereby the adoption of new wall-trench style architecture was piecemeal both within and between sites and individual structures, indicating contestation or negotiation of new Cahokian lifeways and identities (Alt 2001).

Dana N. Bardolph's (2014) study of Cahokian contact situations in the Central Illinois River Valley emphasized that the physical structures are only part of the network of archaeological features associated with households (see also Wilson 2008:130). Bardolph's analysis of culinary features at the Early Mississippian Lamb site demonstrated that some material practices regarded as hallmarks of Cahokian culture (like Ramey Incised and Powell Plain pottery and wall-trench architecture) were adopted by local Late Woodland residents, while the traditional extramural spatial organization of domestic food storage, processing, and production was retained. Looking at Cherokee households at the Townsend site in North Carolina before and after European contact, Marcoux (2008, 2010b, 2012) encountered the opposite pattern. Postcontact domestic architecture indicated short-lived occupations of households, suggesting that maintaining traditional household architecture and socio-spatial organization became increasingly difficult in uncertain times. The demonstrated continuity in ceramic practices, however, indicated that social identities embedded through ceramic traditions were more easily maintained after contact because of their comparative expediency and mobility.

## ARCHAEOLOGY OF COMMUNITIES

While the concept of communities is a longtime focus of inquiry for social theorists, it has only more recently received critical attention in archaeology. The following discussion focuses on archaeological engagements with community rather than on broader anthropological discourse and highlights parallel disciplinary histories with settlement and household studies (see Hegmon 2002; MacSweeney 2011; Varien and Potter 2008; Yaeger and Canuto 2000; the concluding commentary to this volume).

### Community as Natural Coresidential Unit

Early approaches framed the community as a natural social entity founded in coresidence; the community functioned as cultural reproduction at the suprafamily level (MacSweeney 2011; Yaeger and Canuto 2000). This perspective encompassed George P. Murdock's (1949) popular definition of the community as a natural social unit that comprised smaller, basal social units like households and families in regular face-to-face interactions. Community organization was structured by localized daily interactions and shared culture, an approach convenient for archaeologists to operationalize, taking residential proximity as related to the site, and shared normative culture as related to material culture (Yaeger and Canuto 2000:3). For this reason, equations of site with community became ingrained in archaeological thought and practice during the culture-historical period of American archaeology; the site was assumed to be the principal social unit, where spatial propinquity and face-to-face interactions produced shared culture and thus could be identified through similarities in material assemblages. The term *community* was operationalized interchangeably, referring to the site itself as well as the residents of a site, particularly as part of large regional surveys (e.g., Childe 1940; Willey 1953).

For American archaeologists, broad "type-variety" typologies based on spatiotemporal distributions of decorated ceramics were employed to define culture groups. Particularly influential was the type-variety classification scheme established by Philip Phillips, James A. Ford, and James B. Griffin in the *Archaeological Survey in the Lower Mississippi Alluvial Valley, 1940–1947* (2003 [1951]). Trait frequencies and distributions were indicative of artifact types that defined localities and regions that then corresponded to community or local groups (e.g., Phillips and Willey 1953; Rouse 1939). The pervasiveness of type-variety schemes and site-based research during this time cemented nascent definitions of the community as the archaeological site particularly in Mississippian archaeology; phrases like "community plan" or "community pattern" were regularly employed in reports to indicate site plan maps (e.g., Lewis and Kneberg 1946).

## Community as Universal Building Block

New archaeology (processual archaeology) became the dominant paradigm in archaeology, positing functional and behavioral models as a vociferous reaction to the naturalized and normative concepts of archaeological cultures (Binford 1962). The processual focus shifted to the scale of social systems, which framed culture as an adaptation to external environmental forces (MacSweeney 2011; Varien and Potter 2008; Yaeger and Canuto 2000). Understanding the function of complex systems meant understanding the constituent parts, or households and larger communities, as universal organizational units. Communities served as an intermediary between biological units (like the family) and larger, more complex social networks (like polities) (e.g., Flannery 1976). This shift corresponded to a renewed interest in settlement patterns and large-scale regional surveys rather than site-based research. Defining site functions based on size and physiographic adaptation produced settlement hierarchies ranging in size, complexity, and function, from short-term hunting and procurement camps to regional centers; intermediate-sized village settlements became synonymous with community. References to communities as a natural or organizational unit were widespread in the archaeological literature, especially in the emerging household literature; however, communities were rarely addressed directly (MacSweeney 2011:25; Yaeger and Canuto 2000).

The utility of community was attractive for archaeologists for defining settlement patterns and social organization in chiefdom-level Mississippian societies. Mississippian communities were synonymous with village-level social organization, situated between the level of households and the emergence of mound centers and chiefly organization (e.g., Muller 1997). The foundational volume *Mississippian Settlement Patterns* edited by Bruce D. Smith (1978) modeled Mississippian culture as an adaptive niche of floodplain ecosystems, and volume contributors detailed hierarchical site typologies in the Mississippian world, ranging in size from homestead, farmstead, village, and regional center, to simple and complex chiefdoms. These approaches positioned the community as a coresidential unit corresponding to the site or an evolutionary organizational unit in the development of Mississippian complexity.

These themes are salient in Rogers and Smith's (1995) volume *Mississippian Communities and Households*. Despite the subject order of the title, it offered little explicit discussion or definitions of community, and households remained the focus of the volume. Communities were vaguely referred to as coresidential social groups at a scale greater than the household and were operationalized as aggregations of households (see also Mehrer 1995, 2000). Rogers (1995b:10) himself noted that archaeologists were interested in households and "*by extension*, the organization of local communities" (emphasis added). The term *community* was used interchangeably with *site* throughout the volume, especially in terms of intrasite analysis.

## Communities as Socially Constructed

Following prominent themes that emerged during the shift to post-processual theories, communities were defined as variable, dynamic, multiscalar, and socially constructed rather than as natural, territorial, or universal entities (Hegmon 2002; see also the concluding commentary to this volume). Social theorists conceptualized the community as ideational, based on perceptions of commonality and difference, or interactional, based on repeated and patterned social and material interactions. Communities as ideation were born out of notions of group identity and solidarity as a perceived "us" versus "them," unwed to coresidence or interaction (Anderson 1991; Cohen 1985; cf. "moral communities" in Whittle 2003). Particularly influential in archaeology was Benedict Anderson's (1991) conceptualization of "imagined communities," the construction of a sense of commonality and affiliation among large populations that never participate in personal interactions. The collective identities of imagined communities are forged through ideological connections and perceptions of shared knowledge and beliefs. Interactional approaches, based in practice theory and the work of Bourdieu (1977) and Giddens (1984), conceptualized communities as group identities created and maintained through recursive social interactions. Following this formulation, communities were reciprocally constituted by and through patterned social practices and routinized material settings (see Lightfoot et al. 1998:201). Jean Lave and Etienne Wenger (1991) framed everyday activities and performances as learned through social interaction; learning was not isolated but was located within "communities of practice" (see also Lave 1993; Wenger 1998; the concluding commentary to this volume). The interactions between and coparticipation of members in communities of practice (those who learn and those who teach) served to create, maintain, and negotiate group identities. Archaeologists adopted this concept, particularly within ceramic studies, to explore how stylistic and techno-functional choice in production indicate different communities in which embodied learning happens in different ways (e.g., Kohring 2011; Sassaman and Rudolphi 2001).

Archaeologists struggled to reconcile conceptual approaches (e.g., the socially constructed community) with analytical approaches (e.g., the material reality of community) (Hegmon 2002; Knapp 2003; MacSweeney 2011; Yaeger and Canuto 2000). Marcello A. Canuto and Jason Yaeger (2000) brought this tension to the fore and revived the archaeology of communities in their trailblazing volume *The Archaeology of Communities: A New World Perspective*. In part, they attempted to mitigate the disconnect between conceptual and analytical approaches by understanding copresence and shared space as important aspects of community-making, while acknowledging that community cannot be relegated to a sociospatial unit. Yaeger and Canuto proposed a definition based on shared practices and shared geographies whereby the construction of community can be related to coresidentiality or copresence through embodied practices, or what Yaeger (2000: 125) calls "practices of affiliation." However, volume discussant William H. Isbell (2000) implored contributors and archaeologists alike to abandon natural concepts of the community and eschew definitions based on territoriality (e.g., Mehrer 2000). Building on Anderson's (1991) imagined community, Isbell positioned communities as the fluid and dynamic processes involved in producing collective goals and values that are in a constant state of being created and reimagined by multiple individuals and groups with potentially competing or contradictory interests (see also Horning 2000; Joyce and Hendon 2000; Pauketat 2000a; Preucel 2000).

Despite Isbell's (2000) warning, archaeologists tended to gravitate toward modified interactionalist perspectives that recognized dynamic and multiscalar relationships between humans and the landscape (e.g., Gerritsen 2004; Knapp 2003). The social interactions constitutive of community, whether at local or imagined scales, were inherently situated within larger sets of spatial and geographic relationships and could not be detached from a history of place (Pauketat 2008a:240; see also Ashmore and Knapp 1999; Cheney 1992; Gerritsen 2004; Fowles 2009; Joyce and Hendon 2000; Knapp 2003; MacSweeney 2011; Pauketat 2000a; Robin 2002; Tilley 1994; Varien and Potter 2008; Wernke 2007; Whittle 2003; Yaeger 2000). While these places can be physical locations and landscapes, they can also be imagined: sacred geographies, cosmological spaces and places, and remembered homelands (Fowles 2009; Isbell 2000; Pauketat 2013a; Van Dyke and Alcock 2003). Yaeger and Canuto (2000) and other foundational scholars agreed that combining aspects of natural and imagined communities that articulate place-making with communal identity-making may be the best approach to reconciling an archaeology of communities (see Harris 2014; MacSweeney 2011; Varien and Potter 2008; Birch, ed. 2013).

An approach to communities as fluid, historically contingent, and multiscalar blurs the lines between archaeological conceptualizations of households, communities, and other social formations. Indeed, an examination of the life histories of Mississippian communities illustrates the complex intersections of identity-making and place-making (e.g., Boudreaux 2007, 2013, 2017; Hally 2008; Moore 2002a; Wilson 2008; chapter 6 in this volume). Mississippian communities were socially constructed on scales spanning local to imagined (e.g., Betzenhauser 2011; Watts Malouchos 2020a). Reflecting the organization of this volume, this section is thematically organized according to trends in Mississippian studies: (1) community-making at multiple scales, (2) conflict, coalescence, and communitas, (3) community and cosmos, and (4) trading traditions and everyday community-making.

## Community-Making at Multiple Scales

An important theme guiding the archaeology of Mississippian communities has been the notion that communities are constituted by a variety of complex relationships; Mississippian collective identities were multicomponent and multiscalar. Casey R. Barrier (2011:206) noted that "groups operated to create overlapping spheres of identity, belonging, motivation, competition, cooperation, and distinction." At any given time, communities were combinations of coresident interactions and/or remote and "imagined" (*sensu* Anderson 1991) affiliations, but they were always being actively constructed, negotiated, or deconstructed through daily practices and experiences (Betzenhauser 2011; chapters 3, 7, 8, 9, 11, and 13 in this volume).

Influenced by ethnohistorical accounts of intracommunity familial and social groups (e.g., Hudson 1976), a number of Mississippian studies explored sociospatial organizations at levels exceeding the household but not broaching the "site." Wilson (2008:11) contended that "a community's developmental history is a chronicle" of the relationships between intracommunity social and residential groups (see also Boudreaux 2007, 2013, 2017; Knight 1998; Wesson 2008; chapters 4, 5, and 6 in this volume). Spatial organization simultaneously reflected and reinforced the social order; subcommunity groups have been identified in large part through architectural patterns of community organization, defined as clusters of residential structures and domestic features, sometimes in association with communal spaces like courtyards or plazas (Cobb 2003; Emerson 1997a; Fowler 1997; Holley 2000; Mehrer 1988; Pauketat and Alt 2005; Stout 1989; Wilson 2008, 2010; Wilson et al. 2006). At Angel Mounds in southwestern Indiana, Staffan Peterson (2010) identified fourteen discrete clusters of structures and interpreted these groupings as neighborhoods (see also Betzenhauser and Pauketat 2019; chapter 4 in this volume). Dru E. McGill (2013) tested the plain ceramic assemblage across four of the projected neighborhoods with the expectation that different ethnic enclaves may have occupied different neighborhoods at Angel and would demonstrate spatially distinct potting practices. While McGill identified the presence of idiosyncratic manufacture techniques and variation in design attributes that pointed to "communities of practice" (see also Worth 2017; chapters 8 and 11 in this volume), these intracommunity differences in potting practices did not correspond to Peterson's proposed neighborhoods.

Several scholars have interpreted Mississippian communities as constituted by networks of corporate groups—that is, as enduring residential groups with kin ties (e.g., Knight 1998; Wesson 2008; Wilson 2008; chapter 4 in this volume). At Town Creek, Boudreaux (2007, 2013, 2017; chapter 6 in this volume) interpreted the creation of spatially discrete residential areas, the in situ rebuilding of domestic structures, and the repeated burial of group members in household spaces as the establishment of enduring household groups and larger moieties and a strategy for integrating disparate groups into a new, larger multivocal community (see also Cook 2008, 2018; Knight 1990, 1998). Similarly, at Moundville, Wilson (2008, 2010) identified spatially discrete residential areas where groups of house structures were recurrently rebuilt and eventually reconstructed as discrete cemeteries and suggested that the residential-to-mortuary zones represented the inscription of important corporate-kin identities on the landscape. Mintcy D. Maxham (2000) observed a similar phenomenon in the Moundville hinterlands, where repeated feasting events at a farmstead site substantiated commoner kinship communities. Maxham interpreted the high percentage of serving vessels and unusual faunal taxa at one nonmound farmstead site as evidence that corporate groups maintained ties to lineage and land outside of the realms of elite-controlled spaces.

The village and town are the most commonly invoked labels attached to Mississippian sites and have mostly remained uncritically synonymous with Mississippian site and community (e.g., Dye and Cox 1990; Lewis et al. 1998). Victor D. Thompson and Jennifer Birch (2018) recently approached the village as an analytical unit in order to facilitate a breadth of cross-cultural comparisons. They offered the term "village-communities" to describe "a restricted geographic place where some portion of the population lived year-round" with "semiregular face-to-face interactions among the majority of the population" (1). In this approach, village-communities were constituted by several levels of social groupings (households, household and family groups, and other smaller coresidential groupings), and social organization was structured by regular interactions. Their village-scale approach framed community members as the social agents, those responsible for instigating processes of settled village and putting an increased emphasis in place-making as community-making.

Despite the complexity of Mississippian settlements and mound centers (see Baires 2017; Betzenhauser 2017; Pauketat 2003, 2004, 2013b), Cahokia is generally the only Mississippian community to be considered an urban place (but see Peterson 2010). The size and scale of Cahokia's metropolitan landscape were unparalleled in the Mississippian world, pointing to "an agentive capability of its own, as a powerful symbol of a community and identity" capable of drawing thousands of people from local, regional, and extraregional contexts to the Cahokian cityscape (Anderson 2018:xii). Indeed, Pauketat (2003) and others have cited the massive and multiple scales of landscape modification and hypercentralization of locals and foreigners into the American Bottom as the process that motivated Cahokia's urbanization (Betzenhauser and Pauketat 2019; see also Barrier 2017; Betzenhauser 2017; chapter 2 in this volume). The impacts of urbanization of the Cahokian landscape reverberated beyond the American Bottom and created an imagined Cahokian and Mississippian communal identity that transcended kin relations and face-to-face interactions (Anderson 1997:263; Baltus and Baires 2020; Betzenhauser 2017; Cobb and King 2005; McNutt and Parish 2020; Pauketat 2013a; Pauketat and Emerson 1999:304; chapters 3 and 11 in this volume).

## Conflict, Coalescence, and Communitas

Violence and warfare during the Mississippian period have long been topics of discussion, although the larger societal effects of conflict on communities have only been broached more recently (see chapter 7 in this volume). The question of how communities negotiate times of stress and how new communities are founded in the wake of polity dissolution has emerged as an important theme in the understanding of community-making in Mississippian societies. Concepts of coalescence and communitas have been invoked to investigate how Mississippian communities mediate societal and environmental pressures and the processes of community-making that supported the integration of new, multivocal communities (Blitz 2010).

Stephen A. Kowalewski (2006:117–118) described coalescence as the creation of new social formations in response to external stimuli, pressures, and upheaval. Coalescent processes observed in cross-cultural analysis include the formation of new corporate political structures, changes in spatial organization (e.g., strategies for communal defense), restructuring of production, and implementation of integrative activities. Birch (2012) noted that the particularly visible signatures of coalescence relate to transformations of the built environment centered on social integration and collective defense. She (2012:666) argued that "coalescence is not an event, but rather, an ongoing process," wherein communities are integrated and ordered through labor investment in public architecture and the subsequent interactions and activities in communal spaces (see also Birch 2013). The transformation of Mississippian groups into new confederacies as a response to the wide-scale sociopolitical upheaval experienced across the postcontact Southeast was the impetus for the coalescence of new communities and societies (Ethridge 2009; Ethridge and Hudson 2002; Kowalewski 2006; Marcoux 2008, 2010b, 2012).

Archaeologists have pointed to aggregation at mound centers and towns as a response to widespread competition and conflict during pre-Mississippian and Late Mississippian periods (Kowalewski 2006). Certainly, large demographic shifts accompanied the establishment of Mississippian mound centers. At the onset of the Mississippian period in the American Bottom, local farmers, villagers, and immigrants from across the midcontinent and mid-South resettled at Cahokia, regional mound centers, and smaller agricultural settlements in the countryside (Alt 2006a; Pauketat 2000a; Pauketat and Lopinot 1997; Slater et al. 2014). Pauketat (2003:39) argued that these large-scale population movements, including "displacement, resettlement, and migration," were integral to the process of constructing a Cahokian culture (see also Barrier and Horsley 2014; Betzenhauser 2017). Moreover, Pauketat (2004, 2007) suggested that part of what brought people to Cahokia and rapidly spread a Cahokian ideology across the midcontinent was a *pax Cahokiana*, an enforced degree of peace and security as a response to territoriality and violence in Late Woodland societies (Emerson et al. 2000) and strategy to mitigate intercommunity conflict and interpersonal violence (see also Boudreaux 2007, 2013, 2017; chapter 6 in this volume). Adam King (2003) argued that at Etowah, the aggregation of competing groups was ameliorated by the invocation of cosmological ideology through mound building and the construction of large communal buildings (see also Cobb and King 2005; chapter 8 in this volume). Similarly, Sullivan (2018) described the transformation from small, dispersed settlements to large Mississippian villages in southeastern Tennessee as coalescence driven by instability and the threat of violence due to sustained drought and an influx of immigrants into the region (see also Buchanan 2015a).

Victor Turner's (1969) concept of communitas—experiences of communality constituted through rites of passage, pilgrimage, or liminality—has been more casually invoked in explanations of Mississippian social integration, particularly in studies that cast mound building as an act of solidarity (Emerson 1997b; Knight 1981:52, 1986, 2006; see also chapter 7 and concluding commentary in this volume). Jennifer D. Bengtson and Jodie A. O'Gorman (2016) explicitly invoked communitas to investigate Morton Village, a multiethnic Mississippian and Oneota community in the Central Illinois River Valley. They argued that culture contact at Morton Village would have created a liminal space for Oneota community members as they negotiated their identities in a newly Mississippianized landscape. The incorporation of Mississippian symbols and objects into the burial of Oneota infants and children was an avenue for transforming collective identities (see also Emerson 2003), as young community members were important and powerful actors in community-making.

## Community and Cosmos

One of the prominent themes in understanding Mississippian communities has been exploring how Mississippian sites were designed as cosmological referents and integrative landscapes (e.g., Lewis and Stout 1998). The quadrilaterals seen in community organization and monumental architecture have been thought to model the cardinal or four-corner directionality common in southeastern belief systems (e.g., Brown 1997; Hudson 1976; Kidder 2004; Knight 1981:46, 1986, 2006). Rectangular platform mounds, plazas, and public buildings symbolized the quadripartite cosmos in their shape, institutionalizing creation stories and embedding religious narratives in the landscape. These monumental and public works created community centers, axes mundi that anchored communities within the cosmos and connected them to sacred origins and ancestral realms (Rodning 2015a; chapter 10 in this volume; see also Skousen 2012).

Mounds, plazas, and public buildings not only communicated cosmological principles but further served as the settings for important religious ceremonies and social events that brought would-be community members together for shared experiences. Group identities were consummated through participation in integrative activities like mound building and the construction of public works (Alt et al. 2010; Barrier and Horsley 2014; Brennan 2014; Cobb and King 2005; Dalan 1997; Dalan et al. 2003; Hally 2008; Mehta 2015; Stout and Lewis 1998; chapters 2 and 4 in this volume) and events like feasting, the game of chunkey, mortuary rites, and annual renewal ceremonies (Baires 2017; Blitz 1993; Holt 2009; Pauketat 2004, 2013a; Pauketat et al. 2002). Periodic festivities and monumental constructions created "instances of community" that inculcated a sense of group solidarity through shared experience between disparate and new community members (Barrier and Horsely 2014:298; Yaeger and Canuto 2000:6; Betzenhauser 2017). As Pauketat (2007:95) explained, the embodied experiences enacted within cosmic spaces were "highly charged with symbolic meanings and memories" and inscribed collective memories onto the monumental landscape (see also Dalan et al. 2003; Demel and Hall 1998).

In fact, Pauketat and Alt (2003, 2005; see also Pauketat 2000a) suggested that the physical acts of erecting post monuments and building mounds as part of the creation of Cahokia's unprecedented urban landscape helped negotiate newly localized group identities. The construction of sacred architecture by city dwellers, rural farmers, and foreign visitors was the corporeal convergence of diverse lived experiences in the material genesis of a new Cahokian social memory (see also Rodning 2015a; chapter 10 in this volume). In this way, memory-making is community-making, and the newly localized Cahokian cosmos and unified Cahokian community were memorialized in the grand scale of the monumental and metropolitan landscape (Pauketat and Alt 2003:166; see also Pauketat 2001). Cosmologically charged communal spaces and architecture would also empower the peoples, things, and practices that inhabited and experienced Mississippian landscapes (see Watts Malouchos 2020b). For example, the monumental architecture of Cahokia's central precinct was built along an axis oriented 5 degrees east of north, an organizational principle that referenced the movements of the moon and reflected a mirror image of cosmic organization (Pauketat 2013a; Romain 2015; see also Baires 2017; Pauketat et al. 2017). For Pauketat (2013a), the directionality of Cahokia's metropolitan landscape aligned and informed the bodily dispositions of inhabitants, entangling them with the power of place (Pauketat et al. 2015).

*Trading Traditions and Everyday Community-Making*

A consideration of the life histories of communities and everyday practices of community members is important for understanding how collective identities are materially and spatially constituted. This angle is particularly salient when thinking about the negotiation of group identities and traditional practices in multivocal and multiethnic communities. Pauketat (2000a, 2001, 2004, 2007) has noted that the creation of new communities involves the blending of potentially different notions of history and identity, whereby traditions are reimagined, restrained, or rejected to unify disparate constituents; processes of tradition-making are processes of community-making.

As Cahokia was experiencing its big bang, there was a centripetal movement of immigrants and pilgrims into the city and a centrifugal movement of Cahokian ideas, objects, and persons to outlying parts of the American Bottom, the midcontinent, and the mid-South (Baltus and Baires 2020; McNutt and Parish 2020). Several researchers have discussed the material ramifications of culture contact between Cahokians and regional Late Woodland groups both in the American Bottom and farther afield. Early interactions on the Mississippian frontier resulted in the establishment of new and multivocal communities that variously adopted, rejected, or localized new Cahokian practices (Bardolph 2014; Friberg 2018; Watts Malouchos 2020a). Philip G. Millhouse (2012) explored Cahokian culture contact and community-making in the Apple River Valley of northwestern Illinois through the lens of creolization. At the John Chapman site, Cahokian Mississippian immigrants lived alongside local Late Woodland peoples and negotiated new identities by blending traditional symbols with Cahokian practices: Cahokian-style plazas and platform mounds were constructed, while traditional residential architecture, ceramic styles, and subsistence practices were retained.

In the American Bottom, villages in Cahokia's uplands transformed into multiethnic communities as people from across the midcontinent and mid-South immigrated during Cahokia's florescence (Alt 2001, 2002, 2006a). As new groups with disparate identities interacted, new Cahokia-influenced social identities were being navigated. Applying Homi K. Bhabha's (1994) concept of hybridity, Alt suggested that upland villages transfigured into "third spaces"—spaces of innovative culture-making—through the novel interactions between upland villagers, immigrants, and new Cahokian lifeways. New wall-trench architectural styles and shell-tempered pottery were adopted at different rates, in different ways, and in different communities throughout the uplands. However, the traditional practice of arranging residential structures around courtyards with central marker posts persisted, rather than shifting to the rigid orthogonal alignment that structured Cahokian city residences. Alt argued that group identities may have been more strongly affirmed across household or courtyard groups, as upland villagers were more willing to experiment with or adopt wall-trench architecture than to alter or abandon the way they organized communal space (see also Betzenhauser 2011; Pauketat and Alt 2005; chapter 9 in this volume).

Similar processes of manipulating, negotiating, and suppressing traditions when integrating diverse groups of people have been noted at other mound centers across the Mississippian world (see chapter 12 in this volume). During the repeated abandonment, reoccupation, and reconfiguration of the Etowah mound center, group histories and traditions were reinvented by different interest groups (Cobb and King 2005; A. King 2003, 2007; King et al. 2011; chapter 8 in this volume). As Etowah was reestablished after AD 1250, the introduction of a new suite of Braden-style symbols was paired with a renewal of traditional communal building architecture on mound summits; communal buildings associated with mounds were co-opted at the same time that identities were tied to new foreign objects and symbols. Charles R. Cobb and Adam King (2005:170) suggested that cycles of abandonment and reoccupation allowed for the manipulation of traditional lifeways, an integral part of the establishment of new communal identities.

## Communities and the Ontological Turn

Following the larger posthuman theoretical movement in the social and physical sciences (e.g., Barad 2003; Latour 1993, 2005), archaeologists gradually began to address material and other-than-human agencies, personhood, and relational principles (but see Deloria 2003; Echo-Hawk 2009; Sundberg 2013; Todd 2016; V. Watts 2013). A diverse body of literature has unfolded in archaeology to engage "alternative ontologies," that is, non-Western and nonmodern understandings of past worlds (Alberti and Bray 2009; see also Alt and Pauketat 2019; Baires 2018; Baires et al. 2013; Harrison-Buck and Hendon 2018; Pauketat 2013a; Skousen and Buchanan 2015; C. Watts 2013; concluding commentary to this volume). The shift to alterity requires archaeologists to break down the dualisms of modern ontologies that divide nature/culture, human/thing, and subject/object. The social world is made up not just of humans, but also of nonhumans that are animate and have agency to generate social change (Alberti and Bray 2009; Bird-David 1999; Deloria 2003; Echo-Hawk 2009; Hallowell 1960; Harvey 2006; V. Watts

2013). The archaeology of communities discussed thus far framed communities as essentially human experiences, as entities wherein only humans have agency to alter and mediate their worlds. Following the ontological turn, archaeologists understand that community membership is not limited to humans, and that community-making exceeds human-to-human relationships. As Graham Harvey (2006:9) described, the animate social world is "a community of living persons, only some of whom are human." Moreover, all constituents of the social world (human and nonhuman actors alike) are entangled in intricate networks of relationships in which all things are or have the potential to be related (Alberti and Marshall 2009; Hodder 2011; Ingold 2011). Relationality, or relational ontology, emphasizes the ways in which the past was practiced, experienced, and understood through complex webs of agents, peoples, places, and things that only existed in relation to each other. Relational worlds have the capacity for infinite relationships that are simultaneously multiscalar, multidimensional, and ever-emergent (Watts 2013).

Oliver J. T. Harris (2013, 2014; following DeLanda 2006; Deleuze and Guattari 2004) argued that an understanding of communities as relational assemblages—the interdigitated relationships of humans and nonhuman actors—addresses the anthropocentrism inherent in traditional archaeological conceptions of community (see also Cipolla 2017; Hamilakis and Jones 2017). The emergent quality of assemblages dereifies typological and hierarchical conceptualizations of community, instead emphasizing the relationships and processes through which community assemblages are manifest (Joyce 2019). As Pauketat and Alt (2018:73) described, communities are sets of relationships, "physical properties, experiential qualities, and other flows or movements of substances, materials, and phenomena that become attached to, entangled, or associated with others and, in the process, define not only people but other organisms, things, places, and the like." Communities are constituted through the intentional gathering and arranging of bodies, materials, substances, and powers bound together by their relationships to each other. While communities cannot be reduced to their constituent parts, Harris (2014:91, 2017) has suggested that archaeologies of community should examine how community actors are assembled in meaningful ways by recognizing archaeological finds across different contexts and tracing the relationships between those contexts.

In the Mississippian world, Pauketat (2013a:27) has invoked the concept of bundling to parse the relationships that brought the Cahokian world into being. Like assemblages, he defined bundles as a "set of otherwise distinct things, substances, or qualities" articulated in unique relationships (Zedeño 2008; see also "caching," Murray and Mills 2013). For Pauketat (2008a:240, 2008b), bundling is the positioning of animated things within large relational fields connected to place—that is, how people, places, things, and powers are gathered together in associative networks. Bundling is the gathering of things with their own social entanglements to relate them in the generation of something new (see also Baltus

2018a:87). Pauketat (2013a) has suggested that the new Cahokian world emerged through appropriating and repositioning the ways in which people, places, things, and powers related, making way for the establishment of a new cosmic realm at Cahokia. The reconfiguring of pre-Mississippian spatial discourses for a new Cahokian order aligned to the moon allowed for a communal and cosmic ethos to be established at Cahokia.

Other archaeologists researching Cahokia have embraced a relational framework to explore Cahokia's emergence and decline. Pauketat and Alt (2018) have outlined how the Cahokian community was constituted through entanglements between substances and elements, namely, corn, shell, clay, water, and fire, the "raw materials of Mississippianization" (see also Baltus and Baires 2012). For example, the relationships of riverine mollusk shells were transformed by fire and re-related in the Cahokia world: shell was fired and crushed into temper and then recombined with earth, water, and fire in the transmogrification to Cahokian pottery. In the same way, Melissa R. Baltus (2018b, see also 2014, 2018a) acknowledged pots as agents of social change as they reassociated producers and consumers with cosmic elements (earth, fire, and water) and were connected to otherworldly networks through the decorative inscription of powerful symbols and containment of powerful substances (see also Friberg 2018; Pauketat and Emerson 1991; Watts Malouchos 2020a).

Indeed, other archaeologists envision entanglements with earth, water, and the built environment as integral to Cahokian community-making (see Baltus and Baires 2012; Baires and Baltus 2016). B. Jacob Skousen (2015) reiterated that the Cahokian community was continually constructed through the movement and convergence of peoples, practices, and things in particularly aligned landscapes. Skousen envisioned recurrent pilgrimages to the Emerald site in the Cahokian uplands as transformative journeys through which people were entangled with new relationships to the moon, water, smoke, and fire (see also Alt 2017). Sarah E. Baires (2017) approached Cahokian religion as founded through the creation of a multidimensional landscape (see also Pauketat 2013a). She sees worlds of the dead as interdigitated with worlds of the living through the construction of urban watery landscapes and unique ridgetop mounds housing ancestral mortuaries in downtown Cahokia that connected inhabitants and visitors to underworld realms (see also Buchanan 2015b). Likewise, Alt (2019) explored how watery spaces animated Greater Cahokia's vibrant landscapes (*sensu* Bennett 2010), linking living and ancestral realms. She suggests that caves and sinkholes were portals to underworld realms and assembled the worlds of the living with the dead.

Just as Cahokia emerged as a new way of experiencing and relating to the world, Baltus (2014, 2015) explained that Cahokia's thirteenth-century unmaking and eventual abandonment required the untangling of foundational assemblages. She cites the termination of classically Cahokia material practices (e.g., production of Ramey Incised pottery and construction of specialized architecture) and shifts in politico-religious ties from northern to southern networks as important parts of the intentional unraveling of Cahokian relationships. In the wake of Cahokia's dissolution, Meghan E. Buchanan (2015a) proposed that disparate groups mitigated tumultuous physical and social landscapes by coalescing at the Common Field site in southeastern Missouri. Community members invoked physical and spiritual protections by assembling galena (and its powerful associations with the Ozark Mountains) with the construction of a palisade fortification wall (see also chapter 7 in this volume).

Relational approaches have not yet saturated Mississippian archaeology or the archaeology of the midcontinent and Southeast broadly, but a few archaeologists have embraced relational frameworks to consider Mississippian mortuary practices and monumental landscapes. Marcoux and Wilson (2010) employed Bruno Latour's (2005) actor-network theory to interpret Mississippian mortuary rites. Looking at Moundville cemeteries, they suggest that the interment of clan group members in discrete mortuary-residential zones transformed the deceased by connecting individuals to new networks of ancestral communities in cosmological realms. Moreover, Cobb and Brian M. Butler (2017) explored Mississippian plazas as relational spaces. They argued that plazas are important founding features in Mississippian communities as they act as both axes mundi (anchoring community in cosmological space and time) and literal and theoretical relational fields (facilitating relationships through their open and flexible space). Plazas were spaces that animated relationships, community integration, and cosmology through performance.

## MOVING FORWARD IN THE ARCHAEOLOGY OF HOUSEHOLDS AND COMMUNITIES

As this chapter has illustrated, archaeological investigations of households and communities require a careful consideration of the myriad ways social relationships are materially constructed from the extraordinary to the ordinary. I offer relational ontologies, particularly assemblage theory, as the "next logical step" in challenging fundamental notions of who and what were involved and how they related in the ever-emergent processes of group identity formation and community-making. Accordingly, the chapters that follow offer significant contributions in moving understandings of Mississippian societies forward by engaging with emerging social theories, applying innovative methods, and analyzing new datasets. These contributions complicate Mississippian histories and set the stage for future developments in the archaeology of households, communities, and beyond.

# 2

## MAKING MOUNDS, MAKING MISSISSIPPIAN COMMUNITIES IN SOUTHERN ILLINOIS

Tamira K. Brennan

Communities are social entities that emerge through practice and are promoted through relationships, affected by history, and reified by events and their outcomes on a daily basis (Dobres 2000; Harris 2014; Khan et al. 2015; Pauketat 2000a; Yaeger 2003). The relationships on which pre-Columbian communities were constructed included people (both living and dead), places (Ingold 1993; Joyce and Hendon 2000; Knapp 2003), and material objects with unique biographies (Chapman 1996; Fowler 2004; Gosden and Marshall 1999). The nested and crosscutting nature of communities (*sensu* Preucel 2000; Yaeger and Canuto 2000) means that they are best understood when examined at multiple scales. These include both spatial scales that explore the connection between real, imagined, and affective communities (Harris 2014; Isbell 2000; Yaeger and Canuto 2000:10; see also Wilson et al. 2006) and temporal scales that account for the role of event and history to their formation, maintenance, or change (*sensu* Clark et al. 2019; Gilmore and O'Donoughue 2015; Robb and Pauketat 2013).

This chapter employs a multiscalar approach to communities to interpret new data at two major Mississippian-period settlements in southern Illinois: East St. Louis, a precinct of Cahokia located within the American Bottom, adjacent to modern-day Saint Louis, and Kincaid, a large mound center located in the Black Bottoms along the Lower Ohio River (Figure 2.1). At both sites, I tack between phases to show the recursive relationship between community-building events, landscape, and the material assemblage. I highlight mound building specifically and landscapes more generally as two examples of how events and the resultant places they created were used both actively and nondiscursively to forge, maintain, or alter communities. I also discuss pottery practices and settlement organization for their potential to gauge the success of those more overt and inclusive measures.

At Kincaid, I focus on how longevity in repeated and successful claims for spaces lent legitimacy to claimants by creating a naturalized sense of place. I also discuss how intrasite dynamics were affected by major changes to the landscape, and how mounds were manipulated to rewrite history and direct the future. At East St. Louis, I also compare spatial scales, considering how neighborhoods, the

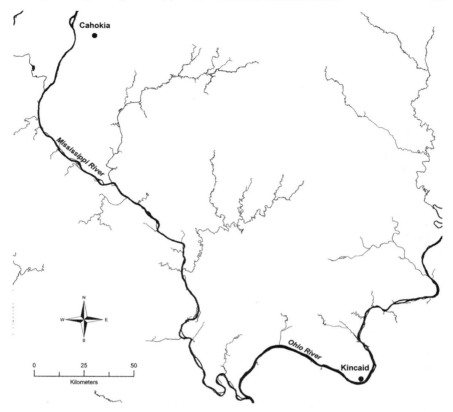

Figure 2.1. Regional map of southern Illinois, showing the locations of Greater Cahokia and the Kincaid site. (Courtesy of Miranda Yancy)

settlement, and the region contributed to the formation Greater Cahokia as both a real (physical) and "imagined" community at the beginning of the Lohmann phase, circa AD 1050 (*sensu* Anderson 1991; Betzenhauser 2011; Hegmon 2002: 268; Pauketat 2008a:240). This formation included not only the emplacement of new monuments and material culture but also the active obliteration of older landscapes and traditional household groupings, each at variable paces. I briefly touch on how the homogeneous material assemblage of the Stirling phase is a realization of the earlier Lohmann communities' efforts, and one that reveals the increasing hegemony that accompanied it (*sensu* Emerson 1997a, 1997b).

## BACKGROUND
Southern Illinois is an area rich in archaeological history, with a Mississippian period that both begins and ends early (AD 1050–1450) relative to the timeline of the greater Southeast (Bareis and Porter 1984; Milner 1998; Muller 1986). The

earliest and largest Mississippian sites appear in an expansive floodplain known as the American Bottom, adjacent to modern-day Saint Louis, while less-nucleated occupation followed shortly thereafter along the waterways farther south. The formation of Mississippian communities is abrupt in some areas and more gradual in others, with notably few instances of the in situ growth of Mississippian cultures exclusive from Late Woodland ones (see Wilson 2017). Changes in internal site structure, potting practices, subsistence, settlement patterns, and architecture are all physical markers of the onset of Mississippian culture.

In Greater Cahokia, the Mississippian period was in progress for several generations, peaked, and underwent population decline and dispersal starting circa AD 1200. Communities farther south persisted into the fifteenth century and present evidence of less rapid decline and associated social restructuring. Instead, they persist, and in some cases grow, until what appears to be a near-abandonment of the region by AD 1450 (Williams 1990; but see Cobb and Butler 2002, 2006; Edging 2007; Fortier et al. 2006). Population density undoubtedly played a role in the pace of these regional declines and the communities' responses to the events that spurred them, as did the particular histories of each place, which I briefly cover below.

## Greater Cahokia

The Greater Cahokia area includes the American Bottom and its surrounding uplands. This region has a rich and deep history of human occupation. Large-scale transportation projects such as FAI-270 (Bareis and Porter 1984) and the New Mississippi River Bridge project (Emerson et al. 2018), as well as large, multiyear research projects (e.g., Pauketat 2003; Pauketat et al. 2017), offer insights into Mississippian communities at an unparalleled scale (see also Collins 1990). These projects cover a broad geographic area as well as large portions of individual sites, together revealing full village plans and regional settlement data. This mound-rich region hosted three of the largest Mississippian centers ever to exist, which we now understand were precincts of the urban area known as Greater Cahokia: Cahokia, East St. Louis, and St. Louis (Emerson 2018a, 2018b). Dozens of smaller and single-mound sites, as well as outposts, villages, and farmsteads, dapple the American Bottom and its uplands in what was a strongly interconnected regional community (Alt 2006b; Emerson 1997a, 2018b; Kelly 1990a; Mehrer and Collins 1995; Milner 1998; Pauketat 2000a).

Here the onset of the Mississippian period occurred circa AD 1050 or perhaps slightly earlier, following a distinctly different Terminal Late Woodland (TLW) occupation that began 150 years prior. Although some TLW settlements in the region were appreciable (see Betzenhauser 2019; Kelly 1980; Kelly et al. 2007; Pauketat 1998, 2013b), they pale in comparison to the size and complexity of the Mississippian ones that followed. The most notable among the latter is the largest and most populous pre-Columbian site in North America, Cahokia. The rapid increase in population density from the TLW to the Mississippian period and recent analyses of strontium isotopes from human remains in this region both indicate that "Cahokian Mississippian" was a coalescent society composed of peoples from diverse locales, and that they immigrated to the area in multiple waves (Brennan 2018a:Table 8.2; Emerson and Hedman 2016; Milner 1986; Pauketat and Lopinot 1997:Table 6.2; Slater et al. 2014). Birch (2012:646, after Kowalewski 2006) has noted that coalescence brings about "transformations in the social, political, ideological, and economic fabric of these . . . societies" (see also Pauketat 2007:85). The material culture within Greater Cahokia supports this assessment, revealing influences from multiple distant locales at the onset of the period, influences that quickly coalesced into a distinctive American Bottom material culture (Betzenhauser et al. 2018; Holley 1989). Later assemblages indicate that subsequent immigrants to the area willingly adopted Cahokian material culture and practices, yet their own origins had some influence on local assemblages (see Holley 1989; Lansdell et al. 2017; Pauketat 2013a). This finding suggests either coalescence-in-progress as migrant waves arrived in Greater Cahokia, or the retention of select homeland practices under the metaidentity that subsumed the varied traditions carried to this region at the time (*sensu* Clark et al. 2013; Clark et al. 2019).

In Greater Cahokia, overt unifying changes occurred at the beginning of the period. Most notable are the obliteration of older landscapes and abandonment of the TLW architectural vernacular. The former took the form of borrowing, filling, leveling, and mound building, to an extent that is still not fully appreciated (see Dalan et al 2003; Kolb 2007, 2018). Within major settlements, it also included the planned construction of large plazas, which simultaneously integrated politics, ideology, and power. The latter involved a change in the practice of constructing houses. The small, square domestic structures of the TLW period with their singly set bent poles forming a domed roof were abandoned in the Mississippian period in favor of larger, rectangular structures built with separate wall and roof elements, the walls of which were emplaced in trenches. These breaks in tradition were accompanied by brand-new, specialized buildings, including forms such as L-shaped, T-shaped, circular, and oversized structures. This "architecture of power" (Emerson 1997a; see also Alt 2017; Betzenhauser and Pauketat 2019) was a physical manifestation of the supradomestic roles of certain community members, and of elite status, power, or control (*sensu* Payne 2002).

By the second phase of the Mississippian period (Stirling, c. AD 1100), the region's population peaked, and material culture was more uniform than in the preceding phase. This uniformity, and the production of an ideologically charged vessel form, Ramey Incised jars, indicates a level of elite control over certain material items, and over ideology as well (Lansdell et. al 2017; Pauketat and Emerson 1991). Shifts toward more private storage and alterations in community layout belie changes in social structure that focus the household on the nuclear family (Brennan 2018a; Collins 1990; Mehrer and Collins 1995; chapter 9 in this volume). One hundred years later, the Moorehead phase marks another shift, where larger structures were grouped near monuments or other focal points, indicating a return to broader household networks and perhaps the reemergence of homeland traditions and identities previously subsumed by new Cahokian ideologies (Brennan and Hargrave 2018:245; Emerson and Hargrave 2000:18–19). Increased emphasis on serving wares and the waning of Ramey and other specialized ceramics were accompanied by a dispersal from Cahokia and, by AD 1300, from most of the American Bottom. The entire region was largely abandoned by AD 1400 (Baltus 2014; Hamlin 2004; Pauketat 2013a).

Recent excavations and analyses from one precinct of Cahokia—East St. Louis —contribute to a better understanding of the formation and maintenance of Mississippian communities in the region (Emerson et al. 2018; Fortier 2007; Pauketat 2005b). The most recent of these projects is the New Mississippi River Bridge (NMRB) project, carried out by the Illinois State Archaeological Survey for the Illinois Department of Transportation. This work resulted in the exposure of a contiguous 4 percent of the 290 ha site and uncovered over 6,000 features containing roughly 13 metric tons of cultural materials (Figure 2.2) (Emerson et al. 2018). Data from this project indicate that East St. Louis began as a small TLW I (AD 900–975) settlement nestled within a crook of Cahokia Creek and bounded by natural swales. It rapidly grew into a very large TLW II (AD 975–1050) settlement that included over two dozen courtyard groups of small, densely clustered houses (Betzenhauser 2019). Courtyard groupings of extended families were typical and included domiciles, associated pits, central working spaces, and sometimes marker posts. Diversity and heterogeneity were common within and between TLW settlements in the American Bottom (Pauketat 2000a), and East St. Louis was no exception. It was, however, exceptional in its size. At 8.4 ha of dense and continuous features, it was the largest documented TLW settlement in the region. It included 372 structures and an estimated population of up to 166 people at any one time within the NMRB corridor alone (Brennan et al. 2018:Table 6.3). While most contemporaneous settlements waned or were abandoned by the Mississippian period, East St. Louis expanded.

There is no break between the last TLW II settlement at East St. Louis and the first Mississippian-period one. The latter was constructed in the footprint of the former and expanded southward across a natural swale and into previously unoccupied territory. Habitation continued to be densest in the core of the former TLW II settlement and in many ways carried on TLW II traditions. These include a greater frequency of TLW II–style pottery than is seen at Cahokia at the same time, construction of houses with single-set post walls, and the occasional arrangement of houses and pits into courtyards reminiscent of a TLW II layout

(Figure 2.3) (Brennan et al. 2018). These structures remained in courtyard formations for a generation or so in one neighborhood of the site. Remnant courtyards were more loosely arranged than their TLW II predecessors and included or were adjacent to novel, special-use buildings. These buildings pulled focus away from the spatially discrete extended family group and toward a settlement-wide community, thus promoting integration and a broader "social whole" (Birch 2012; Kowalewski 2006). This new layout at East St. Louis served as a referent to the

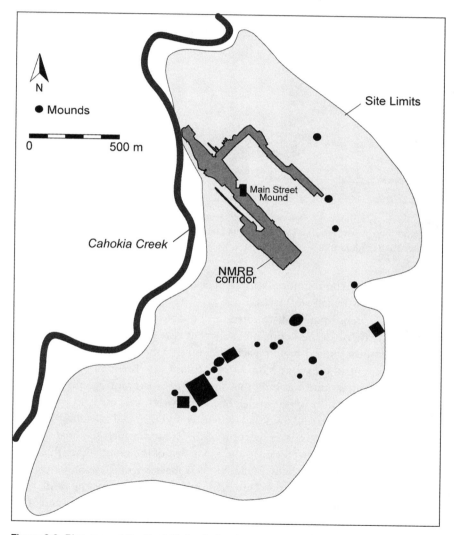

Figure 2.2. Plan map of the East St. Louis Precinct. NMRB = New Mississippi River Bridge. (Tamira K. Brennan; after Brennan 2018d:Figure 1.2)

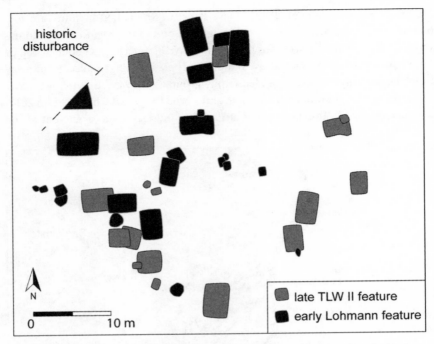

Figure 2.3. Early Lohmann single-set post structures overprinting a late Terminal Late Woodland II courtyard group. TLW = Terminal Late Woodland. (Tamira K. Brennan; after Brennan 2018a:Figure 8.3)

larger, "imagined" communities (*sensu* Anderson 1991) of Greater Cahokia and to the new Mississippian worldview.

Special-use architecture is distributed throughout the Lohmann settlement. It is particularly dense in the Lohmann settlement core adjacent to what is one of the earliest known mound-building activities on site: the construction of a large, ridgetop monument known as Main Street Mound (see Brennan 2016, 2018b). This 42 m × 16 m mound was built into the side of a natural ridge slope, which would have increased its apparent height from a westward (outside) approach. Preparation for Main Street Mound was extensive and included the filling of older borrow pits, perhaps for the core portion of the mound, which the final monument ultimately overprinted. Prior to the expansion of the mound over this borrow, the landscape was specially prepared via a mass burning event across the surface of the then-filled borrow. This event included tobacco, white sand, and disarticulated human remains. It was then built up to the level of ground surface and covered with an extremely clean, silty fill, where the footprint of the mound was to expand. This long monument was composed of variegated dark and light fills from different sources. These could have been in reference to particular places or laden with symbolism of war and peace (Hudson 1976; Sherwood

and Kidder 2011). It largely appears that ridgetop mound building in this manner were events unique to the Cahokia region (Baires 2017; Pauketat et al. 2010).
Main Street Mound was used for many generations as a place for the interment
and processing of deceased community members. It remained active through the
site's early Mississippian (Lohmann and Stirling phase) occupation (see Nash et
al. 2016:Table 3.6), but there is no indication from NMRB excavations that its use
persisted into the final, early Moorehead occupation of the site.

Lohmann-phase special-use architecture is even denser within a 350 m long
excavation block referred to as the Exchange Avenue corridor, located 200 m east
of the core community area noted above. Within this 30–50 m wide corridor,
seven rectangular and one T-shaped special-use structure were observed, indicating a newly established area of intense ceremonial activity that illustrates the
rapidly growing complexity of the site during the Lohmann phase (Figure 2.4).
Lohmann-phase features that are not, or could not be, assigned to the early sub-
section of that phase reveal a settlement whose organization is more intentional
than organic. The negotiation evident in the earliest Lohmann community appears to have resolved into a site structure and material assemblage that is strik-
ingly consistent with that at the Cahokia site and beyond.

Not only did the ultimate reorganization of structures at East St. Louis by the
end of the Lohmann phase preclude central kin-based storage, but the larger floor
areas and separate roof elements of the new wall-trench architectural form afforded the possibility of increased private or house-level storage (see also chapter 9 in this volume). This new type of wall carried heavy social implications of
a change in the labor of house construction, a change in community interaction
(Alt and Pauketat 2011; chapter 8 in this volume), and, importantly, the abandonment of a traditional vernacular, discussed below.

The Lohmann settlement ultimately expanded into previously unoccupied territory and took on a less organic settlement structure: buildings show a strong
preference for cardinal orientations as opposed to the more varied orientations
that occur in TLW II courtyard groupings (Brennan et al. 2018:Table 6.6). Several
distinct Lohmann-phase cemeteries, one adjacent to Main Street Mound and one
200 m to its northeast, are further evidence of the development of (or the pen-
chant toward) physically expressing subcommunity identities within the growing
population of East St. Louis (Brennan and Nash 2018).

## The Black Bottoms

Just as Greater Cahokia declined, population density was picking up in far southern Illinois and in adjacent regions surrounding the confluence of the Mississippi
and Ohio Rivers (Lewis 1990; Muller 1986). Settlement patterns here differed from
those of Greater Cahokia. Smaller and more dispersed sites characterize the region, with fewer—and often singular—large centers (Riordan 1975). Within the
Black Bottoms, Kincaid Mounds was that center from approximately AD 1100 to

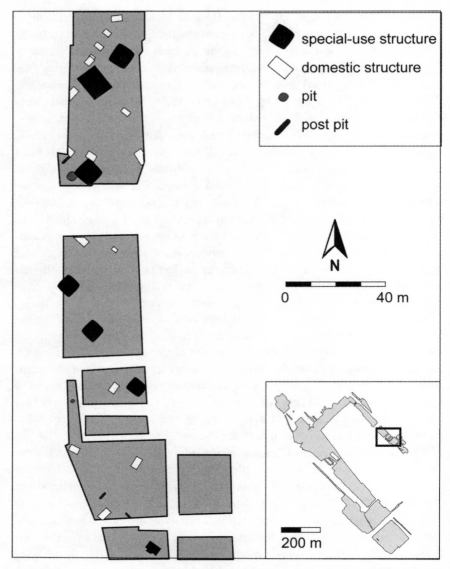

Figure 2.4. Dense special-use architecture in the Exchange Avenue corridor of the New Mississippi River Bridge Project. (Tamira K. Brennan; after Brennan 2018c:Figure 3.19)

AD 1450 (Figure 2.5). Kincaid is located along Avery Lake, a remnant channel of the Lower Ohio River, the latter of which now runs 1.6 km to the south of the site. Kincaid is approximately 80 river km upstream from its confluence with the Mississippi River and 220 km southeast of Greater Cahokia as the crow flies. With more than 26 mounds, multiple plaza areas, and dense concentrations of structures in some areas, it is one of the largest Mississippian mound centers on record (Butler et al. 2011; Cole et al. 1951). Little is known of its early phase, which likely began a generation or two after the start of Greater Cahokia. Present data indicate that Early Kincaid included only a small population centered beneath what ultimately grew into the site's largest mound and plaza group. Middle and late phases (spanning AD 1200–1450) are better documented. They reveal Kincaid as a major center until well after Cahokia's decline. The coeval timing of Cahokia's decline and Kincaid's rise in complexity and craft intensification may not be coincidental, despite the fact that little evidence of interaction between the American and Black Bottoms exists (Brennan and Pursell 2019).

When compared with its contemporaries of a similar scale, Kincaid is understudied. Extensive excavations took place at the site from 1934 to 1944 as part of the University of Chicago's graduate field schools and the Works Progress Administration, although the onset of World War II left the results only summarily published (Cole et al. 1951). The breadth and caliber of excavations were great, but the excavations offered a biased glimpse of the site since mounds and not their adjacent communities were the primary focus of these investigations. More recent research conducted through the Center for Archaeological Investigations and Southern Illinois University Carbondale has begun to provide a more representative sample of the community, although one that is biased toward the state-owned two-thirds of the site due to access issues. These recent investigations are largely guided by a large-scale magnetometry survey of the site (reported in Butler et al.

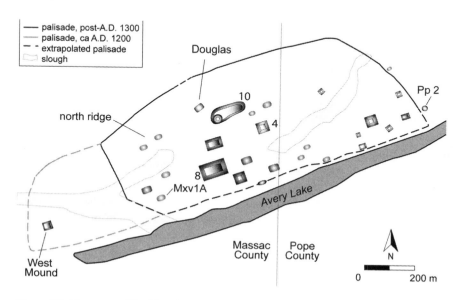

Figure 2.5. Plan map of the Kincaid Mound center. (Tamira K. Brennan; after Brennan 2014:Figure 4.1)

2011) that revealed a compilation of what have thus far proven to be features of the Middle to Late Kincaid phase (Brennan 2014).

The largest mound and plaza group is roughly central to the site (in Massac County), with a smaller mound and plaza group at the eastern site periphery (Pope County). Isolated at the western site boundary are a single low mound and its short-lived community, dating to the Middle Kincaid phase (West Mound). Several iterations of a palisade enclose the site, the latest of which was to the exclusion of the West Mound community. Natural sloughs dissect Kincaid, with the densest housing found atop natural ridges. Many ridges are adorned with low, accretional mounds resulting from the repeated burning, burial, and rebuilding of domestic or supradomestic houses in the footprint of their predecessors.

Early-phase houses have only been excavated in a few places on site, despite targeted investigations to locate them. Among these locales are the basal levels of several of the site's mounds, both large and small (Cole et al. 1951). Middle- and late-phase houses are densest immediately outside of the larger mounds and on the site's natural ridges. At both ridge and nonridge locations, families or groups often continued to occupy the same spaces over multiple generations. Little investigation has been completed into the central spaces created by adjacent mounds of this type, but limited testing at one suggests that it served as a midden area rather than as a central workspace, though perhaps not initially (Brennan 2014). Workspaces for pottery identified in the University of Chicago's investigations indicate that work areas dedicated to specific tasks did exist (Cole et al. 1951), perhaps as potting gradually shifted from a household level to a broader community endeavor. Analyses of pottery practices support this finding, revealing increasingly more homogeneous ceramic assemblages through time, all while the Kincaid settlement grew more complex (Brennan 2014; Pursell 2016). This material shift follows the dissolution of the brief-lived West Mound community and the restriction of the palisade to exclude it, a move that reduced the total enclosed site area by approximately 25 percent.

At roughly the same time, the intensity of community activities in the core mound area increased, including organizational changes that redirected movement and gaze. For example, the largest mound (Mound 10), which sits at the head of the largest plaza, was transformed from multiple monuments into one linear mound that spanned nearly the entire northern border of the main plaza. At some point after this event, a low, broad monument was constructed immediately northwest of Mound 10 (Douglas Mound; see Campbell 2013; Welch 2013) in what would prove to be one of the final shifts in site organization. This feature is outside of the main mound group and plaza and set at an angle that is at odds with the overall orientation of most of the site's built features. Instead, it aligns with the north ridge, a natural elevated contour on which many late-phase houses and supradomestic buildings were erected. This period marks the final use of the site, circa AD 1450, at which time the entire region was largely abandoned (see

Cobb and Butler 2006). There is no evidence of a catastrophic end to Kincaid, and there are not enough data to pace its decline, although it presently appears to have been rapid. A Late Kincaid house in the plaza, burned with its floor assemblage intact, hints at a potentially catastrophic end, though further data are needed to support that conclusion (Brennan 2014).

## DISCUSSION

The neighborhood, settlement, and region are all important scales of analyses in their own right, but they are also crucial in examining communities, which are best understood in relation to other communities (real or imagined) at many scales (see also chapter 7 in this volume). Small-scale data indicative of community-making are quickly obscured when we fail to examine them at an intrasite level (Wilson et al. 2006; chapter 11 in this volume). Broad regional studies that do not consider everyday minutiae blur details of social processes that are key to understanding how communities come into being. Understanding circumstances unique to community formation at individual settlements is therefore integral to understanding the Mississippian phenomenon in general (Alt 2002; Boudreaux 2013; Emerson 2002; Marcoux 2010b; Pauketat 2005a; Wilson 2008). Yet we cannot understand small-scale details outside of the context of settlement and regional histories, or outside of the broader communities in which they were nested. The actions and events of the smallest contribute to the largest, and the group identities formed through imagined communities bear on the actions and tangible outcomes of the smallest physical ones. Temporal scales, too, work in this way. We cannot underestimate the impact of brief participatory events or the persistent effects of their material outcomes. No current moment is absent of its precedents, whether actions call on those precedents for legitimacy and support, or instead seek to rewrite them anew (*sensu* chapter 13 of this volume).

The microscale details of East St. Louis's transition from a TLW II to Mississippian settlement and its role in the making of Greater Cahokia illustrate the above, as does the glimpse of Kincaid as it was shaped through small- and large-scale events. These data are but two of innumerable examples of how small but persistent actions, individual and cumulative events, and the transformation of space into place (*sensu* Joyce and Hendon 2000) were all vital aspects of Mississippian community-making. They also illustrate that the physical world is in a recursive relationship with community, both creating it and being created by it through the daily engagement of objects and persons.

At Kincaid Mounds, the notably sparse Early Mississippian presence may indicate a sampling bias on a sizeable site that holds large tracts of land yet uninvestigated. It alternately may indicate that these earliest habitation areas were primarily beneath the site's most prominent mounds, as is suggested by excavations at the plaza-side Mound 4 (Cole et al. 1951). Here, domiciles continued to be built on the mound's earliest layers. As the monument grew in size, these smaller houses were replaced by larger buildings that presumably served a public or ceremonial function. These mounds perhaps memorialized the founding families, whose homes they ultimately displaced: a symbol both of their growth in prestige or power, and of their ability to organize and command the labor needed to assert their status. Continuity between a space's first residents and those who sponsored and maintained the later mound is not assured, but similar persistent claims to space seen elsewhere on site and discussed below suggest that a "biography of origins" (Connerton 1989:17) was an important and common practice at Kincaid and other Mississippian sites (see also Pauketat 2008b, 2010; Wilson 2010; chapter 13 in this volume).

In one well-documented location (Mx$^v$1A)—like at many others—the termination of a domicile was marked by intentional incineration of that building followed by its burial with basket loads of dirt, before another house was raised in its place on the newly elevated surface. Mx$^v$1A happened to be on top of a natural ridge at the site (the South Ridge), taking advantage of the status accorded to raised elevation in Mississippian societies from the house's inception. The cumulative results of the burning and burial practice were a notably elevated domiciliary mound. Several domiciliary mounds adjacent to one another created a courtyard of sorts on the South Ridge. It is likely that purification, identity, and place-making were all parts of the ritual of setting these buildings ablaze, burying them, and rebuilding in situ. I have argued elsewhere (Brennan 2014) that these are the spaces of foundational families at Kincaid, whose successful claims to place through this repeated practice asserted the legitimacy of their heritage (Van Dyke and Alcock 2003; Wilson 2010). These domiciliary mounds were not monumental in the same sense as Mound 4 or other plaza-side mounds, but the memories created by the burning and burial events, as well as the memories that these practices called on, created continuity with the past. Continuity lends legitimacy to those who can claim it (Connerton 1989:3; McAnany 1995). The founding of one of the site's Late Kincaid neighborhoods on the previously unoccupied North Ridge may have been an attempt to mimic the successful efforts of the founding communities at Mx$^v$1A (Brennan 2014).

Changes in the broader landscape at Kincaid over time indicate both intentional and nondiscursive manipulation of the day-to-day practices of its residents. Among the former are two large-scale and coordinated events: the restriction of the site's palisade to the exclusion of an entire Middle Kincaid neighborhood (West Mound), and the incorporation of multiple mounds at the northern edge of the plaza into one massive monument, Mound 10.

It is unclear whether the palisade line contracted before the West Mound neighborhood was abandoned, thus intentionally excluding these residents, or whether it contracted following the neighborhood's dissolution. Either way, it marked changes related to Kincaid's most peripheral residents in a manner that was common throughout the Mississippian world (see Price and Griffin 1979;

chapter 7 in this volume). The West Mound neighborhood was always set apart from the rest of Kincaid in several ways. Aside from the neighborhood's physical distance from the site core and location across a seasonally inundated slough, its residents practiced notably different manners of potting, house and hearth construction, and lithic procurement (Butler 2010) than Kincaid's other neighborhoods (Brennan 2014). This evidence suggests that West Mound was not an outgrowth of the core settlement but composed of migrants to Kincaid from the south or west. The abandonment of the West Mound neighborhood could be due to residents' relocation elsewhere on site, ultimately rendering their distinct material culture invisible as they were folded into the communities of practice that were themselves becoming less distinct by the Late Kincaid phase (cf. chapter 8 in this volume). Alternatively, West Mound's residents may have abandoned their settlement for more favorable options off site as community activities intensified in Kincaid's core. The former scenario appears more plausible. When they abandoned their neighborhood, they left their cleaned-out buildings standing. These houses were not incinerated until a much later point in time, after the structural materials began to rot and were thoroughly insect infested (Parker 2013).

Similar to the reconfiguration caused by the contraction of the palisade, the construction of Mound 10 through the subsumption of multiple smaller mounds into one long mound also changed the way that the site was perceived. This mound's presence had been a daily reminder of the structure and organization of society. The major changes it underwent altered those perceptions in active ways (during mound building) and passive ones (given its constant presence in the background of daily life). It is possible that multiple influential families sponsored a joint endeavor in which the now single, larger monument was a powerful symbol of that amalgamation. Alternatively, the co-opting persons may have intended for these efforts not only to obliterate the memories associated with the construction and experience of the individual subsumed monuments (*sensu* Bradley 2003:224), but to terminate the ritual performances and maintenance that would have allowed the influence of these groups to endure (see Pauketat 2007:99). Efforts such as these could have forced the forgetting of a multivocal past or helped legitimate a new, fictitious one (Bradley 1987, 1993; Van Dyke and Alcock 2003; Wilson 2010).

This reworking of Mound 10 was followed by the addition of a conical projection at its southwest corner. A small, house-like structure was placed atop this projection in what is a singular example at the site: a mound-top residence that served only one or several individuals. With these efforts, Mound 10 became the site's largest mound, at approximately 150 m in length. Around the same time, Mound 8 became host to a 380 m$^2$ circular rotunda that could have held up to 850 people (Welch et al. 2008). Both mounds reveal important changes in events taking place at Kincaid. The new Mound 10 structure is seemingly exclusive in its nature, as opposed to the integrative function of the Mound 8 rotunda.

Regardless of the intentions behind their construction and manipulation, mounds and other aspects of the landscape had the power to imprint clear and lasting messages to the people who daily interacted with them (Bender 2002; Ingold 1993). The co-option of multiple monuments at Kincaid appears to have been a unifying effort at a time when complexity was nearing its peak. Because "our experience of the present very largely depends upon our knowledge of the past," which in turn affects the minutiae of everyday life (Connerton 1989:2), mound construction and alteration at this scale would have served both the Mound 8 and Mound 10 scenarios well (see also Pauketat and Alt 2003).

The coordination, collective agreement, and effort that these actions required suggest a growing unification at Kincaid toward the end of the middle and into the late phase. These actions are accompanied by less diverse potting practices, which were likely an unintentional outcome of the more ordered experience within Kincaid's restructured and more restricted physical setting (Brennan 2014; and see Ingold 1993; Joyce and Hendon 2003:143). The stability and duration of this unity at Kincaid are questionable. The aforementioned Late Kincaid neighborhood that developed along the site's North Ridge suggests that the order projected by the largest mounds and plaza did not transfer to the site's youngest neighborhood. Instead, houses here were aligned to the ridge's natural orientation of approximately 55 degrees east of north, and at odds with the alignment of the major mounds and buildings in the plaza (roughly 75 degrees east of north). At the eastern terminus of this ridge and immediately to the north of Mound 10, a new mound with a considerable footprint was constructed at a similar off-grid orientation to the ridge (Douglas Mound). This low monument experienced few moderate building episodes before occupation at the site ceased (Welch 2013). This changing settlement organization may align with changes in how Kincaid's residents—or at least a portion of them—referenced their communities (*sensu* Pauketat 2000a). Too little is known to determine whether the Douglas Mound in fact represents factionalism or a more widely accepted change in settlement structure that could indicate the breakdown or failure of the slightly earlier Mound 10 unification efforts. There is no evidence that Kincaid persisted for any significant period of time following Douglas Mound's brief history. Like most sites across the upper mid-South, Kincaid ceased to host a measurable population after AD 1450 (Cobb and Butler 2006).

Comparison of these data with those from East St. Louis indicate that similar actions and events played a significant role in Mississippian community-making in the American Bottom. As with the Kincaid example, events at East St. Louis include both intentional acts such as major and widespread landscaping efforts, and the outcomes of nondiscursive acts, such as the daily experience of living and interacting within these intentional new landscapes. Such is the case across the Mississippian world. The unique histories of each place lend insight into the effects of these directed experiences, as well as their expected and unintended outcomes. At East St. Louis, interaction with and manipulation of past persons and monuments helped standardize objects, places, and perceptions in a rapid and wide-spread manner at the onset of the Lohmann phase. The construction of a ridgetop monument, Main Street Mound, was only one example of these interactions. Its variegated fills and the individuals' remains interred within it gave it a unique genealogy (*sensu* Pauketat 2010:24) that defined the communities it served. Other ridgetop mounds excavated throughout Greater Cahokia have unique stories of their own, including the inclusion of inalienable items and the manipulation of human remains (Baires 2017; Pauketat et al. 2010). Baires (2017) posits that such ridgetop mounds were foundational monuments essential to the formation of a new Cahokian religion. Their construction and all that they symbolize was an act of community formation, a solidification of ideological beliefs, and a physical reminder of these ideals to anyone who experienced the events or lived daily in the presence of the resulting mound. This and the other processes described here led to East St. Louis's adoption of the technological and ideological changes that swept the region within only a generation's time.

Such shifts were not only clear technological breaks; they were also physical manifestations of a more meaningful break with traditions of the past and an endorsement of the new Mississippian way of life. At East St. Louis, forging these new Mississippian communities involved considerable negotiation. Unlike excavated examples at Cahokia and other bottomland sites in the region (Collins 1990; Pauketat 1998, 2013b), single-set post houses persisted in appreciable numbers at East St. Louis for a generation, making up 58 percent of all Early Lohmann domiciles (Brennan 2018c:Table 3.6). The brief persistence of some of these traditions is of utmost importance, as the earliest Lohmann settlements elsewhere in the American Bottom adopt an innovative new wall-trench construction technique nearly wholesale while abandoning kin-based courtyards for a preplanned and more restricted household-focused settlement pattern. Exceptions exist within the upland territory outside of the American Bottom, but these exceptions are under very different circumstances and manifest in different manners (see Alt 2002, 2017; Pauketat 2003). Yet these more traditionally constructed houses at East St. Louis were still distinct from their TLW II predecessors in characteristically Mississippian ways. The square single-set post dwellings of the TLW II at East St. Louis had bent-pole frames and averaged 6.6 m² in floor area (Brennan et al. 2018:Table 6.1). These were replaced in the Early Lohmann phase by larger (8.2 m² mean) single-set post rectangular buildings that included a higher frequency of interior storage pits and interior support posts (Brennan 2018c:68). The latter fact suggests that some aspects of the vernacular of East St. Louis (floor area and storage strategies) had been abandoned even though the traditional practices associated with wall and roof construction were retained. At the same time, the remaining 39 percent of Early Lohmann structures are built with wall trenches and are notably larger than the single-set post forms, at a mean of 10.7 m² floor area (Brennan 2018c:81).

The above data represent conceptual shifts in what a house should look like and who composed a household. These shifts may not have been easy for community members who had been living the same practices for over a century, but they may have been eagerly adopted by the immigrant portion of the population, who arrived specifically to partake in something new. The fact that the process of house construction may now have involved prefabricated elements means that a different labor force and knowledge set may have also been required for what was once a mundane and kin-focused task (Pauketat and Woods 1986). While the buildings present during the TLW phase had an anonymity to the designer, the new domestic architecture of the Lohmann phase may reveal the emergence of specialists (following Rapoport 1989:89; and see Pauketat 1994). This supposition is supported by the widespread occurrence, for the first time, of a standard suite of special-use structures.

The role of one's dwelling in expressing and solidifying identity cannot be underemphasized here. Vernacular architecture is, by definition, buildings without architects. That is, domiciles are built through a collective understanding of what a domicile is and should be, and that understanding is both unselfconscious and available to any member of society (Rapoport 1969, 1976). Changes in vernacular indicate a change in that understanding and rarely occur as abruptly as is seen in the American Bottom at the transition to the Mississippian period. This shift is rapid and great enough to propose that architecture in Greater Cahokia, very briefly, was no longer vernacular. Further emphasizing the importance of traditional architecture, vernacular elements were manipulated at the upland pilgrimage site of Emerald to mitigate the tensions between the familiar and the new during the early days of Cahokia (Alt 2017).

A more materially homogeneous society was firmly emplaced by the Stirling phase, less than three generations later, at which point the material assemblage and clearly preplanned neighborhoods are a testament to the hegemony of Greater Cahokia's ruling class (Emerson 1997b). Although only the earliest Mississippian phase is emphasized in the above discussion, the fact that Stirling-phase material culture at sites of all types throughout Greater Cahokia reached a new and sustained level of standardization so rapidly (or at all) speaks to the effectiveness of the local and widespread community-building events at East St. Louis and other nascent Mississippian sites (see Betzenhauser and Pauketat 2019).

## CONCLUSION

The physical world, artifacts, buildings, and landscapes all aided in naturalizing new ideologies that accompanied the advent of Mississippian life (Hegmon 2002: 270; Ingold 1993). This naturalization occurred in intentional and active ways, such as group participation in major events (see Khan et al. 2015) and a refiguring of community layouts to promote integration (Kowalewski 2006), but also in nondiscursive manners, as movement, memory, and perception were changed by one's interaction with the physical world (see Mills and Walker 2008; Van Dyke and Alcock 2003; Wilson 2010). Similar shifts in site and settlement structure, potting practices, subsistence, and architecture mark the onset of Mississippian life in the two case studies here, and many others across the Southeast. Together these indicate a paradigmatic shift in how communities were conceptualized and carried out in practice. The construction and maintenance of mounds—activities that Pauketat (2007:42) has noted are equivalent to cultural, political, and ideological maintenance—were key to this conceptualization and to the ideological shifts that made Mississippian society possible. The benefits or associations offered by new imagined communities were attractive enough to draw disparate peoples to seek and enact unified goals. The scale of these communities, spanning great physical and social space, made them subject to co-option or manipulation in ways that the smaller, more spatially associated communities of the preceding period were not.

## Acknowledgments

Thanks are due to the organizations that sponsored excavations resulting in the Kincaid and East St. Louis datasets: the Center for Archaeological Investigations and director emeritus Brian Butler; Southern Illinois University Carbondale field school instructors Paul Welch and Corin Pursell; Southeast Missouri State University; the Illinois State Archaeological Survey and director emeritus Tom Emerson; the Illinois Department of Transportation and chief archaeologist John Walthall, succeeded by Brad Koldehoff; the Federal Highway Administration; and the numerous lab and field crews for each project. Thanks also to Robert Mazrim for providing insightful comments on an earlier draft.

# 3

# THE BATTLE MOUND COMMUNITY

*Interaction along the Red River and*
*throughout the Caddo Homeland*

Duncan P. McKinnon

A rchaeologists often define the study of landscapes using terms such as landscape archaeology, anthropology of place, sacred and ideational landscapes,
ecological landscapes, cosmological landscapes, political landscapes, and socialized
landscapes (Anschuetz et al. 2001; Ashmore 2002; Bailey 1995; Bowser 2004; Brady
and Ashmore 1999; Delcourt and Delcourt 2004; Knight 1998; Krech 1999; Layton
and Ucko 1999; Lepper 2004; Sabo 2012; Smith 2003). Some perspectives focus on
the distribution of "tangible" or physical components and processes in which landscape modification contributes to community membership and cohesion (Brooks
2012; King et al. 2011; Perttula and Rogers 2007, 2012; Vogel 2012; Yaeger and
Cantu 2000). Others are rooted in ideational, social, or "intangible" components
and the way that processes tied to memory, identity, and conception create, shape,
and change landscapes (Alcock 2002; Ashmore and Knapp 1999; Tilley 1994).
Given the integration of the tangible and intangible by the community members
who inhabit, interact with, create, and socialize landscapes, these two perspectives
and processes are not independent (see also chapter 8 in this volume).

In this chapter, I integrate both perspectives by examining community interaction of Caddo peoples situated along the Red River and throughout the Caddo
homeland. I focus on the multiscalar interactions of a Caddo community known
as the Battle community, interactions that served to maintain long-term social
connections within and between communities throughout the Caddo cultural
landscape. I first evaluate intraregional interaction by examining artifact frequencies at known archaeological sites situated within the Battle community. Following, I explore interregional interaction by evaluating distributions of rayed circle
ceramic designs and effigy shell pendants found at farmsteads and community
mound centers located throughout the Caddo homeland. These material objects,
and the representations they embody, reinforced and integrated multiple scales of
the tangible and intangible aspects of community formation, identity, and interaction on the landscape by Caddo peoples during the Middle and Late Caddo period (c. AD 1200–1680).

## THE CADDO HOMELAND

The Caddo archaeological area, as delineated by archaeologists, comprises a 200,000 km² landscape primarily located within portions of what are today southwestern Arkansas, northwestern Louisiana, eastern Texas, and eastern Oklahoma (Figure 3.1). The Caddo archaeological area, which I refer to as the Caddo homeland, is situated within the Trans-Mississippi South, a biogeographic region characterized by a diverse ecological combination of arbor, fauna, climate, and terrain very similar to the woodlands ecology east of the Mississippi River (Minnis 2003; Schambach 1998:8). Around AD 900, the Indigenous inhabitants of this region descended from earlier Woodland period manifestations (often referred to as Fourche Maline culture; see Schambach 1982a) into a Caddo cultural tradition defined by a broad suite of shared social, economic, artistic, ideological, and political characteristics (Girard et al. 2014; Perttula 1992, 2012; Perttula and Walker 2012; Townsend and Walker 2004). As Caddo people, they occupied this landscape as late as the early nineteenth century in some locales, before being removed to the Brazos Reservation in Texas and, by 1859, to Indian Territory within present-day Oklahoma (Smith 1995).

Located on the westernmost frontier of the southeastern cultures of North America (see Muller 1978a), Caddo communities interacted with, and are often included as part of, the culturally and linguistically diverse and widely distributed group of Indigenous populations known to archaeologists collectively as Mississippians (Anderson and Sassaman 2012; Blitz 2010; King and Meyers 2002). In

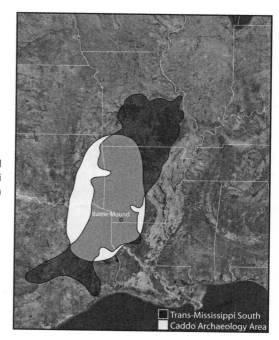

Figure 3.1. Caddo archaeological area and the Trans-Mississippi South. (Duncan P. McKinnon)

addition to its people's interaction and exchange with neighboring Mississippian groups, the Caddo homeland borders the southern plains region to the northwest. In other words, the ancestral landscape that the Caddo occupied was situated between two distinct cultural, geographic, and resource areas (Bell 1961; Perttula 2002; Vehik 1990; Vehik and Baugh 1994). This strategic location not only allowed Caddo communities to exchange goods and ideas with Mississippian communities throughout the eastern woodlands, it also facilitated long-distance direct or indirect interaction and exchange with Caddoan-speaking southern plains groups and likely with other linguistic and cultural groups situated farther to the west. Items exchanged and traded between Caddo and plains groups included bison (hides, hair, meat, and tallow) and important wood resources, such as the Osage orange or bois d'arc wood (*Maclura pomifera*) for use in the construction of bows (Creel 1991; King and Gardner 1981; Schambach 2000, 2003). Further, exchange with southern plains groups has been suggested as part of broader, interregional trade with groups in the Southwest and West in the form of turquoise, ceramic styles, Pacific Coast *Olivella* marine-shell beads, and perhaps cotton textiles (Creel 1991; Jurney and Young 1995; King and Gardner 1981; Kozuch 2002; Lankford 2006, 2012). Certainly, Caddo communities were strategically centered between two ecological and cultural resource zones, which allowed members to participate to varying degrees in economic and ideological exchange with neighboring Mississippian, plains, and Southwest communities.

Generally, archaeologists have subdivided the Caddo homeland into three archaeological subareas. While Caddo people occupied all of these subareas, their communities varied regionally in terms of architecture and mound types, subsistence and economic practices, mortuary treatment and ceremony, and artistic expression (Early 1988, 1993; Eubanks 2014; Girard et al. 2014; Kay and Sabo 2006; McKinnon 2011, 2015; Perttula 2009, 2017; Perttula et al. 2010; Sabo 1987; Sabo et al. 1988; Schambach 1990; Sullivan and McKinnon 2013). The emphasis herein is focused on community and interaction of Middle and Late Caddo (c. AD 1200–1680) within the Central Caddo subarea, along the Red River in southwestern Arkansas.

## CENTRAL CADDO COMMUNITY ORGANIZATION

There is little debate that the communities of Middle and Late Caddo peoples along the Red River were organized in a pattern of dispersed farmsteads situated along the river valley bottoms, where Hernando de Soto's *entrada* of 1539–1542 first recorded a region fully inhabited by Caddo farmsteads (Quinn 1979:143; Schambach 1993:87). One hundred and fifty years later, the Domingo Terán de los Ríos expedition documented a dispersed Upper Nasoni community along the Red River. The frequently referenced 1691 map (known colloquially as the Terán map) depicts several farmsteads containing circular thatch-covered dwellings, open-air storage structures, and ramadas (Hatcher 1932; Perttula et al. 1995; Perttula 2005; Schambach 1982b; Swanton 1942; Walker and McKinnon 2012; Walker and Perttula 2008). On the western edge of the community is an earthen temple mound, seemingly isolated from the surrounding farmsteads (Perttula 2005; Wedel 1978). Until recently, it was suggested that the location of the mound indicated a pattern of vacancy that defined Caddo communities situated along the Red River. While archaeological testing at several Red River farmsteads demonstrates consistencies in the architectural style and form of the circular dwellings on the Terán map (Kelley 1997; Perttula et al. 2008; Trubowitz 1984), recent research questions the applicability of a vacant mound center as a definitive pattern among Red River communities. For example, geophysical anomalies and surface collection artifacts at the Battle Mound site indicate the previous existence of numerous circular Caddo structures within a few meters of the large mound and distributed throughout the immediate landscape (McKinnon 2009, 2010, 2017; McKinnon and Haley 2017).

Nonetheless, the Terán map represents a synchronic view into broader aspects of Red River community organization that can be compared with archaeological data and evaluated beyond analyses of "bounded" archaeological sites, landscapes, and static coresidence. For example, the Upper Nasoni community organization has been suggested by Sabo (2012) to represent a cosmogram embedded in concepts of space and place. Emphasized are the organizational rules associated with Caddo cosmology and the cardinal directions of east and west, which correspond to life and death symbolism. The east, with the rising sun, is associated with life-affirming events and rituals, such as renewal ceremonies, whereas the west, with the setting sun, is connected to life-threatening events and rituals, such as hunting and warfare. Sabo (2012:446) proposes that the layout represents a "hierarchically ordered community," with the temple mound being home to the *xinesi* (priests) and serving as the central point for the maintenance of social relationships with the Upper World, and the *caddi* (chiefs) residence being centrally located within the community and serving as the central point for the maintenance of social relationships with members of the Middle World community (see Reilly 2004; Sabo 1995). These two intracommunity places were connected through the kindling of a sacred fire or axis mundi that was continually reaffirmed through ritual. This sacred fire was subsequently shared with the individual fires within the community farmsteads, thus maintaining symbolic and community membership, cohesion, and identity within a framework of overarching cosmological beliefs and community relationships (see also chapter 10 in this volume).

## BATTLE MOUND COMMUNITY AND INTRAREGIONAL INTERACTION

The Battle Mound site (3LA1) is situated along the Red River in southwestern Arkansas. It represents the largest extant mound in the Caddo homeland and is one of the largest earthen mound constructions in the Southeast (Muller 1978a; Perttula 1992:118; Schambach 1982a:7). The large mound and surrounding landscape of domestic farmsteads, hunting locales, areas of ritual practice, and natural formations compose a dispersed and socially integrated Caddo community that occupied this portion of the Red River during the Middle and Late Caddo time periods (Figure 3.2). While there has been important work identifying and excavating Red River farmsteads, much of what we know today of Middle to Late Caddo communities is from the perspective of larger sites that often contain mounds (e.g., Buchner et al. 2012; Jackson et al. 2012; McKinnon 2017; McKinnon and Haley 2017; Webb 1959). Unfortunately, little fieldwork has been done on farmsteads along the Red River, resulting in a fairly incomplete record of nonmounded farmstead distributions (Schambach 1982b:11). The fragmentary record largely stems from the ephemeral nature of farmstead sites, the damaging sinuosity of the meandering Red River (especially since Caddo frequently located farmsteads and mounds atop sandy ridges within active meanders), modern levee construction, and destructive aspects of modern agricultural practices and land leveling.

Farmsteads such as Cedar Grove (3LA97; Trubowitz 1984), Red Cox (3LA18;

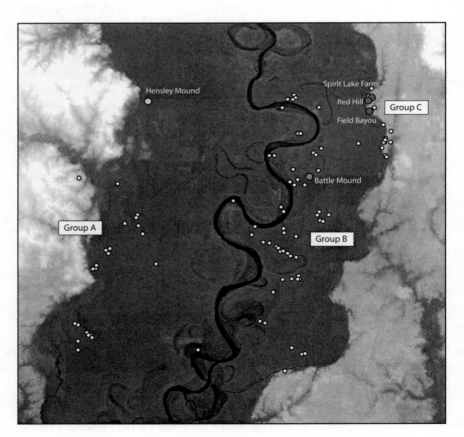

Figure 3.2. Distribution of sites within the Battle community. (Duncan P. McKinnon)

McKinnon et al. 2017), and Spirit Lake (3LA83; Hemmings 1982) represent a few of the domestic spaces in the Battle community and offer initial insights into the processes of intraregional interaction. Although many additional sites remain unanalyzed (or, in some cases, destroyed by cut bank erosion or agricultural production), these analyzed sites are constituents of the broader distributed community, which also includes natural landforms such as the meandering Red River, which bisects the river valley on a north–south alignment. While absolute chronologies are currently unavailable at most sites, ceramic chronology indicates broad temporality and thus can be reviewed as evidence of cumulative use of the landscape by Battle community members (Thompson 2017:137). The sites and natural landforms that constitute the Battle community are defined by their combined functional and symbolic interactions and are embedded with cosmological meaning, purpose, and vision. These sites were fully integrated into the daily lives and functions of the occupants (see Anschuetz et al. 2001; Kornfeld and Osborn 2003; Robb 1998).

The Battle community distribution reflects three spatially distinct groups or community places (A, B, and C). These groupings, based on frequencies of archaeological artifact types, are used to evaluate aspects of intraregional interaction (see Moran 2008:100; Yaeger and Canuto 2000). I propose that these community places are part of an integrated Caddo community of farmsteads, hunting locales, areas of ritual practice, and natural features that represent the location of dynamic social interactions between tangible and intangible components of the landscape and contribute to the formation and reinforcement of community and a shared identity and heritage (Olwig 2001:94).

Group A contains 24 sites, located roughly 6 km west of the Red River and along McKinney Bayou (see Figure 3.2). Calculations of the presence or absence of individual artifact types from both surface and excavated material reveal that lithic debris is present at 97 percent of the sites, ceramic sherds at 29 percent, and faunal remains at 0.04 percent. Faunal remains are present at a single site (3MI92). No human burials have been recorded. While many of these sites have not been examined systematically in the field, and the material currently on record is largely the result of avocational collections, the high occurrence of lithic material and low percentage of ceramics suggest that these sites represent specific-use activities, such as hunting or resource procurement.

The Hensley Mound is a lone mound site within this group and is approximately 6 km (3.72 miles) to the north and west of the larger Battle community. Unfortunately, the mound was destroyed in the early 1970s, and much of the land leveled for agriculture. There are no collections associated with Hensley Mound, so its role as a part of the Battle community is unknown. However, an interesting consideration is based on the Terán map cosmological model presented by Sabo (2012). On the Terán map the mound and associated temple are on the western fringes of the Upper Nasoni community, where it is suggested that the location functioned as a physical and symbolic "gateway." Through this locational gateway, visitors entered the community and were welcomed with various eating, smoking, and cleansing ceremonies and rituals (see Sabo 1995). Importantly, these rituals connected individuals with both the human and spirit realms and reaffirmed membership in the Upper Nasoni community. Perhaps the western location of the Hensley Mound served a similar functional and symbolic purpose for Battle community members.

Group B is located east of the Red River and contains 56 sites (see Figure 3.2). Within this group are six recorded mound sites, including the large and centrally located Battle Mound site (McKinnon 2017). Lithic debris has been recorded at 86 percent of the sites, ceramic sherds at 82 percent, and faunal remains at 28 percent. Human remains have been found at several sites within this group, although the location, degree, or type of burial is not fully understood (many are the product of pot hunting and arcane note taking). The abundance and fairly equal distribution of lithic and ceramic artifacts suggest that these sites represent the domestic constituents of the Battle community, similar to the dispersed set of farmsteads recorded on the Terán map. Included within Group B are the Cedar Grove, Red Cox, and Spirit Lake farmsteads (Hemmings 1982; McKinnon et al. 2017; Trubowitz 1984). Additionally, the presence of human remains suggests the location of cemeteries. Caddo community cemeteries have been noted to contain numerous individuals, with the size of the cemetery corresponding to settlement densities of the surrounding populations (Perttula 1992:83; Story 1990:338–339).

Farther east are 17 sites that define Group C and are located within the upland landscape above the Red River floodplain. Lithic debris has been recorded at 94 percent of the sites, ceramic sherds at 71 percent, and faunal remains at 18 percent. Human remains have not been recorded at any of the Group C sites. Among this group are three mounds: Spirit Lake Farm Mound (3LA239), Red Hill Mound (3LA21), and Field Bayou Mound (3LA22).

While these sites are provisionally defined by the archaeological record, initial considerations of intraregional landscape use and activity can be applied toward an evaluation of intraregional community interaction beyond a simple distribution of archaeological sites. The Battle community, in which Caddo peoples viewed and actively participated in both the "imagined" and "natural" realms (see Isbell 2000), represents a "single affective community" or assemblage of Caddo inhabitants, animals, places, and material objects that were linked together through ritual practice and reaffirmation of community cohesion and identity (Harris 2014). Again following the work of Sabo (2012), along with the corresponding artifact-type frequencies, I propose that the western Group A is a community place that represents the location of activities associated with life-threatening events, such as hunting bear (see Bolton 1987:103; Swanton 1942:137). Group C, situated to the east, represents the location of activities associated with life-affirming ceremonial events, such as seasonal cooking and feasting ceremonies held at important mound places situated along the edge of the uplands above and overlooking the domestic farmsteads distributed along the fertile river valley (see Swanton 1942:226–233). Group B, then, is the domestic sphere of daily life, balanced between the life-affirming and life-threatening places, and represented by numerous farmsteads. It is also the location of the important Battle Mound: the former residence of the priestly *xinesi*, who maintained relationships with the Upper World community, and the chiefly *caddi*, who maintained relationships with the Middle World community (Bolton 1987; Griffith 1954; Swanton 1942). Bisecting the community is the productive Red River as a central element—an axis mundi, perhaps—and a figurative connection to the watery realm of the co-existing Underworld community. In this view, the intraregional community interactions link together the tangible and intangible, and the Battle Mound community "is understood as dynamic, transformative, and emergent through practice" (Harris 2014:79).

## BATTLE MOUND COMMUNITY AND INTERREGIONAL INTERACTION

The Caddo peoples who actively participated in and identified as members of the Battle community also expressed their membership externally through interregional interaction with neighboring communities. Recent research in the Caddo homeland has begun to explore connections of community and identity that existed within and between Caddo groups and their neighbors (see Girard et al. 2014; Perttula 2017; Walker 2014; Wiewel 2014). Here, I highlight two distributional studies that exemplify the processes where material goods, along with accompanying ideologies, were reciprocally exchanged with neighboring groups. Goods and ideas were incorporated into communities and reinterpreted as distinct, yet broadly shared, forms of architecture, settlement, and material culture (Perttula 2009; Sullivan and McKinnon 2013; Walker 2014).

### The Rayed Circle

The rayed circle is defined in Phillips and Brown's (1978:155) Glossary of Motifs as a type of motif present on Spiro engraved shell cups. In Caddo examples, the rayed circle is present on ceramic vessels with two varieties that I have conditionally defined as rayed circle burst and rayed circle overhead (McKinnon 2016). Both are distributed throughout the Caddo homeland (Figure 3.3). While there are variations to the overall theme, the rayed circle burst has a central element, a circle containing a series of small triangles or rays emanating outward in a seemingly rotational movement (see McKinnon 2016:Figure 2a). The rayed circle overhead is a series of cross-hatched triangles that are pointed downward, with a single circular engraving or set of nested concentric circles at the triangle base (see McKinnon 2016:Figure 4).

Rayed circle burst vessels are clustered along the Red River, proximate to and within the Battle community in southwestern Arkansas (48 percent) and to the northeast along the Caddo, Little Missouri, Saline tributary, and Ozan Creek drainage in south-central Arkansas (38 percent). The Battle community cluster contains a greater number of rayed circle burst vessels, yet they exist in more concentrated occurrences and at fewer sites. For example, the vessels found at Battle Mound and the contemporaneous Haley Place mound (3MI1; Hoffman 1970) constitute 49 percent of the total number of vessels and 25 percent of the entire rayed circle burst corpus.

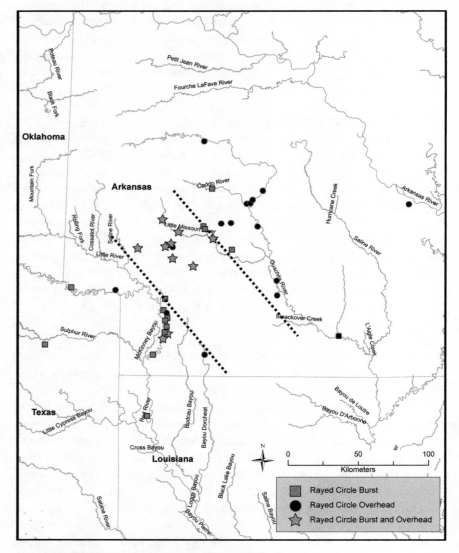

Figure 3.3. Distribution of rayed circle. (Duncan P. McKinnon)

When the distributions are compared across space, they reveal a possible interactional and perhaps ideological corridor bordered to the south by the Little and Red Rivers and to the north by the Little Missouri and Ouachita Rivers (see Figure 3.3). Initial observations suggest a north–south heterogeneity expressed in interregional community interaction, with the rayed circle overhead influence originating at communities in the northeast and the rayed circle burst influence originating in the southwest. Combinations of the two representations are present at all but one of the sites within the corridor and likely represent some degree of interaction with communities to the southwest and northeast. Sites within this corridor include Murf Davis (3PI13), Stokes Mound (3PI17), and Hayes Mound (3CL6; Weber 1971) along the Little Missouri drainage; Mineral Springs (3H01; Bohannon 1973), Flowers (3HE37; Harrington 1920), Jim Cole (3HE59), and Washington Mound (3HE35; Harrington 1920) along the Ozan Creek drainage; and Ferguson (3HE63; Schambach 1996) along Caruse Creek. The Lester (3LA38) and Battle Mound sites—which are located outside of the proposed corridor and are constituents of the Battle community—also contain both varieties. The presence of both rayed circle varieties at these two sites suggests that certain members of the Battle community were active participants in interregional interaction with distant groups and identified as former or current members of those communities.

## Zoomorphic Effigy Pendants

A second distributional study and example of interregional community interaction involves nonceramic Caddo representational art in the form of zoomorphic effigy pendants (Kay 1984; McKinnon 2015; Moore 1912; Perttula et al. 2010; Webb 1959; Weber 1972). The pendants were emblems of identity worn by members of communities as necklaces and crafted from a wide variety of local and nonlocal raw material, such as freshwater mussel shell, *Busycon perversum* (whelk) marine shell, animal bone, and various types of soft stone. The pendants contain a diverse set of representations and likely have ideational elements at a number of cultural levels (Layton 1991:34).

Recent examinations group the zoomorphic pendants into two broad stylistic categories (Dowd 2011; McKinnon 2015). Group A effigies resemble salamanders and have a wide body, discernable feet, triangular heads, and two eye markings or perforations (see Dowd 2011:Figure 9; McKinnon 2015:Figure 2). Group B effigies are slender pendants with an engraved pattern of concentric parallelograms or diamonds, usually with a dot in the center (see Dowd 2011:Figure 10; McKinnon 2015:Figure 4). The upper portion is typically rounded, with perforations just below the top. The pendant style resembles a cicada, with the possibility of the concentric diamond element representing the folded wings resting on the body. The similar insect themes worn as necklaces, yet diverse in presentation, likely suggest expressions of community identity at the individual level that may have been shared between individuals and intrasocial groups (Penney 2004:45).

While these themes are linked broadly to Mississippian groups throughout the Southeast, they are distinctive in Caddo expression and elaboration during Middle and Late Caddo periods (Girard et al. 2014:96).

The pendants have been found at sites across the Caddo homeland, with an apparent north–south heterogeneity in style, similar to the north–south distinctions in the rayed circle distribution (Figure 3.4). Most sites contain fewer than six pendants, and in many cases only a single pendant is represented. In other words, they

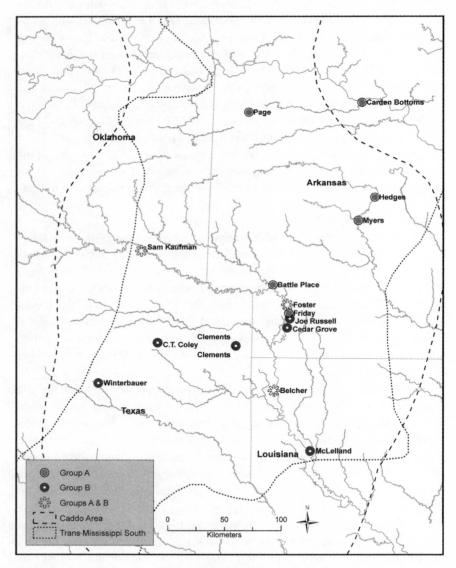

Figure 3.4. Distribution of zoomorphic pendants. (Duncan P. McKinnon)

are rare. Important exceptions include the Belcher (n = 65; Webb 1959), Clements (n = 18; Perttula et al. 2010), and Foster (n = 11; Buchner et al. 2012; Moore 1912) mound sites. Distributional analysis reveals that Group B pendants are primarily located in the southern part of the Caddo homeland. Except for a single freshwater mussel shell pendant, Group B pendants are all made from nonlocal marine whelk. Group A pendants are primarily located in the northern part of the Caddo homeland and have a greater diversity of medium, including soft stone, bone, and whelk and mussel shell. Three sites (Sam Kaufman, Foster [likely a part of the Battle community], and Belcher) are fairly equally spaced along the Red River and are the only examples where both Group A and Group B pendants are documented. This finding suggests that these locales were community "hubs" of socioeconomic importance. Each is a multimound site and has been interpreted as a civic-ceremonial center where archaeological data demonstrates that broad-scale social interaction and trade flourished (Buchner et al. 2012; Perttula 2008; Webb 1959). Additionally, the north–south heterogeneity of stylistic forms suggests the presence of broader cultural narratives of the Beneath World (Dowd 2011; McKinnon 2015).

## DISCUSSION AND CONCLUSION

The Caddo people who lived within the Caddo homeland during Middle and Late Caddo times created and maintained both the tangible, natural, or physical and the intangible, imagined, or social components of community at multiple scales of formation, identity, and interaction. While defined today as archaeological sites with non-Native names, assigned trinomials, and delineated boundaries in site reports, the archaeological sites that define Caddo communities were not simply static locations of coresidence bounded within natural landforms. To the contrary, Caddo landscapes should be evaluated as dynamic assemblages of tangible mounds, farmsteads, animals, natural features, and people that were integrated with the intangible aspects of memory, identity, and conception. These dynamic assemblages were actively linked together to create communities and reaffirmed through the process of ritual, renewal, exchange, and interaction of ideas, material goods, and the Caddo people themselves.

An examination of multiscalar aspects of interaction within the Caddo homeland illustrates how members participated in and maintained distinctive elements that defined the daily and ceremonial components of community. The Caddo people who lived in these communities, and in particular the Battle community during the Middle and Late Caddo times, expressed membership through a variety of intra- and interregional interactions as a single assemblage of social, economic, and political places, ideas, people, and nature (Harris 2014). On an intraregional scale, the places and spaces along the Red River defined as archaeological sites represent an integrated Caddo community of farmsteads, hunting locales, areas of ritual practice, and natural features, linked together both through the movement of daily necessities and as a "socio-political discourse concerning the relations between community, self, and place" (Olwig 2001:94). On an interregional scale, important mound sites, such as Battle Mound, represent the loci of distinct communities that were loosely affiliated by marriage and kinship relations and whose members were socially and politically integrated into a heterogeneous, interregional network of trade and interaction (Perttula 2012:8). Archaeological sites within the Caddo archaeological area have historically been defined in terms of isolated site characteristics or bounded within river and creek drainages. Using the Battle community as a focus of study, this chapter offers one example of how Caddo archaeology is moving beyond these restrictive analyses and toward broader themes related to economic and ideological interaction, connection, influence, identity, and exchange of communities throughout the Caddo homeland and with neighboring Mississippian, plains, and Southwest communities (Girard et al. 2014; Perttula 2017).

This frame of thought continues today, with the Caddo people who visited the ancestral Battle Mound community landscape in 2007. The visit was during a meeting of the annual Caddo Archaeology Conference (Davis and Davis 2009; Gregory 2009). While there, several Caddo gathered small twigs from cedar trees growing on the mound to bring home to Oklahoma. The large and looming earthen mound was a visible reminder of community, identity, and heritage. The cedar sprigs, gathered and deposited into small pouches, were collected to be incorporated and reinterpreted in ritual practice, perhaps, but they were certainly a reminder of the intangible processes of memory and identity and the reaffirmation of community cohesion and membership within a framework of cosmological beliefs and community relationships that persist to this day.

# 4

## NEGOTIATING COMMUNITY AT PARCHMAN PLACE, A MISSISSIPPIAN TOWN IN THE NORTHERN YAZOO BASIN

Erin S. Nelson

Late Mississippian (AD 1350–1541) archaeological sites in the northern Yazoo Basin in Mississippi typically consist of one or more earthen platform mounds adjacent to a large plaza surrounded by multiple residential areas. Sites are closely spaced throughout the region, and evidence for smaller, nonmound settlements is lacking. These observations suggest a distinctive Mississippian settlement pattern for the northern Yazoo, but they only partially address questions about past communities and the people who were part of them. In this chapter, I compare household, site-level, and regional archaeological data to ethnographic descriptions of Historic period (c. AD 1550–1800) Native American communities located nearby. The archaeological evidence indicates that Mississippian people moved across the landscape, founded communities, and arranged their living spaces in ways that are analogous to Historic period Indian towns, notably of the Chickasaw and Choctaw. These communities consisted of people engaged in shared practices that both tied them to one another and rooted them in a particular place. Simultaneously, Mississippian people performed roles and identities that likely have their basis in a clan system of social organization that extended more broadly beyond the limits of the local community. Shifts in practices related to mound building and the organization of space at Parchman Place (22CO511) in the second half of the fifteenth century provide evidence of divergent interests that were likely rooted in these dissonant identities, and that contributed to the short- and long-term trajectory of the community. Despite major disruptions in Mississippian social institutions and practices following contact, a consideration of ethnographic data alongside archaeological data can contribute significantly to our understanding of kinship, everyday social interactions, and relations of authority among Mississippian communities.

## FRAMING COMMUNITIES

Ethnographic descriptions indicate that the descendants of Mississippian people organized themselves according to a number of highly structured social systems.

Clans were generally exogamous social categories based on filial descent through matrilines (though some were patrilineal), and each clan was affiliated with one of two major social divisions understood as both contrasting and complementary in nature (Knight 1990). Patterns of residence crosscut the clan system, with members of multiple clans residing together in towns, referred to by the Choctaw as *oklas* (Galloway and Kidwell 2004) and by the Creek as *talwas* (Ethridge 2003; Knight 1994; Swanton 1946). Historic period towns were autonomous, considered by Urban and Jackson (2004:703) to be the "minimally self-sufficient units of Muskogean social organization." Often, they were associated with shared ceremonial facilities, perhaps including a square ground, ball ground, and council house (Lewis et al. 1998). Town members shared a ceremonial fire, and people of the same town were referred to as being of the same "fire," terminology more broadly used to indicate alliance (Swanton 1928:250). Though towns had a physical presence on the landscape, physicality was not their defining feature. In fact, towns could be nucleated or dispersed across the landscape, and they could move from place to place while retaining their essential character. Rather it was the members themselves and their shared ceremonial practice that constituted a town, much in the way that we think of congregants and their shared religious practice as constituting a church (Scarry and Steponaitis 2016). Though towns were autonomous, alliances and other relationships existed between Historic period towns, "reflecting a broader awareness of community and perhaps tribal identity" (Urban and Jackson 2004:703).

Towns were composed of members of multiple clans, local manifestations of which frequently took the form of small-scale, corporate lineages or subclan groups, as in the "house groups" of the Chickasaw (Brightman and Wallace 2004; Knight 1990; Speck 1907; Swanton 2006 [1928]) and Choctaw (Galloway and Kidwell 2004; Swanton 1931; Urban and Jackson 2004). Taking the Historic period Chickasaw as one example, Knight (1990) describes such lineages or subclan groups as corporate in nature. These groups, composed of related women and their husbands and children, resided together and were tied to estates that included houses, shared communal space, and agricultural fields. Chickasaw estates were named, and their members were thought to share characteristics of personality and custom.

Significantly, the communities just described are of recent historical origin, forged by the descendants of Mississippian people in the wake of major social disruptions caused by European colonization (Ethridge and Hudson 2002; Pluckhahn and Ethridge 2006). Members of these coalescent societies (Kowalewski 2006) found new ways to live with one another that drew on their shared understandings of kinship and other forms of social organization. And though this organization was highly structured, its crosscutting nature meant that these formations were flexible and that people could draw on multiple identities in the context of negotiating, building, and maintaining their communities (Leach 1954).

While attempts to understand social organization have proven extraordinarily productive in the study of coalescent societies, archaeological evidence suggests that Mississippian social formations were also adaptable and that Mississippian people could manipulate their organizing structures by drawing on crosscutting identities. Scarry and Steponaitis (2016:265) point to a changing emphasis on town- versus clan-based identities during Moundville's history. Employing Gearing's (1962) concept of structural poses, they argue that Moundville was transformed from a town to a permanent ceremonial ground incorporating members of multiple towns during the thirteenth century, and that the transformation is consonant with the increased power of clan leaders at the expense of that of town leaders. Cobb and King (2005) discuss political reorganization at Etowah in terms of the relationship between power and the ways that people drew on contrasting conceptualizations of time, understandings that were tied up in various notions of kinship. During Etowah's initial occupation, its residents incorporated ideas related to a shared mythical past (world renewal, fertility) in mound building and other material practices to promote an ethos of egalitarianism within the community. During its subsequent occupation, monumental architecture and burial practices involving repeated intergenerational interment emphasized genealogical time, which promoted an "emerging politics of exclusion" (Cobb and King 2005:181; see also chapter 8 in this volume). These examples and others (e.g., Birch 2012; Knight 1990) demonstrate that concurrently held identities that have their basis in differing social structures and associated temporal concepts are relevant for understanding social questions such as how communities are forged and maintained over time.

In similar ways, archaeological evidence from Parchman Place reveals historical moments in which negotiations took place among people who were drawing on different sets of values. Influenced by practice-based theories of social interaction (Bourdieu 1977; Giddens 1979, 1984), much recent archaeological scholarship has regarded past communities as forms of social organization for which boundaries are constantly maintained and negotiated (Barth 1969; Birch 2012; Díaz-Andreu et al. 2005; Harris 2014; Marcoux 2008; Pauketat 2007). These approaches stress *what people do* (e.g., Pauketat 2008a:240), both as matters of daily routine and as more intentional acts meant to communicate social messages. Significantly, they consider practice as shaped by historical conditions and existing social structures. In turn, those conditions and structures are affected by practice. In line with these approaches, I view communities as defined by people and their interactions, by the physical and social spaces in which practice takes place, and by historical context, including existing social structures and larger political formations. Importantly, processes of community building happen at multiple scales (Rogers and Smith 1995; Yaeger and Canuto 2000).

In the present case, the relevant organizing structures differ in terms of the nature and extent of their flexibility. Clan identity, determined matrilineally, is fixed at birth, and though rankings among clans are flexible, their membership criteria and internal structure are less so. In contrast, town membership can be understood in terms of what Brett Riggs (personal communication 2010) has called "structured autonomy." Though guided by a set of structuring principles, corporate kin groups exercise considerable autonomy in affiliating with other groups to form a town. Consequently, the town is a social entity that requires intention in its formation and maintenance: towns must be constantly built and rebuilt through practice.

In what follows, I consider the ways that Mississippian people living at Parchman Place in the fourteenth and fifteenth centuries went about building, maintaining, and negotiating community ties. In examining the archaeological data, I evaluate the fit between these data and ethnographically documented accounts of kin-based social structures that organized Historic period Native groups, particularly those of the western Muskogean nations. Archaeological evidence from Parchman Place indicates that Mississippian people moved across the landscape, founded communities, and arranged their living spaces in ways that are analogous to Historic period Indian towns, notably of the Chickasaw and Choctaw. However, material practice also indicates that community-building activities were used to negotiate the tensions between leadership and community values and that crosscutting social identities were called on in these moments of negotiation.

## ARCHAEOLOGY OF PARCHMAN PLACE

Parchman Place is a Mississippian period settlement located in the northern Yazoo Basin of northwestern Mississippi (Figure 4.1). The northern Yazoo is a rich floodplain environment created by the meanderings of the Mississippi, Ohio, Deer Creek, Sunflower, and Yazoo Rivers. The alluvial actions of relict river channels resulted in natural levees ideal for the cultivation of maize and other native domesticates, as well as oxbow lakes and adjacent wetlands, which supported an abundance of aquatic resources and migratory birds. The region as a whole was densely occupied during late prehistory, though historical relationships among sites in the region have yet to be fully worked out (Connaway 1984a:83; Hally and Chamblee 2019; Johnson et al. 2016; Phillips 1970:940). In any case, mound sites are closely spaced, and evidence for smaller, nonmound sites is lacking. Radiocarbon dates from Parchman Place span roughly 200 years and indicate that people moved to this location in the early fourteenth century (Nelson 2020). As part of the establishment of their community in this location, Mississippian people built five or more earthen mounds along a natural levee overlooking an oxbow lake. Simultaneously, they established a series of neighborhoods surrounding an open, central plaza. Figure 4.2 shows the results of magnetic gradiometry at the site, with discrete residential areas indicated by clusters of dark magnetic anomalies representing burned Mississippian houses.

More than 40 Mississippian structures have been identified in the magnetometer data based on their size, shape, and strong positive magnetic signatures (typically 20–60 nT) (Johnson and Haley 2006; Nelson 2014). These structures are located on the surfaces of Mounds A, D, and E, as well as in off-mound areas, primarily to the south and east of the main mound group. Excavations have determined that structures identified by magnetic gradiometry are typically located less than 60 cm from the current ground surface and were fired prior to abandonment, a process that enhanced their remnant magnetism. An additional 20-plus houses were identified via surface survey as concentrations of fired daub eroding

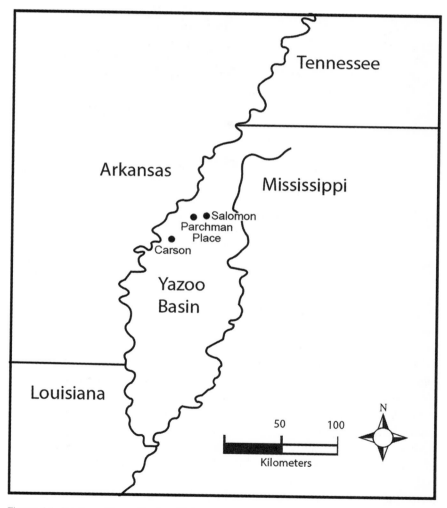

Figure 4.1. Northern Yazoo Basin with locations of Parchman Place and nearby sites mentioned in the text. (Erin S. Nelson)

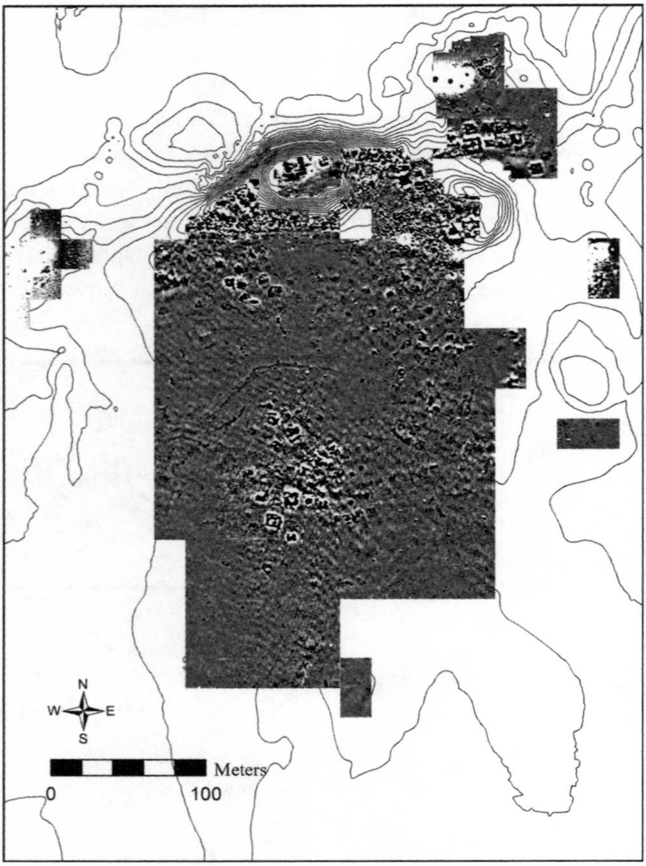

Figure 4.2. Magnetic gradiometry results showing clusters of residential areas surrounding a magnetically clean plaza, Parchman Place. (Courtesy of the Center for Archaeological Research, University of Mississippi)

out of the surface (Connaway 1984b; Nelson 2020:18). Figure 4.3 plots known surface and near-surface structural features on a modern topographic contour map. Excavations in mound and residential areas indicate that these features are the latest iterations of a series of buildings constructed in the same location. In residential areas, excavations revealed from two to five buildings stacked one on top of the next. The summit of Mound E had at least ten such layers.

Residential neighborhoods are identified in the magnetometer data as discrete clusters of houses and other architectural features that are organized around shared outdoor spaces, typically courtyards. Four such neighborhoods flank the plaza (N1, N2, N4, and N5 in Figure 4.3), while a fifth (N3 in Figure 4.3) is located to the east of Mound A, physically separate from other residential areas (Nelson 2020). The building and rebuilding of houses in the same space suggest that these neighborhoods are of significant duration. Radiocarbon samples from four residential contexts indicate that many, if not all, of the plaza-adjacent neighborhoods

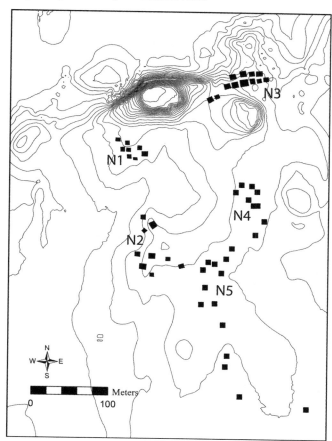

Figure 4.3.
Topographic
contour map
(50 cm contour
interval) showing
domestic struc-
tures identified
via magnetic
gradiometry
and surface
concentrations
of daub,
Parchman Place.
N = neighborhood.
(Courtesy of
the Center for
Archaeological
Research,
University of
Mississippi)

were founded in the early to mid-fourteenth century, coincident with the initiation of mound construction (Nelson 2020:Table 1.2). Within these neighborhoods, people organized their houses and other facilities around central courtyards. Neighborhood 3 is distinct from other residential areas at Parchman Place
in terms of its location, late founding date, and internal organization. Rather than
building their homes around courtyards, Neighborhood 3 residents constructed
two rows of closely spaced houses on either side of a 3 m wide avenue or path
oriented toward a ramp leading to the summit of Mound A (Nelson 2014). In addition to revealing a series of domestic structures, excavations in the vicinity of
Neighborhood 1 revealed activities associated with the founding of the Parchman
Place community and actions taken on the part of those living nearby to further
the well-being of the community. Two sequential deposits in this location are of
particular interest. The earlier of the two consists primarily of food remains that
were trampled into the initial occupation surface, resulting in a dark anthropo-

genic clay that is rich in organic materials and artifacts. The latter is a 30 cm thick deposit of mounded ash that was placed here in at least three discrete episodes.

The earlier of the two deposits dates to the early to middle part of the four-teenth century, around the time that Parchman Place was founded, and when the mounds, plaza, and neighborhoods were initially constructed (Nelson 2020: Table 1.2). It contains a typical domestic pottery assemblage characterized by a mix of cooking, serving, and storage vessels (Nelson et al. 2020). Botanical re-mains from the deposit are also typical of everyday consumption, with broadly even representation of a variety of plant foods, notably maize (*Zea mays*, ker-nels and cupules), chenopod (*Chenopodium berlandieri*), maygrass (*Phaseolus vulgaris*), and erect knotweed (*Polygonum erectum*) (Melton 2013; Nelson et al. 2020). The faunal remains, however, fit most easily into a pattern frequently interpreted as exclusive elite feasting (Jackson and Scott 2003:553–555). Deer (*Odocoileus virginianus*) elements within the deposit exhibit a low degree of fragmentation and high degree of completeness, while the presence of golden eagle (*Aquila chrysaetos*) and American crow (*Corvus brachyrhynchos*) suggests elite and/or ritual ac-tivities (Nelson et al. 2020). Elsewhere, my colleagues and I interpret this deposit as the remains of inclusive potluck-style feasting associated with the founding of the Parchman Place community (Nelson et al. 2020). The presence of a domestic-looking ceramic vessel assemblage (including a majority of cooking vessels), maize remains indicative of food preparation, and prebutchered deer haunches are con-sistent with this interpretation. While "provisioned" deer meat and the presence of rare birds including crow and golden eagle would normally be interpreted as exclusive, elite activity, the nonspecialized ceramic assemblage suggests that these unusual elements may have been important in inclusive ritual or ceremonial prac-tice at Parchman Place.

Directly on top of the deposit just described is a feature consisting of three dis-crete layers of redeposited ash with a combined thickness of 30 cm (Figure 4.4). The ash was also placed here during the fourteenth century, sometime after the initial occupation of the site. The vessel assemblage associated with the ash fea-ture contains a high ratio of serving vessels, including large, wide, shallow bowls suitable for serving large groups of people, as well as small and very small bowls suitable for serving rare, valuable, or perishable goods (Nelson 2020:71; Nelson et al. 2020). Botanical remains are similar to those described above but also con-tain substantive quantities of nutshell, including thin-shelled hickory (*Carya* sp.) and acorn (*Quercus* sp.). Maize kernel-to-cupule ratios indicate that the ash fea-ture has four times the amount of consumable maize than the underlying deposit (Melton 2013; Nelson et al. 2020). The faunal assemblage from the ashy feature is consistent with everyday household consumption; the only notable features are the high proportions of burned (more than 50 percent) and calcined (more than 36 percent) bone, which could only be the result of purposeful burning (Nelson et al. 2020). Based on its contents, we interpret the ashy feature as the remains of everyday household consumption. However, its distinct depositional character bears a striking resemblance to ethnographic accounts related to the special treatment of ashes in preparation for the renewal of sacred fire during annual maize harvest ceremonies such as the busk or Green Corn ceremony (Jackson 2003:198; Nelson et al. 2020). These remains may therefore represent the remains of such fires—that is, ashes from the sacred fire or hearth scrapings of households within

Figure 4.4. Ash heap in Neighborhood 1 excavation trench at Parchman Place. View east. (Erin S. Nelson)

the community that were gathered and deposited together in a specially designated spot, perhaps similar to the "ash heaps" shown on Historic period square ground maps in Oklahoma, as recorded by Swanton (1928; Knight 2006:425).

Excavations in Mounds E and A reveal the complex ways that mound building was used in community building and negotiation throughout Parchman Place's history (Nelson 2020). Early stages of Mound E were associated with ceramic assemblages that differ from the more typical domestic assemblages found elsewhere, but that are remarkably like the assemblage associated with the ashy feature described above. These serving assemblages are characterized by bowls of all types, notably large, wide, shallow bowls and very small serving bowls. In one context, small serving bowls took the form of finely made carinated and restricted bowls that were almost certainly made farther south, in the southern Yazoo Basin or Natchez Bluffs region (Nelson 2020:87; Phillips 1970:49), perhaps indicating a kin- or trade-based relationship with Mississippian groups to the south. Social distinctions made by having or not having fine pottery of distant manufacture suggest that socially distinct segments of the Parchman Place community took part in feasting events related to the founding of the mound and community.

Following the feasting activities that mark the commencement of mound building, people at Parchman Place generally undertook a standard pattern of mound construction that included the addition of earthen mantles and the building and dismantling of summit structures. First, they constructed a mantle that served as a platform for a large residential building. Some mantles were constructed using redeposited midden from nearby locations; others were constructed of sediments (particularly clays) chosen for their desired engineering properties (Nelson 2020:100). Summit buildings were wall-trench structures made of wattle and daub and covered by thatched roofs. Each building was used for some length of time before it was swept clean of artifacts and then burned, typically in a manner that ensured the preservation of large amounts of structural material in the form of fired or vitrified wall daub and sometimes carbonized wall posts, ceiling beams, or roofing material. In most cases the recently destroyed structures were immediately buried in a layer of mound fill, when the building remains were still hot enough to cause oxidation and reduction. This basic sequence of events was repeated many times during the fourteenth century and the early part of the fifteenth century. In fact, this pattern is well documented for Mississippian sites more broadly and is frequently interpreted as a manifestation of the succession of leaders (Anderson 1994; Cobb and King 2005; Hally 1996; Knight 2006; Trubitt 2009).

Sometime during the middle of the fifteenth century, mound building at Parchman Place was punctuated and perhaps disrupted by atypical mound-building practices that include veneering, truncation, and the physical incorporation of one mound by another (Nelson 2020:100–104). The first of these is the addition of a white veneer composed of ash, crushed mussel shell, and kaolin (a fine, silty clay that is white in color) to a mound summit exposed in the Mound E summit excavation (Figure 4.5). In some places, it appears that the materials making up this deposit were mixed prior to their deposition, a preparation described by Sherwood and Kidder (2011:74). There is evidence for at least five (and probably more) white layers, with intermediate gray layers in between the pure white ones (see Pauketat 2008b for discussion of the use of alternating light and dark settlements in mound construction). This finding indicates that the white mound surface was maintained for a period of time before a new structure was built on its surface, in contrast to the previous practice, where new structures were built immediately after the burial of old ones.

The materials used to construct the white mound surfaces were intentionally chosen for their physical properties and cultural associations (Nelson 2020: 100; see also Charles et al. 2004; Kidder and Sherwood 2016). The closest known source of kaolin is nearly 60 km away, and the distance required to transport it is an indication of its significance (Charles et al. 2004:50). The color white has symbolic associations with purification and renewal (Hudson 1976:226; Pursell 2004, 2013:85), and ash and shell likely had cosmological associations for Mississippian people (Baltus and Baires 2012; Hall 1997; Lankford 2004, 2007; Pauketat 2008b:65). We can understand each component of the white veneer, therefore, as referencing one of the three divisions of the Mississippian cosmos: ash, with similar connective and communicative properties as smoke (Jackson 2003), references the Above World; clay and mussel shell, respectively, represent this world and the Beneath World. When gathered together (Bradley 1990, 1998; Mills 2008), these substances represent the entirety of the cosmos and emphasize the importance of ideas related to wholeness and balance between complementary parts for Mississippian people (Nelson 2020:157).

Following a period of maintenance of the white mound surface, at least two stages of Mound E were built in the standard manner, with each mantle supporting summit architecture that was constructed and deconstructed according to the

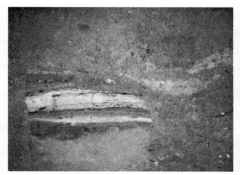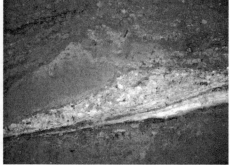

Figure 4.5. White veneer composed of ash, crushed mussel shell, and kaolin, located on an intermediate summit of Mound E at Parchman Place. (Courtesy of the Center for Archaeological Research, University of Mississippi)

common practice. Following these construction stages, Mound E was truncated. That is, someone or some group of people removed an unknown quantity of fill from the top of the mound, all the way down to the white veneer and adjacent floor. Given that the truncation extended to the veneered surface and no farther, I consider these two unusual acts of mound building to be related. That is, the people responsible for the truncation intentionally exposed the veneered surface in order to reference the meanings and circumstances associated with its creation (Nelson 2020:157). Though unusual in the Mississippian world, aboriginal excavations in mound contexts have also been reported in the American Bottom, for example in Mound 49 at Cahokia (Pauketat 2008b:72; Pauketat et al. 2010) and the Main Street Mound at East St. Louis (Brennan 2016:87). Much like Mound A at Parchman Place, the excavations in Cahokia's Mound 49 seem to have intentionally revealed a series of alternating light and dark mantles from an earlier stage of mound construction. According to Pauketat (2008b:75, 77), one possible goal of Native digging was to "reinspect or document the stratigraphy in the exposed profile," thereby revealing "the apparent sedimentary truths that they or their parents or grandparents had buried in the ground."

Following the truncation and re-exposure of the white mantles in the mid-fifteenth century, mound builders at Parchman Place resumed building Mound E in the standard, established pattern: a mound fill layer followed by a summit structure that was destroyed and then buried. The sequence was repeated at least four times before the mound was abandoned, probably in the late fifteenth or early sixteenth century. These final construction episodes represent a return to the standard mound-building practices previously noted. However, they take place within a shifting social context at Parchman Place, reflected in both mound building and the organization of (some) domestic spaces. First, the physical relationship between Mounds E and A changes shortly after the truncation event, when fill from Mound A encroaches on the space formerly occupied by Mound E. This spatial encroachment continues with the next stage of construction, when the swale separating the two mounds is filled in. Subsequently, Mound A was expanded rapidly and dramatically, coming to tower over all other mounds at the site and incorporating a substantial portion of Mound E. By this time, if not before, the people living in Neighborhood 3 had established a spatial relationship with Mound A by orienting the path separating houses toward a ramp leading to the Mound A summit, an orientation that I argue is social as well as physical.

## DISCUSSION

In the beginning of this chapter, I posed a set of interrelated questions. First, does the archaeology suggest that we can think about the Mississippian community at Parchman Place in terms of social categories known to exist among Historic period Indian groups, such as clans, house groups, or towns? The most telling evidence for social organization comes from multiscalar spatial organizational schemes. Households, as Rogers (1995b) points out, have been considered a fundamental building block of society (Wilk and Rathje 1982), though they can be difficult to pinpoint archaeologically. For instance, we do not know whether individual residential structures at Parchman Place can be considered autonomous households, or whether households might be better understood as consisting of multiple dwellings positioned around courtyards. Neighborhoods, in contrast, can be identified based on the close spatial clustering of multiple dwellings with shared communal space in the form of courtyards or paths. In most cases, these clusters are situated at intervals alongside a shared plaza and are separated from one another by unoccupied spaces. At the site level, then, constituent social groups of the community were organized in specific relationships to one another and to major site features, including the plaza and the mounds. Furthermore, each neighborhood may have been affiliated with a single mound. Neighborhood 3 is suggestive in this regard, not only because it is in proximity to Mound A, but also because the path separating its two lines of houses is oriented directly toward the ramp leading to Mound A's summit.

If we look at the site as a whole, then, we can think of the community at Parchman Place as structurally similar in many ways to Historic period Indian towns, and of neighborhoods composed of multiple courtyard groups as structurally similar to the house groups of the Historic period Chickasaw and Choctaw, an argument that has been made for multihousehold groups at early Moundville as well (Wilson 2008:17, 75; cf. Knight 2016; Scarry and Steponaitis 2016). House groups presumably could be equivalent to a single household or could encompass multiple households. Neighborhood 3, with its lines of houses on either side of a path, may also represent a house group, as the concept does not seem to be tied to any particular internal spatial arrangement. In addition to site organization, the simultaneous establishment of the main components of the site plan—mounds, plaza, and neighborhoods—suggests that the population that founded Parchman Place may have moved to this location *as a town*. If this is the case, we might look to nearby sites such as Salomon (22CO504) as possible locations of origin.

Structural similarities, physical proximity (less than 7 km separate Parchman Place and Salomon), and sequential ceramic assemblages and radiocarbon dates (Johnson et al. 2016) indicate a possible population shift from Salomon to Parchman Place around the beginning of the fourteenth century, a situation perhaps analogous to the wholesale relocation of Historic period towns. This pattern of movement may have been typical for the region, given the number of similarly sized sites nearby, and it should be a focus of future research in this region. As Birch (2012:665) has pointed out, "By focusing our attention on historical trajectories of development in contiguous communities over time, we are better positioned to understand the social relations that are encapsulated in settlements as well as the broader historical processes of which they are a part."

If we understand the structural organization of Parchman Place in terms of a town and the multiple house groups that make up its members, the next question we can ask is about the identities of the people who lived there. In matrilineal societies, house structures would have belonged to women, as would have associated courtyards and other workspaces, storage facilities, gardens, and agricultural fields (e.g., Sullivan and Rodning 2011). If we assume matrilocal residence, then the core household members were likely women and their children, though they also may have included other close relatives, perhaps husbands, parents, and unmarried male relatives. The exact composition of households would, of course, have depended on local conventions and individual circumstances, but they would have been organized around principles of matrilineal descent.

In some ways, basic social relationships and organizational principles of house groups would have been similar to households in that house groups would have been composed of related women and their husbands and children, and much of the day-to-day decision-making would have been negotiated among house group members, with senior women in residence having a considerable amount of influence (Sullivan 2001a). Significantly, however, a primary locus of identity at the house group level would have been clan affiliation. For some individuals, clan identities crosscut household-based identities due to the nature of matrilineal descent and exogamous marriage rules. Again assuming matrilocal residence, we can expect that married men would not have been members of the prevailing clan of the house group where they resided. Rather, the clan identities and obligations of married men would have been closely aligned with the house group of their mothers and sisters, whether or not their mothers and sisters resided within the town.

Clan obligations to the entire community would have been fulfilled by members of a house group plus married men of the same clan who resided elsewhere. Ethnographically, clans had defined ceremonial responsibilities within a town (Scarry and Steponaitis 2016:258; Swanton 1946:654–665). At Parchman Place and other Mississippian period sites, these responsibilities likely included roles in annual rites of intensification (Knight 1986), the residues of which can be observed in mound building and the deposition of large quantities of ash in Neighborhood 1. Clan identities would have extended beyond the town to encompass members who resided in nearby communities.

Among other things, broader clan obligations probably included burial. James (2010, 2015) interprets the secondary burial of individuals at Carson (22CO515), a contemporary site located 10.5 km to the southwest, as emphasizing the social importance of corporate groups. Furthermore, she argues that social houses (Lévi-Strauss 1982:174) may have been a key feature of social organization at that site. Significantly, Carson is the only site in the region that does not fit the pattern previously described for mound sites in the northern Yazoo Basin. The site stretches nearly two kilometers in length and has seven large earthen mounds and over 80 smaller ones (Johnson and Connaway 2020). It is also unique in that it was occupied throughout the entire Mississippian period. The relative lack of burials found at Parchman Place and the elaborate mortuary program at Carson may indicate one way in which the sites were connected to each other. Carson may be best understood as a regional ceremonial center with mortuary functions. If people from Parchman Place and other towns within the surrounding region were buried at Carson, that would indicate significant social integration and interaction among late Mississippian communities in the northern Yazoo.

It seems, then, that lineage-based identities are most relevant at the local scales of households, house groups, and towns. While clan-based identities also articulate with house groups, the roles and obligations of clans are most relevant within the town and within the broader region. The most significant overlap between lineage-based and clan-based identities, therefore, occurs at the scale of the *town*: the scale at which shared identities are *intentionally* forged, and consequently, the scale at which there exists the most ambiguity in the relative importance of contrasting social identities.

Recalling the minimal definition of Historic period towns as composed of people and their shared ceremonial practice, I now consider the evidence for activities that Mississippian people engaged in at Parchman Place that speak to the establishment of their community, as well as the ways that community was actively maintained, negotiated, and transformed through time. Spatial organization of the site, mound building, and other founding events all suggest that concepts of wholeness and balance between constituent parts were important components of the proper functioning of a town. The values denoted by these practices signify an effort on the part of community members to forge a shared identity as members of the town, perhaps grounding those relationships in mythical (as opposed to genealogical) understandings of time (Cobb and King 2005:174; Gosden and Lock 1998). In the decades that followed the town's founding, these community values were reinforced, contested, and transformed in various ways, some of which can perhaps be understood as relating to conflicts between town- and clan-based identities.

Apart from establishing the physical layout of the town, Mississippian people at Parchman Place took part in a number of founding activities specifically related to establishing their community in place. Bowl-dominated ceramic assemblages associated with the earliest mound-building stages suggest that activities related to the initiation of mound building involved large-scale feasting on the part of community members, a situation with parallels elsewhere in the Mississippian world (e.g., Pauketat et al. 2002; see Knight 2001 for pre-Mississippian examples). Furthermore, differences in the types of bowls used for serving in different contexts indicate that multiple distinct segments of the population took part in the feasting events. The use of nonlocal carinated and restricted bowls by one of these segments suggests that they had social ties to Mississippian groups in the southern Yazoo Basin or Natchez Bluffs region, perhaps based on kinship or trade relationships. Potluck-style feasting was also a major activity associated with the founding of Neighborhood 1, which was coincident with early mound building (Nelson et al. 2020). All of this evidence suggests that mound building and the activities associated with it are related to the establishment of the town *in a particular place*. Population movements and the establishment or resettling of communities in particular locations offer moments of ambiguity in which previous social structures can be scrutinized, reorganized, and transformed (Cobb and King 2005:170; see also Kowalewski 2006). Here, shared values related to wholeness and balance were emphasized from the town's very establishment.

While community-building activities are most in evidence at the beginning of Parchman Place's occupation, material practice indicates that there was a need for a continued focus on acts of maintenance and balancing, perhaps because of the tendency of clan- and town-based identities to come into conflict. Consequently, ceremonial practice at Parchman Place indicates an ongoing attention to maintaining the well-being of the community and its place in the world. In addition to feasting events associated with the initiation of mound building, the ash deposits in Neighborhood 1 recall historical and modern accounts of putting the old fire to rest in preparation for the renewal of sacred fire during annual ceremonies related to maize harvests and other significant events (e.g., Jackson 2003:198; Witthoft 1949). I suggest that these ash deposits represent the remains of sacred fire or the hearth scrapings of households within the community that were gathered and deposited together in a specially designated location, perhaps analogous to the "ash heaps" shown on Swanton's (1928) map of a Kealedji square ground in Oklahoma (see Nelson et al. 2020). Within this conceptual understanding, an ash deposit that archaeologists might typically consider only as incidental "trash" takes on more significant meaning (e.g., Colwell-Chanthaphonh and Ferguson 2006). It is the first step in an annual rite, the purpose of which was to restore balance within the community and within the world.

The burning and burial of mound-top structures can also be understood in terms of purification and renewal (Hally 1996; Knight 2006). Mound E was constructed following a repeating pattern of mantle construction alternating with the building and use of summit structures. The destruction and burial of these structures after a period of use initiated the next episode of mantle construction. In general, the repeated sequence of building, use, destruction, and burial of mound-top structures on Mound E (and probably Mounds A and B) indicates a remarkable degree of continuity through time. It seems, then, that the rules regarding succession of leaders were well established and happened smoothly throughout Parchman Place's early history, a time when individual mounds were of comparable size, suggesting that leaders from several lineages or clans may have shared power equally, or perhaps that they had different but equally esteemed forms of authority (e.g., Knight 2010:365). Overall, fourteenth-century mound-building practices indicate a continued attention to balance among constituent parts of the community, a primary principle on which the town was founded.

Sometime during the mid-fifteenth century, new mound-building and spatial-organization practices suggest an extended period of negotiation between community members who emphasized values associated with the well-being of the town (balance, wholeness) and attempts to tip the social or political balance in favor of a single clan-based subgroup within the town. The unusual nature of the white veneer as well as its continued maintenance may correspond to some particularly trying event for the Parchman Place community (perhaps a contested succession), and this circumstance was counteracted by an extended focus on community purification and renewal during which some members of the Parchman Place community emphasized values related to wholeness and balance between complementary parts. Furthermore, those responsible for the truncation of Mound E intentionally removed a portion of the mound summit in order to re-expose the veneer (or at the very least halted their cutting activities once it was reached). This act would have reinforced the significance of the white mound surface and the meanings it held for those who created it. If the maintenance of a white mound surface can be interpreted in terms of corporate group values related to balance, wholeness, and renewal, then re-exposing the surface at a later date implies a desire on the part of those responsible to return to those values (see also Baltus 2014).

These extraordinary practices on the part of community members are likely a response to social jockeying by subgroups within the Parchman Place community that escalated over the course of the fifteenth and early sixteenth centuries. Direct evidence for increasing competition between social groups in the post-truncation era includes the spatial encroachment of Mound A at the expense of Mound E's footprint, followed soon after by the rapid and dramatic expansion of Mound A, resulting in the partial incorporation of Mound E. While both mounds continued to be built and used, probably into the early sixteenth century, Mound E remained a modest size, while Mound A came to dwarf all other mounds at Parchman Place. Finally, the manipulation of the site plan late in Parchman Place's history suggests that the inclusive ideals expressed by founding events and other ceremonial practices were not shared by everyone or that they became less important in certain situations. One house group in particular distinguished itself from others by building away from the plaza and orienting its neighborhood toward Mound A at a time when Mound A was beginning to dominate the landscape. As these activities occurred well after the town was founded, they suggest that the cooperative ideals espoused in the rest of the site plan were not shared by everyone and that spatial practice could be used to manipulate these ideals.

There is good reason to suppose that the social competition evidenced by the construction history of Mound A and the spatial discourse of those living in Neighborhood 3 may have its roots in the clan system. Among some Historic period groups, including the Chickasaw, clans (and lineages based on clan affiliation) were ranked with respect to one another, but significantly, the rankings were not mutually accepted (Knight 1990:9–10). Therefore, this particular social institution was internally cohesive but externally flexible. Within the context of a town composed of multiple social groups, there was potential for people to draw on clan-based identities to support their political or social aspirations even as others promoted an ethos of balance and complementarity among town members.

## CONCLUSION

Patterns evident in household, neighborhood, site-level, and regional data suggest that the settlement at Parchman Place can be considered analogous to the Historic period towns of the Chickasaw, Choctaw, and other Native groups. Archaeological evidence from the northern Yazoo suggests that we can understand at least some Mississippian communities in terms of the social categories recorded in the postcontact era. I argue that Mississippian people moved across the landscape, founded new settlements, and organized their living spaces in ways that are similar to those of their western Muskogean-speaking descendants. This similarity can help us think about Mississippian communities in terms of kinship organization, social interactions occurring in everyday and ritual contexts, and the relations and tensions between leaders and other segments of the community (particularly clan-based vs. town-based ones). Thus, material traces of ceremonial and everyday practice in mound building and other contexts can reveal some ways in which people maintained, negotiated, and transformed their community.

# 5

## MISSISSIPPIAN COMMUNITIES AND HOUSEHOLDS FROM A BIRD'S-EYE VIEW

Benjamin A. Steere

In the years since the publication of Rogers and Smith's (1995) important volume on Mississippian communities and households, much has changed in the way archaeologists think about houses and households in the Mississippian world. The "building block" model for interpreting Mississippian households (see Muller 1978b for an early example), which was useful for comparing archaeological assemblages from Mississippian period sites across the Southeast, has been rightly critiqued for its failure to help us appreciate past communities in all their messiness and complexity (Pluckhahn 2010). More broadly, Yaeger and Canuto (2000) and others (see Birch 2012; Harris 2014; Pauketat 2000a) warn about the dangers of conflating archaeological sites with communities in a simplistic one-to-one fashion. Drawing from Bourdieu's (1977) concept of habitus, proponents of a more theoretically explicit archaeology of communities (see Birch 2012; Harris 2014; Whittle 2003; Wilson 2008; Yaeger and Canuto 2000; chapter 1 in this volume) suggest that archaeologists should seek to understand the relationships between the seemingly mundane actions of people in communities (such as house construction) and broader social forces, such as migration, displacement from warfare, and major political and economic changes. These scholars define communities not just as collections of coresident people, but as networks of people, places, practices, and things (Harris 2014:77).

Yet even as they critique earlier iterations of household archaeology in the introduction to their book *The Archaeology of Communities*, Yaeger and Canuto (2000:10) argue that archaeological interpretations of domestic architecture are still vital to understanding past communities, and that houses "will generally form the basic unit of analysis." House design is a shared social phenomenon that crosscuts individual sites and even regions (Blanton 1994; Rapoport 1969). We can see the rise and fall of shared house patterns and construction methods at microregional, regional, and macroregional scales (Hally 2002; Steere 2017:59–63), and this study can help us understand the degree to which communities of practice related to house construction were connected across space and time.

In this chapter I use Harris's (2014:77) definition of the community, a complex assemblage of "things, places, animals, plants, houses, and monuments," as a point of departure for new ways to think about the relationship between houses and people in the Mississippian world. I work from a broad spatial and temporal scale, using a database of 1,258 houses from 65 sites across the Southeast to identify patterns of architectural variation that previous anthropological studies of houses and households have linked to changes in household composition, household economics, architectural symbolism, status differentiation, and settlement systems (Steere 2017:3–5).

Many contributors to this volume show how small-scale changes in domestic architecture, such as post size and placement, house size, and the size and placement of storage facilities, can be used to infer social changes in communities at the microregional scale (Birch 2012; Boudreaux 2013; Cobb and King 2005; Wesson 2008). What I offer here is a large-scale, bird's-eye view of southeastern architectural variation. I describe a set of related patterns that are especially useful for understanding Mississippian communities: changes in the shape, size, wall construction, and segmentation of houses, along with changes in the practice of rebuilding houses in place. This discussion provides a comparative background for the other chapters in the volume and outlines broad patterns of continuity and change in domestic architecture that are useful for inferring social changes in Mississippian communities.

## RESEARCH BACKGROUND AND METHODS

From the Woodland through the Historic Indian period, Native southeastern people built their houses from locally available wood, plant, and animal materials. Post-in-ground construction was the primary building technique. Both rigid posts and flexible poles were used to create walls and frames for houses (Lacquement 2007). The practice of using wall trenches to erect what may have been "prefabricated" walls in houses became widespread during the Early Mississippian period (see Alt and Pauketat 2005; Cobb and King 2005; Pauketat and Woods 1986), but single-set post construction is the dominant wall-building technique in the years before and after. Additional materials such as river cane, grass, split saplings, tree bark, daub, and sinew or hide straps were used to finish walls and cover roofs (Steere 2017:75–80; for historical and ethnographic accounts of house construction, see Adair 1968 [1775]; DuPratz 1972 [1725]; Lawson 1709; Speck 1909). House shape varied over time, but there was a general shift from predominantly circular and oval structures in the Middle and Late Woodland period to rectangular, square, and square-with-rounded-corner floor plans during the Mississippian and Historic periods (Hally 2002; Steere 2017:18–21). In contrast to the large longhouses of the Northeast and contiguous room block structures in the Southwest, southeastern domestic structures rarely exceeded 80 m² in floor area. These structures probably only provided shelter for one or two nuclear or extended families at a time.

In the archaeological record, southeastern Indian houses are most often identified as post patterns with associated artifacts, hearths, storage and refuse features, and burials. In some cases, as when houses burn, or when houses with basins are identified at sites that are not deeply plowed, additional remains such as house floors, timbers, and collapsed daub walls can be identified (Benyshek et al. 2010).

With recognizable house patterns and a robust ethnohistorical record to aid interpretation, the southeastern United States is an excellent laboratory for answering large-scale questions about houses and households. Since the era of New Deal archaeology, houses have been a focus of major excavations, and researchers have made significant contributions to household archaeology for decades (Lacquement 2007; Pluckhahn 2010; Steere 2017:4–7). However, there have been fewer attempts to identify and explain important broadscale diachronic and synchronic changes in domestic architecture.

From 2007 to 2010 I constructed an architectural database with the goal of addressing this gap in our understanding and identifying variation in Native southeastern architecture from a broad geographic and temporal perspective (Steere 2017). The data for my research included site maps and structure drawings from well-documented excavations in North Carolina, Georgia, Alabama, Tennessee, Kentucky, and the southern parts of Missouri, Indiana, and Illinois (Figure 5.1). I targeted sites with broad horizontal coverage and a manageable amount of superimposition from multiple occupations, and I attempted to efficiently capture variation across space and time.

Most archaeological studies of houses and households begin at a fine spatial and temporal scale, usually at the level of a single house or site, and then move out for comparisons with other areas. In contrast, for this study, I started at a larger scale and zoomed in. I examined variation in structures grouped by chronological periods used by other archaeologists in broadscale syntheses in the Southeast: Middle Woodland (c. 200 BC–AD 400), Late Woodland (c. AD 400–1000), Early Mississippian (c. AD 1000–1200), Middle Mississippian (c. AD 1200–1350), Late Mississippian (c. AD 1350–1550), and Historic Indian (c. AD 1550–1800) (following Anderson and Mainfort 2002; Anderson and Sassaman 2012; Bense 1994; Hally and Mainfort 2004).

The final sample included 1,258 structures from 95 components at 65 sites (Table 5.1). I initially selected architectural data sets from sites in the southern Appalachian region, and then I expanded into areas with especially good data. The dataset has a bias toward Mississippian period structures and nucleated sites, which is a function of both the general research bias in the region, and the fact that Mississippian period houses are often better preserved and more easily recognized than earlier structures. Geographic coverage is fairly broad and even over time,

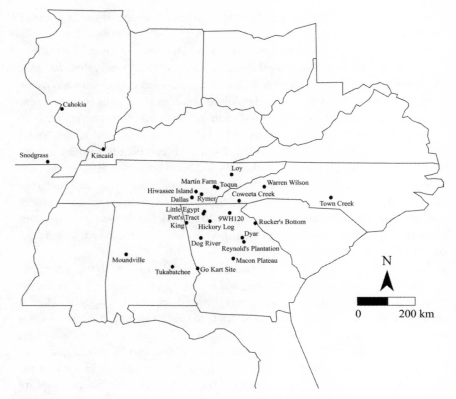

Figure 5.1. Map of Mississippian period sites mentioned in the text. (Steere 2017:Figure 1.1; courtesy of the University of Alabama Press)

although some periods have better coverage than others. For example, despite a long history of large-scale excavation projects in eastern Tennessee, very few Late Woodland period structures have been recorded; the lack of well-recorded houses is not for lack of archaeological research (Sullivan and Koerner 2010). Thus, the sample of sites is not strictly representative in a statistical sense, and it is biased toward well-documented sites, but geographic coverage is broad, temporal coverage is deep, and the data are reliable. (For a more in-depth discussion of the sampling method for this study, see Steere 2017:7–14.)

I scanned site maps and house drawings and converted them to a uniform scale and orientation, then recorded information about architectural variables that archaeological and ethnographic studies of houses have shown to be relevant for understanding variation in households (see Steere 2017:185–190). These variables included structure size and shape; the number, diameter, and spacing of wall posts; the number of interior walls or partitions, the number of interior features; and the number of interior burials. As I entered structures into the database, I classi-

## Table 5.1. List of Archaeological Sites Recorded in the Database

| Site name | State site number(s) | Structures (n) | Reference |
|---|---|---|---|
| 1GR1X1 | 1GR1X1 | 1 | Jenkins and Ensor 1981 |
| 1PI61 | 1PI61 | 4 | Jenkins and Ensor 1981 |
| 9GE1754 | 9GE1754 | 2 | Ledbetter 2007 |
| 9GE1760 | 9GE1760 | 4 | Ledbetter 2007 |
| 9GE1776 | 9GE1776 | 3 | Ledbetter 2007 |
| 9GE1781 | 9GE1781 | 2 | Ledbetter 2007 |
| 9GE333 | 9GE333 | 2 | Ledbetter 2007 |
| 9GE901 | 9GE901 | 5 | Ledbetter 2007 |
| 9GE903 | 9GE903 | 15 | Ledbetter 2007 |
| 9GE922 | 9GE922 | 3 | Ledbetter 2007 |
| 9WH120 | 9WH120 | 2 | Robert S. Webb, pers. comm. 2007 |
| Alarka Farmstead | 31SW173 | 2 | Shumate et al. 2005 |
| Banks III | 40CF108 | 3 | Faulkner 1988 |
| Banks V | 40CF111 | 5 | Faulkner and McCollough 1978 |
| BBB Motor | 11MS595 | 21 | Emerson and Jackson 1984 |
| Bessemer | 1JE12 | 25 | DeJarnette and Wimberly 1941; Welch 1994 |
| Brasstown Valley | 9TO45, 48, 49 | 43 | Cable et al. 1997:148–162 |
| Cahokia | 11MS2 | 253 | Pauketat 1998 |
| Chota-Tanase | 40MR2, 62 | 34 | Schroedl 1986 |
| Coweeta Creek | 31MA34 | 16 | Rodning 2009b |
| Dallas | 40HA1 | 29 | Lewis and Lewis 1995 |
| Dog River | 9DO39 | 1 | Poplin 1990 |
| Duncan Tract | 40TR27 | 5 | McNutt and Weaver 1983 |
| Dyar | 9GE5 | 6 | Smith 1994 |
| Ela | 31SW5 | 15 | Wetmore 1990 |
| Fernvale | 40WM51 | 2 | Steere and Deter-Wolf 2013 |
| Garden Creek | 31HW2 | 1 | Keel 1976 |
| Go Kart Site | 9ME50 | 1 | Ledbetter 1997 |
| Hickory Log | 9CK9 | 16 | Paul Webb, pers. comm. 2006 |
| Hiwassee Island | 40MG31 | 48 | Lewis and Kneberg 1946 |
| Hiwassee Old Town | 40PK3 | 6 | Riggs et al. 1998 |
| Hoecake | 23MI8 | 11 | Williams 1974 |
| Jenrette | 31OR231a | 3 | Ward and Davis 1993 |
| Jewell | 15BN21 | 22 | Hanson 1970:5–14 |
| Kellog | 9CK62 | 1 | Caldwell 1955; Ledbetter et al. 2009 |
| Kimberly-Clark | 40LD208 | 3 | Chapman 1994 |
| Kincaid | 11MX1 | 27 | Brennan 2007 |
| King | 9FL5 | 67 | Hally 2008 |
| Kolomoki | 9ER1 | 1 | Pluckhahn 2003 |
| Little Egypt | 9MU102 | 3 | Gougeon 2002 |
| Lower Saratown | 31RK1 | 2 | Ward and Davis 1993 |
| Loy | 40JE10 | 2 | Polhemus 1998 |
| Macon Plateau | 9BI1 | 12 | Prokopetz 1974; Ingmanson 1964 |

Continued on the next page

Table 5.1. *Continued*

| Site name | State site number(s) | Structures (n) | Reference |
|---|---|---|---|
| Martin Farm | 40MR20 | 12 | Schroedl et al. 1985 |
| McFarland | 40CF48 | 5 | Kline et al. 1982 |
| Mialoquo | 40MR3 | 8 | Russ and Chapman 1983 |
| Mitchum | 31CH452 | 1 | Ward and Davis 1993 |
| Morris | 15HK49 | 12 | Rolingson and Schwartz 1966:114–174 |
| Moundville | 1TU500 | 152 | Wilson 2008 |
| Napoleon Hollow | 11PK500 | 1 | McGimsey and Wiant 1986 |
| Potts' Tract | 9MU103 | 3 | Hally 1970 |
| Ravenswood | 31SW78 | 2 | Keel 2007 |
| Rivermoore | 9GW70 | 3 | Markin 2007 |
| Rucker's Bottom | 9EB91 | 12 | Anderson and Schuldrein 1985 |
| Rymer | 40BY15 | 23 | Lewis et al. 1995 |
| Snodgrass | 23BU21b | 91 | Price and Griffin 1979 |
| Summerour | 9FO16 | 1 | Pluckhahn 1996 |
| Toqua | 40MR6 | 118 | Polhemus 1987; Chapman 1994:74–99 |
| Town Creek | 31MG2 | 45 | Boudreaux 2007 |
| Townsend | 40BT89, 90, 91 | 10 | Marcoux 2010b |
| Tuckasegee | 31JK12 | 1 | Keel 1976; Riggs 2008 |
| Tukabatchee | 1EE32 | 2 | Knight 1985 |
| Two Run Creek | 9BR3 | 1 | Wauchope 1966:223–231, 450 |
| Warren Wilson | 31BN29 | 12 | Dickens 1976; Moore 2002b |
| Yearwood | 40LN16 | 14 | Butler 1977 |
| Yuchi Town | 1RU63 | 2 | Hargrave 1998 |

fied them into four general categories: domestic, nondomestic, storage, and other. Domestic structures are those that appear to have served primarily as dwellings in domestic contexts. Nondomestic structures include large public buildings and smaller special-purpose buildings, like mound-top temples and sweat lodges. The remaining structures could be classified as storage buildings or structures with some other, unknown function.

I focused on a single architectural variable at a time, exploring synchronic variation and diachronic change. This strategy was effective for identifying major patterns of architectural variation over time and also helped me avoid the trap of reifying cultural historical units by instead focusing on concordant changes in architecture. Five patterns in particular shed light on changes in Mississippian communities: shape, size, exterior wall form, segmentation, and rebuilding of houses.

## SHAPE
I grouped structures in the database into five major qualitative shape classes: circular, oval, rectangular, square, and irregular. A small number of houses were T shaped or keyhole shaped. This categorization obscures some finer details of

structure form but captures most of the variation. From a broad view, changes in shape track with breaks between the major chronological periods. There is a general shift from circular domestic structures in the Middle and Late Woodland to rectangular domestic structures in the Late Woodland and Early Mississippian, to square domestic structures and rectangular storage structures in the Late Mississippian, to circular and rectangular domestic structures in the Historic Indian period. Figure 5.2 is a schematic model of houses from each of the major time periods that captures these general trends.

Circular structures occur in all time periods. While the Early Mississippian period does not include any circular domestic structures (unlike all other periods), it does include circular nondomestic structures, possibly earthlodges and sweat houses. This shape is most common during the Middle Woodland period. Over 65 percent of Middle Woodland domestic structures in the database are circular. Only about 7 percent of all Early, Middle, and Late Mississippian structures are circular. They make up a low proportion of structures, mostly nondomestic, in the Mississippian components at Hiwassee Island, Toqua, Macon Plateau, Jewell, Bessemer, Martin Farm, and Cahokia, but they are common at Town Creek, Rucker's Bottom, several sites in the Oconee River Valley in piedmont Georgia, and possibly at Brasstown Valley, where the Late Woodland to Early Mississippian chronology is not entirely clear.

Twenty-three oval-shaped structures (2 percent) were recorded at 13 sites dating to the Woodland, Early Mississippian, and Historic Indian periods. Over half of these houses are from Owl Hollow–phase sites (n = 6) in Tennessee and the Late Woodland occupation at Brasstown Valley in northeastern Georgia (n = 8).

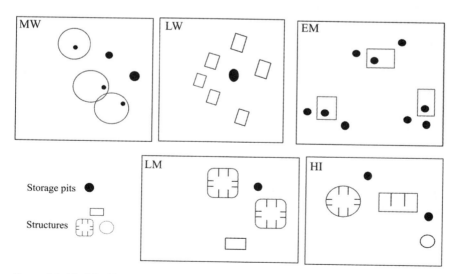

Figure 5.2. Model of household clusters for each chronological period. MW = Middle Woodland; LW = Late Woodland; EM = Early Mississippian; LM = Late Mississippian; HI = Historic Indian. (Steere 2017:Figure 3.1; courtesy of the University of Alabama Press)

Rectangular structures (n = 595, 47 percent) were the most common of all, appearing in all periods, but most frequently in the Late Woodland, Mississippian, and Historic Indian periods. Approximately 80 percent of the Late Woodland and 60 percent of the Early Mississippian structures are rectangular. Nearly half of the Historic Indian structures in the study are rectangular. Rectangular domestic structures are not as common during the Middle and Late Mississippian, but rectangular storage buildings commonly occur at Late Mississippian sites. Only four Middle Woodland structures are rectangular, and these all come from the Yearwood site, which may have been a special ceremonial center (Butler 1977).

Square structures (n = 358, 28 percent) occur in all periods but are especially common in the Middle and Late Mississippian periods. Domestic structures in villages and domestic and nondomestic structures on mound summits are often square with rounded corners. Only seven square structures were recorded from Woodland period sites: one square structure of unknown function with rounded corners in the premound midden at Garden Creek, three square domestic structures at Rivermoore, and three roughly square domestic structures at the Yearwood site. Several square Middle Woodland Connestee-phase structures with rounded corners and a single support post, nearly identical to a square house at Garden Creek, were recorded at the Iotla site at the Macon County Airport near Franklin, North Carolina (Benyshek et al. 2010). Only four of the Historic Indian period structures in the sample were square: two large, nondomestic public structures at Toqua, and single domestic structures at Yuchi Town and Tukabatchee. At the Townsend site, three Cherokee domestic structures described as "octagonal" closely resemble Late Mississippian domestic structures that are square with rounded or truncated corners.

The remaining structures (n = 119, 9 percent) did not fit into these four broad shape categories. Most of these structures (n = 97) have an undefined shape due to poor preservation or incomplete excavation. However, 22 structures had complex or unusual shapes, such as two T-shaped, nondomestic structures at Cahokia Tract 15A.

## STRUCTURE SIZE
Structure size has probably received more attention in archaeological studies of households than any other architectural variable in the database, for both practical and theoretical reasons. Variation in house size within a community is highly visible, broadcasting strong signals about individual and household status (Blanton 1994; Wilk 1983). House size is also easily recorded, and even the earliest and most cursory excavation records in the Southeast include plan-view maps of houses drawn to scale. I was able to record the floor area of 1,054 of the 1,258 structures in the database. Only structures with incomplete floor plans were not measured. Figure 5.3 shows the mean and median size of houses for each of the broad time periods in the Southeast. The median size for all domestic structures

in the database is approximately 28 m². Domestic structures from all time periods very rarely exceed 80 m² in area, and this number appears to represent an upper limit on the size of ordinary domestic structures in the Southeast.

Compared to houses from all other time periods in the Southeast, Middle Woodland domestic structures are relatively large, with a median size of approximately 40 m². The average size of domestic structures declines sharply during the Late Woodland period, particularly in the American Bottom region and the Deep South.

In the western part of the study area, Early Mississippian wall-trench houses are much larger than Late Woodland domestic structures. Specifically, domestic structures from the Late Woodland and Terminal Late Woodland occupations at sites such as the BBB Motor site, Cahokia, and Hoecake average only 7.7 m² in floor area. In contrast, Early Mississippian domestic structures from the BBB Motor site, Bessemer, Cahokia, Jewell, Kincaid, and Moundville have an average floor area of 23 m². Early Mississippian domestic structures at these sites are also spaced farther apart from one another when compared to Late Woodland period household clusters. At Cahokia, Tract 15A, Pauketat (1998:135–135) identified a shift from larger courtyard groups to smaller, nuclear family households as the primary unit of social organization.

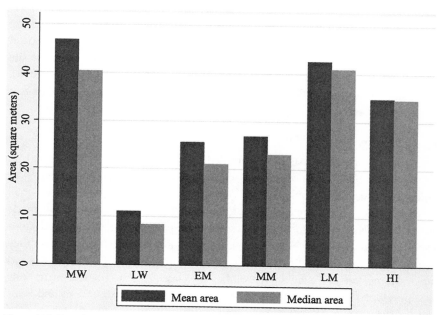

Figure 5.3. Bar chart of average (mean) and median floor area for domestic structures. MW = Middle Woodland; LW = Late Woodland; EM = Early Mississippian; MM = Middle Mississippian; LM = Late Mississippian; HI = Historic Indian. (Steere 2017:Figure 1.11; courtesy of the University of Alabama Press)

To the east, in the southern Appalachian Mountains and the surrounding pied-mont regions, Late Woodland domestic structures from Brasstown Valley and Rivermoore average 28 m². Early Mississippian domestic structures from Chota-Tanase, Hiwassee Island, Kimberly-Clark, Macon Plateau, Martin Farm, Toqua, and Town Creek average 39 m². Thus, in the eastern part of the study area, do-mestic structures increase in size from the Late Woodland to the Early Missis-sippian period, but the increase is not as dramatic as in the west. Because so few Late Woodland sites with broad horizontal exposure have been excavated, it is harder to identify major changes in the spacing of houses from the Late Wood-land to the Early Mississippian period.

From the Early Mississippian period forward, domestic structure size contin-ues to increase, and it plateaus during the Late Mississippian and Historic Indian periods. The sample of Late Mississippian period structures from the database has a median size of 41 m², while the median size of Historic Indian domestic struc-tures is 35.2 m². In the southern Appalachians, Late Mississippian winter houses are generally larger than Early Mississippian wall-trench houses and tend to be arranged in clusters of two or three domestic structures and associated storage buildings that may represent extended, perhaps matrilineal, families (Hally 2002, 2008; Sullivan 1986, 1987).

At this broad scale, changes in house size seem to reflect major, society-wide changes in the organization of households and communities. After the Late Wood-land period, houses generally become larger and more widely spaced, suggesting that small nuclear or extended family households emerge as a basal unit of social organization. These patterns have been documented at the scale of the single site and region (see Pauketat 1998; Peregrine 1992; Pluckhahn 2010; Wilson 2008). There are certainly exceptions, but in terms of house size and the layout of houses in communities, the data suggest these trends may be widespread.

## WALLS AND POSTS

Southeastern archaeologists have identified three kinds of wall construction that capture most of the variation in house construction. First, walls can be made with single-set posts. These walls fall into two types: those with closely spaced, small posts and those with more widely spaced, larger posts. Second, walls can be made of small, closely spaced posts that are set in long, narrow trenches. In some cases the individual posts in the wall trenches can be identified, while in others they cannot. Third, some buildings are made with a combination of wall trenches and single-set posts (see Lacquement 2007). This classification is based on the one first developed at Hiwassee Island and the Chickamauga Basin (Lewis and Kne-berg 1946; Lewis et al. 1995). It is also similar to Pauketat's (1998) typology of wall types at Cahokia Tract 15A and Wilson's (2008:44–45) classification of early Moundville house walls. Walls were made with single-set posts from the Middle Woodland through the Historic Indian period. Approximately 65 percent of all structures in the database are built with single-post walls, and every site in the database has at least one structure with this kind of wall.

Wall trenches are a predominantly Early Mississippian construction pattern, although some houses with wall trenches appear in later periods, particularly in the Midwest, and there is at least one possible Late Woodland wall-trench structure at the Summerour Mound (Pluckhahn 1996). Out of 397 structures with wall trenches, 365 are from the Early Mississippian period. The remaining 32 occur during the Middle Mississippian period at Snodgrass and Kincaid and during the Historic Indian period at Yuchi Town and Jenrette. Sixty-one structures with both wall trenches and single-set posts have been identified at 13 sites in the database, mostly during the Early Mississippian period, but also during the Late Woodland period at 1PI61, the Middle to Late Mississippian period at Martin Farm, and the Historic Indian period at Chota-Tanase, Ravensford, and Jenrette.

I recorded the total number of wall posts for 502 structures. In most cases and in all the time periods, wall posts were regularly spaced, making it possible to infer the location of posts in the event of relatively straightforward overlapping structure patterns. The median number of wall posts per structure for all time periods is 29, and the distribution is positively skewed, with most of the 502 houses falling at or below the mean of 39 wall posts per structure.

The average number of wall posts per domestic structure increases steadily from the Middle Woodland to the Middle Mississippian period, and then it declines during the Late Mississippian and Historic Indian periods. This trend reflects general diachronic changes in wall construction. Middle Woodland, Middle Mississippian, Late Mississippian, and Historic Indian buildings, with larger, widely spaced posts have fewer wall posts than Late Woodland and Early Mississippian structures, with their closely spaced, smaller posts. While wall-trench construction comes in and out of fashion, single-post construction persists throughout the years under examination and is found alongside wall-trench construction.

## SEGMENTATION

Like floor area, measures of the segmentation of interior space have received attention from archaeologists and other researchers looking for meaningful connections between architectural remains and human behavior. Ethnoarchaeologists, cultural anthropologists, archaeologists, and other researchers working from a cross-cultural perspective have examined the division of space within buildings to make inferences about changes in storage (Kelly et al. 2005), sedentism (Flannery 2002), division of labor (Flannery 2002; Gougeon 2002), and political complexity (Kent 1990).

In the Southeast, lines of interior posts and the remains of interior walls provide evidence for the segmentation of houses. I recorded the number of walls and partitions in 502 houses. In general, the number of partitions and walls seems to increase over time. The average number of partitions in structures increases from practically zero during the Middle Woodland period to nearly two per house during the Late Mississippian period. The maximum number of divisions found within houses during each period also increases, and this number jumps noticeably between the Middle Mississippian and Late Mississippian periods.

During the Woodland period, almost no structures have visible interior divisions. I recorded the presence or absence of interior partitions in 34 Middle Woodland houses. Out of this subset, only one structure, a McFarland-phase house at the Duncan Tract site, seems to have a possible interior wall, and its identification is tentative. In general, Middle Woodland houses have round, open floor plans. During the Late Woodland period, when structures are generally very small and rectangular, there is little evidence for interior partitioning. Only three structures had two possible interior walls, five had one possible interior wall, and the remaining houses had none.

Floor area must also be considered when examining interior segmentation. In contrast to many Middle Woodland and Middle to Late Mississippian houses, most of the Late Woodland structures are so small that dividing the structures into two or three sections may have been impractical, severely limiting movement and space for activities. Out of the eight structures with interior walls, five range between only 7 to 16.4 m² in floor area.

There is some continuity in the segmentation of interior space from the Late Woodland to the Early Mississippian period. Many Early Mississippian domestic structures in the sample are small and rectangular, with open floor plans. I recorded the presence or absence of interior partitions in 164 of the 524 Early Mississippian structures in the database. Out of this subset, only 22 structures have interior walls (one or two in each instance). These particular structures vary a great deal in terms of size and function, from small domestic structures to large nondomestic buildings. As in the Late Woodland period, subdividing some of these structures may have been impractical. However, many structures that appear to have open floor plans are quite large, and size would not have been a limiting factor.

Middle Mississippian period structures show more signs of interior segmentation. The presence or absence of interior partitions could only be confidently determined for 16 structures—from Town Creek, Rucker's Bottom, and Hickory Log—and many of these structures are not especially well preserved. However, from this small group, nine out of 16 structures had between one and four interior walls. Along with this change is an increase in structure size, making the division of interior space more tenable.

During the Late Mississippian period there is a substantial increase in the segmentation of interior space. By this time, the winter house—a square house with rounded corners, a central hearth, four interior support posts, and interior daub walls—becomes increasingly common in the southern Appalachian region (see Gougeon 2007; Hally 2002; Polhemus 1987; Sullivan 1986, 1987). I recorded the presence or absence of interior partitions in 132 of the 295 Late Mississippian structures. Out of this subset, 35 structures had at least one interior partition. Among these structures the number of interior walls ranged from one to 12, with an average of approximately four. Partitions were mostly found in the square domestic structures described above, but they also appeared in large square, circular, and rectangular nondomestic structures.

Interior divisions in Late Mississippian winter houses have been well documented. There are especially detailed descriptions of interior partition walls from Late Mississippian winter houses at King (Hally 2008), Little Egypt (Gougeon 2002:17–18, 27–68; 2007), Toqua (Polhemus 1987) and Loy (Polhemus 1998). These walls were sometimes made of split posts, rather than whole ones, interwoven with cane, and covered with daub. These wattle-and-daub partitions radiated out at 90-degree angles from the four central support posts, dividing the winter houses into as many as eight or nine discrete areas for sleeping, storage, and domestic activities (see Gougeon 2006:185–188).

This change in the division of interior space, from basically open floor plans with a likely central/peripheral division of space focused on the hearth to houses divided up into as many as eight or nine small rooms, is one of the most significant changes in house form identified by this study. Prior to the Middle and Late Mississippian periods, occupants probably divided their houses conceptually. It is also likely that during the Woodland and Early Mississippian period, occupants performed different types of activities in different parts of houses, but archaeological evidence for this behavior is not as strong as in later periods.

## REBUILDING

Rebuilding and repair provide strong lines of evidence for understanding architectural investment, occupational duration, the domestic cycle, and architectural symbolism (Hally 2002; Haviland 1988; Whittle 2003:141). In the Southeast, domestic and nondomestic structures and storage buildings were repaired in place, completely rebuilt in place, or rebuilt after being moved or shifted slightly from the original position.

Rebuilding is virtually nonexistent during the Middle Woodland period. There is no convincing evidence for wall repair or the rebuilding of structures in place. In some cases, the walls of circular structures overlap slightly. Analysts generally interpret this pattern as the seasonal abandonment of a structure and perhaps a site, and the construction of a new house in the same area after a hiatus of some time. There is limited evidence of repair and rebuilding during the Late Woodland period.

Rebuilding becomes more frequent during the Mississippian period. Twenty-one percent of the 459 Early Mississippian structures show evidence of rebuilding, and 55 percent of Early Mississippian components have at least one repaired or rebuilt structure. In some cases, structures are repaired or rebuilt as many

as five times in a single place. The rebuilt structures include 73 domestic structures, 23 nondomestic structures, and (at Martin Farm) one structure of unknown
function.

This trend continues in the Late Mississippian period. Twenty-two percent of
the 287 Late Mississippian structures have multiple building stages or repairs, and
25 of these structures were repaired or rebuilt three or more times. Rebuilt structures were identified in 41 percent of sites with Late Mississippian components.
Domestic structures accounted for most of the structures with multiple building
stages (n = 43), but nondomestic structures (n = 12), storage buildings (n = 7),
and one building of undetermined function were also repaired and rebuilt.

Rebuilding is much less frequent after contact with Europeans, when Native
communities often responded to the new biological, social, political, and economic landscape of the Colonial period (AD 1600–1760) with migration and resettlement (see Marcoux 2010b for a Cherokee example). Only 7 percent of Historic Indian structures in the database show evidence of rebuilding or repair, and
in no instance did this repair or rebuilding take place more than once.

## DISCUSSION AND CONCLUSIONS

Changes in architecture—the adoption of new floor plans and wall-building techniques—would have played out on a daily basis at an intimate scale within communities. However, broadscale changes call for explanations that consider social
factors beyond the scale of the individual household or community. Houses are
built using community and even supracommunity labor, often organized along
kin lines (see for example Horne 1994; Kramer 1982). An ethnographic example
from eighteenth-century Creek society illustrates the complex and nuanced social relationships embedded in domestic architecture. Before getting married, a
young Creek man had to raise a crop and build a house with the help of his male
relatives to show his future wife's lineage that he was an acceptable suitor (Hudson 1976:198). Creek society was matrilineal and matrilocal. Older, married men
from the boy's lineage may have been spread out across several towns, living with
their wives' households, and they would have come together to build a house for
their young kinsman. The Creek house, then, is the record of a cultural model for
house building shared by a group of individuals from the same lineage who lived
in geographically distinct communities. Houses are usually constructed by social
groups larger than households, and it is the interaction between these larger social groups that we need to consider in our explanations of architectural variability. Within this tradition of house construction, domestic structures would look
more similar when communities were integrated, with high rates of marriage between groups living in different settlements. Houses would look dissimilar at a
regional and macroregional scale when society was less integrated and marriage
alliances were more localized.

Houses are a major investment of materials and labor, more so than pottery or other classes of material culture. It seems reasonable to suggest that domestic architecture may be even slower to change than some other forms of material culture, given its durability and labor cost. Thus, the nature of house construction, both in terms of material investment and social processes, makes houses especially good indicators of broad changes in social organization. We should expect to see change in domestic architecture track with major changes in social organization identified through other lines of evidence (settlement patterns, subsistence strategies, burial patterns, etc.), and we should expect the scale of these architectural changes to vary depending on the size and scale of integration of societies. Households, even relatively isolated ones on dispersed farmsteads, are always part of larger communities, and those larger corporate groups (e.g., lineages, clans, chiefdoms, polities, regional cultures) are not static. They grow and contract over time in response to political, economic, and social forces. When the larger social groups that communities belong to are more integrated, we might expect houses to look more similar at a broad spatial scale, as the movement of people across the landscape would be less constrained by political and social boundaries.

Several findings from this study support this general theory. During the Late Woodland period, houses become more dissimilar at a macroregional scale, but more similar at the scale of the single site and region. In the western part of the study area, domestic structure size and form are remarkably uniform in sites and across a broad area from the American Bottom southward to west-central Alabama. This pattern is distinct from the southern Appalachian region, which seems to have more architectural variability. This finding could point to a more localized level of social integration: marriages and other alliances and the social process of house construction would have been more circumscribed, resulting in a pattern of regional similarity and macroregional differences in houses. Cobb and Nassaney (1995:217) come to a similar conclusion by examining the distribution of Late Woodland small triangle projectile points, maize, shell-tempered pottery, and shell ornaments.

In the Early Mississippian period, the common occurrence of small rectangular houses and, more specifically, wall-trench houses, points to widespread integration among social groups from the American Bottom to Georgia. There is some regional variation in Early Mississippian house form. Cobb and King (2005:169) state that wall-trench houses were more common in the Central Mississippi Valley, while single-post structures were more common in the southern Appalachians. However, Early Mississippian wall-trench houses occur in eastern Tennessee and northern Georgia, and single-post structures persist throughout the sequence in small numbers on both sides of the Southeast. From a broad view, houses are more similar at a macroregional scale during the Early Mississippian period than during any other time in the Southeast.

Early Mississippian polities may have incorporated large numbers of people; we can infer this from a political landscape with a few large mound centers (e.g., Cahokia, Etowah, and Moundville) that may have dominated large geographic areas (Cobb and King 2005; Wilson 2008). Exchange, competition, and emulation between these polities (*sensu* Renfrew and Cherry 1986) would have created broad avenues for exchanges of people, material, and ideas. Communities could have used wall-trench houses as a symbol of group membership in these large polities, or this structure may have been imposed on communities from the top down through coercion (Alt and Pauketat 2011; Pauketat and Alt 2005).

Wall-trench houses began to disappear after AD 1200, a change that tracks with a general transition from Early to Late Mississippian political organization, which involved a shift from few polities with large centers (Cahokia, Moundville, Etowah) to more polities with smaller centers (e.g., Barnett-phase polities like Coosa) (Cobb and King 2005). If wall-trench houses did have a strong association with the Early Mississippian social order, the large-scale abandonment of the form may be related to the waning strength of the early polities. This change could be the result of bottom-up or top-down processes operating on a large scale. As the political clout of leaders at Cahokia and Moundville declined, corporate groups may have gradually abandoned the old house form, creating symbolic distance between themselves and the old elite (for Cherokee examples, see Rodning 2015b; chapter 10 in this volume). The change in house style could also have been mandated from the top down by new elite filling the power vacuum left by the older, larger polities.

Houses are more similar in the southern Appalachians during Late Mississippian times than during Early Mississippian times, suggesting a high degree of integration and exchange between the polities in eastern Tennessee, western North Carolina, and northern Georgia. Compared to the Early Mississippian period, there is something of a contraction in the spatial extent of shared house patterns, but the complex Late Mississippian winter house form is remarkably consistent in and between sites. This pattern points to the existence of broadly shared ideas about house construction, spread over much of the southern Appalachians (see Hally 2002, 2006). In an interesting contrast to other recent studies and analyses of ceramics and other artifact types (see Harle 2010; Lulewicz 2019b), which suggest regional-scale variation in interaction and organization, the data that I have assembled point to shared practices in the construction of domestic architecture, which is a powerful medium that recursively shapes and is shaped by daily practices.

During Historic Indian times, against a backdrop of disease, violence, and political upheaval, there is less investment in domestic houses, but among historically known groups house form is remarkably uniform. The similarity in domestic structures across a broad geographic area may be the result of refugee groups forming new communities in the southern Appalachians, following Kowalewski's (2006) model for coalescent societies. Sharing architectural patterns at the household level, patterns that possibly refer to older, Late Mississippian public architecture, may have been an important mechanism for integrating newly formed communities (see Rodning 2009a for a discussion of this process at Coweeta Creek; see Baltus 2014 for a discussion of architecture and revitalization movements in the American Bottom region). In a broad geographic area that once had similar Late Mississippian winter houses, we see divergence in architectural forms and architectural similarity at a smaller spatial scale, as these groups become archaeologically and historically visible (Hally 2002).

The in-place rebuilding of houses is extremely rare in the Late Woodland period but then becomes more common in the Early Mississippian period, and more so in Late Mississippian times. During the Historic Indian period, in the wake of the biological, social, political, and economic upheaval of contact with Europeans, the rebuilding of domestic structures diminishes.

During Early Mississippian times, large polities like Cahokia and Moundville may have contributed to increased boundary maintenance and social stability (as in Pauketat's [2004] *pax Cahokiana*), resulting in an uptick in the rebuilding of houses, even in the face of endemic southeastern warfare. In the Late Mississippian period in the southern Appalachians, the in-place rebuilding of houses is even more common. Hally (2006) has argued that these Late Mississippian polities were quite stable at a regional level, even as they were prone to cycling and collapse at smaller scales (see chapters 2 and 6 in this volume).

Widespread changes in southeastern domestic architecture happened concordantly. These changes are the material end result of communities of practice centered on house construction, but they incorporated people beyond the scale of the individual household and settlement. The broad spatial and temporal extent of these changes requires large-scale driving forces, which I suggest are major changes in social organization, as well as in the degree of interaction and interdependence of southeastern societies. The major transitions in house form in the Southeast happen at times of system-wide political and economic change. These include: the Middle Woodland to Late Woodland to Early Mississippian transition, which coincides with the adoption of maize agriculture and the emergence of chiefdom political organization; the breakdown of large, Early Mississippian polities and the establishment of smaller polities and paramount chiefdoms; and the coalescence of Native American groups of the eighteenth century. The expansion and contraction of alliance and exchange networks associated with these major changes would have mediated the smaller-scale processes of house building.

Communities are not just collections of households in settlements; they can span multiple settlements, and they include things (like houses) in addition to people. Following Harris (2014:77), a conceptualization of communities as assemblages of human and nonhuman things, and of houses as a particularly meaningful element of those assemblages, offers new avenues for understanding the Mississippian world. In the years since the publication of Rogers and Smith's *Mississippian Communities and Households* (1995), new theoretical approaches that fall under the umbrella of the archaeology of communities have offered valuable new ideas for reconstructing daily life in the Mississippian world. In those same years, our ability to manage large archaeological datasets has improved dramatically. With these new theoretical and methodological tools, we should use the opportunity to engage in broadscale comparative studies of domestic architecture and communities. Patterns like these can only be identified with large datasets and broad geographic coverage, and the project of explaining them encourages us to consider the impact of large-scale social processes on everyday life.

## Acknowledgments

I thank many individuals for their help with the research that is summarized in this chapter. In particular, Steve Kowalewski, David Hally, Mark Williams, Bram Tucker, Jen Birch, John Chamblee, Tasha Benyshek, Chris Rodning, Paul Webb, Ramie Gougeon, Rob Beck, Lynne Sullivan, Brett Riggs, Jane Eastman, Beau Carroll, Russ Townsend, Johi Griffin, Brian Burgess, and Miranda Panther offered comments, suggestions, critiques, and inspiration. I also extend my thanks to Elizabeth Watts Malouchos and Alleen Betzenhauser for organizing the symposium that led to this volume and seeing the book through to completion. This chapter is dedicated to Joel Jones, a friend and mentor whose passion for archaeology, intellectual curiosity, and kindness were an inspiration to all who knew him.

# II

# COALESCING AND CONFLICTING COMMUNITIES

# 6

# VARIABILITY WITHIN A MISSISSIPPIAN COMMUNITY

*Houses, Cemeteries, and Corporate Groups at the Town Creek Site in the North Carolina Piedmont*

Edmond A. Boudreaux III, Paige A. Ford, and Heidi A. de Gregory

The incorporation of archaeological, ethnohistorical, and ethnographic data to identify and explore the roles of the social groups that constituted Mississippian communities has become increasingly important to Mississippian archaeologists (Blitz 2010:5; chapter 1 in this volume). As a result, Mississippian communities are now seen as consisting of multiple interest groups connected through a variety of economic, political, and ceremonial relationships (Cobb 2003; Emerson and Hargrave 2000; Hally 2008; Kelly 2006:255–256; Knight 1998, 2010; Pauketat 2000a; Sullivan and Mainfort 2010; Wilson 2008). Households, kin-based corporate groups, and noncorporate groups such as clans and moieties were important in Historic period southeastern communities, and this pattern presumably obtained during the Mississippian period as well (Hally 2008:9; Knight 1990). These groups often separately constructed and maintained elements of the community's built environment. For example, corporate groups have been identified archaeologically through the houses or clusters of houses they shared, the monuments they created, and the presence of discrete cemeteries or burial areas within cemeteries (Goldstein 1980, 1981, 2010; Hally 2008; King 2010; Knight 1990, 1998, 2010; Marcoux 2010a; Wilson 2008, 2010).

Although corporate groups were considered in Mississippian studies before Rogers and Smith's *Mississippian Communities and Households* in 1995 (e.g., Goldstein 1980; Knight 1990), that volume placed explicit emphasis on adjusting the scale of analysis from the level of the region or the chiefdom to the household and community. As stated by Rogers (1995b:7), this change in analytical scale was part of a broader trend in the social sciences, where focus was shifting from macro-scale entities, such as systems, regions, or chiefdoms, toward actors, factions, and interest groups (Brumfiel 1992). A consideration of the roles of households and other groups within Mississippian communities has been an important component of many studies since the 1990s (Blitz 2010; Cobb 2003; Pluckhahn 2010; chapter 1 in this volume).

In this chapter, we discuss the Mississippian community represented by the Town Creek site (AD 1200–1400) in the piedmont of central North Carolina. In particular, we focus on the remains of structures and clusters of burials around Town Creek's plaza, places that were created and sustained by members of corporate groups. We compare these structures and cemeteries based on the assumption that their variability reflects differences among corporate groups. While previous studies have assumed a certain amount of homogeneity among household groups at Town Creek (Boudreaux 2007, 2013), our investigations suggest that some important differences exist among households regarding rank, access to exotic materials, longevity, demographics, and the structuring of space within cemeteries.

## CORPORATE GROUPS AND COMMUNITY

In Historic period southeastern Indian communities, and presumably during the Mississippian period as well, corporate groups were primarily coresidential matrilineages that collectively managed access to economic resources such as farmland and its produce (Hudson 1976; Knight 1990). Matrilineal membership was a core element of social identity because one's lineage and clan legitimatized claims to social positions and economic resources (Blitz 2010:9–10; Blitz and Livingood 2004:298–299; Brown 1995; Goldstein 1980, 1981; Knight 1990:9–12, 1998:54; Wilson 2010:6). Ethnographically, matrilineal clans were the most common kin-based social group in the Southeast, and each community consisted of multiple clans (Blitz 2010:14–15; Hudson 1976:186–187; King 2001a:11–12; Wilson 2010:9–10; Wilson et al. 2010:75–77). Although clans were not corporate groups themselves, each clan consisted of several lineages or household groups that were corporate in nature (Hudson 1976:192; Knight 1990:6, 2010:358–360; Wilson 2010).

Archaeologically, Mississippian corporate groups have been associated with individual houses, discrete clusters of houses, public buildings, and mounds (Hally 2008:273; Knight 1998, 2010; Wilson 2008, 2010). One of the distinguishing characteristics of corporate groups worldwide is their persistence from one generation to the next, and one way these groups maintained and legitimized control over resources through time was through the maintenance of bounded cemeteries (Adams and King 2011; Binford 1971; Ensor 2013:61–63; Gillespie 2011; Goldstein 1980; King 2011; McAnany 1995; Saxe 1970). In many Mississippian societies, corporate groups also established and maintained their own kin-group cemeteries on the landscape (Brown 1995; Goldstein 1980; Knight 1998; Wilson 2010:4). In some cases, individuals were interred beneath the floors of public or residential structures affiliated with that group (Brown 1995:13–15; Cushman 1962 [1899]:404; Hudson 1976:335–336; Swanton 1931:183; Wilson 2010:4). In other cases, groups established cemeteries in formerly occupied domestic spaces to intentionally connect past and present generations (Boudreaux 2013; Wilson 2010:10–12; Wilson et al. 2010).

## THE TOWN CREEK COMMUNITY

Extensive investigations at Town Creek since the 1930s have caused much of this Mississippian settlement to be exposed and documented (Boudreaux 2007; Coe 1995). This research includes the identification of over 40 structures, the near-complete excavation of the site's platform mound, and the excavation of over 200 burials containing approximately 250 individuals (Figure 6.1) (Boudreaux 2007, 2011; Coe 1995). The Mississippian community at Town Creek was founded circa AD 1150–1200 (Boudreaux 2017), and it was abandoned by AD 1400. The extent of archaeological investigations at the site allows us to talk about public and domestic spaces across the entire community and the changes in the use of these spaces throughout its history.

The Town Creek site consists of a central plaza surrounded by a ring of domestic and public spaces, all of which were encircled by a palisade early in the site's history (Boudreaux 2007). This circular arrangement of the Town Creek community is the earliest known example of the Piedmont Village Tradition (Jones 2018; Ward and Davis 1999:79), a regional variant of a circular village tradition found across much of the Northeast and adjacent parts of the Southeast from AD 1000 to 1700 (Cook 2018; Jefferies 2018; Means 2007). Public spaces at Town Creek included a central plaza, an area to the east where a series of buildings and a platform mound were located, and an area to the west where one or more structures and a rectangular enclosure were built. These public spaces were the loci of ceremonial activities throughout the community's existence. Some activities appear to have been truly communal and integrative in nature, possibly involving large groups of people as participants or observers. Examples of such activities at Town Creek include feasting, mound building, the raising and removing of monumental posts, and the burial of prominent individuals (Boudreaux 2013:492–495). In the public areas at the west end of the plaza, integrative activities included feasting events and the construction of a platform mound, beginning circa AD 1300. Mound building involved at least three additional construction stages that represent multiple ritually based labor projects and that would have involved large groups of people (see Pauketat 2000b:119). The public area on the eastern end of the plaza contained a westward-facing building early in the community's history, prior to AD 1300. Later, this building was replaced by a large enclosure that surrounded several burial clusters (Boudreaux 2007). Activities in this area may have been related to community-level mortuary rituals (Boudreaux 2013:497).

Domestic areas at Town Creek were located along the north and south sides of the community's plaza. Circular patterns of postholes and clusters of burials are archaeologically visible elements representing the remains of the household

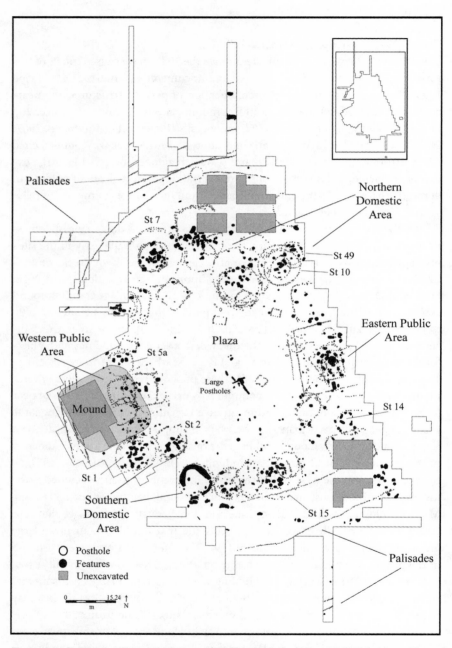

Figure 6.1. Selected architectural elements at Town Creek. (Edmond A. Boudreaux III)

groups that constituted this community. Most, and possibly all, of these spaces appear to have been built early in the community's history, prior to AD 1300, functioning domestically as circular houses with some burials placed in their floors (Boudreaux 2007:71). These circular posthole patterns likely are the remains of flexed-pole structures (n = 14) between 7 and 10.5 m in diameter. Such structures have been identified as houses, both at Town Creek and at other Mississippian sites in the region (Boudreaux 2013:489; Oliver 1992:120; South 2002:Figure 6.6H). This kind of structure persisted into the eighteenth century as the typical house style in a number of communities in the North Carolina piedmont (Ward and Davis 1999:Figures 4.16, 7.6, and 7.10; chapter 5 in this volume).

After around AD 1300, it appears that several groups transformed their houses into large, enclosed cemeteries. In three (Structures 1, 7, and 15) cases—possibly four (Structure 10)—the former locations of houses were surrounded by a large (13–19 m) circular enclosure of wooden posts. These enclosed areas were used as cemeteries after the original houses no longer stood. In the two completely excavated enclosed cemeteries, multiple burials toward the periphery superimposed the postholes of the original structure, indicating that some individuals were interred in these cemeteries after the walls of the earlier houses were no longer present (Ford 2016:83; Rosenwinkel 2013:88–89). It appears that these places began as circular houses with burials in their floors but then persisted as cemeteries after the original houses were no longer occupied.

Most groups, however—including those occupying the nine structures numbered 2, 5a, 6, 8, 14, 17, 21b, 31, and 49—did not transform their spaces into enclosed cemeteries. Instead, these nine structures appear to have always been houses, with the completely excavated examples (n = 4) containing 7–10 burials (Boudreaux 2013:490). Diagnostic ceramics and overlapping features indicate that most groups associated with houses at Town Creek (n = 7) may have vacated their homes some time before former houses became cemeteries, while two groups (inhabiting Structures 2 and 21b) may have continued residing at the site contemporaneous with the cemeteries (Boudreaux 2005:Table 3.6). The transformation of some house locations into cemeteries and the apparent withdrawal of individuals from most other houses coincides with a decline in Town Creek's population, a time when it appears that fewer households were concentrated at Town Creek and households may have been more dispersed across the landscape (Boudreaux 2013:495–497). The placement of houses and then cemeteries in prominent locations around Town Creek's plaza suggests that the corporate groups that maintained these places persisted and played important roles in the community's social, political, and economic life throughout its entire existence. Although just who was buried in the household cemeteries later in time at Town Creek is unclear, it is plausible—based on the relatively large number of individuals these cemeteries contain—that multiple households used the handful of cemeteries at Town Creek later in its history and that the households who had lived in unoccupied locations were now burying their dead in one of the three or four larger cemeteries that had been established in the domestic area. The presence of multiple subgroups within these large cemeteries is consistent with the idea that these spaces were used by multiple households (Ford 2016; Rosenwinkel 2013).

## COMPARISON OF EXCAVATED STRUCTURES

The broad outline of Town Creek's Mississippian community presented in the previous section has been known for some time (Boudreaux 2007, 2010, 2013). Although previous studies have classified Town Creek's domestic-area structures and cemeteries based on their size, demographics, and number of burials (Boudreaux 2007, 2010), these studies assumed a certain amount of homogeneity within structure types. In this chapter, we explore variability among domestic-area structures and cemeteries at Town Creek. We see structures and cemeteries as part of the built environment created by the corporate, household groups that made up the Town Creek community. As such, we assume that variability among houses and cemeteries reflects differences in the histories of these places and the practices of the corporate groups that used them (Adams and King 2011; Hally 2008:525; McAnany 2011; Steere 2017:176–177; Sullivan and Mainfort 2010).

Approximately 20 structures and cemeteries have been identified in domestic areas at Town Creek, but many of these have been only superficially investigated. In approximately half of the area archaeologically investigated at Town Creek, the plow zone was removed and underlying features were mapped, but these features were not excavated (Boudreaux 2013:Figure 4). In this section, we focus on those domestic-area houses (n = 4) and cemeteries (n = 2) that have been completely excavated. We describe and compare these structures based on archaeological observations such as structure size, evidence for structure rebuilding, artifact distributions, burial demography, and the spatial patterning of burials in order to infer some dimensions of the corporate groups that created and used these places.

### Structure Size

Differences of rank among corporate groups are often explored through differences in structure size (Steere 2017:21; chapter 1 in this volume). House size is positively correlated with rank and wealth in many societies; larger houses often contain more productive members, and higher-ranked houses are more successful at recruiting new members (Ames 2008:501). Although the number of completely excavated houses at Town Creek is small (n = 6), a histogram (Figure 6.2) of their distribution by area suggests that there may be two size classes, a smaller class of 45–55 m$^2$ and a larger class of 65–70 m$^2$ (Table 6.1). If there was an association between house size and status at Town Creek, the three larger structures may have been associated with higher-status families. All three larger houses are near the public area on the west side of the plaza, where the mound was built, which may have been a more prestigious location within the community.

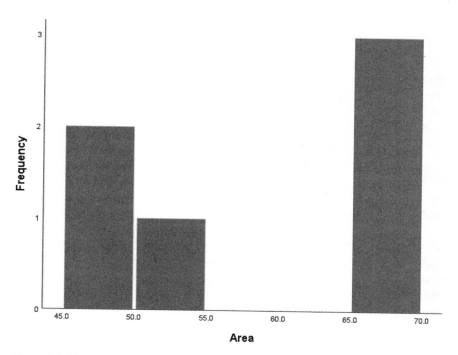

Figure 6.2. Histogram of completely excavated circular houses (n = 6) by size.
Mean = 58.08; standard deviation = 10.105. (Edmond A. Boudreaux III)

## Table 6.1. Size and Rebuilding Data for Excavated Domestic-Area Structures

| Structure | Diameter (m) | Area (m²) | Postholes in 60 cm buffer | Wall post density (posts/m) | Rebuilding ratio |
|---|---|---|---|---|---|
| Enclosed Cemeteries |
| 1 | 14.3 | 161.0 | 90 | 3.11 | 2.05 |
| 7 | 18.9 | 280.3 | 134 | 2.73 | 1.80 |
| Circular Houses |
| 1 | 9.1 | 65.4 | 46 | 1.52 | 1.00 |
| 2 | 9.1 | 65.6 | 92 | 2.88 | 1.90 |
| 5a | 7.9 | 48.7 | 73 | 2.80 | 1.85 |
| 7 | 9.4 | 69.9 | 124 | 3.96 | 2.61 |
| 14 | 7.7 | 46.0 | 42 | 1.76 | 1.16 |
| 49 | 8.2 | 52.9 | 52 | 2.73 | 1.80 |

## Structure Rebuilding

A positive correlation exists at Town Creek between the number of postholes associated with circular, domestic-area buildings and the number of burials they contained (Boudreaux 2013:489–490). This finding suggests that the number of burials reflects how long these structures were in use rather than any contemporaneous variability in household-group size. Thus, the longevity of household spaces varied substantially, which presumably reflects the differential longevity of the social groups associated with them.

Structure longevity can be assessed by using the number of postholes associated with a structure as an indicator of how much it was rebuilt or repaired. This method assumes that the postholes composing an archaeological structure represent both its original posts and those that were used in repairs as older posts rotted and were replaced (Hally 2008:315; Marcoux 2010b:118–120; Pauketat 2003:45–46; Warrick 1988:34–35). Six structures (1, 2, 5a, 7, 8, and 49) were excavated thoroughly enough to estimate the number of rebuilding episodes by using a method developed by Warrick (1988). First, we calculated posthole-density ratios using geographic information system (GIS) software to select all postholes within a 60 cm buffer of each structure's outline to determine the density of postholes per meter. Then, the structure with the lowest posthole density was used as a baseline to calculate a relative rebuilding ratio for other structures, based on the assumption that the structure with the lowest density either had not been rebuilt or had been only minimally rebuilt (Warrick 1988:40). In the domestic-area sample from Town Creek, the interior posthole pattern of Structure 1—presumably the wall of the original house in this location—had the lowest posthole density (1.52/m) (see Table 6.1).

Using the interior pattern of Structure 1 as a model for a minimally rebuilt house, we found what appears to be variability in the duration of structure use, with some houses having been minimally repaired (Structure 14) while others were rebuilt in place at least once (Structures 2, 5a, and 49) and possibly twice (Structure 7). What is more, the amount of rebuilding in place represented by the enclosed cemeteries (Structures 1 and 7) indicates that groups maintained those spaces for a long period of time. Enclosed cemeteries consisted of two constructions—an interior and an exterior circular pattern of postholes—that likely represent continuous but sequential periods of use (Boudreaux 2013:490). The combined rebuilding ratios for both the interior and exterior patterns suggest that these structures were rebuilt in these spaces three or four (or possibly more) times.

## Artifacts

Differences over rank among corporate groups are often explored through the differential distribution of artifacts, which can indicate inequalities in access to resources or intra- and extracommunity connections (Ames 2008:508; Cobb 1993:61;

Hally 2008:525–526; King 2010). Overall, a minority of individuals were interred with artifacts (36.3 percent) at Town Creek, and the overwhelming majority of burials with artifacts contained few items and very few types of artifacts (Boudreaux 2007:90). Most grave goods at Town Creek were either relatively ubiquitous across the site (e.g., shell beads, rocks, projectile points) or singular in occurrence (e.g., quartz crystal, awl, celt) (Table 6.2). Here, we highlight the distributions of several kinds of artifacts that may indicate connections among households, between domestic and public contexts within the community, and between households at Town Creek and the larger Mississippian world.

Copper fragments were recovered from burials in Structures 5a and 7. The only other place copper fragments are found in a sealed context at Town Creek is in a premound public building and a mound-summit context at the west end of the plaza (Armour 2012:Table 3.1; Boudreaux 2017:219). Structure 7 and the western public buildings are also connected in that nearly all of the passenger pigeon remains at Town Creek (98 percent) came from public-building contexts at the west end of the plaza (49 percent, n = 54) or from the Structure 7 vicinity (48 percent, n = 53) (Boudreaux 2017:219).

The presence of Pine Island–style marine-shell gorgets in Structures 14 (n = 1) and 49 (n = 1) suggests a connection between these corporate groups and the larger Mississippian world. Pine Island gorgets, which consist of a cross formed by the removal of four fenestrations, are found across the Southeast, with examples from Spiro, Angel, Etowah, and other sites in between (Brain and Phillips 1996:29–30). The gorgets depict the cross-in-circle, a widespread, fundamental Mississippian motif found on many sacred objects, which is associated with ideas about the sun and the sacred fire, the spiritual center of communal religious and political life in Mississippian and Historic period towns (Lankford 2007:20; Reilly 2004:130; chapter 8 in this volume). In the tripartite cosmos of many southeastern Indian groups, the sacred fire was the representation in the Middle World—the world occupied by humans—of the Sun, a powerful entity of the Above World (Lankford 2007:20–21).

## Burial Demographics

The presence of men, women, and children within each house and enclosed cemetery in the domestic areas at Town Creek indicates that these were burial spaces for members of kinship-based groups (Boudreaux 2007:87–88). Multiple contexts at Town Creek show that criteria for burial in domestic spaces were different than for burial in public spaces at the west end of the plaza. For example, only adults were buried in mound-summit contexts; only women and subadults were buried in some premound buildings; and only older adults were buried in another premound public building (Boudreaux 2007, 2017:216–219). Although domestic-area spaces are generally more inclusive, some important variability does exist

## Table 6.2. Artifacts Associated with Burials by Structure

| Structure | Burial | Awl | Burial covering | Celt | Ceramic vessel | Ceramic sherds | Ceramic beads | Copper axe | Copper fragments |
|---|---|---|---|---|---|---|---|---|---|
| 1 | | | | | | | | | |
| | 2a | — | — | — | — | — | — | — | — |
| | 13 | — | — | — | — | — | — | — | — |
| | 17 | — | — | — | — | 3 | — | — | — |
| | 21 | — | — | — | — | — | — | — | — |
| | 23 | — | — | — | — | — | — | — | — |
| | 27 | — | — | — | — | — | — | — | — |
| 2 | | | | | | | | | |
| | 33 | — | — | — | — | — | — | — | — |
| | 34 | — | 1 | — | — | — | — | — | — |
| | 35 | — | — | — | — | — | — | — | — |
| | 54 | — | — | — | — | — | — | — | — |
| 5a | | | | | | | | | |
| | 47 | — | — | — | — | — | — | — | 7 |
| 7 | | | | | | | | | |
| | 86 | 1 | — | — | — | — | — | — | — |
| | 87 | — | 1 | — | — | — | — | — | — |
| | 89 | — | 1 | — | — | — | — | — | — |
| | 92 | — | — | — | — | — | — | — | 1 |
| | 95 | — | 1 | — | — | — | — | — | — |
| | 98 | — | — | — | — | — | — | — | — |
| | 108 | — | — | — | 2 | — | — | — | — |
| | 111 | — | — | — | — | — | — | — | — |
| | 117 | — | — | — | — | — | — | — | — |
| | 120 | — | — | 1 | — | — | — | — | — |
| | 123 | — | — | — | — | — | — | — | — |
| | 125 | — | — | — | — | — | — | — | — |
| 14 | | | | | | | | | |
| | 43 | — | — | — | — | — | — | — | — |
| | 45 | — | — | — | — | — | 1 | — | — |
| | 50 | — | — | — | — | — | — | 1 | — |
| 49 | | | | | | | | | |
| | 68 | — | — | — | — | — | — | — | — |
| | 68a | — | — | — | — | 1 | — | — | — |
| | 70 | — | — | — | — | — | — | — | — |
| | 75 | — | — | — | — | — | — | — | — |
| Total | | 1 | 4 | 1 | 2 | 4 | 1 | 1 | 8 |

| Projectile points | Rock | Hammerstone | Celt | Quartz crystal | Shell beads | Shell gorgets | Shell ornaments | Total |
|---|---|---|---|---|---|---|---|---|
| — | — | — | — | — | 22 | — | — | 22 |
| 1 | 2 | — | — | — | — | — | — | 3 |
| — | — | — | — | — | — | — | — | 3 |
| — | 2 | — | — | — | — | — | — | 2 |
| 2 | — | — | — | — | — | — | — | 2 |
| 1 | — | — | — | — | — | — | — | 1 |
| 1 | — | — | — | — | — | — | — | 1 |
| — | — | — | — | — | 1 | — | — | 2 |
| — | — | — | — | — | 6 | — | — | 6 |
| — | 1 | — | — | — | — | — | — | 1 |
| — | — | — | — | — | — | — | — | 7 |
| — | — | — | — | — | — | — | — | 1 |
| — | 1 | — | — | — | — | — | — | 2 |
| — | 1 | — | — | — | — | — | — | 2 |
| — | — | — | — | — | — | — | — | 1 |
| — | — | — | — | — | — | — | — | 1 |
| — | 1 | — | — | — | — | — | — | 1 |
| — | — | — | — | — | — | — | — | 2 |
| — | — | — | — | — | — | — | 2 | 2 |
| — | — | — | — | — | — | — | 2 | 2 |
| — | — | — | — | — | — | — | — | 1 |
| — | 1 | — | — | — | — | — | — | 1 |
| 1 | — | — | — | — | — | — | — | 1 |
| — | — | — | — | — | 24 | 1 | — | 25 |
| — | — | — | — | — | — | — | — | 1 |
| — | 1 | — | — | — | 20 | — | — | 22 |
| 1 | 1 | — | — | — | — | — | — | 2 |
| — | — | — | — | 1 | 9 | 1 | — | 12 |
| — | 1 | — | 1 | — | — | — | — | 2 |
| — | 1 | 1 | — | — | — | — | — | 2 |
| 7 | 13 | 1 | 1 | 1 | 82 | 2 | 4 | 133 |

(Table 6.3). For example, houses contain a much higher proportion of women (43.2 percent) than do the enclosed cemeteries (21.1 percent). Women are especially underrepresented in Structure 7, where they are only 16.7 percent of the population, versus 35 percent for Structure 1 and 30.6 percent for Mississippian burials overall. Although the proportions of men are comparable for enclosed cemeteries (31 percent) and houses (27.3 percent), men are overrepresented in Structure 1 (50 percent), especially relative to Structure 7 (25 percent). One of the most striking patterns in Structure 7 is that over half of the burial population (58.3 percent) consists of subadults, which is considerably higher than the proportion of subadults (15 percent) in the other enclosed cemetery (Structure 1), in domestic-area houses collectively (29.5 percent), and in Mississippian burials overall (45.4 percent). This variability in burial demographics among contexts within the domestic area suggests that individual corporate groups at Town Creek used different principles for determining who could be buried within their spaces around the plaza.

## Spatial Distribution of Burials

A comparison of the spatial patterning of burials within completely excavated circular structures suggests variability in how groups organized their spaces and how they might have changed the structures through time. Burials within most structures at Town Creek were arranged so that they formed a square surrounding a central, open space (Boudreaux 2017:212). This is the case in premound public buildings, mound-summit buildings, and domestic-area buildings. Two buildings, Structures 4a and 5a, were located beneath the mound and had not been affected by plowing. In both of these structures, burials were arranged in a square around a hearth, and this arrangement was presumably the case in other structures, where plowing had destroyed all but the deepest features.

In Structure 7, the largest cemetery and the one that was used for the longest time, several distinct subgroups appear to radiate outward from the central square cluster of burials (Figure 6.3) (Rosenwinkel 2013:Figure 5.10). Each subgroup in Structure 7 includes burials that superimpose postholes in the walls of the original structure, indicating that these more peripheral burials took place within this space after the original house was no longer standing (Rosenwinkel 2013:88–89). The square cluster of burials at the center of Structure 7 likely contains the founders of this household and other individuals who were buried in the floor of this structure when it was a house (see Hally 2008:319, 532–534). In addition to including the earliest members of this corporate group, the burials in Structure 7's central square may include individuals from later in the cemetery's history. Between two and eight individuals were interred in each of the four burial pits that make up the central square cluster of Structure 7. Burial within one of these pits seems to have been important, as these central burial pits contain 40 percent of the 50 individuals buried in this cemetery. In addition, since the peripheral burial

Table 6.3. Burials by Gender in Excavated, Domestic-Area Structures

| | St. 1 | St. 2 | St. 5a | St. 7 | St. 14 | St. 49 | All domestic | Enclosed cemeteries | Houses | All Mississippian* |
|---|---|---|---|---|---|---|---|---|---|---|
| | | | | | | Counts | | | | |
| Youth | 3 | 3 | 1 | 28 | — | 2 | 63 | 34 | 13 | 83 |
| Female | 7 | 3 | 2 | 8 | 3 | 4 | 40 | 15 | 19 | 56 |
| Male | 10 | 3 | 1 | 12 | 3 | 3 | 37 | 22 | 12 | 44 |
| Total | 20 | 9 | 4 | 48 | 6 | 9 | 140 | 71 | 44 | 183 |
| | | | | | | Percent | | | | |
| Youth | 15.0 | 33.3 | 25.0 | 58.3 | — | 22.2 | 45.0 | 47.9 | 29.5 | 45.4 |
| Female | 35.0 | 33.3 | 50.0 | 16.7 | 50.0 | 44.4 | 28.6 | 21.1 | 43.2 | 30.6 |
| Male | 50.0 | 33.3 | 25.0 | 25.0 | 50.0 | 33.3 | 26.4 | 31.0 | 27.3 | 24.0 |

*Includes burials from public contexts.

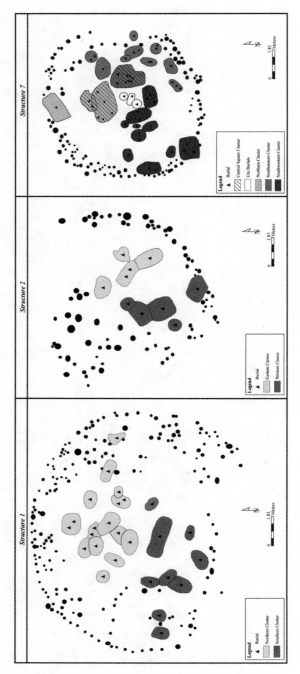

Figure 6.3. Clusters of burials in Structures 1, 2, and 7 at Town Creek. (Edmond A. Boudreaux III)

clusters within the Structure 7 cemetery appear to radiate outward from the central cluster, individuals within the central cluster may also have played significant roles within the peripheral subgroups (Rosenwinkel 2013:59–61).

Unlike Structure 7 and most of the burial spaces at Town Creek, Structures 1 and 2 were not organized around a central square (see Figure 6.3). Instead, the burials in Structure 2 were in a circular arrangement around a central space (Ford 2016:96), and the arrangement of burials in Structure 1 appears to have been more haphazard, with no clear, central area being discernible. In both Structures 1 and 2, the spacing between burials suggests that they may have been subdivided into two clusters (Ford 2016:108).

## DISCUSSION

There is variability among the houses and cemeteries in the domestic areas at Town Creek along several dimensions, including size, associated artifacts, structure rebuilding, and spatial arrangement of burials. Here, we use the patterns discussed in the previous section to develop inferences about possible variability among the corporate groups at Town Creek. The ranking of corporate groups was a common element of social and political life in Mississippian societies (Cobb 2003; Knight 1998). Rank differences among groups could be expressed through the size of dwellings, the spatial arrangement of dwellings and monuments within a settlement, or preferential access to some resources (Knight 1998, 2010; Steere 2017:138–139). The three largest houses in our sample at Town Creek are located in the western part of the community, in proximity to the western public area where the mound was built. At Moundville, Knight (1998:51) argued that corporate groups near the site's largest mound were more highly ranked, and that rank decreased with distance from this mound. At Town Creek, two of the larger houses, Structures 5a and 7, were located within or adjacent to the western public area where the platform was built around AD 1300. Burials at both structures were found with copper fragments, an exotic material often associated with Mississippian religious items, the presence of which is consistent with these having been higher-status households (Brown 2004, 2007).

The only other place where copper fragments were found at Town Creek was in premound and mound-summit public buildings in the western public area, places that likely were associated with community leadership and political decision-making at Town Creek (Boudreaux 2007:88–91, 2013:497). In many southeastern Indian groups, there was a clear connection between some corporate groups and political leadership roles within a town, as one had to be a member of a certain clan to be eligible for political office (Blitz 1993:10; Knight 1990; Sattler 1995: 225; Urban and Jackson 2004:698; Worth 1998:87). The distinctive, artifactual link among public buildings and corporate-group spaces at Town Creek could indicate that community leaders were selected from the corporate group or groups represented by Structures 5a and 7.

Differences in rank can be challenging to identify archaeologically in middle-range societies, such as Mississippian chiefdoms of the Southeast, where economically based class distinctions did not exist (Ames 2008:508; Cobb 2003). In such cases, where rank distinctions were not always starkly expressed in material ways, a constellation of differences can be used to explore rank. Structure 7, in addition to its large size and the presence of copper fragments, is distinctive in two other ways that suggest it was a place associated with a highly ranked, successful corporate group whose members were connected to community leadership roles. First, nearly all passenger pigeon remains from Town Creek were recovered from either the Structure 7 area or the public area at the west end of the plaza (Boudreaux 2017:219). The consumption of passenger pigeon in many Mississippian societies appears to have been limited to special people or special places, as passenger pigeon elements are often associated with high-status areas, elite residences, ritual buildings, and mound-summit contexts (Jackson and Scott 1995:110 and 116, 2003:554). Second, Structure 7 is distinctive because of its longevity. It was rebuilt more than any other domestic-area structure at Town Creek, and it contained more burials, by far, than any other context. The longevity of this place indicates that it was home to a successful corporate group that persisted throughout most, and possibly all, of Town Creek's existence as a community. The importance of this place is suggested by the large number of burials within its central square burial pits, a practice that may reflect a preference for later group members to be buried within the space associated with the group's founders and ancestors (Beck 2007:8; Wilson 2010).

While Structure 7 clearly seems to have been the place of a highly ranked corporate group, distributions of several distinct kinds of artifacts can be used to speak to the roles that other corporate groups played within the community as well. Unusual artifacts—copper-covered wooden discs, cross-in-circle ornaments of mica, a marine-shell pin, and rattles made of pebbles within a wooden container—are mostly found in public areas at the east and west ends of the plaza, with burials of individuals thought to have been political and ritual leaders (Boudreaux 2013:493–494). Some important exceptions to this pattern are the presence of marine-shell gorgets with the cross-in-circle motif in Structures 14 and 49 and the presence of a copper axe in Structure 14. Not only are these artifacts distinctive because they were made from exotic materials, but they are symbolically laden objects whose importance would have been recognized across the Mississippian world. Copper axes have been interpreted as symbols of political authority because many have been found with high-status burials and other distinctive artifacts (Brain and Phillips 1996:362; Peebles 1971:82; Scarry 1992:178–179), while shell gorgets have been seen as items that embody the cosmos or supernatural events (Knight et al. 2001:136; Lankford 2004:207–211). The copper axe and shell gorgets at Town Creek reflect connections between the corporate groups represented by Structures 14 and 49 and the external, Mississippian world. Furthermore, the presence of these ideologically charged items in Structures 14 and 49 demonstrates that such items were not just the purview of public rituals or high-status households. Instead, the presence of ideologically important items across Town Creek suggests that multiple corporate groups were integral to the ritual and political life of the community.

Kelly (2006:255) and Knight (2010:358) have argued that corporate groups at Cahokia and Moundville may have played complementary roles in craft production within a community-wide ritual system of cooperative and reciprocal relationships. According to Knight (2010:360), groups that engaged in the reciprocal exchange of goods and services within a community-wide ritual framework would have been bound to each other in a "fabric of obligation [that] would counter the tendency to fission." At Town Creek, ritually charged items and those made from exotic materials are concentrated in public areas, but they are also found in corporate group spaces in the northwestern (Structure 7), northeastern (Structure 49), and southeastern (Structure 14) parts of the community. This relatively diffuse distribution of important objects across Town Creek is consistent with the theory that multiple corporate groups played complementary roles in the community's ritual life.

Of all the houses that existed at different times in Town Creek's history, only four appear to have developed into enclosed cemeteries. Exactly why these household places persisted and others did not is unclear. The two enclosed cemeteries that have been excavated both developed out of larger houses, so higher-status corporate groups may have been more likely to transform their houses in this way. Beyond this commonality, though, Structures 1 and 7 are different in several ways that indicate significant variability among the corporate groups that created, transformed, and maintained these places. Although multiple indicators suggest that Structure 7 was associated with a high-status corporate group, the artifacts in Structure 1 are not distinctive. Stark differences in the demographics of the burials in these two cemeteries suggest that the corporate groups used different criteria for determining who could be buried in these places.

The spatial arrangement of burials was different within each enclosed cemetery. The burials in Structure 7 were organized around a central square. In southeastern Indian societies, squares were frequently used at multiple scales, ranging from individual objects to the layout of entire towns (Hally 2008:522–523; Hudson 1976:220–221). Squares were cosmograms that evoked beliefs about sacred aspects of the cardinal directions, the Middle World, and the potential for an axis mundi to connect the different layers of the cosmos through ritual (King 2010:61–65; chapters 8 and 10 in this volume). During the Historic period, many Native towns had what were known as square grounds, public spaces for communal gatherings and ceremonies, which consisted of a central hearth surrounded by four benches that corresponded to the cardinal directions (Hally 2008:148; Hudson 1976:220; King 2010:61; Knight 1998:58). When the smoke from the fire in this central hearth rose upward, it was believed to form an axis that connected the Middle World to the Upper World (King 2010:62; Reilly 2004:127). It is possible that the central square arrangement of burials in Structure 7, and within several other houses and public buildings at Town Creek, was created to invoke the structure of the cosmos, and perhaps to facilitate connecting with group ancestors. The importance of the central square burial cluster in Structure 7 is indicated by the later burial clusters that appear to radiate outward from it and by the apparent preference for burial within it. Perhaps the central square contained the founders of this corporate group, and there was a preference for or political advantage to burial in proximity to these ancestors (Beck 2007:8; Wilson 2010).

Structure 1 and the nearby Structure 2 were organized differently than Structure 7 because a central square cluster of burials was not present in either. Instead, Structure 1 was bisected to form northern and southern clusters, while Structure 2 was bisected to form eastern and western clusters. If the layout of Structure 7 was informed by the idea of the square as a cosmogram, then the corporate groups that created Structures 1 and 2 were invoking a different model, perhaps one of opposition, complementarity, and balance (Ford 2016:78), all of which were important concepts within southeastern Indian societies (Hudson 1976). While the full significance of the variability between Structures 1 and 7 is unclear and could be due to several factors (see Emerson et al. 2003:176), this variability indicates, at the very least, differences in practices among the corporate groups that persisted for multiple generations within the Mississippian community at Town Creek.

## CONCLUSIONS

A significant contribution of Mississippian scholarship since the 1990s has been recognizing and exploring the roles played by household and corporate groups in structuring Mississippian societies. Important insights have been developed by considering some fundamental Mississippian activities—such as mound building, the destruction and renewal of public buildings, and feasting—as undertakings sponsored and performed by corporate groups (Knight 2010; Pauketat et al. 2002). Additionally, the complex structures of some large, multiple-mound, civic-ceremonial centers have been rendered more intelligible when they have been viewed as places created and maintained by the collective actions of multiple corporate groups (Kelly 2006; King 2010; Knight 1998, 2010; Pauketat et al. 2002; Wilson 2010). This corporate-group, household-level perspective has contributed to a better understanding of the importance of the groups that made up the Mississippian community at Town Creek as well (Boudreaux 2007, 2013). Significant changes late in Town Creek's history (c. AD 1300) included the construction of a platform mound and the movement of people out of this settlement as households became more dispersed across the landscape. Despite these significant changes, the Town Creek community persisted because corporate groups continued to participate in communal ceremonies and maintained their places around the plaza through mortuary ritual, an important means for constructing and expressing their identity through physical ties to their ancestors and an ancestral place (Adams and King 2011; Bourdieu 1977:89–90; Foucault 1977; Hodder and Cessford 2004; Wilson 2010:4). Such persistent, emplaced mortuary rituals also may have legitimized ancestral ties, literally and figuratively, to a place within the community that included social, political, and ritual rights and obligations as well as claims to economic resources and places on the landscape (Brown 2007; Connerton 1989:72–73; Goldstein 1980, 1981; King 2011; McAnany 2011; Saxe 1970; Wilson 2010). Although important changes took place over time in terms of where corporate groups lived and how they used their space around the plaza, it appears that a key element in the persistence of the Town Creek community was multiple corporate groups demonstrating in various ways the significance of their ties to their ancestors.

Although corporate groups were important throughout Town Creek's history and several of their places around Town Creek's plaza followed the same house-to-cemetery trajectory, our research shows that these groups were not equivalent. Instead, they differed from each other along several dimensions that included rank, longevity, and practice. For example, while it was important for some households to bury members in a square arrangement of graves at the center of a structure or cemetery and—in at least one case (Structure 7)—for later group members to be buried within or in relation to this central square, this was not the case in some other structures and cemeteries where different principles guided the placement of burials and the arrangement of space. This recognition of intracommunity variability is important in order to acknowledge the agency of most of Town Creek's residents (see Pauketat 2000b) and to avoid the pitfall of seeing households or corporate groups as a homogeneous class of interchangeable units (Rogers 1995b:25).

# 7

# MISSISSIPPIAN COMMUNITIES OF CONFLICT

Meghan E. Buchanan and Melissa R. Baltus

Archaeological evidence for physical violence (e.g., palisades, burned villages, bodily trauma) during the late twelfth through fifteenth centuries indicates an increase in intercommunity conflict in the Mississippian Midwest.[1] Warfare has been implicated in the expansion (Larson 1972), maintenance (Gibson 1974), and destruction (Dye 2009) of southeastern Mississippian societies. Previous research regarding midwestern Mississippian warfare has typically focused on the divisive nature of conflict, such as political fragmentation and community fissioning. The onset of palisade construction at Cahokia and other midwestern Mississippian sites is often seen as the beginning of the end for these communities, signaling their inevitable slide into abandonment.

Periods of endemic warfare or even the threat of warfare can have a profound effect on people's daily lives. Day-to-day activities associated with hunting, farming, or resource gathering may become increasingly circumscribed or embedded with fear of potential attack (Milner 1999; Milner et al. 1991; Wilson 2012). Social ties with more distant groups may be severed through decreasing contact or outright conflict between those groups. Even residential groups may be divided by walls intruding across settlements and between houses (Dalan et al. 2003). These impacts often highlight the ways in which conflict can disrupt community.

In this chapter, however, we consider how communities were built *through* conflict. Drawing on comparison of sites from the American Bottom and its surrounding uplands (Cahokia, East St. Louis, and Olin) and part of the central Mississippi River Valley (Common Field), we argue that communities were created through the spatial incorporation or separation of walls and through new or continued (repoliticized) material practices (e.g., mound building, commensality) despite, or perhaps as part of, regional violence.

## COMMUNITIES AND CONFLICT

Within analyses of Mississippian societies, definitions of what constituted community are few and far between. In the *Mississippian Communities and Households* volume (Rogers and Smith 1995), households were defined by multiple authors, but definitions of community are lacking (see introduction to this volume). Instead, throughout the volume communities were implied to be concentrations of many households and, during periods of conflict, concentrations of households behind palisade walls or fortification ditches. Many approaches to the archaeology of communities equate the community with the site, a bounded spatial entity where community was created not only through proximity, but also through face-to-face contact and interaction with other community members (Mehrer 2000; see chapter 1 in this volume for the history of household and community archaeologies). Such a definition can be particularly appealing when we are studying palisaded sites since walls seem to create clear boundaries, enclosing people within protective spaces. Peregrine (1993) argued that in contexts where warfare was present, communities would be structured so that households would not be accessible by those from outside of the community; palisade construction was one such way to structure communities.

Critiques of earlier community concepts and definitions have highlighted that community extends beyond site limits and palisade walls. Yaeger and Canuto (2000) argue that community is social, ever emergent, and structured through daily practices, many of which are spatially constituted. Yaeger (2000:129–131) differentiates between three kinds of practices that are generative of community among Classic Maya sites: daily routines embedded in a shared sense of habitus (see also Joyce and Hendon 2000), practices that reinforce communal identities while at the same time highlighting intercommunity difference (like feasting and monumental constructions), and practices that cite wider, extralocal identities. During periods of endemic violence and warfare, the repetition and routinization of practices were affected by life within palisade walls, but the practices that constituted conceptions of shared community membership could also continue to be extended to people living at other locations.

Kowalewski (2006) has suggested that the concept of coalescence is germane to understanding some southeastern Native communities, particularly those that experienced significant pressure due to factors like warfare or demographic collapse. Birch (2012) argues that coalescence was an ongoing process that could include spatial changes to communities (e.g., formation of large towns, fortification, development of village layout or architecture aimed at community integration) as well as social and political changes (e.g., formation of new rituals or institutions oriented toward community integration or collectivity). In both Yaeger's (2000) formulation of community and Kowalewski's (2006) and Birch's (2012) elaboration of coalescent communities, community was continually renegotiated within walled settlements, between multiple local communities, and between communities throughout entire regions (see also Birch and Williamson 2018; Jefferies 2018; Sullivan 2018).

Harris (2014:86) has further extended this critique of the community concept and highlighted several weaknesses that have relevance for our discussion on Mississippian communities during periods of violence. First, Harris suggests that approaches to the archaeology of communities have largely focused on the positive aspects of community, downplaying violence within and between communities. Second, definitions of community have been anthropocentric. Harris (2014:89) argues that "the communities we study do not impose themselves on particular places; rather they emerge through them." Communities do not exist solely through interactions between people; they are created through the relational connections between people, places, material objects, nonhuman beings, animals, and so on. Periods of warfare require different relations between the diverse actors that constitute communities. And third, approaches to the archaeology of communities have ignored the role of affect. Affects emerge through the convergence of multiple actors; thus, affect is central to community-making, maintenance, transformation, and dissolution. The material culture of communities (houses, pottery, features, built environment) was tied to the affective fields in which they were created. For example, Harris (2014:91) argues that certain types of Late Neolithic pottery allowed for affective connections; vessels created in ritual contexts were later used in domestic activities, tying the larger ritual community to the daily practices of people across great distances.

Previous research on Mississippian communities in the Midwest has focused on the creation of communities during the nascent stages of Cahokia (eleventh-century Lohmann and twelfth-century Stirling phases), related Mississippian centers, and related subsidiary sites (e.g., Betzenhauser 2011; Mehrer 2000; Pauketat 2000a). When the later phases of Cahokian Mississippian communities (thirteenth-century Moorehead and fourteenth-century Sand Prairie phases) are discussed (e.g., Mehrer and Collins 1995), they are framed within a narrative of the overall decline of Cahokia. In other words, rather than the ongoing community-*making* seen during the Lohmann (AD 1050–1100) and Stirling (AD 1100–1200) phases, communities of the Moorehead (AD 1200–1275/1300) and Sand Prairie (AD 1300–1400) phases have been conceptualized as being engaged in the processes of *unmaking* and eventual abandonment.

In what follows, we trace the creation, transformation, and destruction of communities in parts of the Mississippian Midwest, namely the Olin and Common Field sites. Drawing on Harris's critiques of the community concept, we explore community-making through the diverse assemblages of actors present in the American Bottom and central Mississippi River Valley during a period of escalating regional violence and warfare. We focus on palisade/compound construction, mound construction, and commensality in the creation of communities during the escalating violence of the twelfth through fifteenth centuries.

## BACKGROUND: MISSISSIPPIAN VIOLENCE AND WARFARE IN THE MIDWEST

Pauketat (2004, 2005a, 2009) has characterized the first century of Mississippian history in the Midwest as the *pax Cahokiana*. This period of relative peace was not completely devoid of violence; large-scale mortuary events at places like Mound 72 involved human sacrifice (Fowler et al. 1999), and numerous monumental post pits throughout the American Bottom region contained female sacrifices (Hargrave and Bukowski 2010), attesting to politically and religiously sanctioned acts of violence at a time of overall regional peace. These public acts of violence were important agents in the creation of a large-scale Cahokian Mississippian community (Emerson et al. 2016; Pauketat 2010), along with more peaceful communal activities like mound building, burial events, and feasting (e.g., Baires 2014a; Pauketat et al. 2002). Cahokia and other sites such as East St. Louis and Emerald (Illinois) were oriented toward organizational axes that reference celestial events (Pauketat 2013a; Romain 2015). Ramey Incised pottery, decorated with iconography that embodied Cahokian cosmological order and balance, was exchanged throughout the Mississippian Southeast (Pauketat 2004; Pauketat and Emerson 1991). Many of these practices were related to the creation and dissemination of religious practices; some were rooted in the politicization of antecedent Late Woodland traditions (Betzenhauser 2011; Pauketat 2000a) and were involved in the creation of community that extended beyond the boundaries of the Cahokia site and beyond the American Bottom floodplain.

The *pax Cahokiana* came to an end during the latter part of the twelfth century. The earliest known palisade construction at a site entangled within the broader Cahokian community began circa AD 1075–1100, at the site of Aztalan in south-central Wisconsin (Krus 2016). Fortifications were common at Mississippian sites in the central Illinois River Valley (Wilson 2012), and palisade construction spread throughout the Midwest after AD 1200 (Krus 2016). Outside of the American Bottom, there is significant evidence for violent conflict in the central Mississippi and Illinois River Valleys, where entire sites burned and burial assemblages bear the evidence of armed conflict and death (Buchanan 2015a; Conrad 1991; Milner et al. 1991; Morse and Morse 1983; Price and Griffin 1979; Steadman 2008; Wilson 2012). While fortifications were present at Cahokia, East St. Louis, and a single site at the northern fringes of the American Bottom, evidence for extant warfare is less conclusive at and immediately around Cahokia. This is not the case for the Common Field site in the central Mississippi River Valley. The differences in presence and enactment of violence have implications for community construction in these areas, as is discussed through our case studies below.

## CASE STUDIES
### American Bottom: Cahokia and East St. Louis

Palisade and compound construction at Cahokia and East St. Louis began circa AD 1150–1200. At Cahokia proper, a palisade encircled Monks Mound, the Grand Plaza, and the adjacent earthen pyramids. This central palisade was constructed in alignment with Cahokia's 5-degree offset organizational axis (Iseminger et al. 1990), despite residential abandonment of this organizational axis shortly before the construction of the palisade (Collins 1990). A series of bastioned compounds were erected in sequence at Tract 15B, immediately west of this central palisade (Pauketat 2013b). The Tract 15B compounds appear to have encompassed specialized politico-religious or extradomestic buildings as well as a series of reset monumental marker posts (which were perhaps recognized as social persons or ancestors, *sensu* Skousen 2012).

Within the East St. Louis precinct, a series of presumably administrative storage structures, also behind a compound or palisade wall, were incinerated in a catastrophic event around AD 1175 (Pauketat et al. 2013). The burning of this storage compound at East St. Louis might have been the result of a violent attack, but a more likely explanation is that the area was set afire as part of a ritual burning event (Pauketat et al. 2013); other kinds of ritual burnings were common in the American Bottom region (Baltus and Baires 2012).

The period after AD 1175 has been conceptualized as the "beginning of the end" for Cahokia as the population in the region dropped; however, while some sites in the Cahokia vicinity experienced population loss (through migration) and abandonment, other sites were established during the late Stirling and Moorehead phases. Despite the construction of the fortification wall at Cahokia, little evidence exists of violent conflict in the American Bottom during the thirteenth and fourteenth centuries. The only other site in the American Bottom that is known conclusively to be fortified is the small village of Olin, located in the uplands at the northern edge of the American Bottom.

## Olin

Located within the modern town of Bethalto, Illinois, the Olin site is situated on a prominent bluff spur overlooking a tributary to the east branch of Wood River. Occupation of the site spans from the late Stirling phase (after AD 1150) through the middle Moorehead phase (c. AD 1250). Excavated in the 1970s as a series of Southern Illinois University Edwardsville archaeological field schools directed by Sidney Denny, the Olin site is unique as it is one of very few fortified sites located in the American Bottom region. The major mound centers of Cahokia, East St. Louis, and Common Field are the only other sites known to have palisades and compound walls, while the smaller Kruckeberg #1 site has a suspected, but unconfirmed, palisade (Woods and Holley 2000).

Excavations at the Olin site, over the course of six years, revealed a tightly organized, small village incorporated within a set of reconstructed palisade walls. The outermost wall is the original construction, and though excavations did not extend beyond this palisade due to erosion of the landform, occupation also did not seem to extend beyond that outer wall (Sidney Denny, personal communication 2009). The inner palisade wall was built partway through the occupation of the site (c. AD 1200), presumably replacing the outer palisade and effectively separating site occupants.

Approximately 47 structures (including episodes of rebuilding) were excavated. These buildings were initially organized around a small square plaza, with buildings roughly cardinally oriented. A single circular sweat lodge was part of the initial site layout. This structure was located at the eastern edge of the small plaza, within the larger outer palisade and approximately 5 m northeast of a monumental marker post. A structure was later built over this post pit after its removal, citing its location.

Reconstruction of the palisade in its smaller form effectively excluded the sweat lodge from the fortified area, presumably corresponding with its abandonment as a formal structure. Additionally, this inner palisade forced the removal and replacement of the structure built on the former post pit location. The reconstruction of the palisade changed the dynamics of the Olin village by excluding previously important buildings and landscape locations, as well as segregating a portion of the human community from view. A very small number of buildings were incorporated within the rebuilt inner palisade, including a set of paired buildings in the northeast corner and a rebuilt series of structures in the northwest corner. Buildings superimpose both inner and outer palisade walls, indicating that occupation of the site continued after the fortifications were no longer maintained.

Pottery from Olin includes a few late Stirling Ramey Incised jars, numerous Moorehead-phase Cahokia Cordmarked jars, and an abundance of serving vessels (Figure 7.1) (Baltus 2014). Fineware bowls, beakers, and plates were present in high numbers, indicating that practices of commensality continued within the bounds of the Olin palisade. This high proportion of serving to cooking vessels (1:1) mirrors that of Cahokia, as measured from the Ramey Field (Hamlin 2004) as well as excavations at Tract 15B (Pauketat 2013b), indicating that practices of

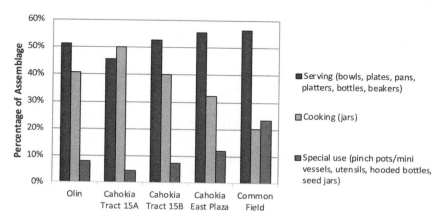

Figure 7.1. Proportions of serving, cooking, and special-use vessels in Moorehead-phase contexts at Olin, Common Field, and Cahokia. (Melissa R. Baltus and Meghan E. Buchanan)

commensality continued to be important and perhaps even increased in scale or intensity during the Moorehead phase (Pauketat 2013b). The pottery from the Olin site, finewares especially, is visually and morphologically quite similar to that recovered from similar contexts at Cahokia itself, suggesting continued connections between the sites.

## Common Field

The Common Field site is located at the southern edge of the American Bottom floodplain, south of the modern town of Ste. Genevieve, Missouri. Although the site was long thought to have been a vacant ceremonial center associated with Cahokia's Lohmann phase (Chapman 1980), a Mississippi River flooding event in 1979/1980 scoured the plow zone from the site, revealing hundreds of densely packed, burned structures and an extensive palisade surrounding the town. A 1980 US Army Corps of Engineers aerial photograph taken shortly after the flood shows at least 300 burned structures (or structure-sized features). Analyses of surface-collected materials following the scouring highlighted the catastrophic nature of the burning event; nearly complete vessels, articulated human remains, and upright, in situ, burned architectural posts were noted by archaeologists in the 1980s and 1990s (F. Terry Norris, personal communication 2010; O'Brien 1996; O'Brien et al. 1982). Systematic excavations conducted by Buchanan in 2010 and 2011 documented six structures, a portion of the palisade, and numerous pits, all of which contained artifacts diagnostic to the Moorehead and Sand Prairie phases. Based on accelerator mass spectrometry (AMS) dates and house-longevity estimates, Common Field appears to have been founded circa AD 1250 and was burned circa AD 1280 (Buchanan 2015b:253).

The palisade was rebuilt once, directly atop the location of the first construction; there are no other building episodes visible in the results from a gradiometer survey conducted over portions of the site. Construction of the palisade included the excavation of a trench (at least 70 cm deep) and the setting in of large posts (approximately 20 cm in diameter) spaced 20 cm apart. Prior to the second construction of the palisade, builders incorporated a prepared fill into the trench, consisting of crushed sandstone, limestone, waterworn pebbles, and pieces of galena (Buchanan 2015a, 2015b).

Structures located within the palisade are oriented either parallel or perpendicular to the palisade walls. Two excavated structures were located less than a meter from the palisade; one was inside the wall, and the other was outside. Buchanan (2015a) has suggested that the structure outside of the wall may have been abandoned and intentionally infilled around the same time the palisade was constructed. This activity suggests that the organizational plan was in place during the initial founding of Common Field. This overriding organizational plan can also be seen in four probable plazas flanking the primary mound (Mound A), oriented the same way as the palisade and structures. This particular orientation appears to reference lunar-aligned sites like Emerald (Buchanan 2020).

The ceramic assemblage at Common Field comprises Moorehead- and Sand Prairie–phase pottery, morphologically and stylistically similar to wares found in the American Bottom, highlighting the continued connections between Common Field and the American Bottom. Large proportions of serving vessels with incised rims (Wells or O'Byam Incised) have been recovered from surface collections and excavated contexts. The proportion of serving vessels to cooking vessels (2:1) at Common Field is larger than seen at American Bottom sites like Tracts 15A and B (Pauketat 1998, 2013b), ICT-II (Holley 1989), and Ramey Field (Hamlin 2004), highlighting the importance of commensal practices at Common Field (see Figure 7.1). More than half of the plates at Common Field were decorated with incised triangles and/or chevrons. While these designs have been interpreted previously as sunbursts (Emerson 1997a:227; Kelly 1984, cited in Hilgeman 2000), Buchanan (2015a) argues that they contain avian- and warfare-related imagery.

## BETTER WALLS, BETTER NEIGHBORS?

No evidence suggests that Olin was ever attacked; the palisade shows no evidence of burning, and likewise no buildings were burned. Additionally, the single intact burial at the site shows no evidence for trauma. A similar pattern may be noted at Cahokia, where no evidence suggests that the palisade or Tract 15B compound were attacked, let alone breached. While the compound at East St. Louis was burned, circumstances surrounding that conflagration remain inconclusive as to extant warfare (Pauketat et al. 2013). In contrast, there is clear evidence that Common Field was attacked and burned. Burned structures (with nearly complete domestic assemblages and in situ burned posts), evidence of burning in the palisade trench, and articulated human remains found in domestic structures all point to an event in which the people living at Common Field were caught unaware, their village was burned, and some people lost their lives.

The initial palisade at Olin appears to have been all encompassing in its form (although portions of the site outside of the palisade may have been affected by erosional forces that destroyed subsurface features). This practice of fortifying an entire face-to-face community is similar to that of fortified villages to the north in the central Illinois River Valley; however, the later reconstruction of the Olin palisade to surround only a plaza area and (potentially) extradomestic buildings is more akin to what we see at Cahokia and East St. Louis (see also chapter 2 in this volume). These differences in fortification practice, while necessarily practical in some respects (especially regarding the logistics of "manning the walls" at a site the size of Cahokia), might also provide insight into community-making processes and practices during times of conflict.

These fortified areas, rather than serving as protection for an entire village or face-to-face community, surround spaces in which people (and likely other-than-human persons [after Hallowell 1975]) might gather for public ceremony—the Grand Plaza at Cahokia and the smaller plaza area at Olin—or buildings associated with politico-religious practices. Such spaces are simultaneously community-building places and elite-status-creating spaces. These concepts are not as contradictory as one might suspect from the surface. Rather, community-building practices are multiscalar: broader community identities emerge through gatherings, ceremonies, and practices that take place in inclusive spaces like plazas, while restricted subcommunities that have potential for the creation of status or class difference emerge through practices occurring in more exclusive contexts and spaces (see the introduction to this volume).

Similar to the initial palisade construction at Olin, the palisade at Common Field appears to have encompassed the entirety of the 17 ha town. One structure was documented outside of the palisade, but it is unclear when that structure was occupied with relation to the timing of the palisade construction. Unlike Olin, the palisade at Common Field does not appear to have been reconstructed to protect the central precinct of the site. Instead, the palisade was reconstructed once in the same trench as the initial wall. Rather than protecting community-inclusive and elite-status-creating spaces (like at Olin and Cahokia), the construction of the Common Field palisade and the organizational orthodoxy of spatial orientation embodied a different kind of community-making process (Buchanan 2019). Like the rigid organization at Cahokia during the Lohmann and early Stirling phases, structures at Common Field (including the palisade) appear to have been oriented based on organizational axes (approximately 58 degrees east of north). The spatiality of Common Field would have created community through the daily, shared practices embedded in the habitus of moving about the planned village (*sensu* chapter 2 in this volume; Joyce and Hendon 2000:154–158; Yaeger 2000:129; chapter 10 in this volume). These daily practices and the site organization itself would have also cited extralocal communal identities through reference to the strict organization at Cahokia and possibly through new/different celestial alignments (see Buchanan 2020). Like the Cahokian politicization of Late Woodland spatial practices during the Lohmann phase, the leaders of Common Field engaged in a new politicization of the Cahokian organizational plan by reorienting the axes.

## DISCUSSION: MATERIAL ENTANGLEMENTS

Like mound building, palisade construction and maintenance would be a practice that engaged a cooperative group of people, working together toward a common goal. This community of practice (see Harris 2014; Lave and Wenger 1991) would potentially crosscut the face-to-face community within which it worked.[2] Additionally, this subcommunity would possibly be engaged in other relational sets of conflict-associated practices: weaponry production, acts of warfare, purification (including use of sweat lodges) before or after combat, dancing and singing in celebration or mourning, and so forth. While the palisade itself may have physically divided the face-to-face community (see Dalan et al. 2003), it simultaneously created other forms of community (see also Birch 2012; Kowalewski 2006).

These bundled practices (Pauketat 2013a; Zedeño 2008) involved in warfare highlight the potential for a community of conflict, with a membership beyond the human. Palisade walls become participants in a community of defense; projectiles (already active participants in a community of hunting) engage in acts of war; other potent materials (e.g., pigments, regalia, poles, trophies and honors, pipes, and personal, clan, or sodality bundles) provide substances needed for purification, supplication, or individual success in acts of warfare (e.g., Bailey 1995; Fletcher and La Flesche 1992; Swanton 2001 [1931]). For example, the palisade at Common Field contained a layer of prepared fill of magico-ritual materials (galena), bundling together physical and spiritual powers (Buchanan 2015b). Additionally, permission for or sanctification of acts of war may have been required from nonhuman beings (e.g., deities, ancestors), while the necessary accoutrements and ceremonial knowledge for preparation may have been the purview of different human individuals or groups (e.g., Bailey 1995; Fletcher and La Flesche 1992). When these elements were assembled in the proper manner, warfare could commence.

The bundled practices of warfare included feasts of preparation and celebration, acts of commensality through which communities emerged. Practices of commensality create and re-create communities in ways that extend temporally and spatially, bringing together those who make the special-use vessels and those (whether human or otherwise; Hallowell 1975) who provide the food. The increased ratio of serving vessels to cooking vessels in the American Bottom and central Mississippi River Valley during a period of conflict certainly speaks to the significance of commensal events in relation to warfare. Remarkably, one important serving vessel type—the rimmed plate—is an innovation that roughly coincides with the first construction of the palisade at Cahokia.[3] Such vessels indicate a shift in cuisine, perhaps including different foods or foods cooked in new ways (Pauketat 2013b). These foods were served in open vessels, a presentation style that allows commensal partners (including nonhuman participants) to witness from above both the food and the iconography around the rim of the vessel. This new vessel type emphasized stylized avian iconography, which was closely associated with the Upper World, warfare, and masculinity throughout the Midwest, Southeast, and plains (see Buchanan 2015a, 2019).

## CONCLUSION: "VACANT" QUARTER
Current evidence suggests a depopulation of Cahokia concurrent with or shortly following the burning of the compound at East St. Louis and the erection of the palisade around the core of downtown Cahokia (Pauketat et al. 2013; Pauketat

and Lopinot 1997). Thirteenth-century Moorehead-phase buildings are fewer in number at the excavated tracts of Cahokia than are buildings from previous time periods (Collins 1990; Pauketat 1998, 2013b; though see Baires et al. 2017); however, floodplain and upland sites continue to have a Moorehead-phase occupation. Evidence from the American Bottom region indicates that continued or new extraregional contacts (Baltus 2014), the introduction of new mortuary practices (Emerson and Hargrave 2000), and limited mound building continued through the late thirteenth century (Baltus 2014; Kelly et al. 2008); the Common Field site was also established during this time (Buchanan 2015a). During this late Cahokian diaspora, we see the founding or florescence of fortified mound centers throughout the greater Southeast (Dye 2009) and the spread of martial iconography, including copper repoussé plates of falconoid figures and flint-clay figurines (e.g., pipes in the shape of warriors) likely produced at Cahokia. By the middle to late fourteenth century, Cahokia and the surrounding American Bottom were abandoned.[4]

Numerous hypotheses have been proposed for the abandonment of what has been called the Vacant Quarter, including environmental degradation, climate change, and the inherent instability of chiefdoms (see Cobb and Butler 2002 for an overview of the Vacant Quarter); in these hypotheses, warfare is seen as a by-product of those larger causal mechanisms. Yet warfare would have also had a profound effect on communities surrounded by and directly affected by violence, whether that violence was directed at them or directed at others some distance away. Violent events and actions would have created new kinds of entanglements, as nonhuman actors, spirits, and places were left behind, and places were abandoned by their human Mississippian inhabitants (Buchanan 2015b). Violence reverberated far beyond palisade walls and individual communities. Once people were compelled to leave what would become the Vacant Quarter, they would have created new kinds of community wherever they ended up (see Buchanan 2020; Cook 2018; Cook and Fargher 2008; Sullivan 2018).

Midwestern Mississippian communities of the late twelfth through fifteenth centuries were more than simple concentrations of households behind palisade walls. The case studies presented here from the American Bottom, Olin, and Common Field demonstrate that community was constructed in many different ways during this period of escalating violence and warfare. Rather than a thirteenth-century "beginning of the end" in the Cahokia region, there was a florescence of new kinds of communities. Community was created through daily bodily movements, citational histories, and shared practices. These communities of conflict included Mississippian peoples connected to one another through multiple cross-cutting relationships (kinship, trading partnerships, sodalities, etc.), as well as nonhuman actors necessary for the practice of war and for protection. Community-making was an ongoing process; when people left the Vacant Quarter, they left some of their community behind, but they continued to engage in new kinds of community-making practices in their new homelands.

## Acknowledgments

Thank you to Alleen Betzenhauser and Elizabeth Watts Malouchos for inviting us to contribute to this volume. Their feedback and critiques have been useful throughout the writing process. Thank you also to the volume reviewers for their helpful feedback. Research at Common Field was funded through a Wenner-Gren grant (Gr. 8366), a Foundation for Restoration of Ste. Genevieve grant, and the Indiana University David C. Skomp Summer Research Fund.

## Notes

1. We generally define the Mississippian Midwest as the region encompassing the modern states of Illinois, Indiana, Missouri, Ohio, and the northern half of Kentucky; this area contains the central Mississippi and Lower Ohio River Valleys.

2. Mound building continued at Cahokia and some outlying sites (e.g., Copper) during and subsequent to this period of conflict (Baltus 2014; Kelly et al. 2008).

3. The earliest iteration of this vessel type appears to be the Wells Incised plate or Wells Everted Rim bowl, appearing at Cahokia in the late Stirling to early Moorehead phase (Holley 1989).

4. There is evidence for an Oneota occupation at a small number of sites, but the dating of this occupation is problematic (Emerson 1997a).

# III

# COMMUNITY AND COSMOS

# 8

# HOUSEHOLDS, COMMUNITIES, AND THE EARLY HISTORY OF ETOWAH

Adam King

Communities are made up of two parts, one that is physical and comprising a landscape and a set of material traditions, and one that is social and made up of relationships among people, the landscape, and things. The physical and the social are inseparable. The social is created, enacted, contested, and negotiated through the creation, use, and interpretation of the physical. People, things, relationships, meaning, history, and identity are bound together through action. In this chapter, I discuss how the first Mississippian community at the Etowah site in northwestern Georgia (Figure 8.1) was created, through a focus on the so-called entanglements among people, material traditions, and meaning.

## THE ETOWAH SITE

The Etowah site is a large and well-known Mississippian town situated on the bank of the Etowah River in the northwestern corner of Georgia (King 2003). The core of the site covers about 22 ha and was surrounded by a ditch and palisade complex. In addition to a clay-lined plaza, that core included a second smaller plaza and as many as six earthen platform mounds. As with most Mississippian mounds, these were used to support mortuary temples and the houses of important people, as well as to host important political and ritual events. Certainly, Etowah's fame derives mainly from the large quantity of elaborately decorated, finely crafted ceremonial objects recovered from the site's mortuary mound (King 2007; Larson 1971). These objects were ritual regalia as much as status markers and are connected to a set of ritual themes and symbols shared widely across the Mississippian region (Waring and Holder 1945).

One of the more interesting aspects of Etowah's history is that the site had a long occupational sequence (c. AD 1000–1550) that was interrupted by periods of abandonment (King 2003). This pattern makes Etowah a unique place to study community formation and its material entanglements. Here I focus on the earliest community, which was established at the site sometime after AD 1000 (see King 2003; cf. Lulewicz 2019a), and which is notably not the same Etowah that dominated a large part of the interior Southeast in the fourteenth century. This was not a community of huge mounds, elaborate objects, and far-flung trade networks.

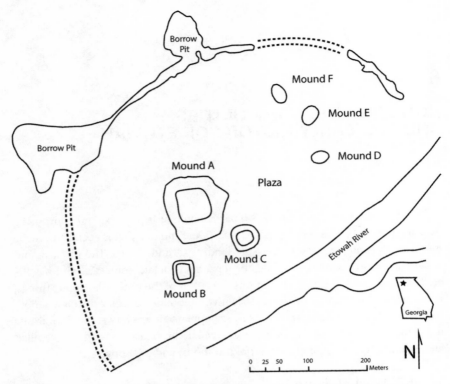

Figure 8.1. Plan map of the Etowah site. (Adam King, Elizabeth Watts Malouchos)

That Middle Mississippian (AD 1250–1375) place was created only after Etowah's first community appeared, flourished, and was abandoned. The story of Etowah's first community is not about the rise of a powerful center, but about the creation of a new way of doing things and a new kind of community in northern Georgia.

## ENTANGLEMENT, COMMUNITIES OF PRACTICE, AND COMMUNITY CREATION

Archaeology has long been challenged to explore the social through the material. While various materialist theoretical frames have been used to accomplish this task, most have fallen short because they emphasize people as reactors to the material conditions of life or treat material objects as static, nonagential things deployed by people. The perspective of entanglement attempts to bridge the gap between things and people by focusing on the intertwining of things, people, and practices, and in particular by allowing things to be agents of change (Hitchcock and Maeir 2013; Hodder 2011, 2012). Entanglement recognizes that social life is defined and practiced through relations with things as well as people. It also recognizes that the meaning and role of things are defined by their relationships with people and with other things. Meaning, identity, and history are continually defined through the entangled relations of people and things. As a result, the creation and use of things are avenues through which differences are contested and new practices and material traditions negotiated.

The idea of a community of practice complements entanglement's interplay between the social and the material by focusing on the importance of learning and enacting practices. A community of practice is a set of social relations that connect people, an activity, and the material world through collective, collaborative action (Lave and Wenger 1991). Social structure and meaning are constructed within communities of practice through participation in the acts of learning a practice and putting that knowledge into action. This process happens in a social context where relations, ideas, and a sense of shared identity are continually negotiated and re-created. The practice entangles people and group identity with the material world. Individuals occupying physical communities are members of many overlapping and intersecting communities of practice.

Taken together, these ideas provide a useful framework for exploring many issues of interest to archaeologists, including the creation of community. A community has both material and social aspects. As a social construct, a community represents some sense of shared identity and history that is made up of competing or antagonistic identities such as genders, lineages, factions, and ethnicities (e.g., Layton and Ucko 1999; Lovell 1998; J. Thomas 2001; Tilley 1994). Community is also physical space or a built environment, whose creation is an active process that is integral to the making of the social (Yaeger and Canuto 2000). Linking people to identity, place, and history are objects and the practices that create them, guide their use, and define their meanings. The creation of the built environment and the objects of everyday life involves negotiating and forging identity and encoding that identity into everyday life, the landscape, and history.

## ETOWAH'S MULTICULTURAL BEGINNINGS

Little (1999) was the first to recognize that the earliest occupation at Etowah appeared to include material traditions found in the vicinity of Etowah along with those from the surrounding region. This realization led him to argue that the earliest community at Etowah was formed by the coming together of people from both northern Georgia and northeastern Alabama. This process—which Kowalewski (2006) later called coalescence—is the X-factor that Pauketat (2007) identifies as key to the emergence of new, complex social forms from Monte Alban to Cahokia. These studies and others argue that the creation of new social forms, communities, and ways of doing things—including Mississippian—often involves the meeting and negotiation of differences. Just as Little (1999) argued for Etowah, coalescence involves some kind of cultural plurality.

The idea underpinning this chapter is that the creation and use of the physical aspects of this new community shaped its social relations, history, and identity. Accepting Little's (1999) argument, we need to understand what came before in the wider region to understand the material and social changes accompanying community-making at Etowah. In northwestern Georgia, the Woodstock phase came immediately before Etowah (Cobb and Garrow 1996; Markin 2007). In terms of material traditions, people in the Woodstock phase made pottery vessels impressed with stamped designs that included nested diamonds and ovals and the line block motif. They lived in nucleated communities, many of them palisaded, which comprised collections of rectangular, single-set post buildings. Some evidence suggests that a few earthen mounds were built at this time, but mounding does not appear to be common (Pluckhahn 1996).

To the north, in southeastern Tennessee, the Hamilton tradition precedes the emergence of Mississippian at Etowah (Schroedl 1998; Schroedl and Boyd 1991; Schroedl et al. 1990). Hamilton pottery is generally either cordmarked or plain and predominantly tempered with limestone. Small amounts of shell and sand-tempered pottery may also be part of the Hamilton tradition. Current research on Late Woodland in the region suggests that people lived in dispersed settlements, moving seasonally and gathering periodically at locales containing large rotundas and groups of burial mounds. No residential structures have been recorded, but most early rotundas were made of single-set posts (Sullivan 2018; Sullivan and Koerner 2010). Those burial mounds were conical, and their graves have been interpreted to contain little evidence of social ranking (Cole 1975).

To the west, just down the Coosa drainage, there are sites belonging to the Coker Ford and Cane Creek phases of the Late Woodland period (Little 1999). Both include evidence for compact, palisaded communities like those of the Woodstock phase. Some sites also include earthen mounds, often faced with rock, containing burials. Structures appear to be made using single-set post architecture, and pottery is predominantly plain and tempered with limestone. A minority of wares tempered with shell and sand are also present in both phases.

The earliest occupation at Etowah exhibits an interesting mix of preexisting practices and traditions of the region. Early Etowah-phase pottery is dominated by shell-tempered types but also includes a significant percentage of both sand- and limestone-tempered pottery (Hally and Langford 1988). In some of the earliest features at Etowah, the frequency distribution of these temper types varies. While these differences could be chronological, the radiocarbon dating done so far does not support that theory (King 2001a). Little (1999) argued that the appearance of limestone tempering at Etowah represented the inclusion of people from northeastern Alabama. Given the prevalence of limestone tempering in the Hamilton tradition of southeastern Tennessee, it is just as likely that people from this area also helped create Etowah.

In 2005, the Etowah Archaeo-Geophysical Survey (EAS) was created to explore the Etowah site using the least destructive approach possible (King et al. 2011). In the gradiometer data collected by EAS (Walker 2009), an interesting pattern was observed that may indirectly support the multiethnic beginnings of Etowah. In those data, we found a magnetic signature that, through archaeological testing, was shown to correspond to wall-trench buildings. In the history of Etowah, wall-trench architecture was only made during the earliest occupation of the site (Hally and Langford 1988). The gradiometer data reveal approximately three times as many wall-trench structures as the later single-set post buildings. More importantly, many are arranged in what appear to be small neighborhoods or subcommunities (Figure 8.2). In the data, multiple clusters of buildings are also present, arranged around small plazas. This sort of arrangement is what one might see in a community established by different social groups. In fact, it is similar to the dis-

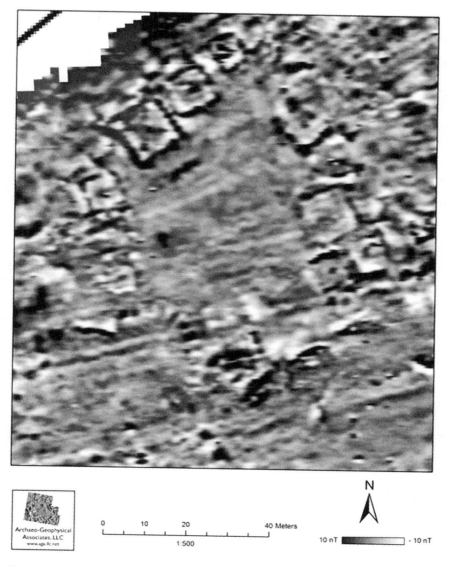

Figure 8.2. Gradiometer map of Etowah neighborhood. (Chester P. Walker; after Walker 2009)

tributions of mound and plaza complexes at Cahokia (Fowler 1997) or the distribution of mounds at early Moundville (Knight 1998).

## COMMUNITIES OF PRACTICE ENTANGLING A NEW COMMUNITY

These patterns in the newly established Etowah reveal alterations to the material practices associated with pottery, architecture, and mound building. Each kind of activity entangled differing communities of practice with material objects and the new Etowah community (Lave and Wenger 1991).

The process of making a pot requires adding a tempering agent to the clay. Compared to the decoration on the outside of the vessel, the choice of tempering agents is more about how the maker was taught (the learned recipe) than about what is to be communicated through the finished vessel. Based on what we know historically about Native people of the Southeast, pottery-making was something learned and practiced by groups of related women (Hudson 1976; Swanton 1946). Before the Etowah community, pottery-making traditions relied mostly on limestone to the north and west of Etowah and sand in the area around Etowah. Shell was apparently also used, but only rarely. After the creation of Etowah, shell became the most commonly used tempering agent, followed by limestone and then sand.

But how did the recipes change as a pluralistic Etowah emerged? Possibly, all potters continued using their traditional recipes but also added shell to some vessels. Alternatively, the different groups who helped form Etowah may have each held to their own recipes, except for one social segment that adopted a new recipe, one that used shell tempering. I tend to favor the former theory. Either way, part of the formation of Etowah included alterations to the practice of making pots.

The rapid rise in the importance of shell has often been attributed to the arrival of new ideas from the core area of Mississippianization, the Mississippi River Valley. However, whether the practice of using shell as a tempering agent was locally derived or inspired by foreign ideas, it surely had meaning. To Native people of the Southeast today and in the Historic period, shell is associated with water, and water is associated with the Underwater or Beneath World of their conception of the cosmos (Lankford 2007). The act of mixing shell with clay dug from the ground may have been both a metaphor for and a real act of creation. The world of people was created when land was brought up from the primordial sea (Hudson 1976; Lankford 1998). In southeastern creation stories, women often play a role in this creation (Lankford 1998).

Wherever the idea came from and whatever it meant, a reliance on shell tempering appears to have represented something new and something distinctly Etowah. By changing pottery recipes and entangling those new recipes with this new community, the women making pots constructed their new identity each time they created a shell-tempered vessel. They taught that new recipe to their children, indoctrinating them into the ways of this new community.

Not only did pottery recipes change, but so too did decorations found on the outside of vessels. In the areas to the north and west of Etowah, most pottery was plain. To the north, some pottery was also cordmarked. Pottery throughout this region was made using the coil and anvil method, where some kind of tool—a stone, a piece of wood, or a shell, was used to help meld the coils of the pot together. In the case of cordmarked and complicated stamped pottery, a wooden paddle was used for this purpose, either wrapped with cord or carved with a design.

When the new community at Etowah was established, those paddles may have been made by someone other than the women who made pottery vessels. Working with Swift Creek paddle-stamped designs, which predate the Etowah phases by several centuries, Pluckhahn and Wallis (2018) argue that wooden paddles used to apply Swift Creek designs were likely made by a set of skilled carvers. Historical and ethnographic information indicates that woodworking was generally a male undertaking among the Native people of the Southeast (Hudson 1976; Swanton 1946), so it is likely that those carvers were men. Smith and Knight (2012), exploring stylistic elements of Swift Creek complicated stamped designs, further argue that designs were drawn onto paddles before carving, leaving open the possibility that design creation was done by someone other than the carver. To the extent that these inferences apply to Mississippian period pottery creation, at least in eastern Tennessee and northwestern Georgia, the process of making pottery may have included a group of people, both men and women, in a chain of labor. Pottery-making was part of a process that could have involved entire households and tied groups of related men and women together.

Given this possibility, a change in how those paddles were made—or the adoption of carved wooden paddles as part of pottery-making—would signal another shift in practice. Figure 8.3 presents the motifs carved into paddles during the beginnings of Etowah. These motifs are all variations of a centering theme that is commonly found on Early Mississippian imagery across the wider Southeast. Iconographers think that this centering theme refers to the sacred center in the Middle World, or earthly realm, which connects this world with the other realms (Lankford 2007; Reilly 2004). Creating a center symbol is an act of creating the

Figure 8.3. Etowah complicated stamped motifs. (Adam King, Elizabeth Watts Malouchos; after Anderson 1994: Figure 74)

cosmos. This centering theme may have been a new idea, or it may have been part of earlier Woodstock-phase pottery traditions. Either way, that theme became associated with new motifs, new pottery recipes, and a new community at early Etowah. The carving of the centering motif by one set of people, maybe men, was enchained to the impressing of that motif into unfired pots by another set of people, probably women. Both activities entangled those doing them with the idea of creation and Etowah as a new community.

Not only through their creation, but also through their use, these vessels enacted and reinforced the ideas fundamental to the new Etowah community. Shell-tempered, complicated stamped vessels were used in both domestic and public contexts in the early Etowah phase. In both everyday activities and important events, the use of the vessels would have entangled the meaning of the symbols impressed in them, the memory of their making (and of that invested meaning), and the foundations of the community.

It was not just pottery that changed with the creation of a new community at Etowah. Architectural forms also changed. Before the emergence of Etowah, buildings were made using the single-set post construction method. In northeastern Alabama, buildings were circular; in eastern Tennessee, only circular rotundas have been recorded; and in northwestern Georgia, domestic buildings were rectangular. As with pottery, architectural form probably had some variability that we simply do not fully understand. At the new community of Etowah, buildings were built using a wall-trench method of construction. In the excavated examples (Hally and Langford 1988), no interior support posts are present in what are presumed to be domestic buildings, suggesting that their construction was bent pole rather than rigid pole.

Whether bent pole or rigid pole, wall-trench architecture seems to be designed for a different organization of labor than single-set constructions. As Alt and Pauketat (2011) argue, single-set post buildings could be built by a small labor force, such as a family group. The wall-trench building form may be more efficiently created using coordinated work parties, each specializing in a particular aspect of building construction. Because walls are placed in trenches, posts cannot be set individually—they would fall over. Instead wall segments have to be prefabricated and then set into the trench. This process makes it possible for one work team to dig the actual trenches while another fabricates the wall segments. Another team could position the walls, bend their tops, and tie them off to create a roof. Alt and Pauketat (2011) argue that this form of architecture was a key part of the remaking of Cahokia's built environment at the site's foundational moment. If the construction effort is broken into specific tasks, it is possible to deploy large labor parties to quickly build lots of houses (see also Pauketat 2004).

No architectural form is just technology devoid of meaning. This new form of architecture was part of the landscape of Etowah, and its meanings became entangled with the identity of this new community. As such, by participating in creating wall-trench buildings, the inhabitants of Etowah physically created their world and constructed their new identities. The fact that wall-trench architecture was best built by teams of workers means that this entanglement and creation would have happened in social groups that transcended the family. The new ideas, identities, and histories of Etowah were enacted in broader social settings that would have served to reach across family ties and even ethnic differences.

As with pottery-making, this new form of building may have had an association with creation as well. Waring (1968) summarized an important connection between the Historic period Creek square ground, domestic architecture, and the community. Waring noted that the Muscogee term for square ground means Big House. That ceremonial space is conceived of as a large house that the community occupied, with the fire in the middle, and beds along the walls. This same footprint is a map of a community, and a map of the Middle World of the cosmos. As others like Hally (2002) and Wesson (2008) have argued, Mississippian domestic architecture has embedded within it key elements of what we think we understand about the Mississippian cosmos and may have been understood as a model of the Middle World. The act of building these structures, like making the pottery vessels, was conceived of as an act of creation—of the world and of the community.

The new Etowah had something else that was rare in northwestern Georgia before its creation: an earthen mound. One mound dating to the Woodstock phase may have been built at the Summerour site in northern Georgia (Pluckhahn 1996), while mounds were common in the Hamilton tradition of eastern Tennessee (Schroedl et al. 1990; Sullivan 2016) and at least present in the Late Woodland traditions of northeastern Alabama (Little 1999). Using linguistic and ethnographic information, Knight (2006) has argued that mounds in the Southeast were earth symbols. Their construction and renewal were part of rites of intensification designed to re-create the world. Taken from this perspective, mound construction was an act of creation.

At Etowah, mound-construction stages dating to the early Etowah phase have not been identified. However, in the 1950s Arthur R. Kelly excavated a series of large, midden-filled pits adjacent to Mound A dating to the early Etowah phase (King 2001b). More than pits, these features were overlapping craters that look like borrow pits and that would have been the source of mound fill. Excavations at Mounds B and C show that neither was begun until after the early Etowah phase (King 2003), so these borrow pits near Mound A likely produced the fill for the first stages of Mound A. Kelly's excavations also showed that these pits were filled rapidly by episodes of feasting events (King 2001b).

In the same way that wall-trench architecture enchained larger groups of people through the construction of buildings, mound building brought together an even larger segment of the new Etowah society. In this case, they were brought together in an act of world renewal and creation. The physical mound was entangled with both the common action of the inhabitants of Etowah and the creation of the new community.

It appears as though the work and feasting that came with mound building took place in an area of Etowah that may have been devoted to a host of integrative activities. On the western edge of the scatter of borrow pits, the inhabitants of Etowah built several large buildings. Two of the largest—on the order of 30 m long—would have hosted events attended by large groups of people (King 2003; Larson 2004). Another large building had a red ocher floor and clay altar inside that we can assume had some ritual significance. In these spaces, collective action involving pottery, buildings, these items' meanings, and the memories of their making all came together to create, reinforce, and memorialize the communitas of Etowah.

## DISCUSSION

Why would various groups come together and go through this process of community-making? The efforts of one or more social segments to create something new following new ideas and their own self-interest may have been inspiration enough. However, Little (1999) offered a more pressing motivation. At least in northern Georgia and northeastern Alabama, Late Woodland communities tend to be palisaded or located in defensible positions, suggesting that intercommunity violence may have been a concern. In the same way that the Great League of the Iroquois was formed to quell violence (Fenton 1998), Etowah's emergence may have been an attempt to dampen fighting.

In the Iroquois example, the idea for the Great League was divinely inspired and carried with it the notion of spreading the Great Tree of Peace (Fenton 1998). In the case of Etowah, I argue that it was the renewal of the world that brought people together. Creation and the making of the world are themes apparent in the nature and creation of pottery vessels, domestic architecture, and even earthen mounds. The establishment of this new kind of community at Etowah was designed to remake the world—to reset creation and remake the world with a new social order.

## CONCLUSIONS: IN THE WIDER REGION

Etowah is by no means alone in the region when it comes to the process of Mississippian community creation. A similar process seems to have been at work in a variety of places across northern Georgia and eastern Tennessee at roughly the same time. The appearance of shell-tempered pottery stamped with centering motifs extends from the Etowah River Valley northward into the Chickamauga Basin in Tennessee. The same applies to both mound construction and a shift to rectangular, wall-trench buildings. Similar material records have been recovered at sites like Hiwassee Island (40MG31), Davis (40HA2), and Sale Creek (40HA10) in the Chickamauga Basin of southeastern Tennessee (Sullivan 2016); and Sixtoe Field (9MU100) on the Coosawattee River of northwestern Georgia (Hally and Langford 1988; Kelly et al. 1965). Even the practice of feasting in conjunction with foundational mound-building episodes was not limited to Etowah. Midden-filled pits like those found at Etowah also were excavated near the mound at Six-toe Field (Kelly et al. 1965).

Regional ceramic seriations and limited radiocarbon dates place the emer-gence of these sites in the period circa AD 1000–1200. Radiocarbon dates from the midden-filled pits at Etowah suggest that the site was occupied as early as AD 1000 (King 2001a). The single radiocarbon date from Sixtoe Field suggests a mid-eleventh century date for that site's occupation (Hally and Rudolph 1986), and the small number of dates from the Chickamauga Basin place early Missis-sippian developments in the early twelfth century (Sullivan 2016). While Etowah has produced the earliest dates, our understanding of the timing of these develop-ments is not precise enough to know where these new sets of practices may have come together first. Apparently, Etowah was one of many communities across this region that were created or transformed through changes in material practices. These new material traditions were entangled with new ways of doing things and new reasons for doing them, creating a new sense of identity, a revised under-standing of history, and new Mississippian places.

# 9

# UNPACKING STORAGE

*Implications for Community-Making during*
*Cahokia's Mississippian Transition*

Elizabeth Watts Malouchos and Alleen Betzenhauser

I nterpretations of Mississippian foodways have traditionally been framed through political economic models connecting the adoption and intensification of maize agriculture to the origins of complex hierarchical polities (e.g., Anderson 1994; Beck 2003; King 2003; Knight and Steponaitis 2007; Welch 1991, 1996; cf. Cobb 2003; Pauketat 2007). In these chiefly scenarios, aspiring elites established control and fostered loyalty through redistributive networks, exchanging wealth items for tributary payments of surplus maize crops. Under elite authority, surplus crops were stored in central crib and granary structures. DeBoer (1988) and Wesson (1999) have suggested that a reorganization of household food storage during the Mississippian period in the Greater Cahokia American Bottom region reflects opposition to elite domination. They argue that an increase in intramural subterranean storage served as resistance to tributary payments of surplus crops stored in elite-controlled granaries (see also Mehrer 2000; Pauketat 2000a, 2004). They posit that the decentralization and concealment of subterranean storage within residential structures masked the visibility of stored goods, effectively obscuring maize crops from elite oversight. In these models, food storage facilities are relegated to a utilitarian byproduct in the emergence of sociopolitical complexity, rather than being significant elements of community landscapes in their own right (e.g., Collins 1990, 1997; Mehrer 1995; Mehrer and Collins 1995).

However, the processes and practices involved in the preservation of food are inextricably tied to everyday lived experiences; the routine tasks involved in the procurement and storage of food were deeply ingrained in tradition and would have been a significant part of mitigating new Mississippian social landscapes. VanDerwarker and colleagues (2017:40) suggest food production was entangled in larger processes of community-making, wherein "surplus production aided in the support of craftspeople and the fueling of community events that simultaneously reinforced status differences and community cohesion." To explore changes in community-making during the Mississippian transition, we approach communities as multiscalar assemblages of agentive humans and other-than-humans (*sensu* Harris 2013, 2014, 2017). Utilizing data from the Greater Cahokian American Bottom region in southwestern Illinois, we contend that subterranean storage practices, namely the processes of earth moving and deposition, mediated the ways that collective identities were materially constructed and affected how people moved around, interacted with, and related to food, objects, stores, pits, and one another, reconfiguring how communities were assembled.

In this analysis, we (1) approach communities as dynamic assemblages; (2) problematize the equation of subterranean pits with the storage of maize; (3) provide a more accurate portrait of the changes and continuities in storage practices during the Late Woodland to Mississippian transition, a portrait that calls previous interpretations of interior storage into question; and (4) demonstrate a more nuanced understanding of how storage practices are enmeshed in larger Mississippian sociopolitical relationships. We begin by considering how subterranean storage facilities worked and what was stored in them, after which we describe Terminal Late Woodland (TLW) and Mississippian settlements and storage practices at two sites in the American Bottom: Cahokia and the Range site. Through these examples, we illustrate how storage practices were altered during the shift to Mississippian lifeways and how they relate to changing communities and group identities.

## RECONSIDERING COMMUNITIES

The archaeology of communities has developed from site-based and adaptational models to an understanding of communities as socially constructed at multiple scales through routine practices and lived experiences (see chapter 1 in this volume). More recent studies have explored how communities are not inherently tied to singular locations (Anderson 1991; Betzenhauser 2011; Harris 2014; Holland et al. 1998; Isbell 2000), yet communities undeniably occupy space and are situated in some tangible arrangements of persons, places, and things (Pauketat 2008a:238; Schatzki 2002; Yaeger and Canuto 2000). Communities are created through shared bodily experiences informed by landscapes, and collective lived relationships are constructed through these material arrangements (Ashmore and Knapp 1999; Basso 1996:55; Gerritsen 2004; Knapp 2003; Wernke 2007). Communal identities are embedded in and enacted through the built landscape and the ways in which people inhabit and perform daily activities in those spaces. Therefore, life histories of the built environment are inextricably entangled with social biographies of community, through shared bodily movements of community members recursively shaped by the landscape (Joyce and Hendon 2000:144).

As part of the recent ontological turn in archaeology, new animist and new materialist frameworks problematize anthropocentric notions of community and emphasize that community-making involves not only human persons, but more-than-humans: places, objects, animals, and other-than-human beings (Alberti and

Bray 2009; Bird-David 1999; Harris 2013, 2014; Harvey 2006; Pauketat 2013a). Similarly, theories of relational ontology explore how people understand and experience their worlds through complex webs of interactions and associations between human and nonhuman actors, and how communities emerge through relationships (Alberti and Marshall 2009; Hodder 2011; Ingold 2011). Accordingly, Harris (2014:89) suggests that conceptualizing communities as assemblages (*sensu* DeLanda 2006; Deleuze and Guattari 2004)—that is, as agentive aggregations of humans and nonhuman actors—better captures the diverse, emergent, and relational qualities of community (see also Harris 2013). As Bennett (2010:34) explains, assemblages are living confederations of vibrant matter, and "an assemblage owes its agentic capacity to the vitality of the materialities that constitute it." Therefore, assemblages are multiscalar, and all assemblages are constituted by other assemblages; in this way, communities are more than the sum of their constituent parts (DeLanda 2006; Harris 2017). By tracing how community actors are intentionally gathered and related across different contexts, we can parse the ways in which communities are assembled, reassembled, and disassembled.

## CONSTRUCTING THE CAHOKIAN COMMUNITY

Mississippian culture first flourished on a large scale at Cahokia, the largest Mississippian polity and mound center, around AD 1050 (Pauketat 2004). In the early eleventh century, Cahokia was a large Late Woodland village, but around AD 1050, significant shifts occurred in the production of material culture and settlement patterns in the American Bottom region with the onset of a new political, social, economic, and religious polity centered at Cahokia (Alt 2018; Baires 2017; Emerson 1997a; Pauketat 2004, 2013a). Dramatic transformations in everyday lifeways and material practices at Cahokia—from the way pots were made, to house construction methods, to regional settlement practices—precipitated the rapid spread of Mississippian lifeways in the American Bottom and across the midcontinent and Southeast.

Socio-spatial practices were reconfigured as every scale of the built environment was reimagined during Cahokia's establishment (Baltus and Baires 2020; Betzenhauser 2011, 2017; Dalan 1997; Dalan et al. 2003; Emerson 1997a; Emerson et al. 2020; Pauketat 2004, 2013a; Pauketat and Emerson 1997, 1999). During this transition, significant portions of the regional population left large villages and hamlets. Some of them presumably relocated to Cahokia and other regional mound centers, where the construction of monumental architecture and feasting events bolstered the creation of a new Cahokian communal ethos. Late Woodland villages and hamlets that were not entirely depopulated or abandoned were reconfigured or replaced with smaller rural Mississippian farmsteads (Betzenhauser 2017; Emerson 1997a, 1997b; Kelly 1990b; Mehrer 1995; Pauketat 2003; Pauketat and Alt 2003). Pauketat (1998, 2000a, 2001, 2003, 2008a) suggests that the disruption of traditional spatial discourses supported large-scale political consolidation during the establishment of a new Cahokian community (see also Dalan et al. 2003; Pauketat and Emerson 1997; chapter 1 in this volume). Moreover, the manipulation of spatial relations was a part of the spread of Mississippian lifeways outside of the Cahokian heartland; different scales of Cahokian architecture, both monumental and vernacular, were variously adopted or rejected in hinterland communities (Bardolph 2014; Millhouse 2012; Watts Malouchos 2020a; see chapter 1 in this volume).

Changes in subsistence practices were contemporaneous with these transformations of the regional landscape. During the Late Woodland period (AD 600–1050), both localized aquatic and terrestrial habitats were exploited for subsistence (Kelly 1997). White-tailed deer, fish, and locally available weedy annuals, squash, and nuts were dietary staples, while maize was not widely or consistently cultivated or consumed until after AD 900 (Simon 2014, 2017; Simon and Parker 2006; VanDerwarker et al. 2017). The incorporation of maize into the diet as part of new Mississippian lifeways would have not only shifted daily agricultural and culinary practices but also altered senses of taste. For instance, Rachel Briggs (2016) argues that the slightly bitter taste of maize hominy was similar to traditional plants consumed during the Late Woodland period. The continuity in flavor profile provided a more palatable transition for the newly Mississippianized while other aspects of foodways were dramatically transformed.

During the Mississippian period in the American Bottom, the presence and consumption of maize significantly increased, although its utilization remained quite variable (Ambrose et al. 2003; Simon and Parker 2006; VanDerwarker et al. 2017). Other components of diet did not change drastically, and Mississippian communities still relied heavily on locally available nonagricultural resources and would have continued to store these foods in addition to maize. For example, the consumption of nuts remained common, and horticultural crops like chenopod, maygrass, knotweed, marsh elder, sunflower, squash, and gourds continued to be utilized as dietary staples. The greatest disparities in diet were not between Late Woodland and Mississippian populations, but between elite and nonelite Mississippians (Ambrose et al. 2003; Lopinot 1997). For example, Kelly (1997) indicates that elite refuse deposits at Cahokia contained higher frequencies of high-utility cuts of deer meat along with a greater variety of food resources. Later isotopic studies conducted on elite and nonelite burials in Mound 72 at Cahokia have also demonstrated that elites consumed significantly less maize than the nonelite population (Ambrose et al. 2003; Yerkes 2005).

## IDENTIFYING STORAGE PRACTICES: FACILITIES AND STORES

Halperin (1994:167) defines storage as an "activity involving the placement of useful material resources in specific physical locations against future need." Several different kinds of fixed and portable precontact storage facilities have been identified, including large bulk-storage pits, small cache pits, storehouses, and above-ground granaries. Other types of storage may have included ceramic vessels, baskets, platforms, shelves, and benches, which leave more equivocal archaeological remains that may not inherently be equated with a storage function. The type of storage facility likely influenced what was being stored and for how long. Cultural factors—including whether the stores were held in common, belonged to individuals or family groups, or were intended for tribute—would have affected the form and location of storage facilities (Hendon 2000b; see also Pauketat and Alt 2004).

Experimental studies and historical accounts have demonstrated that subterranean pits have been successfully utilized to store food and seed grain for extended periods (Currid and Navon 1989; Reynolds 1977; Wilson 1917). Observing modern Maya storage practices, Smyth (1991:25) notes that certain morphological traits of subterranean pits are associated with a storage function, including the combination of a large volume with a relatively small orifice. Deep cylindrical or bell-shaped pits are thus more conducive to long-term food storage than are those with basin shapes or small volumes (DeBoer 1988). Currid and Navon (1989) note that food storage in subterranean bell-shaped pits continues to be a common storage practice in modern-day Argentina, Cyprus, and several regions of Africa (e.g., Sudan and Rhodesia), and there are archaeological examples across the globe of crop storage in deep cylindrical and bell-shaped pits. During the Formative period (1500 BC–AD 100) in the highlands of Mexico, large (more than 1 m diameter) bell-shaped pits carved into bedrock were quite common. Results of palynological analyses of bell-shaped pits in Oaxaca Valley revealed higher percentages of maize pollen, suggesting that these features were used for the long-term storage of maize (Winter 1976). Deep cylindrical and bell-shaped pits (1–2 m wide and 2–3 m deep), some of which were lined (with ash, rock, and plaster), were common in Iron Age Palestine and could have been used to store grain (Currid and Navon 1989; see also Bowen and Wood 1968; Reynolds 1979). Subterranean pits were also used to store domesticated millet throughout China during the Neolithic Age (Lu et al. 2009). These cross-cultural examples indicate that deep pits with large volumes and restricted orifices were conducive to the long-term storage of grains including maize.

Determining whether a pit feature in the archaeological record served as a storage facility for comestibles or specifically maize can be difficult. In situ evidence for stores is often lacking; pits that may have been initially used to store food were adapted to store noncomestibles (Hendon 2000b; Tringham 1995; Winter 1976) or were repurposed for refuse disposal (DeBoer 1988; Mehrer 1995; Winter 1972). The subterranean storage of nonmaize cultigens and other organic and inorganic commodities was an important aspect of the seasonal routine for centuries prior to the Mississippian period, across the eastern woodlands (DeBoer 1988; Mehrer 1995). In the Savannah River Valley and wider coastal Southeast, deep cylindrical pits dating to the Late Archaic period (3000–1000 BC) were common and likely were used for mast storage (Sanger 2017; Sassaman 2010; Sassaman et al. 2006). Likewise, large, deep, bell-shaped and cylindrical pits in the American Bottom also date back to the Late Archaic (McElrath et al. 1984; McElrath and Fortier 1983). Subterranean storage pits were in use long before the appearance of maize, throughout the initial forays into maize horticulture, and as maize became an agricultural staple. Therefore, it is clear that stores themselves are only one component of the processes and practices of storage, and we cannot assume that deep pits functioned *solely* to store maize.

Complicating matters, natural and cultural formation processes and modern agricultural practices have extensive deleterious impacts on these features, truncating the deep pits and rendering them shallower in the archaeological record. In light of these issues, we trace general trends in all subterranean pit features that were interpreted and classified as storage pits by analysts (that is, not posts, monumental post pits, hearths, smudge pits, burials, middens, etc.). Rather than limiting our considerations to pits with particular dimensions or volumes associated with long-term maize storage, we consider all storage pits as potential facilities in the storage of maize, other comestibles, and noncomestible items. This inclusive approach allows us to trace how storage practices related to everyday community-making and investigate how storage pits, not just their contents, were integral to transformations in community landscapes.

## CHANGING COMMUNITIES AND STORAGE PRACTICES IN THE AMERICAN BOTTOM

We turn now to our analysis of feature evidence from three areas of Cahokia (the tracts 15A/Dunham, 15B, and ICT-II) and the Range site in the southern American Bottom. Both Cahokia and Range exemplify changes in community organization during the Mississippian transition given the evidence for continuous or repeated occupations during the Late Woodland and Mississippian periods, as has been revealed through large-scale excavations. For present purposes, we focus on the four phases that define the temporal range of the Mississippian transition: George Reeves/Merrell (AD 900–975), Lindeman/Edelhardt (AD 975–1050), Lohmann (AD 1050–1100), and Stirling (AD 1100–1200) (see Fortier et al. 2006). The first two phases belong to the latter half of the TLW period, and the last two correspond to the first half of the Mississippian period. In the following sections, we also calculate pit-to-structure ratios as a comparative measure of the amount of subterranean storage in relation to the number of houses, assuming that domestic structures were associated with household groupings. We also employ measures of floor area and a width-to-length (W:L) ratio for structures (Baires et al. 2017; Baltus 2014; Milner et al. 1984; Pauketat 1998, 2013b). Earlier structures tend to have higher W:L ratios (i.e., closer to 1), indicating that the structures were squarer in plan shape, while later structures tend to have lower ratios (i.e., closer to 0.5), indicating that the structures were more rectangular.

## Communities and Storage Practices during the Mississippian Transition at Cahokia

Salvage excavations of Cahokia's 15A, Dunham, and 15B Tracts were conducted in the early 1960s under the direction of Warren L. Wittry, but Pauketat (1998, 2013b) ultimately synthesized and reported the data. The tracts ranged in size from 1.5 ha to 4 ha and were located only 250 m and 800 m west of Monks Mound in an area referred to as Downtown Cahokia. The TLW Merrell- and Edelhardt-phase occupations are characterized as large villages, comprising several adjacent courtyard groups (Pauketat 1998, 2013b). These courtyard groups were composed of an open space with central pit and post features surrounded by domiciles (Figure 9.1, *left*). In some cases, four large storage pits were arranged in a quadrilateral around a central post. One courtyard contained a complicated series of monumental posts and associated ramps adjacent to a quadrilateral arrangement of 20 large storage pits, indicating that the pattern was intentional and repeated, possibly over several generations.

At least 111 pits and 64 structures were affiliated with the Merrell-phase occupation of Downtown Cahokia (Pauketat 2013b). This count produces a moderate pit-to-structure ratio of 1.73 (Table 9.1). Merrell-phase domestic structures have

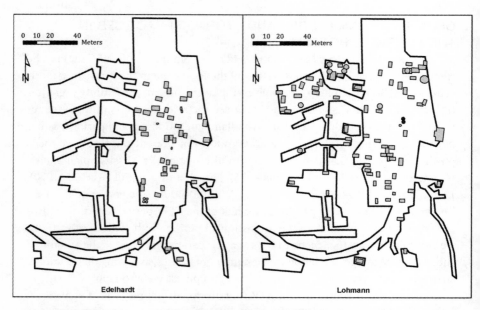

Figure 9.1. Changing community at Downtown Cahokia (Elizabeth Watts Malouchos and Alleen Betzenhauser; after Pauketat 1998:Figures 6.16 and 6.34)

Table 9.1. Comparative Data for Terminal Late Woodland and Early Mississippian Occupations at Cahokia and Range

| Component | Total structures (n) | Total houses (n) | Total pits (n) | Pit-to-house ratio | Rectangular-to-circular pits | Deep storage pits (n) | Exterior-to-interior pits | Interior pits (%) | Floor area (m²) | Width-to-length ratio |
|---|---|---|---|---|---|---|---|---|---|---|
| Downtown Cahokia | | | | | | | | | | |
| Merrell (15B) | 64 | 64 | 111 | 1.73 | 60:40 | 60 | 109:2 | 1.8 | 9.8 | 0.68 |
| Edelhardt (15A/15B) | 28 | 28 | 59 | 2.11 | 30:29 | 29 | 57:2 | 3.4 | 8.0 | 0.58 |
| Lohmann (15A) | 96 | 78 | 75 | 0.96 | 15:56 | 48 | 70:5 | 6.7 | 13.9 | 0.53 |
| Cahokia ICT-II | | | | | | | | | | |
| Lohmann | 23 | 10 | 52 | 5.20 | 7:45 | 17 | 45:7 | 13.5 | 13.4 | 0.56 |
| Stirling | 53 | 33 | 118 | 3.58 | 11:107 | 63 | 80:38 | 32.2 | 18.7 | 0.56 |
| Range | | | | | | | | | | |
| George Reeves | 151 | 147 | 267 | 1.82 | 120:124 | 132 | 247:20 | 7.5 | 5.6 | 0.81 |
| Lindeman | 141 | 132 | 407 | 3.08 | 99:243 | 150 | 370:37 | 9.1 | 5.8 | 0.76 |
| Lohmann | 14 | 12 | 24 | 2.00 | 5:17 | 10 | 17:2 | 8.3 | 9.2 | 0.51 |
| Stirling | 13 | 7 | 25 | 3.57 | 1:20 | 10 | 6:19 | 76.0 | 14.8 | 0.58 |

*Note:* Structure and house totals include rebuilds; house totals exclude special-use structures. Pit totals exclude hearths, smudge pits, and post pits. Special-use structures were excluded when calculating floor areas, width-to-length ratios, and pit-to-house ratios. Cahokia 15B Merrell-phase sample includes indeterminate Terminal Late Woodland features because most of these likely date to the Merrell phase. Pit plan shapes for Cahokia ICT-II were estimated from published maps.

an average width-to-length ratio of 0.68 and floor area of 9.8 m², indicating that
the houses were larger and more rectangular than contemporary structures elsewhere in the region. Only 59 pits and 28 structures were classified as Edelhardt-
phase features (referred to as EM2 and EM3 in Pauketat 1998), yielding a pit-
to-structure ratio of 2.11 (Pauketat 1998, 2013b). The Edelhardt houses have an
average width-to-length ratio of 0.58 and floor area of 8.0 m², indicating that the
houses were slightly smaller and more rectangular than the Merrell-phase structures. For both phases, most pits were circular in plan, but rectangular plan shapes
were also common (Figure 9.2). More than half of the pits were deep cylindrical or
bell-shaped types conducive to long-term storage. The vast majority of pits were
located exterior to houses, with only four pits (3 percent) on house floors. Interior pits were typically basin shaped and smaller than exterior pits.

At the beginning of the Lohmann phase (c. AD 1050), the large TLW village
was dismantled as the immediate landscape was rapidly urbanized through the
construction of earthen pyramids, monumental structures, and large public plazas, concurrent with an influx of population, both from within and without the
region (Alt 2006a; Dalan et al. 2003; Fowler 1997; Pauketat 2004, 2013a; Schilling
2013; Slater et al. 2014). The new Cahokian city was constructed according to a
newly established grid with a primary axis based on celestial referents and set at
5 degrees east of north (Baires 2014b; Betzenhauser and Pauketat 2019; Fowler
1997; Pauketat 2013a; Romain 2015). Courtyards and central pit features were
abandoned in favor of larger open plazas, often with central posts but without
centralized sets of pits. Individual structures were realigned according to the new
city plan rather than oriented in relation to courtyards or exact cardinal directions (Figure 9.1, *right*).

During the Lohmann phase, there were 96 structures and 75 pits in excavated
areas of Downtown Cahokia (Tracts 15A and 15B), resulting in a pit-to-structure
ratio of 0.96 (Pauketat 1998, 2013b). Nearly all structures were built using a new
architectural style of wall trenches instead of single-set posts. Houses average
a width-to-length ratio of 0.53 and a floor area of 13.9 m², indicating that they
were substantially larger and slightly more rectangular than the earlier structures.
The frequency of internal storage pits increased, but they were still low in number
(n = 5), while external storage pits remained overwhelmingly common (93 percent). Pits with circular plans slightly outnumbered those with rectangular plan
shapes, and deep pits conducive to long-term storage predominated (64 percent).
Interior pits varied in depth and morphology, with examples of both shallow,
basin-shaped and deep, bell-shaped pits found on structure floors.

Also during the Lohmann phase, entire neighborhoods were newly constructed
in previously unoccupied areas of the site (Betzenhauser and Pauketat 2019). For
instance, the ICT-II Tract, located 500 m southeast of Monks Mound at the edge
of the Grand Plaza, exhibited no evidence for a TLW occupation (Collins 1990).
During the Lohmann phase, a planned neighborhood was established, complete
with residential domiciles, storage pits, and specialized structures. These features

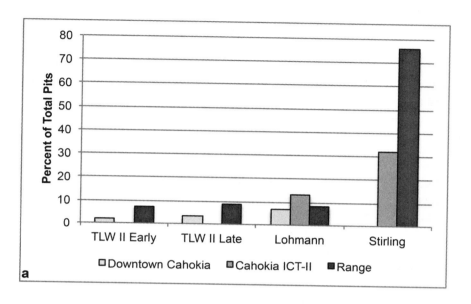

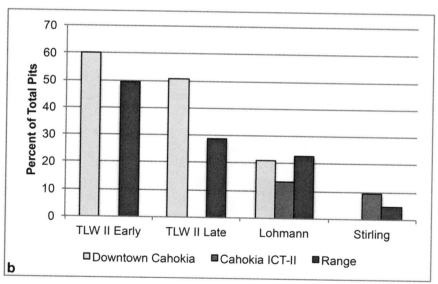

Figure 9.2. Percentage of total pits that are inside structures (a) and that have rectangular plan shapes (b). TLW = Terminal Late Woodland. (Elizabeth Watts Malouchos and Alleen Betzenhauser)

were oriented along the same grid as contemporaneous structures in Downtown Cahokia (5 degrees east of north). In total, 23 structures and 10 pits were associated with the Lohmann-phase occupation of the ICT-II Tract. The houses have an average floor area of 13.4 m² and average width-to-length ratio of 0.56, indicating that they were similar in size and shape to contemporaneous houses elsewhere at the site. Fewer than one-third of the pits were conducive to long-term storage. The pit-to-house ratio (5.2) is much higher than in Downtown Cahokia and the highest calculated for all samples in this analysis. Only 16 percent of the pits exhibited rectangular plan shapes. Additionally, the only evidence of central granaries or storehouses at Cahokia dates to the late Lohmann and later Stirling phases (Collins 1990).

## Communities and Storage Practices during the Mississippian Transition at Range

Now, we shift our analysis to the Range site (Figure 9.3). This multicomponent habitation site is located in the southern American Bottom, approximately 19 km south-southwest of Cahokia and 3 km north of Lunsford Pulcher, a Mississippian mound site. The settlements at Range were nearly completely exposed and excavated as part of the extensive FAI-270 project of the 1970s and 1980s. Materials and data collected were synthesized by Kelly (1990b) and colleagues (1987, 1990, 2007) and by Hanenberger (2003). The prominent floodplain ridge was continuously occupied circa AD 650–1500, the Late Woodland Patrick phase through the Oneota phase, providing an unprecedented glimpse into the history of the region from a single locale.

The TLW George Reeves–phase (AD 900–975) occupation at Range consisted of structures arranged in circular courtyard groups flanking two rectangular plazas (Kelly 1990b; Kelly et al. 2007; Mehrer 1995). In total, 151 structures were recorded, including four oversized square structures that possibly served as public meeting houses. All structures were built using single-set post architecture. Houses average a width-to-length ratio of 0.81 and floor area of 5.6 m². These morphometrics demonstrate that the houses were significantly smaller and squarer in plan than contemporaneous features at Cahokia. The north end of the settlement included a central cluster of large, limestone-lined pits in a plaza and a complex of marker posts central to a courtyard. The southern plaza and two flanking courtyards had quadrilateral pit arrangements. Several sets of central pits were re-excavated or renewed in place, in some cases maintaining the quadrilateral pattern. Pit features were nearly equally divided between circular and rectangular plan shapes, with rectangular pits occurring more frequently than in earlier occupations at the site. The high number of storage pits (n = 257) results in a pit-to-structure ratio of 1.71. Nearly half of the pits were deep cylindrical or bell-shaped pits conducive to long-term storage. Only 20 pits (8 percent) were located inte-

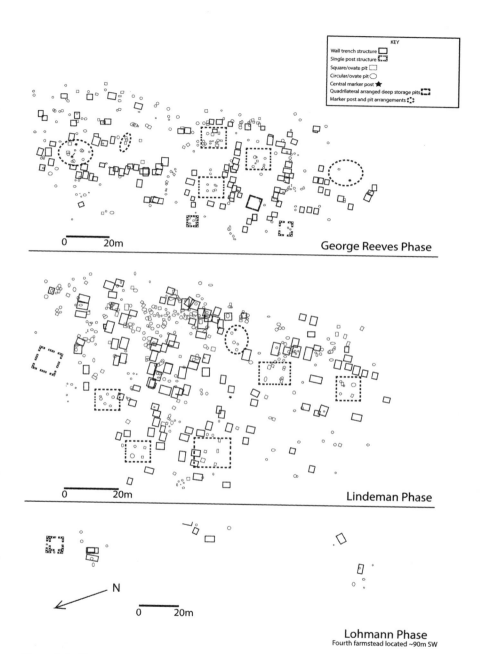

KEY

Wall trench structure ▢
Single post structure ▢
Square/ovate pit ▢
Circular/ovate pit ◯
Central marker post ★
Quadrilateral arranged deep storage pits ▦
Marker post and pit arrangements ◌

0      20m

**George Reeves Phase**

0      20m

**Lindeman Phase**

N

0      20m

**Lohmann Phase**
Fourth farmstead located ~90m SW

Figure 9.3. Changing community layout at the Range site. (Elizabeth Watts Malouchos and Alleen Betzenhauser; after Kelly 1990b:Figures 40 and 42; Hanenberger 2003: Figure 5.1)

rior to structures. The interior pits were small and shallow cache or processing pits rather than deep storage pits.

The subsequent Lindeman-phase (AD 975–1050) occupation at Range is described as an even larger village (Kelly 1990b; Kelly et al. 2007; Mehrer 1995). Community organization was similar to the preceding occupation, with a total of 141 structures (including nine oversized square and possible circular structures) arranged around plazas and courtyards with central post and quadripartite pit arrangements. Architectural style remained consistent with that in the previous George Reeves phase, although the average floor area slightly increases to 5.8 m², and the structures were more rectangular in shape, with an average width-to-length ratio of 0.76. The number of subterranean pits increased to 407, resulting in a higher pit-to-structure ratio of 3.08. Pits were primarily circular in plan shape, but rectangular pits were also frequent, accounting for 41 percent. Pits were commonly deep cylindrical and bell-shaped storage pits (37 percent) and remained exterior to structures, although 37 (9 percent) were excavated interior to structures. The interior pits were evenly split between small, shallow pits and deep cylindrical and bell-shaped types. The early Lindeman peak was followed by a much smaller village with only three courtyards and fewer central features, although the quadripartite pit pattern remained evident.

The Mississippian Lohmann-phase (AD 1050–1100) occupation at Range is characterized by a series of four spatially discrete farmsteads composed of two-to-three contemporaneous structures and a handful of exterior pits (Kelly 1990b; Hanenberger 2003). Unlike Cahokia, Range lacked monumental plazas and mounds. In total, only 14 structures date to the Lohmann phase, including two special-purpose buildings. The public structure and one residence were built using single-set posts, but the rest were built using the new wall-trench architectural style. The average structure floor area again increases from the preceding phases, this time more dramatically, to 9.2 m², but the structures were smaller on average than those at Cahokia. The average width-to-length ratio is 0.51, indicating that they were more strongly rectangular than earlier houses at the site. The number of pits also dramatically decreased, down to 26, with a pit-to-structure ratio of 2.0, which is less than the preceding phase. Only two pits were located interior to structures. Deep storage pits account for 42 percent of all pits. Plan shapes were primarily circular with only five being rectangular.

Although the size of the habitation decreased dramatically, evidence exists for suprahousehold communal activities, most notably in the form of the possible council house located in the northern settlement, and a large refuse pit possibly associated with feasting or Green Corn ceremonialism located in the next settlement to the south (Emerson 1997a). The presence of such features suggests that the residents of these farmsteads were also involved in hosting activities and events that, as Emerson (1997a, 1997b) suggests, served to integrate rural populations into the Cahokian community. One aspect of integration may have included the centralized storage of foodstuffs and important objects for a much larger, dispersed community.

## Mississippian Stirling-Phase Communities and Storage at Cahokia and Range

Excavating storage pits within structures did not become a common practice in the American Bottom until the twelfth-century Stirling phase (Mehrer 1995). At Cahokia, evidence from tracts 15A/Dunham and 15B suggests that these areas transitioned to extradomestic use through the construction of circular sweat lodges, L- and T-shaped temples, large circular rotundas, walled compounds, and monumental post circles (woodhenges) rather than typical rectangular residences (Betzenhauser and Pauketat 2019; Pauketat 1998, 2013b). However, the ICT-II Tract remained predominantly residential. This tract held 46 Stirling-phase structures arranged around an open plaza. A total of 111 pits results in a pit-to-structure ratio of 2.41. The majority of pits remained exterior to structures (n = 73), but 34 percent of the pits were placed interior to structures (n = 38). Pits were circular in plan and ranged from smaller, shallower, basin-shaped pits to larger, deeper, belled and cylindrical pits. Interior pits were larger and deeper than their Lohmann-phase counterparts. One large, deep, bell-shaped pit contained a human burial and negligible domestic debris. Structures have an average floor area of 17 m² and remained more rectangular in shape with an average width-to-length ratio of 0.57. One granary structure with a floor area of 2.8m² and a width-to-length ratio of 0.7 was identified.

At the Range site, the Stirling occupation consisted of two discrete clusters of structures situated in reference to the physiographic landscape, a linear sand ridge along an oxbow lake (Kelly 1990b; Hanenberger 2003). Twenty-five pits and 12 structures date to the Stirling phase. Eight structures are rectangular, and four are small circular structures that likely served as sweat lodges or granaries, indicating continued communal, integrative, or extralocal activities (Emerson 1997a, 1997b). All rectangular structures were built with wall trenches with the exception of one small, single-set post structure. The pit-to-structure ratio is 2.08, and 68 percent of pits were located on the interior of structures (n = 17). All pits were circular in plan shape. Interior pits were split evenly between deep, cylindrical, bell-shaped and shallow, basin-shaped pits. Structures have an average floor area of 11 m² and remained rectangular in shape with an average width-to-length ratio of 0.69.

## Summary

As evidenced at Cahokia and the Range site, TLW villages in the American Bottom were composed of several houses, possibly the residences of related kin or familial groups, located on the periphery of open courtyards. In some cases these communal spaces were marked with central features including marker posts and/or a configuration of four large storage pits (Fortier and McElrath 2002; Kelly

1990b). Domiciles were typically small and built using single posts set into square or slightly rectangular semi-subterranean basins, and storage and other pit features were primarily located outside of structures (Kelly 1990b; Mehrer 1995). Exterior storage pits were often densely clustered around small, tightly aggregated houses. Interior pit storage facilities were rare, and their morphology varied significantly. Kelly (1990b; Kelly et al. 2007) noted the regular distribution of stone and ceramic pipes in central pit features during both the George Reeves and Lindeman phases at Range, suggesting that they were communal possessions rather than owned and used by individuals.

In contrast, early Mississippian communities varied widely from densely occupied mound centers to relatively isolated farmsteads consisting of two to three contemporaneous structures (Kelly 1990b; Mehrer 1995). Houses were larger and built predominantly using wall trenches set into shallower basins. The increase in house size and change in wall form suggest that Mississippian roofs were hipped, in contrast to the traditional bent-pole construction of single-set post buildings (Lacquement 2007). This new architectural style would have opened a great deal of overhead storage space. Most domiciles were built using the new method of wall-trench construction, but large communal or special-use buildings were still built using single-set posts. Internal storage pit and hearth features became more common, but external pits remained dominant.

The most significant shift in storage practices during the Mississippian transition was not a wholesale adoption of interior subterranean storage, but rather the decommissioning of large pits centrally arranged within courtyards. With the transformation from Late Woodland to Mississippian traditions, the storage of food and commodities in communal subterranean pits was no longer at the literal or figurative center of communities. Moreover, the increase in interior storage during the Late Mississippian period coincided with another region-wide reorganization of communities. During the Stirling phase, politico-religious factioning and the splintering of the Cahokian community were reflected in the reemergence of courtyard groups. Some have suggested that this change demonstrates the increasing autonomy of individual households and privatization of domestic economic activities (Collins 1990, 1997; Holley 1989; Mehrer 2000; Mehrer and Collins 1995; Pauketat 1994, 2000a). However, Baltus (2014) argues that it is indicative of a disruptive political transformation that deemphasized early Cahokian socioreligious orders. The arrangement of communities and residential landscapes was integral to the making and unmaking of the Cahokian community.

## DISCUSSION

Hendon (2000b:42) notes that storage in the archaeological record is typically conceptualized as either a location or an activity. We contend that storage transcends this dichotomy. Storage facilities were an important aspect of the social construction of the built environment and shaped how community was experienced, understood, and organized. Storage pits, quite literally potential pitfalls, played a prominent role in physically creating spaces, affecting movements, and altering bodily dispositions by restricting the ways in which persons and things moved through and related to residential and public spaces. It stands to reason that changes in community organization (of which storage was integral) were not just logistical; they were ontological (Alt 2019; Baires 2017; Baltus 2014; Harris 2013, 2014; Pauketat 2013a; Pauketat and Alt 2018).

The practice of subterranean storage mediated connections beyond pits and stores, relating acts of earth moving and deposition to communal landscapes. Indeed, community-making through the modification of the landscape and the manipulation of earth was not limited to the mounding of earth but extended to the mining and deposition of soils associated with the construction of public works and sacred spaces at multiple scales (Alt et al. 2010; Baires and Baltus 2016; Brennan 2014; Dalan 1997; Dalan et al. 2003; Pauketat 2008b; see also Nelson 2020; chapters 2 and 4 in this volume). Earth and soil tend to be considered as animate and powerful only when their manipulation culminated in an earthwork; however, soil mining for other purposes must be taken into account when we think about transformations in the Cahokian built landscape (Dalan 1997; Pauketat 2008b; Pauketat and Alt 2018). As Baires and Baltus (2016:985) indicate, excavating and using domestic features (like semi-subterranean house basins and storage pits) still required earth moving and deposition, experiences of moving in and out of the earth that transcended the mundane and would have mediated connections to other realms (see also Alt 2019; Pauketat 2008b, 2013a).

In the American Bottom, storage activities surpassed simple subsistence sustainability, and stores themselves were but one component of the more complex assemblages that emerged through the comingling of noncomestible objects and elements in earthen pits. We suggest that during the Late Woodland period, the deliberate combination and deposition of materials within centrally located subterranean storage pits created powerful assemblages that acted to center communities (*sensu* Harris 2013, 2014, 2017; cf. "bundling" in Pauketat 2013a). For example, many central storage pits at Range that contained pipes also eventually contained seemingly domestic refuse (Kelly 1990b; Kelly et al. 2007). The intentional deposition of these pipes would have constructed new relationships through and with storage, infusing the assemblages of objects and the dynamic substances of earth and vibrant matters of soil with the transformative powers of fire and smoke (*sensu* Bennett 2010; see also Baires and Baltus 2016; Baltus and Baires 2012; Pauketat 2008b). Moreover, the central location of these pits in association with marker posts suggests cosmological relationships since posts may have embodied ancestral spirits (Skousen 2012) and the emplacement of large posts created axes mundi connecting to other worlds and spirit dimensions (Pauketat

2013a; Skousen 2015; Rodning 2015a). The practices of storage enacted assemblages, imbuing materials, substances, elements, places, people, and other-than-human participants with meanings and powers, mediating times and realms (Buchanan and Skousen 2015), memories (Hendon 2000b), and emotions (Gilmore 2015; Harris and Sørensen 2010; Pollard 2008; Sørensen 2015; Tarlow 2012).

During Cahokia's foundation and the transition to Mississippian lifeways, centralized subterranean storage pits were no longer tied to shared communal spaces nor were they fundamental to maintaining communal relationships. Community-making through earth moving and deposition in pits at the center of communities shifted to mound and monument construction (Pauketat and Alt 2003, 2005), feasting (Pauketat et al. 2002), theatrical mortuary events (Baires 2017; Zimmermann Holt 2009), and celestial religious observances (Pauketat 2013a) at Cahokia and outlying mound centers. At the same time, multiple scales of spatial discourses were transformed: vernacular architectural techniques, the alignments of houses and neighborhoods, and the occupation of the surrounding floodplain and uplands (Alt 2017; Betzenhauser and Pauketat 2019; Pauketat 2003, 2013a). Pauketat (1998, 2000a, 2001, 2003, 2008a) cites the deconstruction of Late Woodland communities as an important precursor to the establishment of new group identities and community relationships at the foundation of Cahokia. The Late Woodland quadripartite organization of space was co-opted and politicized on a monumental scale at Cahokia with the institution of rectangular pyramidal mounds and plazas and a citywide reorganization along a grid system (Pauketat 2001; Pauketat and Emerson 1997, 1999; see also chapter 1 in this volume). As Baires and Baltus (2016:975) describe, early Mississippians were "learning to relate to new social persons or to familiar social persons in new ways" (see also Alt 2019; Baltus 2018a, 2018b; Pauketat 2013a; Pauketat and Alt 2018; Watts Malouchos 2020a). Meanings attached to the ways that residential landscapes and the built environment were constructed transformed as part of the establishment of a Cahokian communal ethos.

## CONCLUSION

Rather than representing a shift toward (or resistance to) elite control of maize surplus, the changes in storage practices and the movement of some large storage pits to the interior of structures during the Mississippian transition were—we suggest—closely linked to the dissolution of Late Woodland courtyard groups and an ideological shift toward community building through monument construction and integrative events. Group interactions and the constant re-creation of communal identities were no longer enacted through the shared central spaces of the courtyard or related to deposition in and extraction from communal subterranean storage pits. The disentanglement of stores and storage pits from the center of communities at the onset of the Mississippian period served to reinforce a new spatiality and newly enacted Cahokian community. Animate objects, elements, and substances were gathered in pits, which were arranged with posts and structures in broader landscapes, assembling and situating persons, beings, and communities within a new Cahokian order.

## Acknowledgments

We are grateful to the Illinois State Archaeological Survey for permission to use its data in this chapter.

# 10

# THE SOCIAL LIVES AND SYMBOLISM OF CHEROKEE HOUSES AND TOWNHOUSES

Christopher B. Rodning and Amber R. Thorpe

S tructures are architectural manifestations of social groups within cultural landscapes. Domestic architecture forms containers, of sorts, for household activities and material symbols of household identities. Public architecture does the same for larger communities, including the towns that were part of the Mississippian and protohistoric landscapes of the Southeast. Household dwellings and community structures known as townhouses formed symbols of identity within

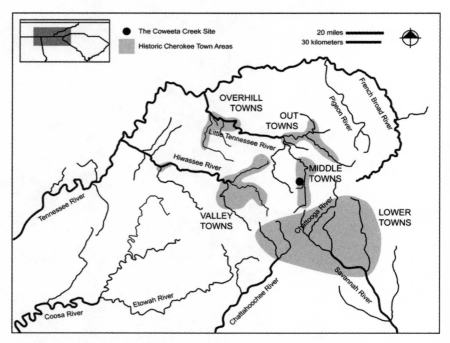

Figure 10.1. Cherokee town areas and the Coweeta Creek site. (Christopher B. Rodning; after Rodning 2010a)

the Cherokee landscape of the southern Appalachians, and several aspects of these forms of architecture created connections among households within Cherokee towns (Figure 10.1) (Rodning 2002a, 2002b, 2009a, 2009b; Steere 2017). This chapter relates Cherokee oral tradition about houses and townhouses to archaeological evidence of these architectural elements of the Cherokee landscape at the Coweeta Creek site, located in the upper Little Tennessee Valley of southwestern North Carolina (Figure 10.2) (Dickens 1978; Rodning 2001b, 2013, 2015a, 2015b). Archaeological evidence from Coweeta Creek reflects patterns that are more broadly visible at Mississippian and protohistoric sites across the greater southern Appalachians. The combination of oral tradition and archaeological evidence demonstrates the active role of architecture as cosmograms, social agents, and actors within the Cherokee landscape.

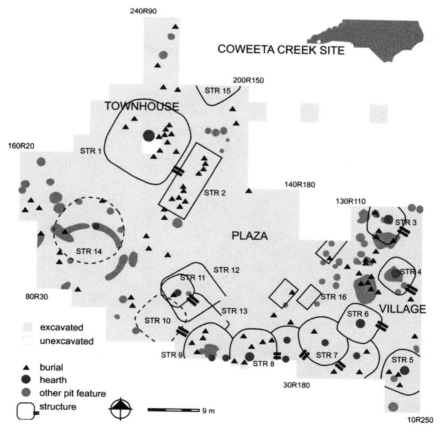

Figure 10.2. Settlement layout at the Coweeta Creek site. STR = structure. (Christopher B. Rodning; after Rodning 2010)

For good reason, many approaches to household archaeology concentrate on domestic activities that took place within houses, status relations and status differentiation among households, and economic and political inequality. From these perspectives, households are conceptualized as fundamental social groups within communities, and households are thought of as microcosms for the broader social landscape of which they are a part. Our approach here focuses on houses and households as basic conceptual groups within communities and also as part of broader ideological and ideational landscapes.

Households are social groups, of course, and they are not precisely the same as houses, outbuildings, and other material signatures of domestic activity, but houses are visible manifestations of household identity. Just as houses are architectural manifestations of households, public architecture is a visible manifestation of community. This public architecture includes the townhouses and plazas present at Mississippian and postcontact Cherokee town sites in the southern Appalachians. References to houses and townhouses in Cherokee oral tradition shed light on the ideational and ideological aspects of household dwellings and community structures, and they form an interpretive framework with which to consider patterns in the archaeology of Mississippian and protohistoric settlements in the greater southern Appalachians.

## ORAL TRADITION

Cherokee oral traditions refer to townhouses as community symbols and settings for public life, and they refer to houses as dwellings and settings for the social lives of households and kin networks (Corkran 1969; Mooney 1900). Townhouses are associated with dancing and feasting, town councils and other diplomatic events held by people and by animals, events related to purification of warriors and preparation for war, events related to warriors' return home from warpaths, and chunkey games. Also referenced in Cherokee oral traditions are mountain summits, where bears, the spirit folk known as the Nûñnĕ'hĭ, and the spiritual forces known as the Thunders have all had townhouses. Houses noted in oral traditions are associated with domestic activities, including the preparation and consumption of food, games, courtship, and the maintenance of matrilineal kin networks and matrilocal households. Some houses are the dwellings of animals, while houses in the sky and at the point where the sun sets are associated with spiritual forces. The Sun is said to visit the house of her daughter every day during her traverse of the sky (Mooney 1900:252). Thunder is said to have lived near the point where the sun sets in the west; when his son (Lightning) went there to look for him, Lightning found Thunder in the latter's house (Mooney 1900:311–315). Oral traditions also reference the houses of chiefs within towns, as well as rules about where newcomers and visitors could live or stay within individual settlements. There is at least one reference to the dwelling of a bear as a house

(Mooney 1900:328), and at least one reference to a townhouse as analogous to a cave (Mooney 1900:327), which are illustrations of a broader phenomenon in the greater southern Appalachians in which timber-frame earth-covered houses were "caves above the ground" (Hally 2002). If at least some aspects of recorded Cherokee oral traditions are clues about the conceptual map of Cherokee culture and cosmos, then they must also be clues about the symbolism of Cherokee houses and townhouses themselves. Townhouses and houses structured public life and dwelling within Cherokee towns, and the built environment of Cherokee towns was an atlas of sorts of Cherokee cosmology.

Major sources of Cherokee oral traditions from the 1700s and 1800s include James Mooney's (1900) compilation based on ethnographic fieldwork conducted in western North Carolina in the late nineteenth century, and the postscript to Alexander Longe's journal of life in Cherokee towns during the early eighteenth century (Corkran 1969). We have recently attempted to create an index, of sorts, of references to houses and townhouses and to activities taking place in them in these written accounts of Cherokee oral traditions. We may not have recorded every single instance of such references in Mooney's compilation and Longe's postscript, but we have recorded many of them, and here we draw on those we deem most relevant to our consideration of the social and symbolic lives of Cherokee houses and townhouses.

Several written accounts of Cherokee oral traditions chronicle the lives and activities of animals, including oral traditions about the origins of animals and their characteristics, ballgames between birds and land animals, the relationships between game and human hunters, and animals holding councils in townhouses. One oral tradition, "The Bear Songs" (Mooney 1900:325–327), recounts the transformation of an old Cherokee clan known as the Ani'-Tsâ'gûhĭ, who decided to withdraw from settlements to live as bears (yâ'nû) in the woods and the mountains, who invited people to hunt them when they needed food, and who taught the people the bear songs with which to call them. Another oral tradition, "The Bear Man" (Mooney 1900:327–329), describes interactions between hunters and bears. After a hunter wounded a black bear with his bow and arrow, the bear led the hunter to "a large cave like a townhouse," which was "full of bears—old bears, young bears, and cubs, white bears, black bears, and brown bears—and a large white bear was the chief," and after the bear council and dance were done, they went to another cave in the side of a mountain, where the black bear lived (Mooney 1900:327).

Within these oral traditions, the lives of animals are structured, in a sense, within a landscape that includes houses and townhouses, the same architectural forms present in the cultural landscape of Cherokee towns. The structures themselves are not described in detail, but they probably therefore had the same characteristics as the houses and townhouses where people lived and where towns were emplaced within the landscape. Several aspects of those houses and town-houses probably resembled the characteristics of the earth island, as noted in several oral traditions.

The cosmogonic myth "How the World Was Made" (Mooney 1900:239–240) begins as follows:

> The earth is a great island floating in a sea of water, and suspended at each of the four cardinal points by a cord hanging down from the sky vault, which is of solid rock. . . .
>
>    When all was water, the animals were above in Gălûñ'lătĭ, above the [sky] arch; but it was very much crowded, and they were wanting more room. They wondered what was below the water, and at last Dâ'yuni'sĭ, "Beaver's Grandchild," the little Water-beetle, offered to go and see if it could learn. It darted in every direction over the surface of the water, but could find no firm place to rest. Then it dived to the bottom and came up with some soft mud, which began to grow and spread on every side until it became the island which we call the earth. It was afterward fastened to the sky with four cords, but no one remembers who did this.

For our consideration here of Cherokee houses and townhouses, the main points to derive from this narrative are that the earth is suspended from the sky by four cords, one at each of the cardinal points. This cosmological model is manifested in the architecture of Cherokee houses and townhouses, which often have four roof-support posts spaced around hearths, and walls and roofs made of wood and earth.

A historical myth, "Mounds and the Constant Fire: The Old Sacred Things" (Mooney 1900:393–397), records the practices of building mounds and town-houses as follows:

> Some say that the mounds were built by another people. Others say they were built by the ancestors of the old Ani'-Kĭtu'hwagĭ for townhouse foundations, so that the townhouses would be safe when freshets came. The townhouse was always built on the level bottom lands by the river in order that the people might have smooth ground for their dances and ballplays and might be able to go down to water during the dance.
>
>    When they were ready to build the mound they began by laying a circle of stones on the surface of the ground. Next they made a fire in the center of the circle and put near it the body of some prominent chief or priest who had lately died—some say seven chief men from the different clans [there were and are seven matrilineal Cherokee clans]—together with an Ulûñsû'tĭ stone [a quartz crystal (Rodning 2011, 2015a)], an uktena scale or horn [probably represented by an engraved rattlesnake gorget (Muller 2007)], a feather from the right wing of an eagle or great tlă'nuwă' [a mythical hawk], which lived in those days, and beads of seven colors, red, white, black, blue, purple, yellow, and gray-blue. The priest then conjured all these with disease, so that, if ever an enemy invaded the country, even though he should burn and destroy the town and the townhouse, he would never live to return home.
>
>    The mound was then built up with earth, which the women brought in bas-

kets, and as they piled it above the stones, the bodies of their great men, and the sacred things, they left an open place at the fire in the center and let down a hollow
cedar trunk, with the bark on, which fitted around the fire and protected it from
the earth . . . the earth was piled up around it, and the whole mound was finished
off smoothly, and then the townhouse was built upon it. One man, called the fire
keeper, stayed always in the townhouse to feed and tend the fire . . . just before the
Green-corn dance in the old times every fire in the settlement was extinguished
and all the people came and got new fire from the townhouse. This was called atsi'la
gălûñkw'ti'yu, "the honored or sacred fire." . . .

Some say this everlasting fire was only in the larger mounds at Nĭkwăsĭ', Kĭtu'hwâ,
and a few other towns, and that when the new fire was thus drawn up for the Green-
corn dance it was distributed from them to the other settlements. The fire burns yet
at the bottom of these mounds.

For our considerations here, the most salient points from this oral tradition are
that, in an effort to protect the town and its people, burials were placed in the
ground and items were cached in the ground before a townhouse was built; that
a constant fire was kept in the hearth; and that the fires kept in the hearths of
household dwellings were periodically rekindled from fire taken out of Cherokee
townhouse hearths.

Another historical tradition, "The Removed Townhouses" (Mooney 1900:335–
336), refers to rocks, mountain peaks, and earthen mounds that represent mythical townhouses and landmarks to ancestral generations of Cherokee towns:

Long ago, long before the Cherokee were driven from their homes in 1838, the
people on Valley river and Hiwassee hear voices of invisible spirits in the air call-
ing and warning them of wars and misfortunes which the future held in store, and
inviting them to come and live with the Nûñně'hĭ, the Immortals, in their homes
under the mountains and under the waters.

The people were afraid of the evils that were to come, and they knew that the
Immortals of the mountains and the waters were happy forever, so they counciled
in their townhouse and decided to go with them. Those of Ani'sgayâ'yĭ town came
all together into their townhouse and prayed and fasted for six days. On the sev-
enth day there was a sound from the distant mountains, and it came nearer and
grew louder until a roar of thunder was all about the townhouse and they felt the
ground shake under them. Now they were frightened, and despite the warning some
of them screamed out. The Nûñně'hĭ, who had already lifted up the townhouse with
its mound to carry it away, were startled by the cry and let a part of it fall to the
earth, where now we see the mound of Sĕ'tsĭ. They steadied themselves again and
bore the rest of the townhouse, with all the people in it, to the top of Tsuda'ye'lûñ'yĭ
(Lone peak), near the head of Cheowa, were we can still see it, changed long ago to
solid rock, but the people are invisible and immortal.

The people of another town, on Hiwassee, at the place which we call now Du'staya-
lûñ'yĭ, where Shooting creek comes in, also prayed and fasted, and at the end of

seven days the Nûñně'hĭ came and took them away down under the water. They are there now, and on a warm summer day, when the wind ripples the surface, those who listen well can hear them talking below. When the Cherokee drag the river for fish the fish-drag always stops and catches there, although the water is deep, and the people know it is being held by their lost kinsmen, who do not want to be forgotten.

When the Cherokee were forcibly removed to the West one of the greatest regrets of those along Hiwassee and Valley rivers was that they were compelled to leave behind forever their relatives who had gone to the Nûñně'hĭ.

In Tennessee river . . . is a place the Cherokee call Gustĭ', where there once was a settlement long ago, but one night while the people were gathered in the townhouse for a dance the bank caved in and carried them all down into the river. Boatmen passing the spot in their canoes see the round dome of the townhouse—now turned to stone—in the water below them and sometimes hear the sound of the drum and dance coming up.

Another historical tradition, "The Spirit Defenders of Nĭkwăsĭ'" (Mooney 1900: 335–337), refers to the protective powers of Nûñně'hĭ dwelling within earthen mounds, and to the role of Cherokee townhouses as places of community convergence and refuge.

Long ago a powerful unknown tribe invaded the country from the southeast, killing people and destroying settlements wherever they went. No leader could stand against them, and in a little while they had wasted all the lower settlements and advanced into the mountains. The warriors of the old town of Nĭkwăsĭ', on the head of Little Tennessee, gathered their wives and children into the townhouse and kept scouts constantly on the lookout for the presence of danger.

One morning just before daybreak the spies saw the enemy approaching and at once gave the alarm. The Nĭkwăsĭ' men seized their arms, and rushed out to meet the attack, but after a long, hard fight they found themselves overpowered and began to retreat, when suddenly a stranger stood among them and shouted to the chief to call off his men and he himself would drive back the enemy. From the dress and language of the stranger the Nĭkwăsĭ' people thought him a chief who had come with reinforcements from the Overhill settlements in Tennessee. They fell back along the trail, and as they came near the townhouse they saw a great company of warriors coming out from the side of the mound as through an open doorway. Then they knew that their friends were the Nûñně'hĭ, the Immortals, although no one had ever heard before that they lived under Nĭkwăsĭ' mound.

The Nûñně'hĭ poured out by hundreds, armed and painted for the fight, and the most curious thing about it all was that they became invisible as soon as they were fairly outside of the settlement, so that although the enemy saw the glancing arrow or the rushing tomahawk, and felt the stroke, he could not see who sent it. Before such invisible foes the invaders soon had to retreat, going first south along the ridge to where joins the main ridge which separates the French Broad from the Tuckasegee, and then turning with it to the northeast. As they retreated they tried to shield themselves behind rocks and trees, but the Nûñně'hĭ arrows went around the rocks and killed them from the other side, and they could find no hiding place. All along the ridge they fell, until when they reached the head of Tuckasegee not more than half a dozen were left alive, and in despair they sat down and cried out for mercy. Ever since then the Cherokee have called the place Dayûlsûñ′yĭ, "Where they cried." Then the Nûñně′hĭ chief told them they had deserved their punishment for attacking a peaceful tribe, and he spared their lives and told them to go home and take the news to their people. This was the Indian custom, always to spare a few to carry back the news of defeat. They went home toward the north and the Nûñně′hĭ went back to the mound.

This narrative refers to an entire town gathering in its townhouse for refuge and safety, and it refers to mythical warriors coming forth from an earthen mound. The Nûñně′hĭ are thought to live anywhere, and they kept townhouses atop many mountains, especially the tallest peaks with bald summits, where drumming can sometimes be heard. The Nûñně′hĭ periodically cared for travelers in those townhouses and guided them home, and they were known to have come to the aid of Nĭkwăsĭ′ and also other Cherokee towns (Mooney 1900:330–331). Within townhouses in Cherokee settlements, and within mythical townhouses in the mountains surrounding Cherokee towns, resided spiritual forces and protective powers.

Many of these oral traditions, of course, refer to townhouses rather than to houses. Given similarities between public structures and household dwellings at precontact and postcontact towns in the southern Appalachians (Hally 2008; Schroedl 1998; Sullivan 1987), it is likely that at least some symbolic properties of townhouses are associated with household dwellings. If we accept that premise, then we may conclude that houses and townhouses were cosmograms: they were architectural symbols of the earth island, they were anchors for spiritual forces, and they were containers for the hearths that themselves were containers for fire. The "constant fires" (or, sometimes, "everlasting fires") kept in Cherokee townhouse hearths were probably conceptualized as earthly manifestations of the sun, and they were the spiritual essence of Cherokee towns. The hearths in Cherokee dwellings were periodically rekindled from the fires kept in the central hearths of Cherokee townhouses, maintaining social and spiritual connections between households and towns and among households within towns.

Along with the clues about the symbolism of houses and townhouses derived from Cherokee oral traditions (Mooney 1900), some written descriptions exist about how structures were actually built (discussed in detail in Schroedl 1986). William Bartram, the Quaker naturalist who visited Cherokee towns in 1775, described the architectural details of Cherokee townhouses, hot houses (known as *asi*), and cabins, but these descriptions refer to structures from the late eighteenth century, and therefore they may be missing some important details about the kinds of structures that were present at Cherokee settlements during late prehistory and the contact period (Waselkov and Braund 1995). Lieutenant Henry Timberlake visited Cherokee towns in eastern Tennessee during winter and spring

1761 and 1762 (Chapman 2009; Randolph 1973; Schroedl 2009; Williams 1927, 1928, 1930). He described a Cherokee townhouse as "raised with wood, and covered over with earth, and has all the appearance of a small mountain at a little distance" (King 2007:17). He attended several events in Cherokee townhouses, including feasts and dances, recounting of war deeds by warriors upon returning home, and diplomatic gatherings at which articles of peace and alliances between Cherokee town leaders and the English colony of Virginia were formed (King 2007:17, 18–21, 45–47). Alexander Longe, the colonial trade agent who lived in Cherokee towns during the early eighteenth century, wrote in the 1725 postscript to his journal that people from many towns—or, perhaps, residents from many settlements who thought of themselves as members of the same community— participated in building townhouses (Corkran 1969:36). Timberlake describes the placement of thick posts directly in the ground in the plan of a house (and presumably a townhouse), with a smaller post between the larger posts, "and the whole wattled with twigs like a basket, which is then covered with clay very smooth" (King 2007:31).

Of course, archaeological evidence can and does shed light on the architectural details of houses and townhouses at Mississippian and Cherokee settlements in the southern Appalachians, from late prehistory through the 1500s and 1600s (Dickens 1976; Gougeon 2006, 2007, 2015, 2017; Hally 2008; Lewis and Kneberg 1946; Lewis et al. 1995; Moore 2002a, 2002b; Polhemus 1987, 1990; Riggs and Shumate 2003; Rodning 2001b, 2002b, 2009a, 2009b, 2015a, 2015b; Sullivan 1987, 1989, 1995; Ward and Davis 1999), and from the 1700s and early 1800s (Baden 1983; Chapman 1994; Faulkner 1978; Keel 1976; Riggs 2008; Rogers 2009; Russ and Chapman 1983; Schroedl 1989, 2000, 2001, 2009). The architecture of houses and townhouses reflects the raw materials available, the performance demands and design principles involved, the topographic contours and landmarks of particular places, and the social histories of households and communities. This architecture also reflects the ways in which Cherokee households and towns conceptualized the architectural spaces and places they called home, and the relationships between household dwellings, public architecture within Cherokee towns, and the larger world in which they were situated.

## ARCHAEOLOGICAL EVIDENCE

Cherokee oral traditions form an interpretive framework with which to consider the archaeology of houses and townhouses at the Coweeta Creek site in southwestern North Carolina and other Mississippian and protohistoric sites in the greater southern Appalachians (Dickens 1978; Rodning 2015a). The site is located in the area of the Middle Cherokee towns, close to towns such as Cowee, Nequassee, and Joree (Rodning 2001a). The site is attributed to the Qualla phase, and it dates from the 1400s through the early 1700s (Rodning 2007, 2008, 2010b). Several household dwellings were situated around a plaza, and beside the plaza was a townhouse. The townhouse, including a square structure with rounded corners and a rectangular ramada situated between the entryway to the townhouse and the plaza beside it, was built and rebuilt in place at least six or seven times, forming a low mound encompassing the burned and buried remnants of the townhouse itself, and deposits of white clay and river boulders (Figure 10.3). Several domestic structures were built and rebuilt in place in multiple stages, although not as

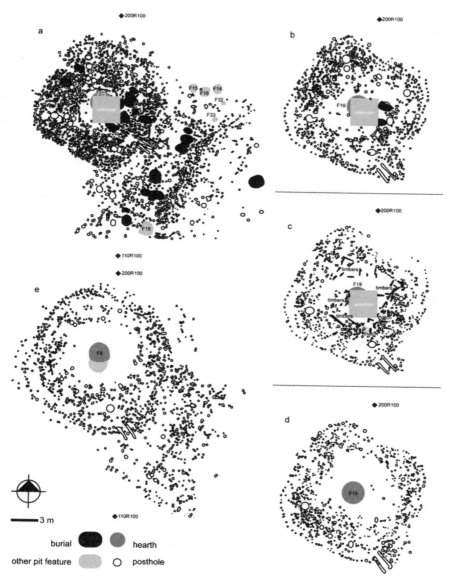

Figure 10.3. Sequence of townhouses at Coweeta Creek: *a*, first stage; *b*, second stage; *c*, third stage; *d*, fourth stage; *e*, fifth and sixth stages. F = feature. (Christopher B. Rodning; after Rodning 2009a)

many as in the case of the townhouse, the architectural symbol of the town and the setting for public life within the community (Figure 10.4).

Domestic structures at Coweeta Creek include houses that date to the fifteenth or sixteenth century, and others that date to the seventeenth century (Rodning 2007, 2015a). Structures dating to the seventeenth century have an area of roughly 5–7 m², with rounded corners, paired entrance trenches, and arrangements of four deeply set roof-support posts surrounding central hearths. Late prehistoric structures at the site are slightly larger and more rounded, up to 8 m in diameter. Domestic structures were built and rebuilt in place, maintaining the placement of dwellings and the households associated with them within both an overarching town plan and specific points within it. Burials are situated inside and beside

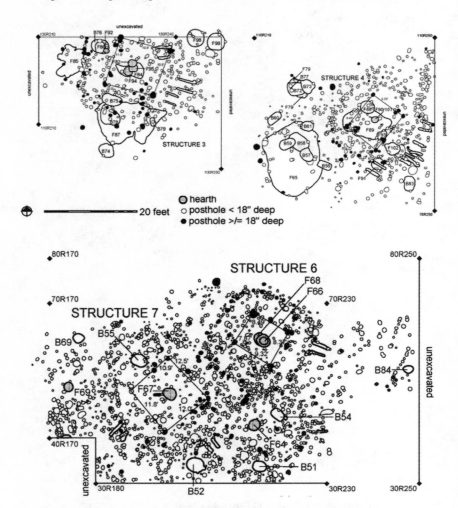

Figure 10.4. Selected domestic structures and sequences at Coweeta Creek. (Christopher B. Rodning; after Rodning 2009b)

these structures, further anchoring households to points in the town plan and the broader cultural landscape.

The townhouse at Coweeta Creek follows the same architectural template as household dwellings, but it is built at a larger scale (Rodning 2010a, 2015a). Early stages of the townhouse were 14 m² in area, with rounded corners, and the latest stages were 16 m across. The entryway to the first stage of the townhouse was situated at the midpoint of the southeastern edge of the structure, and it was later moved to the southernmost corner. The alignment of the townhouse and its entryway was consistent in all stages, and this alignment connected the townhouse to household dwellings within the town. This alignment, and the broader town plan, was consistent through several generations of the community, as well as through several generations of the townhouse and the houses themselves.

Other archaeological clues exist about community longevity and generational continuity within the Coweeta Creek town plan. The four roof-support posts and four corners of the townhouse itself were analogous to the four cords connecting the earth island to the sky vault (Rodning 2010a). Many burials were associated with the first stage of the Coweeta Creek townhouse (Rodning 2001a, 2011), comparable to the burials of town elders noted in Cherokee oral tradition about townhouses and mounds. These burials, and material goods in them, probably served in part to protect the town in the future, as noted in oral tradition about the spirit defenders of Nequassee (Nĭkwăsĭ'). Oral tradition about the Nequassee townhouse also refers to the gathering of the entire town inside the townhouse, illustrating the point that such structures, in a sense, housed a whole town. The cumulative effect of building and rebuilding the townhouse in place was to create a mound, which in Cherokee oral tradition is conceptually related to the even more monumental and more permanent landmarks of mountain summits and peaks. The central hearth in the Coweeta Creek townhouse was kept in place in successive iterations of the townhouse (Rodning 2009a, 2010a), consistent with the "everlasting fire" and the "constant fire" noted in Cherokee oral tradition.

Fire and hearths formed another material element connecting the townhouse and houses within the Coweeta Creek community. Given references in Cherokee oral tradition to taking fire from townhouse hearths to kindle fires in the hearths of household dwellings, it seems likely that this practice was done at the Coweeta Creek site. Not only did houses and townhouses resemble each other architecturally, but they were also connected by fire, and perhaps even by the columns of smoke emanating upward toward the sky from hearths inside structures within the community.

## CONCLUSIONS

Guided by Cherokee oral tradition, an archaeological consideration of Cherokee architecture at the Coweeta Creek site reflects ideational aspects of houses and townhouses, and the ways in which households and the community as a whole were anchored within a social landscape. Houses and townhouses are landmarks in the map of Cherokee cosmology, they are present along the paths of movement of the sun across the sky and down to the horizon, and they form dwellings for mythical animals and spiritual forces in the mountains and streams surrounding Cherokee towns. Townhouses and earthen mounds were architectural manifestations of the earth island, from when the world and the land were new, and houses followed the same template at smaller scales. Townhouse hearths contained fire that symbolized the sun and that manifested the spirit and vitality of Cherokee towns. Fires kept in household dwellings were periodically rekindled from townhouse hearths, thereby connecting houses to towns, and creating enduring connections between households within towns. Houses and townhouses structured daily life and ceremonial life within Cherokee towns, and they anchored households and towns within settlements, within the Cherokee cultural landscape, and within the Cherokee cosmos. From these perspectives, Mississippian and protohistoric architectural forms in the greater southern Appalachians were cosmograms, and they were social agents and actors within the social landscape. Our focus here has been a single archaeological site, but the kinds of structures and the overarching settlement plan at Coweeta Creek resemble aspects of the built environment at other Cherokee town sites, and at Mississippian and protohistoric sites throughout the greater southern Appalachians.

## Acknowledgments

We are grateful to Elizabeth Watts Malouchos and Alleen Betzenhauser for the opportunity to contribute to these conversations about household and community in the Mississippian Southeast. We appreciate the support of the Department of Anthropology, the School of Liberal Arts, and the Paul and Debra Gibbons Professorship at Tulane University, and the Research Laboratories of Archaeology at the University of North Carolina at Chapel Hill.

# IV

# MOVEMENT, MEMORY, AND HISTORIES

# 11

# MOVING TO WHERE THE RIVER MEETS THE SEA

*Origins of the Mill Cove Complex*

Keith Ashley

The late pre-Columbian history of northeastern Florida has been long inter-preted as a continuous series of in situ cultural developments interrupted only by sixteenth-century European arrival. Over the past two decades, however, research in the region has taken a new tack by considering archaeological data in ever-broadening spatial and social scales of analysis that incorporate the geopolitical contexts of northern Florida and beyond (Ashley 2003, 2012). This perspective privileges historical contingency, permits people to move across the landscape, and interrelates extralocal interactions and local processes. Such a broadened geographic and temporal outlook offers a new take on the region's cultural history. Here I propose that groups from the middle St. Johns River Basin migrated north around AD 900 and contributed to the founding of the Mill Cove Complex near the river's mouth (Figure 11.1). The reinvigoration of dormant long-distance exchange networks at this time combined with the opportunity to participate in these interactions partly precipitated this move and resettlement. Tenth-century community building at Mill Cove and elsewhere along the lower or northern St. Johns, however, was not simply the outcome of migration.[1] Rather, it was a more complex coalescence that involved a mix of newcomers and locals.

## COMMUNITIES OF PRACTICE

Archaeologists worldwide are reconceptualizing the term *community*. The conventional view of communities as static collections of domestic units living within a bounded space and sharing daily experiences and cultural lifeways is being replaced by more dynamic and interactive notions of communities as networks of social relations that exist at multiple scales and result in various types (e.g., Varien and Potter 2008; Yaeger and Canuto 2000; chapter 1 in this volume). Moreover, any given person is involved in an ever-changing array of communities that do not necessarily require socially visible boundaries or copresence in a sharply defined group. People are members of communities that—through recurring practices—create principles that organize their lives and shape their identities. Herein, I en-

Figure 11.1. Location of Mill Cove Complex and early Mississippian world. (Keith Ashley)

gage a specific type of community known as a community of practice by considering the learned technological process of making St. Johns pottery and exploring
how population movements from the south fueled the spread of this ceramic technology into northeastern Florida.

A community of practice is "a set of relations among persons, activity, and
world" that entails the collective learning of a practice in which the creation of
social structure and meaning are part of an ongoing negotiation through social
participation and collaboration over time (Lave and Wenger 1991:98). The practice intertwines learning, meaning, and group identity because "learning is not
merely a condition for membership, but is itself an evolving form of membership" (Lave and Wenger 1991:53). Individuals participate in multiple communities of practice that embed them within broader social fields, meaning that communities of practice "cannot be considered in isolation from the rest of the world,
or independently of other practices" (Wenger 1998:103). Instead, they must be
viewed "in relation with other tangential and overlapping communities of practice" (Lave and Wenger 1991:98).

Not all forms of joint work are communities of practice. What sets a community of practice apart from other groups is a sense of cohesion obtained through the "mutual engagement" of its members in the negotiation of a "joint enterprise" involving a "shared repertoire" (Wenger 1998:73–85). These three dimensions of community are wellsprings of learning and knowing rooted in individuals doing things together, creating a sense of place, purpose, and common identity, and settling their differences. Shared repertoires include "routines, words, tools, ways of doing things, stories, gestures, symbols, genres, actions or concepts that the community has produced or adopted in the course of its existence, and which have become part of its practice" (Wenger 1998:73). A community of practice gives form to the experience "by producing objects that congeal this experience into 'thingness,'" a process and product referred to as reification (Wenger 1998:58).

A community of practice approach lends itself to the archaeological study of ceramic production at the household level (e.g., Eckert 2008; McGill 2013; Sassaman and Rudolphi 2001; Stark 2006; Worth 2017). In fact, the pottery-learning networks described among interacting potters in the ethnographic record conform nicely to the framework outlined in a community of practice (e.g., Arnold 1998; Herbich 1987; Smith 2000; MacEachern 1998). In her study of ancient Pueblo potters, Eckert (2008:2) defines communities of practice as "social networks in which Pueblo potters learn their craft from other women in the community . . . [through] a shared history of practice and not by spatial constraints." She further notes that "multiple communities of practice can exist within a given village, while a single community of practice can cross cut multiple villages" (Eckert 2008:2). Potters are also engaged in a wide range of networks of interaction of which pottery-making is only one (Herbich 1987:202).

It is widely assumed that women were the potters in the American Southeast (Hudson 1976:264). Young girls learned from other women in their household group how to collect and process clays and make and decorate pots as part of the domestic routine. Among potters, a community of practice provides a "learning environment and deviation reduction mechanisms," whereby practitioners are taught how to make culturally accepted pottery types and forms (MacEachern 1998:114). Apprentices initially learn by observing, long before being allowed to join in; this process is what Lave and Wenger (1991) refer to as legitimate peripheral participation. Ceramic production begins well before a pot is fired and follows an operational sequence marked by technological choices largely guided by their historically situated shared technological dispositions materialized in the form of a local ceramic tradition (Smith 2000:22). These shared conscious and unconscious habitual routines are what Bourdieu (1977) refers to as habitus, durable dispositions that develop within a sociohistorical context as a practical way of doing something. In effect, interacting groups create a shared identity predicated on repeated and habitual routines such as organizing space and performing domestic tasks (e.g., pottery and craft production).

Along these lines, Lemonnier (1986:149, 1992) has shown that insightful information on social relations and identity formation can be gleaned through examination of technological styles or *chaîne opératoires* (operational sequences), "a series of operations which brings a primary material from its natural state to a fabricated state" (Cresswell 1976:6). The premise here is that a group of individuals or community of practice choose between a number of equally viable options, with choices going beyond mere technical logic or material efficacy. In some cases, different social groups create virtually identical products, but the way or order in which tasks are executed sets the groups apart. With respect to pottery manufacture, ethnography has demonstrated that most potters perform their craft as taught to them early in life and hesitate to change an operational sequence that required years of learning and practice (Sassaman and Rudolphi 2001).

Beyond the relatively stable communities of face-to-face interaction among members working directly with one another, communities of practice connect at a broader scale through "constellations of practice." Wenger (1998:127) mentions several factors that lead communities of practice to form larger constellations, such as sharing historical roots, facing similar conditions, having members in common, sharing artifacts, and having overlapping styles. With respect to pottery production, these might constitute what archaeologists often label as regional ceramic traditions or style zones. Worth (2017:139) envisions these regional style zones as communities of practice, "fundamentally based on the routine practices of and interactions between the very craftspeople whose behavior generated the patterned distribution of material culture that archaeologists study."

## TERMINAL LATE WOODLAND ARCHAEOLOGICAL RECORD OF THE LOWER ST. JOHNS

Traditional interpretations of the emergence of the Mill Cove Complex and Mount Royal presume that each developed organically out of local St. Johns I populations, indicating cultural continuity between the St. Johns I (Woodland) and St. Johns II (Mississippian) periods (Milanich 1994:263). While such a claim may hold merit for groups within the middle and upper reaches of the St. Johns River, this is not the case for the lower St. Johns, where St. Johns I culture sites are rare (Figure 11.2). Excavations and radiometric dating over the past decade bolster a refined ceramic chronology for extreme northeastern Florida (Table 11.1), but one similar to that originally proposed by Sears (1957). In this update, a long-standing tradition of sand tempering characterized the local Woodland period. Plainwares prevailed, while check stamping (Deptford) and complicated stamping (Swift Creek) underwent separate episodes of florescence as a minority type. St. Johns Plain pottery occurs occasionally, perhaps as an import from the south. A brief and localized Late Woodland temporal phase (and culture) known as Colorinda immediately precedes St. Johns II. By the early tenth century, any trace of Colorinda pottery had largely vanished, and St. Johns II series pottery dominated on all local sites dated between AD 900 and 1250.

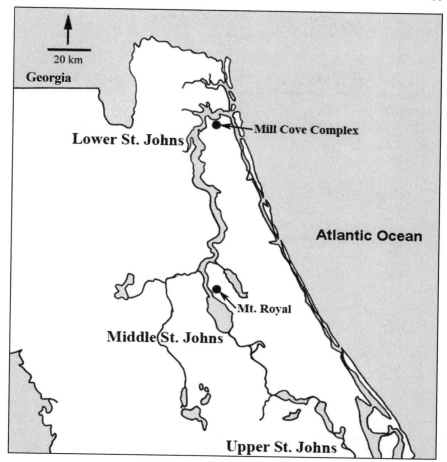

Figure 11.2. Mill Cove Complex and Mount Royal. (Keith Ashley)

Apart from being short lived, Colorinda ceramic assemblages are distinctive and consist of sand-tempered plain, ground sherd–tempered plain (Colorinda), sponge spicule–tempered plain, and sponge spicule–tempered check-stamped (St. Johns series) (Sears 1957). The former two types predominate, whereas the latter two, combined, typically account for approximately 10 percent of the Colorinda ceramic assemblage (Ashley 2006). While St. Johns wares are a minor part of the assemblage, the ground sherds used as temper in Colorinda vessels most often de-rive from St. Johns pots. Thus, the makers of Colorinda pottery also either manu-factured small numbers of St. Johns vessels or acquired them through some form of exchange (e.g., trade, marriage relations, alliance building). Regardless of their origins, St. Johns pots were eventually ground up for use as temper.

Sometime during the early tenth century, St. Johns II assemblages replaced

**Table 11.1. Comparison of Middle and Lower St. Johns
Region Chronologies after AD 500**

| Date | Middle St. Johns | SE United States | Lower St. Johns |
|------|------------------|------------------|-----------------|
| 1600 | St. Johns IIc | Mississippian | San Pedro |
| 1500 | St. Johns IIb |  | San Pedro |
| 1400 | St. Johns IIb |  | St. Marys |
| 1300 | St. Johns IIb | Mississippian | St. Marys |
| 1200 | St. Johns IIb |  | St. Johns II |
| 1100 | St. Johns IIb |  | St. Johns II |
| 1000 | St. Johns IIa |  | St. Johns II |
| 900 | St. Johns IIa |  | St. Johns II |
| 800 | St. Johns IIa | Woodland | St. Johns II |
| 700 | St. Johns Ib | Woodland | Late Swift Creek |
| 600 | St. Johns Ib |  | Late Swift Creek |
| 500 | St. Johns Ib |  | Late Swift Creek |

Colorinda throughout northeastern Florida. These assemblages are composed almost exclusively of sponge spicule–tempered St. Johns series wares, in which check-stamped sherds dominate in frequency on all sites, followed closely by plain, and distantly by incised, punctated, and other types. A hallmark of local St. Johns II assemblages is the presence of grit-tempered Ocmulgee Cordmarked, a type locally made and imported from south-central Georgia, but absent in Colorinda assemblages. Concomitant with the tenth-century change in ceramic technology, the archaeological record of the lower St. Johns demonstrates shifts in the size, location, and structure of settlements.

Colorinda sites consist mostly of a small number of low-density artifact scatters and shell middens along the lower St. Johns River and Florida barrier islands to the north (Ashley 2006). The McCormack (8DU66) and Dolphin Reef (8DU276) sites, with larger and thicker refuse deposits, differ from the norm (Ashley and Hendryx 2008; Richter 1993). Each also contains a major and more widespread St. Johns II component. At Dolphin Reef, Colorinda and St. Johns II middens are mixed, although only Colorinda was identified approximately 300 m away at the adjacent Tillie Fowler site (8DU17245). Radiometric assays on soot from separate sherds taken from context-secured St. Johns II and Colorinda deposits at these two sites are statistically identical at the 2 σ level (AD 900–1020). At McCormack, a pure Colorinda area was positioned about 300 m from a pure St. Johns II sand burial mound (Goodman Mound), although mixed shell middens occur in the intervening area. Figure 11.3 shows the location of select Colorinda and St. Johns II sites.

At least four early St. Johns II village-mound settlements—Dolphin Reef, McCormack, TR Preserve (8DU58), and Caracasi/Atosi (8DU97)—along the south side of the river, as well as the Grand site (8DU1) on Big Talbot Island to the north, contain rare Colorinda sherds in St. Johns contexts dating to circa AD 900–1100. At the Mill Cove Complex, Colorinda pottery is somewhat common in shell middens beneath and adjacent to the Grant Mound but virtually absent several hundred meters away near the Shields Mound. The other seven known St. Johns II habitation-mound sites are either undated chronometrically or date to a slightly

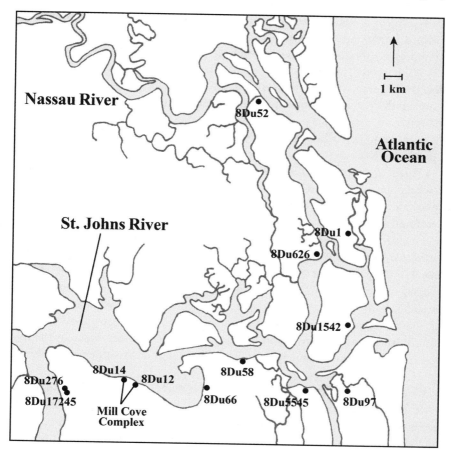

Figure 11.3. Select Colorinda and St. Johns II sites along lower St. Johns River. (Keith Ashley)

later period based on a single radiocarbon date from each site (Ashley 2012). With the exceptions discussed above, most St. Johns II village sites occurred in locations previously unoccupied by Colorinda groups. Admittedly, because of the nearness in age of the radiometric assays from Colorinda and early St. Johns II contexts, it is difficult to assess confidently whether these occupations are concurrent or closely sequential during the late ninth and early tenth centuries.

A unique aspect of Colorinda, distinguishing it from earlier Swift Creek and later St. Johns II cultures, is its mortuary practices. While the other two cultures constructed continuous-use burial mounds, the only confirmed Colorinda cemetery (McCormack site) is not mounded and includes a high percentage of prone (facedown) burials.[2] Nonmound cemeteries marked by extended prone interments are not associated with the St. Johns River Valley. To the north, however, such burials are a defining characteristic of the coeval Kelvin culture on St. Simons Island and the adjacent mainland coast of southern Georgia (Cook 1979, 2013). Moreover, Kelvin assemblages include appreciable amounts of complicated stamped pottery and grog tempering (Cook 2013:31–50), suggesting that Kelvin represents terminal Late Swift Creek along the lower Georgia coast (Ashley and Wallis 2006:11; see Cook 2013 for an alternative interpretation). The simultaneous appearance of grog tempering and similar mortuary practices alludes to active ninth-century relationships or interactions between northeastern Florida and southeastern Georgia peoples. A similar connection between the two regions has been demonstrated empirically through paddle design matches and neutron activation analysis during earlier Late Swift Creek times (Wallis 2011).

While it is tempting to render Colorinda a transitional assemblage produced by local populations on their way to fully adopting a St. Johns ceramic technology, Colorinda can also be considered in another way. Taken as a whole, ninth-century Colorinda assemblages evince a "blending of the long-standing, local tradition of sand tempering, the sherd tempering of the Georgia coast (e.g., Wilmington), and the spicule tempering (St. Johns) of the St. Johns River valley to the south" (Ashley 2006:96). The presence of small amounts of St. Johns pottery on Colorinda sites— whether made locally or imported—spotlights contact with St. Johns groups to the south. I propose that these connections in concert with broader-scale historical trends sweeping across the Southeast opened the door for a downriver (northward) intrusion of St. Johns II people from the middle St. Johns, whereby the region's small Colorinda population quickly became part of a resettlement process.

## WHO MADE ST. JOHNS POTTERY IN NORTHEASTERN FLORIDA?

What does the replacement of Colorinda ceramic assemblages by St. Johns II in the early tenth-century archaeological record of extreme northeastern Florida signify? Does it merely represent the acceptance of a new ceramic repertoire by local populations, or does it point to the arrival of immigrants from the south? One thing beyond doubt is that St. Johns II ceramic assemblages in northeastern

Florida are remarkably similar to those found throughout the river valley and adjacent Atlantic coast at the time. Moreover, the roots of this ceramic technology extend back to the Early Woodland period (Milanich 1994). We also should bear in mind that the changes witnessed in the archaeological record are not simply the addition or replacement of a decorative style but are the wholesale adoption of an entire ceramic tradition that required a different production procedure or *chaîne opératoire*. The learned practice of processing and firing certain raw clays to achieve a chalky texture and buff/gray exterior color distinguished St. Johns pottery from neighboring ceramic traditions for more than two millennia. While more stylistically malleable aspects of pottery like surface decoration underwent episodes of change, the way St. Johns pots looked and felt did not.

A paste containing microscopic sponge spicules and a tactual softness routinely described as chalky defines St. Johns pottery (Borremans and Shaak 1986). How sponge spicules got into the paste is a source of debate. Traditionalists argue that these biosilicate pieces naturally occur in raw clays used by St. Johns potters (Borremans and Shaak 1986; Cordell and Koski 2003). Others contend that freshwater sponges were collected and purposefully added to clay as temper during paste preparation (Rolland and Bond 2003).[3] To date, no workable clays containing common-to-abundant sponge spicules have been identified in investigations of raw clay sources in Florida and southeastern Georgia (e.g., Cordell 1984:57–77, 1992:113–127; Crusoe 1971; Espenshade 1983). This absence is astonishing given the fact that hundreds of thousands of St. Johns sherds have been recovered from Florida.[4]

Because the paste of St. Johns pottery across the broad St. Johns region is consistently fine and compact, clay processing must have involved extensive levigation and/or the utilization of natural clays with fine compositions. No modern researcher or ceramicist has been able to successfully manufacture vessels (or test bars) that match actual St. Johns pots in terms of texture, paste consistency, and abundance of sponge spicules. With respect to firing, St. Johns wares routinely exhibit well-oxidized, light-gray to pale-buff interior and exterior surfaces. These thin outer lenses bracket a dark reduced core, an outcome generally true regardless of vessel thickness. Thus, the production of St. Johns pottery apparently required techniques, sequences, and motor habits different from those employed in making other Florida pottery types.

What appears to differentiate St. Johns from other wares in the region then is not only the pottery's outward appearance but also the technological style or technical choices employed in rendering chalky wares. Evidence that St. Johns potters shared a learned *chaîne opératoire* is suggested by the results of Rolland's (2004:132–150) oxidation study. Her analysis of St. Johns sherds from a variety of geographically dispersed sites demonstrates remarkable consistency in refired colors. Eighty percent of the refired St. Johns sherds revealed pale colors not observed in other Late Archaic through Mississippian period sherds in her sample.

Because the St. Johns specimens were from vessels undoubtedly made of different clays, the degree of similarity is astonishing and appears to be tied to a standardized clay processing and paste preparation. This theory is reinforced by ethnographic "travel data" that suggest that "ancient potters would probably travel no more than 1 km to obtain their clays and tempers and few would travel more than 7 km" (Arnold 1998:357). Therefore, a specific recipe for preparing and tempering certain fine clays combined with a forming and firing routine was essential in the manufacture of distinctive looking and feeling St. Johns pots. In other words, there was a "shared repertoire" or specific way of working among a community of St. Johns potters. Ethnographies also reveal that chants, rituals, or taboos often accompanied or guided various production steps, thereby combining physical acts, spoken words, or other social rules in the production of a pot (Rice 1987:115).

By the early tenth century, groups throughout the entire St. Johns River Valley shared a St. Johns ceramic technology.[5] The rapid and complete shift from Colorinda to St. Johns II ceramic assemblages implies an influx of potters with intimate knowledge of the technological tradition of how to make St. Johns pottery. The migration of individuals or families, along with intermarriage, would have expanded the production of St. Johns pottery quickly over a vast area. As St. Johns potters moved into northeastern Florida, local Colorinda potters appear to have modified their ceramic assemblages to mirror those of the immigrants. While these new arrivals brought in different technical behaviors, local potters had been aware of St. Johns pottery through trade or other forms of exchange. Potters familiar with the St. Johns ceramic tradition taught locals how to make the chalky wares. The similarity of St. Johns wares across such a vast region reflects shared stylistic and technological practices learned among regularly interacting potters. Potter interaction has been shown to be a "significant factor" in shaping local styles, with both frequency and quality of interaction representing important variables (Herbich 1987:201).

Ethnographic data worldwide show that the process of making pottery is often conservative, as groups of interacting potters produce a consistent style and form through time. The learning of motor skills and muscle memory are key aspects of pottery production, and it is difficult to change them (Minar and Crown 2001:375). In fact, many potters are reluctant to alter the learned operating process and motor habits that might have taken years to master (Smith 2000:22; MacEachern 1998:114). Movement from one community of practice to another demands a significant "transformation" (Wenger 1998:103). Arnold (1998:357) estimates that "changes in the motor habit patterns required for pottery forming technologies may take at least a generation to change." Based on ethnoarchaeological and ethnographic data, Clark (2001:12–22) suggests that ceramic technological style, or nondecorative manufacturing processes, is a useful marker for detecting instances of migration in the archaeological record.

Refuse deposits at a few northeastern Florida sites such as Dolphin Reef, McCormack, and the Mill Cove Complex (near the Grant Mound) evince mixed assemblages suggestive of a transition from Colorinda to St. Johns II. In contrast, nearby sites with coeval or even slightly earlier radiometric dates contain essentially pure St. Johns II habitation middens. Thus, the former sites may represent Colorinda communities that converted to the production of St. Johns II pottery, while the latter lean toward communities of immigrants with full knowledge of how St. Johns pots should look and feel. The grossly homogeneous nature of the physical characteristics of St. Johns assemblages is part of a broader constellation of practice throughout the entire St. Johns River Valley between AD 900 and 1250. However, beneath this veneer of homogeneity, we may be able to distinguish smaller communities of practice at a microscale (Herbich 1987:196). Detailed ceramic attribute analyses can help draw out subtle variabilities or microstyles indicative of smaller interacting communities of potters (e.g., McGill 2013). At present, such technological data are lacking for large assemblages across the region, but these questions should be the focus of future research.

## THE MILL COVE COMPLEX

If we were to look across the Florida landscape one thousand years ago, two civic-ceremonial centers would stand out with respect to the quantity of imported exotic stone, metal, and other minerals deriving from the early Mississippian world. One is Mount Royal, a large, single mortuary-mound site along the northern middle section of the river between Lake George and Little Lake George. The other, situated nearly 100 km to the north near the river's mouth, is the Mill Cove Complex. Perched on a 10 m high bluff overlooking a broad cove in the river channel, this site incorporates two prominent architectural features, known as Shields (8DU12) and Grant (8DU14) Mounds. Spaced about 750 m apart, these dissimilar-looking yet coeval communal cemeteries bracket domestic areas consisting of refuse scatters, variable-density shell middens, and subsurface pits of various sorts (Ashley 2005a, 2005b, 2012). Near the Shields Mound is Kinzey's Knoll, a ritual or special-event midden containing the remains of ceremonial feasting, ritual artifact production and use, and burial preparation (Ashley and Rolland 2014). Radiometric assays from various contexts date the mound complex to circa AD 900–1250. Kinzey's Knoll and other areas closest to Shields Mound date to the late tenth and early eleventh century. Middens adjacent to Grant Mound also date to this early time frame. In fact, these contexts from Mill Cove provide some of the earliest St. Johns II dates in northeastern Florida.

Grant and Shields are similar yet morphologically different. Both were above-ground, accretionary cemeteries with an abundance of human remains and grave goods, including both local and exotic items (Ashley 2012:104–107). Each was built with reference to existing topographic features in the form of high relict dune landforms, further heightening and altering their visual prominence, depending on perspective. Like the mound at Mount Royal, Grant and Shields each had a

distinctive set of embankments that approached the mound from the side opposite the river.[6] Moore (1895:473) described Grant's shape as the "usual truncated
cone," 8 m tall, and Shields as a platform mound "unlike in form any aboriginal
earthwork on the river." Shields was more than a mound; it was a linear feature
about 180 m long, 45 m wide, and 3–6 m tall. Moore focused his excavations on
the flat-topped mound at the northern end, where he encountered hundreds of
human burials. What looks to be a second mound, untouched by Moore, sits atop
the southern terminus of the linear ridge. Limited testing of the mound in 2014,
however, failed to generate any artifacts, colored sands, or evidence of human construction. It is still unclear how much of the linear feature composing the Shields
Mound is natural dune ridge and how much is anthropogenic fill.

Moore's excavation of the Grant and Shields Mounds produced roughly the
same materials, but certain artifact categories varied greatly in quantity between
the mounds (Ashley 2012:122). For instance, copper and ground-stone tools such
as celts and tobacco pipes were much more prevalent in the Grant Mound. Compared to the "meager list of copper" from Shields, Moore's (1895:465–466) excavation of Grant yielded copper beads, pins, and embossed geometric plates as
well as rare copper-covered biconical earspools and two long-nosed god mask-
ettes. These last items likely were manufactured between AD 1000 and 1200 in
the American Bottom (Kelly 2012). In addition, various thin sheets of distinctly
hammered copper with embossed dots and circular rings from Grant, Shields,
and Mount Royal are "nearly identical" to the Cummings-McCarthy headdress
plate from the American Bottom, which likely "found its way to Illinois by way
of the emerging Mississippian trade routes," circa AD 900–1050 (Sampson and
Esarey 1993:463, 468). Through optical emission spectrographic analysis, Goad
(1978:137–148) linked a sample of 23 copper artifacts recovered by Moore from
Grant and Mount Royal to five "ore clusters" in the Southeast (Appalachian Mountains) and four "ore clusters" in the Great Lakes region. Finished artifacts crafted
of this ductile metal were undoubtedly making their way to these St. Johns River
settlements by the tenth and eleventh centuries.

In contrast, heirloom or salvaged Archaic period (c. 6000–1000 BC) artifacts,
such as bannerstones and stemmed projectile points, were far more common in
the Shields Mound. Shields also produced at least one red jasper bead similar to
those found on Archaic sites in Florida. Two uniquely shaped ground-stone spatu-
late celts of Mississippian origins were also recovered from this mound. Only five
other such celts have come from Florida sites, including three from the mortuary
mound at Mount Royal and one from Amelia Island to the north. While human
burials were interred in various ways in both mounds, Moore's brief, impression-
istic, and at times ambiguous excavation descriptions hint at primary burials being more common in Grant Mound, and secondary bundled interments being
more frequent in Shields.

Unit testing beneath and adjacent to the Grant Mound in the 1980s and 1990s demonstrated deep middens containing materials that predate and postdate St. Johns II occupations (Thunen 2005). We have recently begun a reanalysis of the pottery recovered during these excavations. Preliminary indications suggest an extensive Woodland component that contains moderate amounts of Colorinda pottery. The situation is completely different near the Shields Mound, where intensive shovel testing and unit excavations over the past twenty years have revealed an essentially pure St. Johns II component (Ashley 2005b:295). Of the more than 20,000 sherds recovered thus far, only a small handful are Colorinda, and even fewer sherds date to earlier or later times. An understanding of what the difference between the Grant and Shields vicinities might mean benefits from a broader regional perspective.

## PUSH-PULL FACTORS OF ST. JOHNS II POPULATION MOVEMENTS

When espousing migration as explanation, researchers must demonstrate the historical or antecedent circumstances for population movement within both the place of immigration and the place of emigration (Cameron 2000:555). In effect, we must identify the historically specific push-pull factors at the points of origin and destination that structured any given migration. Though a diverse array of circumstances might stimulate demographic displacement, potential movers often search for new homes in areas where they have some degree of familiarity, through social interaction, alliance, or kinship (Anthony 1990:900). Migrants are unlikely to move to locations about which they have little or no information.

The tenth century witnessed the first-time appearance of St. Johns II sites along the lower St. Johns. In fact, the movement of St. Johns II populations into the region appears to have been part of a wholesale reordering of settlements along at least the northern third of the St. Johns River. Current archaeological evidence reveals population aggregations near Mount Royal and Mill Cove Complex, the two mound centers that gained regional prominence during the early Mississippian period. Few confirmed habitation-burial mound sites date specifically to AD 900–1250 in the intervening area (Ashley 2012:102). If this was the case, what historical conditions might have enticed communities to move downriver (north) and resettle along the lower reaches of the St. Johns?

The dating of the advent of St. Johns II sites in northeastern Florida to circa AD 900 provides a tantalizing clue. The tenth century set the stage for a radical turning point in southeastern Native American history (Kelly 2012; Pauketat 2004; Pauketat and Emerson 1997). This era marks the materialization of the urban landscape of Cahokia, which straddled the Mississippi River near present-day St. Louis (see chapter 2 in this volume). In its wake, smaller mound center polities sprouted across the Southeast. Subsistence in many locations shifted from foraging and small-scale gardening to extensive floodplain maize farming. Long-distance interaction networks, mostly inactive for the past few centuries, reanimated. What followed during Mississippian times (AD 1000–1500 and beyond) was an extraordinary flow of domestic and exotic materials that enmeshed polities in a vast Indigenous world system that articulated communities of varying sizes across much of eastern North America (Brown et al. 1990; King and Freer 1995; Pauketat 2004). Exchange, however, was merely one of several mechanisms of interaction responsible for bringing nonlocal materials to northeastern Florida.

An unanticipated opportunity to engage in these interaction networks in some capacity, perhaps as suppliers of marine shell and other Florida resources, prompted broadscale settlement changes as groups jockeyed to gain access to strategic locations and resources. No mound centers in Florida or along the Atlantic coast, dating to the opening centuries of the Mississippian period, received more exotica from the interior Southeast and Midwest than did Mill Cove Complex and Mount Royal. The success of these two centers and the chance to be a part of what was going on there likely drew people to these locations. Although the move north might have been primed by the rebirth of long-distance interaction and exchange, the decision to move was much more than an automated reaction to a distant demand for shell and other resources. It was a calculated outcome of social and political choices made by individuals and small groups who eventually chose to leave their homeland and start anew in the north. The eventual coalescence of St. Johns and Colorinda communities, however, would have necessitated new means of social integration, conflict resolution, and community identity formation that likely required constant negotiations between peoples of different cultural backgrounds (Birch 2012; Kowalewski 2006).

Although established 96.5 river km from one another along different segments of the St. Johns River, the Mill Cove Complex and Mount Royal have similar natural settings and layouts. The section of the lower river channel near Mill Cove is remarkably similar to that of the northern middle St. Johns basin immediately above Lake George. A broad river channel, distinct shorelines, large coves, and in-river islands characterize the immediate vicinity of both Mount Royal and Mill Cove Complex (Ashley and Rolland 2014:268). Rather than being positioned closer to the coastal estuary on lands adjacent to or surrounded by expansive tidal marshes, as are most St. Johns II sites in the area, the Mill Cove Complex is situated along the river's south side on a higher bluff overlooking a broad bend in the river channel. Thus, the Mill Cove Complex locality is physiographically analogous to the middle St. Johns and was perhaps chosen because it "looked like home" (Goldstein 2002:357 makes a similar argument for colonization of Aztalan in Wisconsin).

Another feature of the Mill Cove Complex reminiscent of the middle St. Johns is Shields Mound itself. Randall (2013) has drawn attention to the historical value of Archaic period shell and sand monuments to later St. Johns communities of the middle St. Johns. Millennia ago, Archaic period populations modified certain low-lying banks of the middle St. Johns River by piling freshwater shells into small heaps and massive annular and linear mounds, fashioning an undulating anthropogenic landscape hundreds of meters long, at least 50 m wide, and as much as 10 m high. Later in time, some of these large linear shell mounds, abandoned for centuries or perhaps millennia, were co-opted as sacred constructions on which post-Archaic St. Johns mortuary took place in the form of conical sand mounds. In fact, Indigenous populations of the middle St. Johns had a long history of constructing sacred places on the remains of ancient human-built features. One site, the Juniper Spring Run Dune, presents "a potential example of St. Johns [II groups] interacting with a natural feature that may have been mistaken for a shell mound in antiquity" (Randall 2013:19).

Upon the migrants' arrival at Mill Cove, a new sacred precinct might have been emplaced on a foreign landscape, which may have required the reconfiguration of cultural meanings and behaviors. To ease this transition, the St. Johns interlopers might have sought out a landscape that reminded them of their homeland: perhaps one relatively free of evidence of previous habitation and in proximity to a linear topographic feature, albeit of sand, somewhat similar to the shell ridges of the middle St. Johns. The natural rolling topography and dune ridge may have served as a cosmic footprint to structure the foreign community's village plan, with the mortuary mound placed on a preexisting dune ridge (Shields Mound) and another natural rise selected for ritual, mortuary preparation, and feasting (Kinzey's Knoll).

Feasting appears to have preceded the erection of the Shields cemetery, as evidenced by discrete deposits of St. Johns II shell midden on the premound ground surface (Moore 1895:467). This opening act may have been part of a transformational process with which they sanctified the space and rendered it their own. In effect, the new arrivals were imprinting the lower St. Johns landscape with a middle St. Johns cultural signature. The presence of Archaic bannerstones and more than 100 projectile points at Shields—and Archaic stone points at the nearby ritual midden at Kinzey's Knoll—speak to rituals that forged a connection to their sacred primordial past (Ashley and Rolland 2014). Acquisition of these pieces of antiquity may have required them to maintain connections to distant kin or engage in quests to seek out such items. The bannerstones and red jasper bead might have even come from Mount Taylor mound sites in northern Florida. Mount Royal itself contains a rich Archaic component from which scores of chert bifaces have been recovered (Jones and Tesar 2001), suggesting that Mount Royal may have served as a source for some of the lithic artifacts at Mill Cove.

As for Grant Mound, with its more traditional conical shape and underlying Colorinda deposits, might it represent a cemetery associated with local populations, who coalesced with the St. Johns II newcomers and came to share their ceramic technology and other aspects of culture and ideology? The two mounds composing the "complex" might betray a social division, with one segment of the Mill Cove population affiliated, socially or ceremonially, with the Shields Mound, and the other affiliated with Grant Mound. Perhaps a social duality of local and newcomer or earth and sky or summer and winter existed. The process of coalescence or fusion of formerly distinct communities has been proposed for the creation of Mississippian settlements with multiple mound centers elsewhere in the Southeast (Blitz 1999). At Mill Cove, periodic social gatherings that involved mound building, mortuary, ritual, and feasting provided mechanisms through which residents negotiated community integration, solidarity, and identity.

The residents of Mill Cove had a rich and varied ritual life focused on death and burial, where the living, recently departed, and revered ancestors shared space in sacred areas of the site (Ashley and Rolland 2014). The internal structure of the two burial mounds, based on Moore's description and what we currently know about other Florida mounds, suggests that Grant and Shields formed slowly and episodically, as rituals were acted out and new burials or mortuary items were added. The reality of paired mounds or paired social groups was common among southeastern Indians (Hudson 1976). In fact, moieties or social divisions were purportedly present among contact period Timucua of northern Florida (Milanich 2004:222). These social institutions often assumed certain complementary social, ritual, or political functions performed to reaffirm membership and history for the good of the entire community. Perhaps the differing material items from Grant and Shields highlight specialized rituals attributable to each mound (and social group who controlled the mound).

In time, the Mill Cove Complex undoubtedly gained regional prominence, as it distinguished itself from other St. Johns II sites in the region by housing the two largest mortuary mounds with the most interments and greatest amount and range of exotica north of Mount Royal (Ashley 2012:104). In fact, the other ten contemporaneous mounds are all much smaller in size and height, and the quantity of in-mound grave goods pales in comparison to those from Grant and Shields. Contributing to the aura of Mill Cove Complex may well have been the fact that it was the founding St. Johns II settlement in the region, a strong possibility based on its early radiocarbon dates from deposits near the Shields Mound. Thus what constitutes what we know today as St. Johns II in extreme northeastern Florida may not be the result of local development exclusively through cultural diffusion or population movement and replacement, but rather a more complex and nuanced process that was part of a large-scale demographic change.

Considering all these factors, the Mill Cove Complex manifests some of the cross-cultural features commonly associated with coalescence. These include movement to a new place for certain resources, increased community size, intensification of trade, communal leadership and political economy (Ashley 2012:116–124), and structured community integration via corporate kin groups or moieties. Coalescence is also a common response to "social upheaval and/or external pressures" (Birch 2012:648; and see Kowalewski 2006:117). In the Mill Cove case, conditions of stress may have involved not the initial St. Johns populations but local

Colorinda groups, as suggested by their mortuary patterns. As mentioned previously, Colorinda and Kelvin (southeastern Georgia) burials often contain facedown individuals. In fact, excavations at the McCormack site revealed five prone interments, including four facedown individuals in a single pit with one lying atop the other three. Among other populations worldwide, it has been argued that burial in a prone position was performed "to ensure that the deceased did not return . . . and directed the dead on a journey away from the living" (Jacobi 2003:102). Moreover, facedown burial is often set aside for enemies and individuals somehow different from other community members. Thus, Colorinda populations may have been at odds with groups to the north, and their coalescence with immigrant St. Johns peoples may have helped stabilize the situation.

## CONCLUSION

This chapter offers an alternative explanatory framework for exploring St. Johns II origins along the lower St. Johns River of northeastern Florida. Using a community of practice approach, I interpret the emergence of the St. Johns II ceramic technology in northeastern Florida around AD 900 as the result of the immigration of peoples from the south with intimate knowledge of the St. Johns pottery-making tradition. St. Johns wares required specially processed clays, tempering materials, and firing conditions to create chalky textured, buff- to gray-colored pots. This shift in ceramics was part of a broader suite of changes that involved a population increase with more village-mound settlements (including some in new locations and others on landforms similar to those of the middle St. Johns), larger forms of monumental architecture, and differing ritual and mortuary practices that were similar to those taking place at Mount Royal to the south. Taken together, these new features further suggest a northern displacement of St. Johns II people, who attempted to imprint their middle St. Johns homeland onto the lower St. Johns landscape. Impetus for this relocation was sparked to some extent by emerging Mississippian interactions in which coastal resources were in demand. The end of the production of Colorinda pottery occurred shortly after the arrival of St. Johns II groups, suggesting that the region's small Colorinda population was drawn into the new St. Johns II social order by the early tenth century.

Among the earliest St. Johns II radiometric dates in northeastern Florida are those from the Mill Cove Complex, the largest settlement and the site of the two most significant mortuary mounds in the region. The presence of the Shields and Grant Mounds at Mill Cove hints at a social duality whose formation, I suggest, might be traced to a merger between locals and newcomers. Once these communities were established, the sacred geography of Mill Cove and Mount Royal became magnetics that restructured the demography of the northern half of the St. Johns River Valley during the early Mississippian period. Both communities forged contacts connecting them to far-off Early Mississippian centers such as Macon Plateau and Cahokia and enabling the acquisition of exotic materials and artifacts for local ritual, mortuary, and social reproduction. Only through a historical and multiscalar approach can we begin to account for the complex and multidimensional array of human relationships that contributed to the origins of the Mill Cove Complex.

## Acknowledgments

I thank Liz Watts Malouchos and Alleen Betzenhauser for their invitation to participate in this volume and for their help throughout the process. Thanks also to Vicki Rolland for reading an earlier version of this chapter and Mike Boyles for his help with the figures. I also greatly appreciate an anonymous reviewer's comments and information on prone burials.

## Notes

1. I use the term *migration* to mean the movement and enduring resettlement of people in a new location that encompasses changes in both their physical and social milieu. As such, this relocation or population movement does not have to cover a great distance but does involve a deliberate and permanent transfer of people beyond their recognized social territory or normal settlement-subsistence range.

2. Two sand burial mounds, Browne (8DU62) and Walker Point (8NA48), have been tied loosely to local Colorinda populations (Ashley 2006:92–93), although establishing the precise cultural affiliation of each mound has proven problematic. In fact, no direct evidence exists linking either mound to the Colorinda period.

3. Lollis and colleagues (2015) have added a new wrinkle to the natural versus temper debate by proposing that spicule-laden organic muck (either dry or burned) was used as temper. They posit that such tempering adds sponge spicules to the paste and contributes to the characteristic soft chalky texture of St. Johns pottery. Preliminary laboratory test bar firing suggests that high frequencies of sponge spicules are not correlated with the soft kaolinite or "chalky" texture (Lollis et al. 2015:105).

4. Sponge spicules have been identified in varying quantities in other soil matrices (Espenshade 1983; Schwandes and Collins 1994). However, in these instances clay or sponge spicule volume was too low to render St. Johns chalky pottery.

5. The only other time we see one dominant ceramic tradition distributed across this same region was during the Late Archaic, when Orange fiber-tempered pottery diffused from its origin points along the Atlantic coast. Sassaman (2010:75) attributes its spread to population movement, although in the opposite direction. He argues that coastal Orange groups "relocated to the middle St. Johns where they coalesced with Mount Taylor groups with whom they had a pre-established alliance."

6. According to descriptions by Moore (1895), Shields, Grant, and Mount Royal each had a causeway consisting of two low and parallel earthen berms that banked a slightly depressed avenue. At Shields and Mount Royal, the causeway linked the mound to a pond hundreds of meters away. Soil scraped from the avenue and perhaps mined from the pond is believed by Moore to have been used in berm construction. These Early Mississippian period sand monuments are the only ones in Florida with such causeways. The Rattlesnake Causeway at Cahokia is contemporaneous, but its construction consists of a high and wide earthen embankment bordered on each side by a linear ditch (Baires 2014b). Though these berms are morphologically different, similar dates of construction suggest that some sort of connection might exist between those along the St. Johns River and the one at Cahokia.

# 12

# RESILIENCE IN LATE MOUNDVILLE'S ECONOMY

Jera R. Davis

> *Persistence of the normal is usually greater than the effect of disturbance.*
>
> —Barbara Tuchman, *A Distant Mirror: The Calamitous 14th Century*

The Moundville site of west-central Alabama has received ample scholarly attention as the seat of a Mississippian polity that incorporated numerous settlements once scattered along a 40 km stretch of the Black Warrior River and its tributaries (Figure 12.1). At its political apex, it had all the monumental hallmarks of a Mississippian capital town: a built ceremonial landscape composed of over two dozen earthen mounds arranged around a plaza, all of it enclosed within a wooden palisade of 1.5 km in length (Blitz 2008). In a noted pattern of precontact decline throughout the Mississippian world (Anderson 1994; Blitz 1999; Blitz and Lorenz 2006; Knight 1997; Pollack 2004), Moundville's influence slowly diminished following rapid coalescence, a development mirrored in population dispersal and decreasing rates of monument construction. As Moundville's once lively neighborhoods gave way to cemeteries and as all but its northernmost mounds went silent, hinterland populations burgeoned (Maxham 2004; Scarry et al. 2016). New communities formed, centered on small-scale single-mound sites and other nodes of religious expression. For a time, outlying communities maintained ancestral grounds at Moundville itself (Wilson 2010) and perhaps gave deference to its high-status caretakers (Jackson et al. 2016), but by the beginning of the fifteenth century alternative cemeteries and religious specialists had appeared in the hinterlands, signaling that Moundville's overarching relevance in valley life was at last coming to an end.

It is within this cultural and historical context, hinterland Moundville from the late fourteenth to the end of the sixteenth centuries (Table 12.1), that the present study is situated. This study is intended as a small step toward understanding one aspect—economy—of the latter phases of Moundville's history. To this end, I draw on data made available in recent attempts to explore the social and ritual mechanisms that fueled production, exchange, and consumption. I address four kinds of objects: shell beads, sandstone "paint palettes," greenstone celts, and stone pen-

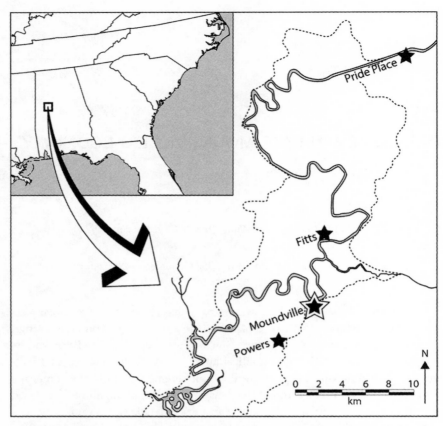

Figure 12.1. Black Warrior River Valley with locations of sites mentioned in the text.
(Jera R. Davis)

### Table 12.1. Mississippian Phases and Sequences for the Black Warrior River Valley

| Years calibrated | Ceramic phase | Developmental phase | Residential and ceremonial phase |
|---|---|---|---|
| AD 1520–1690 | Moundville IV | collapse and reorganization | — |
| AD 1400–1520 | late Moundville III | | outmigration and necropolis |
| | early Moundville III | paramountcy entrenched | |
| AD 1250–1400 | Moundville II | | |
| | | regional consolidation | consolidation and emplacement |
| AD 1120–1250 | Moundville I | | |
| | | initial centralization | — |

*Source:* Adapted from Porth 2017:Figure 1.4.

dants. Because these objects are argued to have been critical in the maintenance of different kinds of relationships, their analysis here permits a more focused understanding of the various motivations underlying late Moundville's economy. As the analysis here makes clear, the differences between earlier and later economic life in the valley are less radical than one might expect given the degree to which political life had changed in the intervening centuries. Indeed, they have enough in common to warrant an application of resilience theory.

## RESILIENCE IN ANTHROPOLOGICAL PERSPECTIVE

Recent research into polity decline has dispelled the notion that decentralization of the sort that occurred across the late prehistoric Southeast equates with a simple reversion to pre-complex social, political, and economic relationships. Moreover, total civilizational collapse, a prevalent notion in popular anthropology (e.g., Diamond 2005) is, on closer inspection, exceedingly rare in human history (Eisenstadt 1988; McAnany and Yoffee 2010; Tainter 2006). Instead, archaeologists note that the age-old attitudes and beliefs implicated in polity formation outlive polity decline. For this reason, they often employ the vocabulary of resilience theory to understand how societies respond to political instability (Redman 2005). Resilience, a concept outlined and popularized in ecological systems theory (Holling 1973), is "the ability of a system to absorb disturbance and still retain its basic function and structure" (McAnany and Yoffee 2010:10). As applied to cultural systems, it is the capacity of a community to recover or regenerate in the wake of environmental, anthropogenic, or sociopolitical disruption (Adger 2000; Butzer 2012; Butzer and Endfield 2012; Dunning et al. 2012; Faulseit 2012; Fisher and Feinman 2005; Fisher et al. (ed.) 2009; Gotts 2007; McAnany and Yoffee 2010; Redman 1999; Redman and Kinzig 2003; Rosen and Rivera-Collazo 2012; Streeter et al. 2012).

The point of resilience theory is not that some structures survive disruption unchanged. Rather, it is primarily a statement about different *rates* of change. The concept of resiliency is an old one in anthropological scholarship. In a sense, Redfield was addressing resiliency in his landmark work *The Little Community and Peasant Society and Culture* (1989). He described how the "little tradition" drives the restructuring of social, political, and economic relationships that accompanies the transition to an acephalous society. Though intertwined in innumerable ways with the "great tradition" of elites, the little tradition was always present, upheld without much scrutiny as it played itself out in the lives of the general population. For the purposes of this chapter, we may think of the little tradition as those economic relationships embedded in kinship and community, slow-to-change drivers of production and exchange relationships that have been important throughout human history. Thus, while political change can be rapid and episodic, other aspects of culture are far more conservative. It is to those aspects that we must look when attempting to understand the twilight years of politically complex societies.

While resilience is a more accurate term than collapse for describing how societies respond to distress, not all societies are equally resilient. For example, those
that encourage broad political participation are generally more resilient than those
in which leadership is more rigidly defined (Gunderson and Holling 2002; Holling
2001:394; Peregrine 2017). Diversity and flexibility in decision-making promote
innovation and empower community members to exercise their specific gifts in
the interest of efficiently solving problems. Likewise, resilience also describes societies in which immaterial forms of capital constitute primary funds of power,
for those societies are defined by a greater degree of reciprocity, trust, and cooperation than those in which power is a function of one's ability to control access
to essential material resources. Of course, politics in early complex societies like
Moundville are rarely so straightforward. Aspiring community leaders and their
supporters may draw on material and immaterial forms of capital simultaneously
and may transition in their emphases over time (Blanton et al. 1996). Thus, any
given society's capacity for resilience may fluctuate in tandem with shifts in that
society's political culture. With this in mind, I turn now to the social and political context of disruption at Moundville.

## ECONOMY IN EARLY MOUNDVILLE

To understand late Moundville's economy, one must first grasp what it had been.
Fortunately for the purposes of this chapter, Moundville has served as a sort of
staging area for research into the economic underpinnings of early complexity
in the southeastern United States and beyond. The most influential statement
has undoubtedly been Welch's (1991) political economy model, which positioned
elites as beneficiaries of an exploitative arrangement designed to extract labor and
goods from nonelite producers (see also Marcoux 2007 for a slightly stronger re-
statement). Welch's model accounted for what was then interpreted as a three-
tiered settlement hierarchy wherein administrative middlemen at single-mound
sites funneled goods from the hinterlands to elites at the local center. With reference to Peebles and Kus (1977), the model described a tributary relationship
in which subsistence producers filled centralized stores in exchange for axes and
hoes, indispensable tools made of durable nonlocal stone that elites controlled by
virtue of their privileged position in long-distance trade networks. In this way,
elites amassed subsistence wealth that they, in turn, used not only to fund monument construction, military forays, and lavish displays, but also to support arti-
sans who, under their supervision, converted local raw materials into craft items
destined to be traded for exotic "prestige goods" (*sensu* Frankenstein and Rowlands 1978). Success in these endeavors demonstrated elite efficacy and reinforced
institutionalized inequality.

As with any good archaeological model, Welch's produced clear expectations.
In so doing, it provided a framework for future research that in the ensuing two-
and-a-half decades directly or indirectly inspired several peer-reviewed publica-

tions in addition to at least two doctoral theses (Thompson 2011; Wilson 2005), six master's theses (Barrier 2007; Barry 2004; Davis 2008; Marcoux 2000; Phillips 2006; Salberg 2013), and numerous conference presentations. Though nearly all of its claims have been contradicted, the array of investigations that Welch's model stimulated has made Moundville's economy one of the best understood of any major Mississippian polity. This research deserves a more thorough synthesis than the necessarily brief and incomplete summary I embark on now.

There is little archaeological basis for statements regarding what might have passed for a political economy in the preceding Late Woodland phase that Alabama archaeologists call West Jefferson (Jenkins 1976). However, the populous villages that West Jefferson hunter-gatherers occupied during the warmer months have yielded such high numbers of microdrills (tools involved in the production of shell beads [Ensor 1991:36; Knight 2010:58]) that several archaeologists infer incipient competition between tribal leaders who used shell valuables as primitive wealth (Pope 1989; Steponaitis 1986). At the same time, increasing reliance on maize brought people into closer relationships with specific plots of productive land than ever before (Scarry 1993). The shift toward maize-centric foodways is also reflected in changing cooking pot forms, from ovaloid jars adapted to preparing foods by direct-fire cooking to globular jars designed for slow boiling (Briggs 2016; Hawsey 2015).

By AD 1120, many had dispersed across the high terrace at Hemphill Bend into a loosely patterned settlement centered on at least two platform mounds and a small plaza (Davis et al. 2015). Emerging leaders manipulated a modest assortment of local and nonlocal valuables, including embellished serving wares, sandstone palettes, and large bifaces of the sort wielded as daggers by the supernatural "Birdman" in contemporary iconography (Steponaitis 1992). Judging by the size of this assemblage, we can assume that distinctions between these leaders and the rest of the community were largely symbolic, a factor not so much of the ability to make material demands of nonkin, but of their ability to demonstrate a special connection between themselves and the temperamental supernatural forces that governed community well-being.

Around the turn of the thirteenth century, the populace undertook a near-total reorganization of the built environment in a deliberate attempt to spatialize and make timeless the status distinctions that had gradually taken hold over the course of the previous century (Davis et al. 2015). They gathered en masse at Moundville (Hammerstedt et al. 2016; Maxham 2004:126). The product of their combined labor—Moundville's mound-and-plaza arrangement—has become an oft-cited example of a sociogram in which the size and position of mound pairs around the central plaza corresponded to the size and prestige of the corporate group that built and used them (Knight 1998).

The core mound arrangement was a blueprint for sociopolitical interaction during Moundville's height, a sort of council house with assigned seating writ large. Yet the tensions inherent in this configuration are not obviously replicated in other material domains, for finished goods of every category have been identified across all investigated areas (Knight 2010:358; Thompson 2011; Wilson 2001, 2008). The same is true of the specialized tools and raw materials used to make them, though the latter concentrate in supposed production locales atop mounds (Knight 2010) and within off-mound households here and there throughout the site (Thompson 2011). The overall pattern is one of iconic redundancy (à la Renfrew 2001:18), in which economic interdependency between Moundville's corporate groups afforded everyone, regardless of rank, with the same types of essential valuables—ritual gear, display items, utilitarian objects, and other valued goods (Thompson 2011:225). Some distinctions did exist. For example, while most Moundvillians wore pendants of hematite, sandstone, and coal, elites donned ones of hammered copper. This finding suggests that some categories of objects were defined according to a gradation of value (Davis 2016; Thompson 2011). Because "the evaluation of objects can serve as metaphors for the evaluation of people" (Lesure 1999:28), the patterns summarized here imply a heterarchical social order of internally stratified peer groups bound to one another through complementary crafting and exchange (Knight 2010:365).

There is no reason to believe that Moundville's social order—which was negotiated during Moundville's rise, materialized in the sociogram, and reinforced in reciprocity—was rendered irrelevant when, in the fourteenth century, households began migrating out from under the direct gaze of mound-dwelling elites and into the hinterlands (Maxham 2004:129). Indeed, the fact that they soon returned to establish group cemeteries exactly where they once had lived is a sign that claims to ancestral ground at the local center remained fundamental to identity and, therefore, social interaction (Wilson 2010). Nonetheless, this out-migration represents a dramatic break in the constitution of community and the use of space (Wilson 2016), one predicated on a constellation of factors. For one, the defensive palisade that once encircled the site had been allowed to fall into ruin for the first time in over a century, presumably because a former menace no longer posed a threat. If it were not for the fact that Moundville was abandoned in a patterned way, archaeologists would likely conclude, therefore, that the subsequent dispersal was principally in response to a decreased concern for common defense. However, because low-status locales on the southern plaza periphery were the first to be abandoned, internal factionalism is also perceived to have played a significant role: those who had the least to gain from the social order were the first to leave.

One wonders how the decision to leave affected these households' responsibilities in the intricate web of reciprocal obligations that had for so long countered the tendency to fission. On the one hand, in traditional societies it is virtually impossible to sever those ties without antagonizing peers, so the fact that households resettled nearby suggests that they left on passably good terms. On the other hand, their absence in day-to-day affairs would be obvious to everyone left behind, a constant reminder of their lesser involvement in the affairs of the center. And yet, all involved had come to rely on the goods and services ensured through active participation, not only for the furtherance of society at large, but also for the reproduction of its constituent groups. Until those needs could be met by other means, efforts were likely made to maintain some semblance of the status quo.

## ARCHAEOLOGICAL CONTEXTS

By the fifteenth century, life in the Black Warrior Valley had assumed a very different character. So far as is currently known, the Moundville site itself was largely abandoned, home to only a fraction of mound-centered households and some poorly understood dwellings on the site's western periphery (Davis et al. 2015; Knight 2010; Porth 2017). In the hinterlands, community life centered on isolated single-mound sites distributed from the fall line to approximately 40 km south, separated from one another by uninhabited zones (Myer 2003). Most people lived in nonmound settlements that Mississippian archaeologists have typically called "farmsteads," though many now question the applicability of that label (Scarry et al. 2016). In the Black Warrior Valley, these were organized on the landscape with respect to several factors including proximity to navigable water, well-drained soils, and single-mound sites (Hammerstedt et al. 2016). Proximity to Moundville proper was at most a secondary concern.

This chapter is focused on three such sites occupied contemporaneously during the Moundville III and early Moundville IV phases: the Pride Place site (1TU1; Davis 2016; Marcoux 2007), the Fitts site (1TU876; Myer 2003), and the Powers site (1HA11; Welch 1998:146–148). These sites yielded a great amount of data, much of it analyzed in accordance with Knight (2010) by me and also by University of Alabama graduate students and employees of Moundville's Office of Archaeological Research (OAR). With the permission of those archaeologists, I gratefully applied those data to this research. Though complete reports are not available for any of these sites, some statements have been made regarding their behavioral, cultural, and historical contexts.

Of course, the nature of the archaeological record obviates a full investigation of Moundville's economy, but it can provide vignettes. For such I turned to the most durable aspect of Moundville's archaeological assemblages: lithics. Lithic objects represent a cross-section of much that once constituted Moundville's economy, from the mundane and profuse to the sui generis; thus, conclusions grounded in lithic assemblages reflect important aspects of the valley's economy as a whole (Cobb 2000; Whittaker 1994). The Pride Place, Fitts, and Powers sites illustrate this point in that the residents of these sites seem to have made the same sorts of items while also disproportionately contributing certain kinds of artifacts to the larger economy (Figure 12.2).

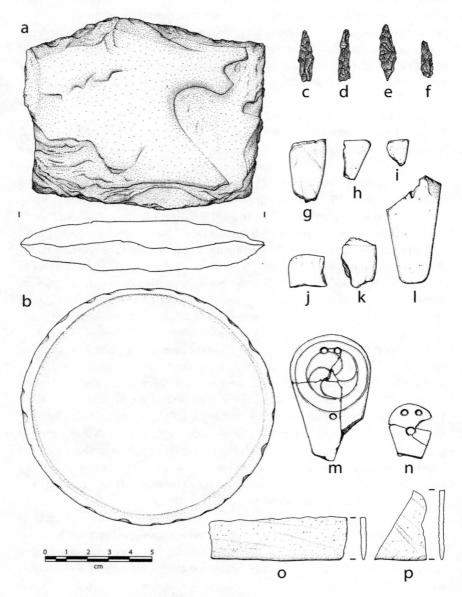

Figure 12.2. Examples of craft objects and tools recovered from the Pride Place, Fitts, and Powers sites: *a*, a greenstone celt preform from the Powers site; *b*, fine gray micaceous sandstone paint palette from the Pride Place site; *c–f*, microdrills from the Fitts site; *g–l*, pendant fragments from the Fitts site; *m–n*, pendants from the Powers site; *o–p*, ferruginous sandstone saws from the Pride Place site. (Jera R. Davis)

## Pride Place (1TU1)

The Pride Place site (Figure 12.3) sits atop a Holocene age first terrace overlooking the falls of the Black Warrior River approximately 23 km north of the Moundville site at the polity's supposed northern boundary. The Moundville III component there is spread across 0.25 ha of a natural rise located about 50 m from the river. Pride Place has attracted archaeological interest for nearly 90 years, beginning with excavations conducted by the Alabama Museum of Natural History in 1933 under the direction of David L. DeJarnette and Walter B. Jones. In 1998 OAR conducted the most extensive excavations there to date, later supplemented by annual University of Alabama field schools in 2007, 2008, and 2009. The Mississippian component at Pride Place includes a palimpsest of two domestic structures, associated pits, a broad sheet midden, a tiny, special-purpose flexed-pole construction, and nine graves including several of the "stone box" style, the southernmost examples in the Mississippian world (Jacobi 1999). In the Cumberland and Tennessee River Valleys, stone boxes are found with and without human remains, the latter often referred to as empty graves or "cenotaphs." These had temporarily housed corpses in preparation for defleshing, bundling, and later reburial (Brown 1981). Pride Place's stone box graves suggest that ritual on the outskirts of the polity catered to a minority population with exotic funerary customs. One wonders whether Moundville's religious leaders sanctioned this behavior.

People at Pride Place worked and manipulated sandstone "paint palettes," portable altars wielded by important religious figures at Moundville and elsewhere (Knight 2010:72–169; Steponaitis 2016); one member of the mortuary population was buried with his head resting on a notched and incised palette. I evaluated whether palettes had been made at the site (Davis 2016). To summarize: excava-

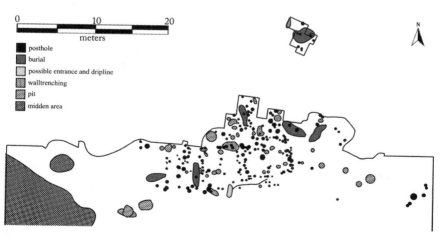

Figure 12.3. Pride Place site map. (Jera R. Davis)

tions at Pride Place produced abundant debitage, sawn scrap, small discs, incomplete palettes, and other objects made out of Pottsville sandstone, which outcrops less than 200 m east of the site. Experimental attempts to chip and then grind palettes and small discs out of Pottsville sandstone produced an assemblage of debitage that in its form and size-grade distribution closely matched debitage retrieved from Mississippian contexts at Pride Place. I concluded on this basis that the finished sandstone objects found there had also been made there.

## Fitts (1TU876)

The Fitts site (Figure 12.4) is located in a plowed field on the west floodplain of Black Warrior River, approximately 4 km north of the Moundville site. Under the direction of Vernon J. Knight Jr. and Jennifer L. Myer, the Black Warrior Valley Survey discovered the site in summer 2000 and undertook test excavations there over the course of summers two and three years later. They exposed the remains of two small constructions—a short line of six postholes interpreted as part of a building and four posts arranged in a square possibly representing the footprint of a corn crib (Myer 2003)—but the data I highlight here mostly derive from Fitts's numerous refuse-filled pits.

Ferruginous sandstone saws and chert microdrills are present in low numbers throughout the Black Warrior Valley, but both are abundant at Fitts. These tools are tough enough to work marine shell and stone, the former for scoring material before snapping it into shape, the latter for perforating finished products. Myer

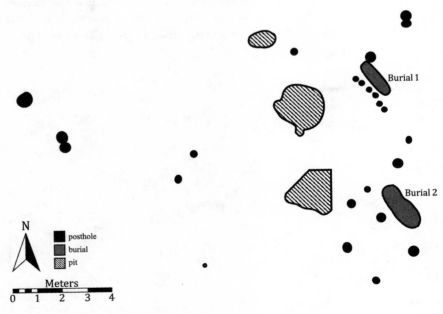

Figure 12.4. Fitts site map. (Jera R. Davis)

recovered one whole and six fragmented pendant "blanks," as well as ground, polished, and sawn scrap made out of a variety of materials including sandstone, ferruginous siltstone, and pink schist. Some fragmented blanks appear to have broken while being drilled, providing at least one explanation for the abundance of chert microdrills also recovered.

## Powers (1HA11)

The Powers site is located on Millians Creek, approximately 4 km southwest of Moundville (Figure 12.5). Though it appears to be roughly 1 ha in size, no systematic survey to define site boundaries has been conducted. Walter B. Jones and David L. DeJarnette surface collected the site in the 1930s, but the vast majority of artifacts analyzed for this research derive from the University of Alabama field schools conducted there in the 1980s and early 1990s. Aided by accumulations of daub brought to the surface by plowing of the site, students under the direction of Richard Krause located and excavated three rectangular structures of single-set post construction, one of which qualifies as a "Class III structure," a building so abnormally large that it is assumed to have served as a communal space for

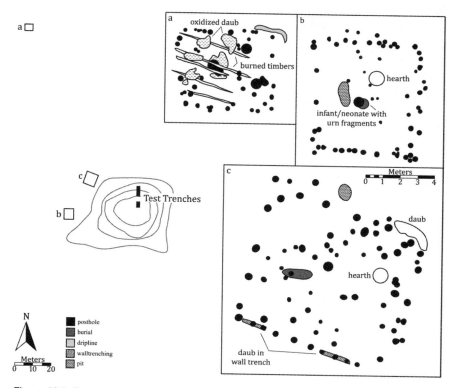

Figure 12.5. Powers site map; a, b, c = excavation units. (Jera R. Davis)

nearby households (Wilson 2008:57–59). Excavations encountered the extended burial of an adult male beneath its floor.

In contrast to the Mississippian residents of Pride Place and Fitts, those of the Powers site cannot conclusively be said to have focused in any way on nonsubsistence crafting. Rather, Powers is exceptional among the sites discussed here for the nature and magnitude of its greenstone artifact assemblage, which includes metates, ferruginous sandstone saws, abraders, unpolished greenstone debitage, and a possible celt preform. These items are what one would expect to find at a place where celts were made. The possible preform deserves additional comment; it is a large chunk of greenstone knapped into a thin rectangle, and if it is truly a preform—the premier evidence of celt manufacture—it is unique among all Black Warrior Valley archaeological assemblages. Its presence contradicts the notion that greenstone entered the valley from elsewhere in the form of finished celts that, once spent or broken, were recycled into other objects (Wilson 2001). Likewise, much of the greenstone debitage from Powers lacks polished surfaces, another indication that greenstone arrived as raw material and was subsequently worked on site.

## Abundance Measures

Abundance measures add a quantitative dimension to this research. They are calculated by way of straightforward mathematical formulae, wherein the numerator is the number of one kind of object recovered from a defined context and the denominator is some measure of background activity for that context (e.g., sum of utilitarian ware sherds as an index of cooking), a fraction that is finally multiplied by some multiple of ten to produce an index of occurrence (Knight 2010:352–353). The denominator controls for bias in artifact counts generated by assemblages of different sizes. Once the measures are calculated, it is a simple matter to determine which activities are "salient" for any given context, a descriptor that Knight (2010:353) applies to measures that are 50 percent higher than the pooled value (or measures expected for similar contexts).

The formulae most relevant here are those Knight devised for sandstone saws and greenstone. To these, I have added a similar formula for measuring microdrill abundance. They are as follows:

Sandstone Saw Index: total sandstone saws divided by total sherds × 10,000
Greenstone Index: total of three categories of greenstone (celt fragments + polished
    chips + shatter) divided by total sherds × 10,000
Microdrill Index: total microdrills divided by total sherds × 10,000

The data used in my calculations are tabulated in Table 12.2. Salient values by time period are displayed in bold. For comparison, Table 12.2 also includes data from datasets generated in accordance with Knight's classificatory scheme, spe-

## Table 12.2. Counts, Abundance Measures, and Pooled Values for Moundville Contexts

| | Total pot sherds | Sandstone saws | | Greenstone | | Microdrills | |
|---|---|---|---|---|---|---|---|
| | (n) | (n) | (index) | (n) | (index) | (n) | (index) |
| | | | Moundville III phase | | | | |
| Fitts | 6,230 | 143 | **229.5** | 15 | **24.1** | 55 | **88.3** |
| Powers | 5,299 | 14 | 26.4 | 16 | **30.2** | 15 | 28.3 |
| Pride Place | 5,598 | 5 | 8.9 | 6 | 10.7 | 31 | **55.4** |
| Mound E | 13,746 | 12 | 8.7 | 9 | 6.5 | 3 | 2.2 |
| Mound G | 3,638 | — | — | 1 | 2.7 | — | — |
| Mound P | 18,618 | 1 | 0.5 | 23 | 12.4 | 6 | 3.2 |
| Mound Q | 14,346 | 1 | 0.7 | 20 | 13.9 | 3 | 2.1 |
| Mound R | 796 | 6 | **75.4** | 15 | **188.4** | 1 | 12.6 |
| Totals | 68,271 | 182 | 26.7 | 105 | 15.4 | 114 | 16.7 |
| | | | Moundville II phase | | | | |
| Group A | 1,510 | 13 | **86.1** | 0 | 0.0 | — | — |
| Group C | 3,640 | 19 | **52.2** | 17 | **46.7** | 1 | 2.7 |
| Group E | 1,442 | — | — | 2 | 13.9 | — | — |
| Mound F | 2,526 | 2 | 7.9 | 14 | **55.4** | — | — |
| Mound G | 1,860 | 1 | 5.4 | 0 | 0.0 | — | — |
| Group H | 746 | 1 | 13.4 | — | — | 1 | **13.4** |
| Group J | 598 | — | — | — | — | 2 | **33.4** |
| Mound Q | 6,210 | 2 | 3.2 | 4 | 6.4 | 1 | 1.6 |
| Totals | 18,532 | 38 | 20.5 | 37 | 20.0 | 5 | 2.7 |
| | | | Moundville I phase | | | | |
| Group K | 1,957 | 4 | 20.4 | 2 | 10.2 | — | — |
| Group L | 1,132 | 13 | **114.8** | 11 | **97.1** | — | — |
| Totals | 3,089 | 17 | 55.1 | 13 | 42.1 | — | — |
| Overall Totals | 89,892 | 237 | 26.4 | 155 | 17.2 | 119 | 13 |

Note: Bold numbers indicate salient values (i.e., values that are 50% higher than expected for that context).

cifically Knight (2010), Thompson (2011), and Porth (2017). Due to the general lack of recent investigations outside of Moundville proper, Pride Place, Fitts, and Powers are the only hinterland sites that have contributed data to these tables. Similarly, because most recent excavations have focused almost exclusively on late Moundville contexts, data pertaining to early Moundville are underrepresented. For example, microdrills are not truly absent from Moundville I phase contexts overall, but they are absent from those assemblages that have been analyzed using Knight's (2010) classificatory scheme. These data and their significance to Moundville's economy through time are discussed in the remainder of this chapter.

## DISCUSSION

The abundance measures demonstrate that practically all households were working with greenstone, saws, and drills, and that this pattern held across centuries
of sociopolitical change. Archaeologists argue that while some early Moundville
households concentrated more than others on making certain kinds of objects,
households in general were self-sufficient (Thompson 2011). Craft items and other
valuables were exchanged across Moundville's various corporate groups, binding
the populace into a network of reciprocal economic obligations (Knight 2010).
According to the evidence presented here, that same pattern held during the late
Moundville period. Though the artifact categories touched on above constitute a
minuscule percentage of the objects circulating at any given time during Moundville's history, each signifies a different domain of Moundville's overall economy.
Therefore, they permit a few brief statements about how craft production figured
into late period social and religious life in the valley.

If it is the case (1) that shell beads were socially valued goods made to be exchanged on the occasion of births, marriages, deaths, and other life-cycle crises
(Lesure 1999; see also Pope 1989), and (2) that microdrills excelled at and thus
were primarily used for perforating shell beads (Ensor 1991:36; Knight 2010:58),
then we may consider microdrills to be a cornerstone of Moundville's social economy.
It is no wonder that microdrills are overwhelmingly salient in off-mound contexts—
that is, contexts associated with nonelites, who were likely less concerned with political prestige than they were with upholding social and ritual contracts among
peers. Considering that microdrills are abundant in contexts spanning almost the
entirety of Moundville's history—from West Jefferson (Pope 1989) to the early
Moundville IV phase—these off-mound assemblages reflect a concern with tradition that mound assemblages do not.

Greenstone—which has been petrographically and geochemically sourced to
outcrops along Hatchet Creek over 150 km from Moundville (Gall and Steponaitis
2001)—was perfectly suited for heavy-duty tools. Its microfibrous structure lends
it flexibility, while its mineralogical composition imparts shock resistance and
durability. That the Moundville people were aware of these traits is attested to by
the fact that fully 96 percent of greenstone artifacts recovered from Moundville
are petaloid celts (Gall and Steponaitis 2001), implements that—once embedded
into hardwood handles—were used to clear fields, build houses, and occasionally
bludgeon foes. Celts were necessary for household survival. It is for this reason
that greenstone celts were once considered the linchpin of Moundville's political
economy (Welch 1991); if they could be controlled, so, too, could the common
people who depended on them. However, the data herein eliminate the possibility
of an economy thus structured: there was never a time in Moundville's history
when both prestigious and lowly households were not working greenstone, though
some worked it more than others. Furthermore, an apparent celt preform at Pow-

ers, unanticipated by Wilson's (2001) conclusion that celts were only made outside of the valley, reminds us that abundance measures cannot tell the whole story.

Sandstone saws were typically used to create grooves and notches in tabular materials such as fine gray micaceous sandstone and ferruginous sandstone. The people of Moundville preferred the former for paint palettes, while fine-grained, colorful varieties of the latter were used for pendants. Both objects were made in Moundville's hinterlands during the polity's twilight years.

At Pride Place, palettes were first roughed out of Pottsville sandstone, then abraded into blanks, and finally notched and incised with sandstone saws (Davis 2016). If palette production or ownership was ever restricted to certain individuals—and it certainly was (Steponaitis 2016)—the rules governing membership in the cult or sodality that used palettes in rituals had slackened by the late Moundville III phase, a pattern mirrored in the concurrent democratization of other esoterica (Knight 1997; Porth 2017). Palette manufacture at Pride Place, then, signifies the efforts of rural people to meet the religious needs of a dispersed population that was increasingly asserting its religious independence from Moundville itself.

Craftspeople at Fitts snapped pendants into simple geometric shapes along sawn grooves. Many broke in the process and were discarded in one large on-site pit, alongside the tools used to make them (Myer 2003). As with shell beads, stone pendants may have been conferred during a rite of passage, albeit a highly specific kind in which warrior status was granted to those who had earned it (Blitz 1993). If so, they were the sorts of object that one provided under threat of public disgrace. Their production at Fitts is a measure of the extent to which social obligations motivated crafting and exchange as a means of knitting a dispersed population into a community whole.

## SUMMARY AND CONCLUSIONS

This research presented crafting data from three nonmound sites in Moundville's hinterlands. Each was occupied during the centuries following initial polity formation and reorganization; their residents almost certainly descended from the people who had left Moundville after the construction of the mound-and-plaza complex. The data suggest that traditional valuables remained important well into the latter years of the valley's Mississippian occupation and that the locus of their production remained within the household. Moreover, the distribution of crafting debris and finished objects is comparable in significant ways to what Thompson (2011) observed for early Moundville contexts: an "iconic redundancy" (Renfrew 2001) in which essentially the same sorts of objects were being made and used across all domestic contexts. It is a testament to the strength of the bonds of reciprocity wrought among early Moundville's populace that the organization of production remained essentially the same across centuries of political, social, and demographic change.

Insofar as they relate to the notion of collapse, these comments echo those of other scholars who urge more precise approaches to abrupt culture change (Eisenstadt 1988; Porth 2017; Tainter 1988, 2006). Even in history's rare instances of near-total societal breakdown, "collapse" emerges as radically different on closer inspection than one might expect. Such was Tuchman's (1978) impression—expressed in this chapter's epigraph—of plague-ridden, war-wracked Europe in the fourteenth century. The economy of the Late Mississippian Black Warrior Valley presents observers with another sort of "distant mirror," its reflection one of social contracts established at a society's founding and sustained over centuries of change.

# 13

# MULTISCALAR COMMUNITY HISTORIES IN THE LOWER CHATTAHOOCHEE RIVER VALLEY

*Migration and Aggregation at Singer-Moye*

Stefan Brannan and Jennifer Birch

S inger-Moye is a large mound-and-plaza complex located in the Lower Chattahoochee River Valley of southwestern Georgia. In this chapter, we explore historical and social dynamics of the community centered there. Our approach is informed by theoretical trends that situate processes of cultural change in multiscalar, historicized frameworks. We take as our starting point a conceptualization of Mississippian communities as active fields for the negotiation of social identity, collective memory, and the production of place (Cobb 2005; Isbell 2000; Pauketat 2007:107). This approach requires considering the "recursive interactions between individuals and institutions, commoners and elites, agency and structure, and top-down and bottom-up processes" (Carballo et al. 2014:116). As such, rather than reifying communities as scalar units in larger social systems, we acknowledge that theoretical perspectives on the community are flexible and should permit the interrogation of relationships between settlement patterns, sociopolitical and economic practices, and cultural production and reproduction (Birch 2013; Boulware 2011; MacSweeney 2011; Thompson and Birch 2018).

We focus on how processes of migration, aggregation, and integration at the community and regional scales shaped the occupational history of Singer-Moye and the settlement landscape of the Lower Chattahoochee River Valley. Our analysis combines archaeological and geophysical data from mound and off-mound contexts to develop an occupational history for Singer-Moye. This history includes initial occupation at discrete locations, integrative practices, the demarcation of restricted and public spaces, the defining of residential loci, and episodes of population aggregation and dispersal. When this history is situated in meso- and macroregional histories of interaction and exchange, a narrative emerges that illustrates how the Singer-Moye community contributed to, and was influenced by, larger processes of sociopolitical change.

## SINGER-MOYE SITE AND ENVIRONMENT

Singer-Moye was occupied circa AD 1150–1500 (Brannan 2018), though perhaps not continuously (Blitz and Lorenz 2002, 2006). The most prominent features of the built environment at the site are the remains of five platform and three dome-shaped mounds arranged around two plazas, which together constitute the site core. Traditionally, platform mounds were built with the express purpose of elevating a flat space above the surrounding landscape. These elevated spaces contained structures or large open features, or they served as stages (Lindauer and Blitz 1997). In contrast, dome-shaped mounds were created by the intentional capping of a structure or other feature by piling earth over its footprint, without the intent to create an elevated, usable space.

Of the eight mounds, four platform mounds (A, C, D, and F) and two dome-shaped mounds (E and H) have been the subject of further investigations using traditional excavation methods and/or shallow geophysical survey. Mound A is the tallest platform mound, rising 14 m above the surrounding plaza and residential spaces. It is pentagonal in shape. At least three structures were built on its summit, with an open corridor down the center of the summit connecting two ramps (Birch et al. 2015). Mound C is the earliest platform mound and is the only one excavated below the terminal summit stage. In 1968, archaeologists associated with the Columbus Museum excavated a large vertical trench in the north face of the mound. They exposed the construction sequence from the summit to the submound ground surface. Mound D had approximately half of its terminal summit excavated, and shallow geophysical survey identified at least one additional stage of construction below the terminal one (Brannan and Bigman 2014). Mound F is the smallest of the platform mounds. Systematic excavations have not been conducted yet, but magnetometry and ground-penetrating radar (GPR) surveys indicate that several structures or other features are present. Both dome-shaped mounds (Mounds E and H) capped a submound structure consistent with a slightly larger than average single-set post Mississippian-style house. Both houses have been completely excavated, though it is not known whether additional architectural features underlie them.

Systematic shovel-test survey has revealed 36 ha of occupation to date. While approximately 6 ha of this area constitute the site core, we believe that the remaining 30 ha consisted of residential occupation and associated land use on well-drained upland terraces. These lands appear to have been occupied contemporaneously when the town reached its greatest size in AD 1300–1400. Additional Mississippian-component habitation areas are likely present on other well-drained landforms and in the floodplain of Pataula Creek, beyond the survey boundaries.

Singer-Moye is the only multimound center in the region not located near the Chattahoochee River (Figure 13.1). Other mound centers are situated in the floodplain of the Chattahoochee, which marks the boundary between modern-day southeastern Alabama and southwestern Georgia and provided the residents with easy access to riverine resources and transportation networks. Singer-Moye, in contrast, is situated next to a small tributary some 30 km east of the river as the crow flies, or 45 km from the confluence of the stream and the river. As most major Mississippian mound centers are located in riverine floodplains, Singer-Moye's location at first seems anomalous. However, we believe that the decision to settle in the uplands was strategic and related to the site's location on an ecological and cultural frontier, factors that contributed to the site's enduring importance in the region.

Singer-Moye is located on a boundary between two neighboring ecoregions: the hilly gulf coastal plain and the coastal plain red uplands (Griffith et al. 2001). The former is a heterogeneous region consisting of dissected plains and low hills

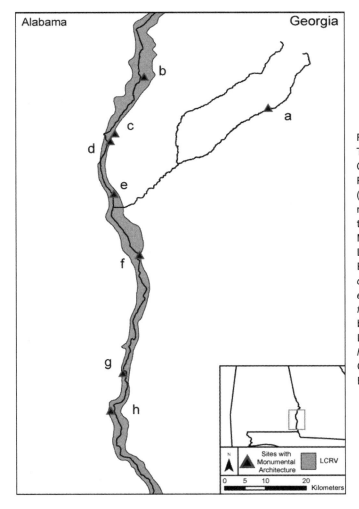

Figure 13.1. The Lower Chattahoochee River Valley (LCRV) and sites mentioned in text: *a*, Singer-Moye; *b*, Roods Landing; *c*, Gary's Fish Pond; *d*, Cool Branch; *e*, Mandeville; *f*, Cemochechobee; *g*, Purcell's Landing; *h*, Omussee Creek. (Stefan Brannan)

with broad tops, northward-facing cuestas, and numerous streams with abundant floodplains. It was covered by oak-hickory-pine forest, some southern mixed forest, and some southern floodplain forest, which contributed to significant microclimate diversity (Schnell and Wright 1993; Schnell et al. 1981; Wharton 1978). The coastal plain red uplands, in contrast, consist of dissected plains, broad, gently sloping ridges, and interstream divides (Griffith et al. 2001). It was covered by a different forest makeup, consisting primarily of southern mixed forest interspersed with oak-hickory-pine forest (Wharton 1978). A location near an ecotone meant that a wider range of resources would have been available to the community at Singer-Moye, contributing to the desirability and resilience of the locality (Brannan and Birch 2017). This upland location would have also offered easy access to the Chattahoochee and Flint River drainages and the flows of people, goods, and information that traveled via those corridors.

## MIGRATION: SETTLING THE COMMUNITY, CIRCA AD 1150–1300

Initial occupation at Singer-Moye, beginning circa AD 1150, was focused within the site core and consisted of multiple, spatially discrete settlement loci (Figure 13.2). Evidence for this stage of occupation includes shell-tempered ceramics with incised arcades, reminiscent of ceramic types originating to the west in Alabama and within regions influenced by the Moundville polity. One locus of early activity is under and near Mound C. The second is approximately 300 m to the south, near Mounds A and H, where several wall-trench structures were encountered in an exploratory trench (Russell and Gordy 2012). Another possible early locus may be just north of Mound B, based on the limited presence of early-phase ceramics.

One platform mound, Mound C, was erected over an early occupational locus, placing its construction sometime after Singer-Moye's initial settlement. Yet, the ceramics recovered from all mound stages, as documented by a trench excavated into the mound's north side, suggest that its formation dates to the same early period in the site's settlement history (Brannan 2018). The precise use of this monument (e.g., funerary mound, viewing platform [Lindauer and Blitz 1997]) is unknown; however, a recent magnetometer survey did not identify structural remains (Birch et al. 2015), suggesting that it did not function as the base for an elite residence. Mound A may have also potentially been in existence during this early phase of occupation, though only the terminal stage has been investigated to date (Blitz and Lorenz 2006).

These data suggest that the original inhabitants of the site may have comprised socially or economically differentiated household clusters that shared common material and ceremonial practices. It is possible that these household clusters represented clan groups or the residents of previously distinct communities (Scarry and Steponaitis 2016; chapter 4 in this volume) who, while sharing the same landscape, were as yet incompletely integrated (see for example Birch 2012). The monumental landscape of the site at this time is difficult to delineate with any cer-

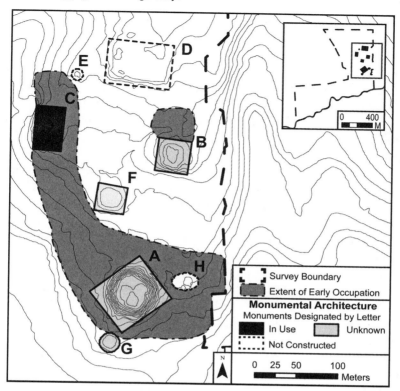

Figure 13.2. Singer-Moye site plan, circa AD 1100–1300. Monuments in use and residential occupation. A–H = monuments. (Stefan Brannan; after Brannan and Birch 2017)

tainty. Mound C was clearly the center of group-oriented construction and emplacement. But it is unknown whether Mound C formed a distinct ritual setting, or whether an early stage of Mound A was also in use at this time.

The initial occupation of Singer-Moye coincided with the appearance of other communities that also erected platform mounds or repurposed Woodland period mounds in the Lower Chattahoochee River Valley (see Figure 13.1): Cool Branch (Huscher 1971), Mandeville (Kellar et al. 1962), and Purcell's Landing (Blitz and Lorenz 2006). Gary's Fish Pond and Roods Landing were also occupied, but no secure evidence for monumental construction has been found in either location (Blitz and Lorenz 2006). The monumental core at Cool Branch was surrounded by a bastioned palisade (Huscher 1971), possibly suggesting a concern for collective defense, although residential occupation appears to have also extended beyond the fortification (Brannan 2018). The site was destroyed by reservoir development in the 1960s, but it remains the only example of a defensive palisade in the region.

Less is known about contemporary sites lacking monumental architecture, due to incomplete survey coverage. Most surveys in the region were conducted in advance of reservoir construction in the 1950s and 1960s and consisted of surface collections only (e.g., DeJarnette 1975; Huscher 1959). Surveys conducted in the last 30 years have been limited to the boundaries of extant reservoirs or of state and federal property, or defined by a narrow area of potential effects (APE) in the case of road and pipeline projects (GASF 2015; e.g., Knight and Mistovich 1984).

The first major population aggregation in the valley occurred circa AD 1200–1300 at Cemochechobee, located 50 km southwest of Singer-Moye, directly on the Chattahoochee River (Blitz and Lorenz 2006; Schnell et al. 1981). Coeval with the founding of Cemochechobee, mound construction may have ceased at all single-mound centers, though we are not certain whether those settlements were abandoned or whether aggregation occurred at one or multiple later mound centers after these populations relocated elsewhere. Cemochechobee was the first multi-mound settlement in the valley. It includes two platform mounds that were constructed over large premound structures and a third burial mound. Based on surface distributions of archaeological materials, we know that more than 61 ha of residential habitation surrounded the monumental site core (Schnell et al. 1981).

Some ceramic vessel motifs identified at Cemochechobee have analogs in the Fort Walton region of northwestern Florida. At this same time, AD 1200, Fort Walton populations were increasing in social complexity, and settlement aggregation was taking place (Blitz and Lorenz 2002; Marrinan and White 2007). Blitz and Lorenz (2002) have argued that this transformation was the result of interaction between extant Late Woodland populations in the Apalachicola region and the settled migrants in the Lower Chattahoochee River Valley.

## AGGREGATION: CONSTRUCTING COMMUNITY AT SINGER-MOYE, CIRCA AD 1300–1400

Sweeping changes in settlement configuration took place at Singer-Moye circa AD 1300–1400, evidencing a significant population increase compared to the site's early occupation. The scale of demographic expansion suggests that this change was accomplished through aggregation as opposed to in situ population growth. At its height, we postulate the settlement was home to more than 2,000 people (Brannan and Birch 2017). We believe that the process of aggregation happened in two stages, based on ceramic seriation and radiocarbon dates (Brannan 2018). Each stage involved a reconfiguration of the central site and the sequential construction of two monumental plazas. A dense residential occupation is suggested by a concentrated residential midden ring that encircles the southern plaza, connects all of the mounds facing it, and extends along the flanks of the north plaza as far as Mound E to the west and Mound B to the east, creating a lopsided U shape (Figure 13.3). The density of material recovered from the southern plaza complex rivals the densest concentrations of materials from residential habitation at other well-surveyed large mound centers, including Moundville (Brannan 2018; Thompson 2011). During the same interval, residential occupation is evi-

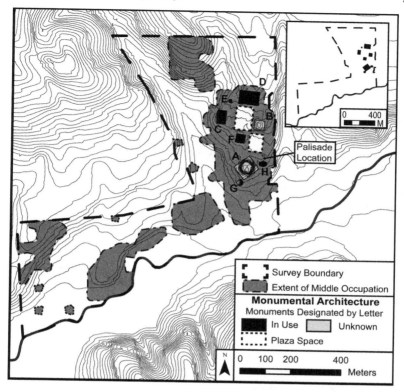

Figure 13.3. Singer-Moye site plan, circa AD 1300–1400. Monuments in use and residential occupation, including settlement on outlying landforms. A–H = monuments. (Stefan Brannan and Jennifer Birch; after Brannan and Birch 2017)

dent for the first time on landforms adjacent to the site core. Ceramic diversity increased during this phase in the site's settlement history. Ceramic modes connected to the early component and similar to those found across central and western Alabama continue to be used. These are joined by pottery bearing decorative motifs characteristic of Fort Walton and Lamar varieties, originating in northwestern Florida and northwestern Georgia, respectively. Other types of material culture, including copper (Brannan 2012), a fragment of a shell gorget (Russell and Gordy 2012), saltwater marine shell (Little 2013), and nonlocal lithic material also hint at increased connections between regions. All evidence points to a meso-regional population aggregation, as well as the incorporation of or connections to populations from farther afield.

The initial occupation of the site, circa AD 1100–1300, may have included a public space, but if so it has been obscured by later occupations. The south plaza served as the footprint for the large-scale aggregation that characterized the AD 1300–1400 phase (see Figure 13.3). In all likelihood, this plaza set the footprint for the growing town (e.g., Dalan 1997; Holley et al. 1993; Stout and Lewis 1999). It was constructed from the infilling of much of the southern edge of the landform to achieve a level surface (Brannan and Bigman 2012). Our excavations, GPR survey, and magnetometer data suggest that this process involved the incorporation of as much as 2 m of fill in the area immediately north of Mound A (Blank et al. 2015). The act of plaza construction is often cited as an example of communal activity through labor mobilization and the setting aside of public space, which furthers the interests of specific social units and the community as a whole. Plazas provided a setting for events such as competitive ceremonies and feasting among descent groups (Cobb and Butler 2017; Kidder 2004; Knight 2010:4–5; Lindauer and Blitz 1997).

Mound A's enduring place as a focus of the natural and built environment is clear. It dominates the landform on which the site core was constructed, anchors the south plaza, and, along with Mound C, overlooks the approach from Pataula Creek. If Mound C anchored the early community, Mound A together with the south plaza anchored this aggregated phase of occupation. Mound F was likely constructed in the early 1300s adjacent to the north side of the south plaza (Brannan 2018; Brannan and Bigman 2014). Mound B, which fronts both the north and south plazas, was probably constructed during the first or second stage of the site's reconfiguration.

In 2015, we identified a linear anomaly, tentatively thought to be a palisade, that divided the south plaza from the residential area immediately to the south. This feature consisted of a ditch measuring 90 cm deep and 75 cm wide that was filled with mottled red, white, and yellow clay fill and was found to contain a series of white clay-filled post molds of 10–20 cm diameter. Ceramic seriation and radiocarbon dates from the surrounding strata, trench, and posts suggest that the palisade was constructed in the early AD 1300s, coincident with the reconfiguration of the site core (Kilgore et al. 2015). It lacks bastions and does not seem to have been defensive in nature. We believe that it served to demarcate space within the community, perhaps setting aside or screening space around Mounds A and H (or the structure beneath what would eventually become Mound H) from public access.

The continued occupation of the southern plaza complex from the early phase of the community history suggests that those occupying this location may have been associated with the site's founders or their social memory. Lineages with longer-lived ties to settlements may have achieved elevated status due to their relative emplacement within towns and associated territories. In the context of population relocation in the US Southwest, local resources, rights, and decision-making were controlled by relatively stable individuals and groups, rather than by the community as a whole (Schachner 2012:24). This process may have played out at Singer-Moye, with the groups that first occupied the site retaining the balance of political influence, or this location becoming a locus of social or political authority (see also Arkush 2018).

The second stage of this aggregated phase of occupation involved an expansion of the original site core. The northern plaza was added (see Figure 13.3). The top of a large natural rise on the north side of the plaza was leveled and turned into an elevated platform, Mound D. The summit of Mound D is enigmatic; excavators have identified a series of uniformly spaced ash-filled pits oriented to the long axis of the mound whose function remains unknown. Another large rectangular structure was constructed abutting the northern plaza. This structure was excavated in 1967/1968 by the Columbus Museum under the direction of Frank Schnell. It is believed to have been an earthen-embanked structure, and the excavation produced intact standing wall timbers and a range of materials dating to the late AD 1300s (Blitz and Lorenz 2006; Brannan 2018). This structure was later capped beneath Mound E. The midden ring extended to Mound E but did not surround the northern plaza on the north and east sides.

These major building programs, including the expansion and definition of a town plan, are suggestive of extensive place-making, sociopolitical consolidation, and community building circa AD 1300–1400. The planning and construction of the original site core centered on Mound A and the south plaza may have been an exercise aimed at materializing a community-based identity during initial aggregation at the site. Approximately 50 years later, the reconfiguration of the site core and addition of a second plaza and associated monumental architecture may have been undertaken as a large-scale labor project as part of negotiations between incoming residents and extant populations (see, for example, Dalan 1997). The fact that Mound C, the oldest extant monument at the site, was incorporated into this expanded community plan may have linked the original site residents to the newcomers in space and time.

The construction of new mounds and plazas during the expansion of the community that centered on Singer-Moye included the creation of settings for the formation and renegotiation of community-based identities. While collectivizing events including feasts, religious ceremonies, or other integrative practices may have taken place, the extension of the residential footprint of the community in keeping with the prevailing logic of the site's original design, as conceived by its inhabitants circa AD 1300 or earlier, suggests that the process of community planning also served to integrate extant residents and recent migrants. The reconfiguration of the built environment in order to create and consolidate community-based identity is a practice that has been repeatedly documented in middle-range and early-state societies elsewhere in the world (e.g., Alt 2002; Betzenhauser 2011; Birch 2012, 2013; Haggis 2013; Lipe and Hegmon 1989; Rautman 2013, 2014).

According to Kowalewski (2013:213–214), large-scale construction projects were not necessarily directed by the actions of specific people or groups. They may also have been carried out by the hidden hand of multiple actors, with the realization of the built environment being beyond the comprehension of any one participant. No singular entity, whether a person or a group, was doing the directing or redirecting, but the results came about from the purposeful actions of many people (Pauketat 2000b). These actions may have consequences that could not have been predicted by any participants but that may have, nevertheless, bolstered a sense of community. Thus, while aspects of the built environment may have been co-opted after construction by groups or persons for specific purposes, collective actions facilitated the construction of these monuments and drove the institutions and practices that made use of the spaces (e.g., Blanton and Fargher 2008; Carballo 2013; Stanish and Haley 2005).

The act of constructing the initial mound-and-plaza complex, as well as all subsequent events in and around these features of the built environment, was key in the lived experiences of the inhabitants, charged with symbolic meaning and the creation of social memory (e.g., Blitz 2012; Pauketat 2007:95; see also chapters 2 and 8 in this volume). In this way, repeated reconfigurations of the built environment can be viewed as practices of place-making, whereby community building constitutes a continually emergent historical process rather than a specific outcome (Cobb 2005; Pauketat 2003; Varien and Potter, ed. 2008).

During the circa AD 1300–1400 interval, the settlement footprint expanded considerably beyond the site core, indicating a large influx of new permanent community members. Adjacent landforms to the west and northwest were occupied, evidenced by a uniform distribution of artifacts on all well-drained areas within the current survey area. Settlement also likely continued farther to the north, west, and east along the adjacent landforms, and possibly south across Pataula Creek (Brannan and Birch 2017). There is no evidence for monumental architecture outside of the site core.

At this same time, almost all smaller single-mound sites in the region were abandoned, as was Cemochechobee. Conversely, the multimound center of Rood's Landing, located approximately 30 km northwest from Singer-Moye, was occupied during this time. Rood's Landing included eight mounds and at least one plaza, and it rivaled Singer-Moye in terms of the size of its central precinct. Notably, the largest platform mounds at both sites are pentagonal in shape. Unfortunately, no systematic survey has been conducted to date in off-mound contexts at Rood's Landing. As we have argued elsewhere (Brannan and Birch 2017), we believe that settlement growth and changes in the complexity of the built environment at both Singer-Moye and Rood's Landing were due to peer-polity interaction and cooperation and competitive emulation as opposed to conflict (Renfrew and Cherry 1986). Both sites developed in a similar fashion and at about the same pace. Both are located centrally in the Lower Chattahoochee River Valley, separated by about a day's travel by foot. A double ditch surrounds the site core at Rood's Landing (Caldwell 1955), but the village extends at least 700 m beyond it along the landform to the northeast (Knight and Mistovich 1984). At Singer-Moye, residential settlement was dispersed, spread out over several land-forms, and would have been difficult to protect with a palisade. We have no reason to believe that either community was concerned about collective defense during this phase of settlement aggregation. The only additional location in the valley with monumental architecture, Omussee Creek, was a small single-mound center located 80 km south of Singer-Moye.

## DECENTRALIZING COMMUNITY AT SINGER-MOYE, CIRCA AD 1400–1500

After 1400, a shift in settlement patterns occurred at Singer-Moye and in the Lower Chattahoochee River Valley as a whole, evidenced by the reorientation of inter-regional interaction, a decrease in polity size, and the shift to a dispersed settle-ment pattern. Mound centers were shorter lived, and the scale of construction at those centers is smaller than in the thirteenth and fourteenth centuries. At the same time, there is a veritable explosion of small, nonmound settlements, al-though the lack of systematic survey coverage in the region makes it difficult to quantify the true extent of this demographic decentralization. This shift in settle-ment patterning occurred at roughly the same time in both the Lower Chatta-hoochee River Valley and several other regions across the greater Southeast (e.g., Anderson 1994; Beck 2013; King 2003; Knight and Steponaitis 1998; Meeks and Anderson 2013). While the reasons for such a shift may vary by region, the mag-nitude of this transition should not be overlooked.

Ceramic assemblages dating after AD 1400 are marked by a shift away from local traditions that had been in place for approximately 300 years. Notably, ar-cades are no longer incised on the shoulders of jars, as had been the case since the initial occupation at the site. The two newer styles that had been introduced circa AD 1300, Fort Walton and Lamar, now dominate ceramic assemblages. It is not known whether extant groups abandoned Singer-Moye, after which time it was resettled by people producing different ceramics, or whether this change represents a period in which local populations fully adopted new forms of mate-rial culture whose origins lay elsewhere in the Deep South. If the site was aban-doned, it was not abandoned for long before being reoccupied.

The final phase of occupation at Singer-Moye included a contraction in the to-tal settlement size and a decrease in the number of mounds in use (Brannan 2018). The specific settlement footprint is tentatively defined, but it is wholly contained within the boundaries of the earlier settlement (Figure 13.4). Only the summit of Mound A exhibits straightforward evidence of utilization during this phase. Oc-cupation of off-mound locations was restricted to the central site core, likely con-centrated on the southern edge of the landform near Pataula Creek and Mound A.

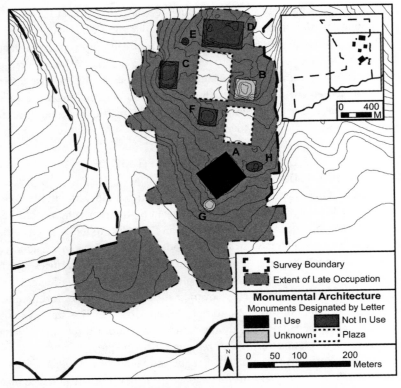

Figure 13.4. Singer-Moye site plan, circa AD 1400–1500. Monuments in use and residential occupation. *A–H* = monuments. (Stefan Brannan and Jennifer Birch; after Brannan and Birch 2017)

Radiocarbon dates from the summit of Mound A indicate an occupation between AD 1400 and 1500 (Brannan and Birch 2017). Here, excavations revealed a single large structure, which has been interpreted as an elite residence blocked off from view below by a low berm of earth (Blitz and Lorenz 2006). This structure contained artifacts that have commonly been linked to broad interregional interaction spheres, including copper, a greenstone celt, and pipe fragments. A recent magnetometer survey revealed the footprint of two additional structures, divided by a thoroughfare connecting the northern and southern ramps (Birch et al. 2015). One ramp provided access to the southern plaza, and the second ramp pointed in the direction of Pataula Creek and the residential area south of Mound A. It is possible that at this time Singer-Moye was a focal point in the landscape for dispersed populations, serving a population larger than that which continued to inhabit the site core. It is unclear to what extent any new construction and/or maintenance of the site's monumental landscape were enacted by the inhabitants or individuals and social groups drawn from the wider landscape. However, it

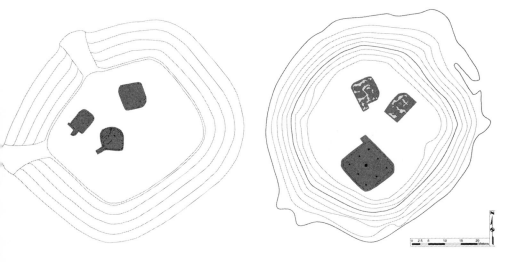

Figure 13.5. Mound summit architecture at Singer-Moye (*left*) and Rood's Landing (*right*). (Stefan Brannan and Jennifer Birch; adapted from Caldwell 1955)

would appear that many areas that had anchored the aggregated AD 1300s community had now fallen out of use.

Only a few other mound centers were occupied at this time. A single mound was constructed at Gary's Fish Pond, a small center that had been occupied as long as Singer-Moye (Blitz and Lorenz 2006). Blitz and Lorenz (2006) argue that Rood's Landing was not occupied at this time. However, the architecture on the summit of the largest mound at Rood's Landing was configured similarly to that of Mound A at Singer-Moye, with the exception that both ramps opened onto the plaza at the former (Figure 13.5). Both ceramic assemblages do resemble each other superficially, but additional radiocarbon dates are needed to resolve their contemporaneity. It may be that these once-large settlements were reconceptualized as vacant ceremonial centers serving a dispersed population, with only a few inhabitants residing there as caretakers (see Knight and Steponaitis 1998).

## SUMMARY AND CONCLUSIONS

In keeping with perspectives on Mississippian community building and place-making advanced by Pauketat (2003) and Cobb (2005), we believe that processes of migration, population movement, and resettlement were foundational to the imagining, reimagining, and emplacement of the community centered on Singer-Moye. This connection is especially evident during the period in which the site seems to have been the focus of sub- and extraregional population aggregation. During these processes of resettlement and integration, massive construction projects played a key role in transforming the social and physical landscape and re-articulating relationships between locals, newcomers, space, and place. The construction of one or more monuments by the initial inhabitants of the site emplaced the earliest occupants in a hitherto unoccupied landscape, circa AD 1150–1300. During the period in which the site served as a focus for regional settlement aggregation, circa AD 1300–1400, the expansion and reconfiguration of the monumental site core provided a focus for the practices that established relationships and identities among residents and newcomers. During the site's final occupation, circa AD 1400–1450, long-established monumental foci were given new life as elite precincts in the context of a dispersed settlement strategy. These events served as settings for the negotiation of power, access to local and nonlocal resources, and the organization and control of rituals and ceremonies. The settlement of areas within the site core and adjacent landforms likely also involved negotiations between residents and newcomers in a process that constructed the social landscape of the Singer-Moye community through the mundane activities of day-to-day living. Through the successive reworking of the landscape, each iteration of the settlement emplaced and materialized community-based identities and ideologies within the Lower Chattahoochee River Valley and the wider Mississippian world.

# COMMENTARY

# THE ARCHAEOLOGY OF MISSISSIPPIAN COMMUNITIES AND HOUSEHOLDS

*Looking Back, Looking Forward*

Jason Yaeger

In a volume that examines the legacy of a foundational text in the field 30 years after its publication, it seems appropriate to begin with a look backward, to trace the intellectual path that we have taken to arrive at this volume. In many ways, the late 1980s and 1990s constituted a watershed period in the household archaeology of the pre-Columbian Americas. Household archaeology was a mature and robust paradigm, strongly influenced by behavioral and functional definitions of the household (e.g., Netting 1982; Wilk and Rathje 1982). Several well-received and influential edited volumes showed the wide range of questions that scholars could address productively using the household approach in regions across the Americas, including Mesoamerica (Santley and Hirth 1993; Wilk and Ashmore 1988) and the Southeast. The latter region was the focus for Rogers and Smith's (1995) foundational *Mississippian Communities and Households*, which is the inspiration for this volume. Interestingly, those volumes also revealed—perhaps unknowingly—the limits of the household archaeology paradigm through their invocation of "community," indicating an interest in processes and dynamics above the level of the household. This word appeared in the title of both Rogers and Smith's text and Wills and Leonard's *The Ancient Southwestern Community* (1994).

Given this growing interest in ancient communities and the close attention to defining and operationalizing the construct of the household, the paucity of explicit definitions of community in these publications is surprising. Instead, most took the community for granted as a natural social unit (see also Murdock 1949), archaeologically indicated by a site. Although most household archaeologists allowed that households (as social and economic institutions) and houses (as residential compounds) were not coterminous (see Ashmore and Wilk 1988), the archaeology of social organization and settlement archaeology of the time were heavily influenced by scalar thinking, mapping putative social units onto the spatial units that formed our archaeological units of analysis: from the individual person to the household (house), to the community (site), to the polity (region), to the culture. Indeed, the ubiquitous metaphor of the household as "building block" of society spoke precisely to this kind of hierarchical, scalar configuration.

Thus, "community" was an empty vessel, waiting to be filled, and within the paradigmatic context of household archaeology, a functionalist theory of community made sense (Kolb and Snead 1997): communities have roles, integrating households into larger administrative and decision-making structures, and serving in turn as building blocks for polities in more complex societies. Kolb and Snead's theory of community was compatible with household archaeology, contextualizing households at a larger scale. It also provided an analytical unit for cross-cultural study, satisfying the comparative commitment that is central to the social sciences (Smith et al. 2012), in much the same way that the construct of the neighborhood does (Smith 2010; see also Arnauld et al. 2012).

While this approach to community is useful, it also has its limitations. Conflating an analytical unit in the archaeological record with a past social institution creates two epistemological pitfalls (Canuto and Yaeger 2012). First, it obviates the need for bridging arguments that allow one to evaluate whether the analytical unit in fact represents the inferred social unit. Second, it treats the social units (households, communities, etc.) as self-evident (Varien and Potter 2008), rather than problematizing their nature and composition. As Wesson (2016) has cogently pointed out, one danger of a functionalist construct of community is that we can become overreliant on our understanding of how communities are *supposed to* work, letting those a priori expectations shape our interpretations of the data.

Perspectives emerged in the 1990s that troubled functionalist notions of household and community, however. Some scholars focused our attention on social categories that crosscut households and communities, such as gender (Gero and Conkey 1991) and class (Saitta 1994). In her classic 1992 article in *American Anthropologist*, Brumfiel exhorted us to break open the black box of society as a system and focus on the complex internal dynamics that shape societies and motivate social change. Her critique was equally applicable to both the household, as she herself demonstrated (Brumfiel 1991), and the community.

It was these latter approaches to ancient societies, focused more on social dynamics and generative practices, that inspired *The Archaeology of Communities* (Canuto and Yaeger 2000). For us (Yaeger and Canuto 2000), an archaeology of communities did not necessarily prioritize the community as an object of inquiry per se. It certainly could, and we defined the community as the confluence of people, place, and premise (following Watanabe 1992). However, we believed that the archaeology of communities could also embrace the study of processes and dynamics that are manifest in interactions that take place within the venue or arena of communities. In that sense, we believed that the community could serve as the central framing device for an approach that occupied the epistemological middle ground between methodological holism and methodological individualism (after de Montmollin 1988).

This rather unconstraining construct of community proved productive, as the contributors could focus on phenomena at multiple scales, while keeping their interpretive gaze focused on interactions and practices that occurred in particular locations. Collectively, the contributors to *The Archaeology of Communities* shifted our research focus to the social construction of communities, emphasizing, in turn, the complex negotiations involved in their development (e.g., Isbell 2000). As archaeologists, though, most retained an abiding concern with the spatial and material aspects of community (for similar concerns, see Lipe 1989; Varien and Potter 2008).

The archaeology of communities has blossomed in the decades since the publication of *Mississippian Communities and Households* and *The Archaeology of Communities*, and scholars have incorporated new perspectives, several of which have become particularly influential. Perhaps the most important broad trend has been to pay closer attention to the material dimensions of community and to the dialectical relationships between the social and the material. Some scholars have focused on how physical settings (community as place) frame and shape interactions and practices of affiliation (community as identity), and how those enduring settings structure subsequent generations of practice (Hendon 2010; Hutson 2010).

More narrowly, many scholars have found the construct of communities of practice to be a useful way to examine the interrelationships between the material and the social. Developed by Lave and Wenger (1991) and drawing on social learning theory, a community of practice is a group of people who are bound together—in their social relationships, their attitudes and orientations, and sometimes a shared identity—because they have learned the same repertoire of steps to accomplish a particular task. A community of practice is not a totalizing institution or identity, and individuals can participate in multiple, overlapping communities of practice. This approach dovetails with the increasing interest among archaeologists in social learning (Tehrani and Riede 2008), systematic approaches such as *chaîne opératoire* to reconstruct detailed steps needed to produce complex artifacts and features (Dobres 2000; Lemonnier 1992), and the ways in which production and technology can shape identity (Dietler and Herbich 1998). Thus, it is unsurprising that archaeologists, including many contributors to this volume, have found communities of practice to be a useful construct.

Other scholars have focused more strongly on the material dimensions of community, inspired by symmetrical archaeology (Olsen 2007; Webmoor 2007; Witmore 2007), actor-network theory (Latour 2005), and object agency (Pauketat and Alt 2005). These approaches eschew anthropocentric constructs of community that privilege people and their interactions; instead, they posit equal roles for a wide range of human and nonhuman actors in community dynamics. One prominent advocate of this perspective has been Harris (2014:77), who defines communities as assemblages of "humans, things, places, animals, plants, houses, monuments." Many contributions in this volume draw on Harris's formulation of community as assemblage, while others are informed by Hodder's (2012) notions of human-thing entanglement.

Another welcome development in the archaeology of communities has been to emphasize the complexity of interactions that occur within a community. Harris (2014) posits that the term *community*—cognate to communitas and commensal—brings implicit connotations of social harmony, which in turn leads scholars to neglect the importance of conflict and competition in community dynamics. While there have been exceptions to this critique, scholars are increasingly viewing communities (in multiple senses of the term) as arenas for negotiation and contestation, a crucible where agents with different goals interact and sometimes compete to forge social constructs and institutions, each bringing a different capacity to influence a particular outcome (e.g., situational power).

These developments are manifest in the excellent contributions to this volume. Collectively, they show how the archaeology of communities and households has matured in the last 30 years, and the ways in which *Mississippian Communities and Households* laid the foundations for these developments. Rather than summarize each contribution in turn, I focus my discussion around several salient themes, the key threads that run through the warp and weft of the complex tapestry of this volume, highlighting contributions that exemplify those.

## DEFINING COMMUNITY

The contributors to this volume all problematize the term *community*, refusing to accept it uncritically as a social synonym for an archaeological site. From that shared point of departure, they go on to develop a variety of approaches to the community. Most present an explicit definition of community, while a few define the community only implicitly. As is appropriate for a volume revisiting Rogers and Smith's 1995 volume, many emphasize houses and households. Given that many embrace a multiscalar perspective, it is surprising that no chapter develops a landscape-oriented definition of community (e.g., Wernke 2015), although McKinnon (chapter 3) and Rodning and Thorpe (chapter 10) both invoke concepts of landscape productively.

Most contributions employ a practice-theory perspective, defining the community as the historically contingent and emergent product of practices, and most prioritize the social dimensions of community above place or premise. Brennan (chapter 2) succinctly summarizes this approach in the first line of her contribution: "Communities are social entities that emerge through practice and are promoted through relationships, affected by history, and reified by events and their outcomes on a daily basis."

The generative practices and events described in the contributions include both quotidian activities and rarer events. The former often entail individuals or small groups of actors undertaking activities related to the reproduction of domestic lifeways, such as pottery-making, house construction, storage of and access to food, and burial of the dead. Rarer events often involve larger segments of the community and are presumably more salient in the experience and memories of community members. These include larger construction projects such as mounds, palisades, and plazas, and large-scale events such as feasting and warfare. Although several authors (Ashley, chapter 11; Buchanan and Baltus, chapter 7; Steere, chapter 5) deploy the community of practice approach to good effect, most embrace broader approaches to practice.

While Brennan acknowledges the nondiscursive dimensions of daily activities, she and the other contributors generally eschew a simple dichotomous relationship in which nondiscursive identities are reproduced through quotidian practices, while more salient practices form the basis of explicit community identities. Instead, the contributors find meaning in the mundane. For example, Steere (chapter 5) shows how the construction of a wall-trench house could activate a community of practice that operationalized the broader norms of pan-Mississippian vernacular architecture with local details, while at the same time recognizing the participants' membership in a broader regional cultural phenomenon that included Cahokia. Similarly, Ashley (chapter 11) shows how the production of spicule-tempered St. Johns pottery evoked the shared origins of the potting community of practice, while contrasting its members with their neighbors who had distinct origins. Practices like these can be just as powerful in the constitution of communities as the construction of a community palisade (Buchanan and Baltus, chapter 7), although the latter had a material longevity that allowed it to participate in the community and structure relationships and interactions long after its construction (see also McGuire and Schiffer 1983).

Several authors highlight the synergistic effect of multiple related practices. In particular, Buchanan and Baltus argue convincingly that sets of related practices that revolved around conflict and warfare—the production of weapons, the construction and maintenance of defensive palisades, acts of warfare, pre- and post-warfare rituals and celebrations, and so forth—constituted a set of bundled practices (after Pauketat 2013a; Zedeño 2008) that would have linked smaller, overlapping communities of practice. At the same time, these smaller practices—and the people who engaged in them—were bound by their contribution to a larger goal, that of defending the town, which in turn was plausibly a powerful generative logic for an identity focused on the defended town, as it placed the different goals of the town's members in stark relief from those of its attackers, a classic case of "us" versus "them," which Barth (1969) argued was the basis for ethnogenesis. In a similar vein, Ashley uses the term "constellations of practice" (after Wenger 1998) to explain how smaller face-to-face communities of practice could be united in a broader, regional community.

As mentioned, many archaeologists studying communities today consider communities to be constituted not only through human practices, but also through interactions among animals, plants, objects, buildings, and places. While earlier approaches to material culture considered how the material world shapes human interactions, new thinkers seek to move beyond "the social" by positing theories of action, being, and becoming that are more symmetrical, as they de-center humans (Webmoor 2007). This broader, symmetrical understanding of how communities are constituted is one of the more influential developments in the archaeology of communities in the last decade, in part, I believe, because it highlights the role of the material world, which forms the empirical core of archaeological inquiry. The contributors to this volume employ constructs of assemblage (De-Landa 2006; Harris 2014; see McKinnon, chapter 3; Steere, chapter 5; Watts Malouchos and Betzenhauser, chapter 9) and entanglement (Hodder 2012; see Buchanan and Baltus, chapter 7; King, chapter 8).

King (chapter 8) provides a powerful example from early Etowah. He argues that the production of stamp-decorated, shell-tempered pottery united men and women in an act of creation with cosmogonic parallels. Women collected the clay and shells—the latter associated with the feminine, watery realm—to create the paste and form the body of each pot. Men made the paddles that were used to stamp designs onto that pot, designs that evoked the world's center and, by extension, processes of centering and cosmogonic creation. Shell tempering and the centering motifs were innovations in the region, and King points out the parallel between cosmogonic creation (as cited through the combination of novel elements in pottery production) and community creation (of Etowah, through the coalescence of multiple social groups): the production of these pots "entangled [the producers] with the idea of creation and Etowah as a new community." King argues that building houses with a novel architectural form, wall-trench construction, created similar entanglements, in this case encompassing the larger work teams that participated in the construction. In both examples, the subsequent use of those pots and houses recalls those entangled relationships. In this contribution, the metaphor of entanglement is particularly evocative as a way to emphasize the broader logics and premises that can be invoked through instances of practices and endure as the basis for a community long after each instance has ended.

Buchanan and Baltus (chapter 7) postulate a more active role for entangled objects, as palisades are conceived of as active participants in bundled practices centered on warfare. These entanglements could also endure after abandonment, they argue: "Violent events and actions would have created new kinds of entanglements, as nonhuman actors, spirits, and places were left behind, and places were abandoned by their human Mississippian inhabitants." This idea raises the possibility of social communities that are separated temporally by generations or millennia, yet connected by the entangled objects they share, as I discuss below.

## CREATING COMMUNITIES: FOUNDING, COALESCENCE, TRANSFORMATION

An essential dimension of most definitions of community is place. The practices that constitute a community occur in places, and often some of the strongest, most overt community-generating practices are also place-making, transforming a space or preexisting place on the landscape into a new place. That place can, in turn, serve as an ideological anchor for a community identity, entangling that identity with that place (to paraphrase King, chapter 8). That can be true of face-to-face communities as well as imagined communities (*sensu* Anderson 1991; see also Isbell 2000; Yaeger 2000, 2003) and diasporic communities (Goldstein 2000), for which a distant location that is the community's shared origin place or homeland (real or putative) is no longer visited, but is recalled and remembered through stories, art, and reenactments.

In this vein, Ashley (chapter 11) argues that new arrivals to the Mill Cove Complex in the St. John II period evoked their homeland in the middle St. Johns region through a series of founding events. These began with a feast that produced a shell midden reminiscent of those in their homeland and was followed by the construction of Shields Mound, which was placed on a linear ridge of sand to mimic the cultural landscape of the middle St. Johns. The deposition of Archaic bannerstones and points in the mound and the nearby ritual midden further evoked the group's deep history in their homeland. Thanks to the physicality of the mound, these material references to the middle St. Johns would have endured for generations after the founding.

In a similar example, Brennan (chapter 2) documents how the construction of the Main Street Mound was preceded by a series of events that included infilling, a ritual to prepare the locale by burning tobacco and depositing white sand and human remains, more infilling, and then the construction of the mound by depositing layers of dark and light variegated fills intermingled with human remains. The mound then served as a locale for the processing and interment of community members for generations.

Many other case studies demonstrate a widespread pattern across the Southeast of foundational events that brought people together in a salient collaborative act that helped establish a community. The foundational event was usually tied to a physically salient and durable place, and it entangled that community with that place, materializing the intangible community (also DeMarrais et al. 1996). These places usually served as the locus for socially powerful practices that reproduced the community over generations. Note, however, that while places like these can shape a community by the ways in which they structure action and interaction and by the symbolic meanings they encode, they do not overdetermine a community, whether in terms of its membership, its underlying premises or logic, or the way it is reproduced. Places are notoriously polyvalent and polysemic. Furthermore, access to them can be contested and change over time, and the events held at them also change. Indeed, foundational places can be powerful venues for practices and events that transform communities, precisely because of their role in the initial founding and subsequent constitution of communities.

Boudreaux and colleagues (chapter 6) document the role of place-making in the constitution of smaller-scale social groups at Town Creek, through the conversion of residences into group cemeteries. The tradition at Town Creek was to place burials under house floors. Around AD 1300, however, at least three residences were turned into dedicated cemeteries; they were encircled with large enclosures of posts, and burials continued within the enclosures after the destruction of the houses. The houses chosen for these cemeteries were those that had the longest occupations, suggesting that they were the houses of founding families, the leaders of the community's more powerful corporate groups. Although the subfloor burial tradition persisted at the site, the authors argue that the establishment of these suprahousehold burial locales and their continued use over time were practices that some corporate groups used to reconstitute themselves and legitimize their control over resources.

Nelson (chapter 4) describes an inclusive potluck-style feasting event associated with the founding of the Parchman Place community. While the feast was not followed by mound construction, the event and the deposit it left behind established that place as a node for later community rituals, as it was overlaid by three ashy lenses that she interprets as the remains of Green Corn ceremonies that brought the community members together to rekindle their hearths from a new sacred fire. As Rodning and Thorpe (chapter 10) discuss for the Cherokee, this new fire ritual established a vital connection to every household at Parchman, as all of the hearth fires of the community—which were fundamental to everybody's daily sustenance and thus survival—shared their origins in a single source.

Many case studies presented in this volume examine the challenges of negotiating community in a heterogeneous society formed by the immigration of several groups of people into a single settlement. Birch (2012) calls these coalescent societies, and examples can be found across the Indigenous Americas, at places like Cahokia, Grasshopper Pueblo, and Kotyiti in North America; Teotihuacan in Mesoamerica; and Tiwanaku in the Andes. These social contexts provide some of the most interesting case studies for studying community formation, as strong differences must be engaged and negotiated to forge community in the face of plurality.

Brannan and Birch (chapter 13) provide an illuminating example. The first occupants at Singer-Moye lived in socially or economically differentiated household clusters, but their similar lifeways and ceremonies suggest basic shared understandings of the world and of ways to act within it. During the fourteenth century AD, however, the site underwent demographic expansion, the rate of which suggests significant immigration into the site. Immigration would have brought challenges of integrating newcomers into the community's social fabric. The construction of a large public plaza, several mounds, and a palisade encircling the entire settlement provided opportunities to bring together large groups of people, including members of established groups and new arrivals, to find common cause and work together. The palisade demarcated the boundaries of the settlement, thus effectively materializing the new community's spatial reach, while the plaza provided a venue for ceremonies and gatherings that engaged large groups of community members in commensal activities, reaffirming the bonds among them. After approximately 50 years, the town plan was reconfigured to accommodate continued immigration and growth of the settlement, with the addition of a second plaza and another mound. The fifteenth century witnessed the abandonment of much of the settlement, as residents dispersed to smaller settlements distributed across the broader landscape. Mound A continued to be occupied, but it became the location of an elite residence, arguably the home of regional leaders whose authority was legitimated through their connection to the focal place of the earlier community.

Another example of coalescence can be seen at Mill Cove. As described above, Ashley (chapter 11) has argued that the construction of the Shields Mound was part of a sequence of founding events that were essential to the establishment of a community of immigrants. Built on virgin soil, the Shields Mound was paired with the site's other mound, Grant Mound. Grant Mound's conical shape conforms to established local traditions, and it was built atop deposits dating to earlier periods of the site's history. Ashley suggests that Grant Mound may have been associated with preexisting populations at Mill Cove, distinct from but integrated with the newcomers mentioned above. The presence of very different exotic assemblages in the two mounds supports that inference. Ashley argues that the two mounds may also have symbolized complementary phenomena, perhaps winter and summer, or earth and sky. If so, this cosmological integration of a complementary dualism—necessary and codefining differences—could have served as a cosmic metaphor that justified the integration of the site's two social groups into one coalescent community. Rodning and Thorpe (chapter 10) document a similar linking of spatialized social relations and cosmological relationships, using the examples of Cherokee townhouses.

Features and events that were particularly salient to past societies have tended to capture the attention of archaeologists as well, as the examples above demonstrate. Yet Watts Malouchos and Betzenhauser (chapter 9) show that the constitution of coalescent communities is a process that entails practices at multiple scales, penetrating deep into households and small settlements. They eschew the dominant explanations of the changing storage practices that accompanied the founding and rise of Cahokia, which are grounded in political economy and envision storage pit location as the outcome of increasing elite control of agricultural production. Instead, they argue that storage pits formed parts of assemblages at multiple scales that included people, storage features, and the food within them. From this perspective, storage pits are not passive products of political and social strategies; they are agents in the constitution of communities.

One critique of the archaeology of community that Harris (2014) raised was that it overlooks conflict and competition within communities. The contributors in this volume, however, amply document the role of conflict in southeastern communities. Buchanan and Baltus (chapter 7) indicate the central generative role of conflict and warfare in constituting communities in the American Bottom, and Nelson (chapter 4) argues that practices that maintained community identity, particularly new fire ceremonies, were important in the context of competing clan-based identities. Many others demonstrate ably how communities served as arenas or social fields for the negotiation and accommodation of difference, whether in socioeconomic standing, sociopolitical status, ethnicity and origins, or gender. Communities can also provide an arena for competition between the groups that compose them. Many contributions to this volume show that such differences were not necessarily eliminated by the constitution of a new community; indeed, they could be essential to that community.

As noted, communities are historically contingent and thus, necessarily, emergent phenomena. They can change in their composition, underlying logics and premises, and scale and spatial configuration. Many case studies document the ways in which communities change over time, such as Singer-Moye, discussed by Brannan and Birch (chapter 13). The most striking example, however, is Moundville, analyzed by Davis (chapter 12). The earliest occupation of Moundville included a ceremonial nucleus of two mounds and a plaza and was ruled by emerging leaders whose relatively weak authority was largely legitimated through religion and ritual. Around a century later, Moundville was remade as a sociogram in what Davis calls "a deliberate attempt to spatialize and make timeless the status distinctions that had gradually taken hold over the course of the previous century." The construction of the mounds and plaza that made up this new town plan arguably sought to manage the contradictions and tensions that had arisen within the community as it expanded in size and complexity, as the inequalities in power and wealth of its constituent corporate groups increased, and as the authority of its rulers grew. Davis argues that differences among corporate groups and stronger political institutions were inherent in the new political community that was inscribed in the new town plan and reproduced through practices in its ceremonial heart. Those differences were also essential to the community's reproduction, however, as different corporate groups apparently controlled the production and distribution of distinct goods that were valued and used throughout the community, creating an economic interdependence predicated on those differences and mediated through reciprocal exchange relationships. Davis argues that this heterarchical economic dimension of the community proved remarkably resilient, as reciprocity and exchange were practices that continued to bind social groups together in a larger political community after people dispersed outward into smaller settlements when Moundville was largely abandoned in the early fourteenth century.

## REMEMBERING COMMUNITIES

Communities are not just founded and created; they must be reproduced. The contributors to this volume problematize community continuity, as described above, but with the exception of Brennan (chapter 2), the authors do not engage explicitly with constructs of social memory. Given the clear connections between many case studies and the archaeology of memory (e.g., Van Dyke and Alcock 2003), however, this is a topic worthy of a brief exploration.

It is striking that, at many sites, houses were built and rebuilt over generations if not centuries, a kind of citation. At Parchman Place, houses were rebuilt sequentially in the same locations, creating stacks of up to five houses (Nelson, chapter 4). Mound E at the site witnessed at least 10 iterations of building, use, destruction, and burial of structures atop the mound. Through these construction efforts, community members reproduced the society's social organization and political authority, inscribing (*sensu* Connerton 1989) it materially in the town's basic fabric. Brennan (chapter 2) documents a similar process at Kincaid, while the rebuilding of palisades can be interpreted in a similar vein (Buchanan and Baltus, chapter 7). The repeated burial of the dead in both domestic contexts (Boudreaux et al., chapter 6) and dedicated cemeteries and mounds was another practice in which community members reproduced the multiple social bonds that joined them together, while also citing and remembering past instances of those practices. Commemorative performative practices like these are powerful sources of embodied social memory (Connerton 1989). As Boudreaux and colleagues note, however, these citations can also change subtly in nature or context, such that they can be essential to the production of social change, as well.

Rebuilding events, cyclical rituals, and repeated burials can recall past instances of those events, reinscribing the communities they generate. Material components of communities can also be erased, however. Sometimes these erasures are relatively minor, perhaps reflecting a shift in priorities rather than signaling the production of new social forms. For example, Buchanan and Baltus (chapter 7) show how a sweat lodge and adjacent post pit that were important to the early community at the Olin site were destroyed, the location of the post pit apparently marked by the placement of a new structure. Subsequently, this structure was excluded from the town by construction of a new inner palisade. This example suggests a gradual "forgetting": as the sweat lodge and post pit and associated activities became less important, they were eventually left outside the town's new boundaries.

Erasures can also be planned and intentional, seeking to create a tabula rasa for a new program of community-making. A striking example is the active destruction of preexisting landscapes and buildings at Cahokia and its surroundings at the onset of the Mississippian period (Brennan, chapter 2). In this case, it seems the leaders at Cahokia sought to set the stage for a new coalescent community at the site, one that was constituted through new forms of domestic architecture and ritual practice that represented a significant departure from earlier Late Woodland traditions.

Erasure from the landscape does not necessarily erase social memory, however. Abandoned, destroyed places can remain salient on the landscape, reminders of past events, their causes, and the groups involved in them. Buchanan and Baltus (chapter 7) document the destruction of Common Field, circa AD 1280, which left the town in ashes, perhaps only 30 years after it was founded. The palisaded settlement was sacked and burned, the articulated bodies of its inhabitants left in the smoldering remains of their houses, alongside their household goods. The destruction of Common Field may have erased the settlement from the landscape, but the fact that people never returned to rebuild the site, nor even to bury their relatives or recover valuable objects among the destroyed buildings, suggests that the event and town remained in the social memory of the region's inhabitants, plausibly making it a place to avoid, as Snead (2004) has suggested for the sacked Ancestral Pueblo community of Burnt Corn.

The reinscriptions of communities involved repeated practices with a rather short temporal rhythm, on the order of years or decades. Thus, as each citation invokes and relies on the past instance, it facilitates a relatively continuous process of community production and reproduction. In other cases, communities are constituted through reference to social memories of a deeper past, memories that are often anchored in places and things. For example, the newcomers to Mill Cove interred Archaic materials in the Shields Mound to commemorate their non-local history (Ashley, chapter 11), and the inhabitants of the dispersed settlements formed during the abandonment of Moundville established group cemeteries at the site, where they could return to bury their dead, thus maintaining a community connection to the place (Davis, chapter 12).

In other cases, the temporal scale stretches further, into the centuries. In these cases, places and the communities that existed there may still occupy an important place in social memories of descendent groups, as is indicated by contemporary Caddo people visiting the ancestral Caddoan Battle Mound (McKinnon, chapter 3). Many generations separate the human social community that once occupied the Battle Mound site and their descendants who activate the site, its buildings, and its plants in contemporary community building. The linking elements are the material components of the assembled community: mounds, artifacts, landscape. These material bridges unite the two human communities into some larger community, what we might call a longitudinal community, that is an assemblage of entangled people and more durable objects, places, and landscapes, very different from most senses of community. The durable material members of a longitudinal community serve as touchstones to the past, however, connecting us with older peoples and places in a way that is emotionally and intellectually compelling. Indeed, this communion with the past is one reason that many people find a passion for archaeology, whether as an avocation or as a career.

## METHODS AND EPISTEMOLOGY

The contributions to this volume clearly demonstrate that the archaeology of communities has benefited from new methods and interpretive approaches. The first of these is geophysical remote sensing, which has been refined to a remarkable extent in the Southeast. While the interpretation of remote sensing data is not transparent, it can be incredibly useful for identifying houses and other subsurface features and documenting a site's configuration. King (chapter 8), for example, uses gradiometer data to determine that there are roughly three times as many wall-trench buildings than later single-set post buildings at Etowah, documenting a population decline at the site. Both King and Nelson (chapter 4, at Parchman) show the power of remote sensing to document the layout of southeastern towns and the clustering of houses. Finally, Brannan and Birch (chapter 13) use ground-penetrating radar and magnetometry to document the scale and extent of infilling employed to create the southern plaza at the site.

The archaeology of communities has also benefited tremendously from an emphasis on multiscalar approaches. Canuto and I found the construct of community to provide a useful analytical scale between the household and polity (Yaeger and Canuto 2000), but as many contributions in this volume document, face-to-face, local communities (*sensu* Isbell 2000) can be more fully understood when they are embedded in larger-scale phenomena (see also Goldstein 2000; Joyce and Hendon 2000; Wernke 2007). For example, many contributors acknowledge the role of Cahokia as a center of pan-regional material phenomena that manifested in house construction, pottery styles, and trade networks beginning in the mid-eleventh century AD (Pauketat 2000a, 2004; see Brennan, chapter 2; Steere, chapter 5). At a smaller scale, Ashley (chapter 11) argues that the emergence of a coalescent community at Mill Cove required mediating the differences between local people and newcomers whose historical geography encompassed connections to the south.

Three contributions (McKinnon, chapter 3; Davis, chapter 12; Brannan and Birch, chapter 13) show the power of tacking back and forth between scales. Davis and Brannan and Birch document how the material dimensions of a community shape and constrain its history. At both Moundville and Singer-Moye, nucleated communities dispersed, but the places that had been integral to the reproduction of the nucleated community remained important. Indeed, they may have been even more important than in earlier times, as they served as venues for practices that constituted communities of people who did not have the same degree of face-to-face interaction as their ancestors.

Finally, a number of the contributors (McKinnon, chapter 3; Nelson, chapter 4; Steere, chapter 5; Boudreaux et al., chapter 6; Rodning and Thorpe, chapter 10) engage productively with the rich ethnographic and ethnohistorical literature available for the Native societies of the Southeast. Although archaeologists in the Southwest and other regions in the Americas have become increasingly skeptical of ethnographic analogy, direct analogies with descendent communities have great potential to interpret aspects of social organization and cosmology of the societies of their ancestors. Of particular note are Boudreaux and colleagues (chapter 6), who make a strong argument that competition between corporate groups—

analogous to ethnographically documented matrilineal clans—was an important factor in the negotiation of community at Town Creek. In another noteworthy case, Rodning and Thorpe (chapter 10) present a detailed analysis of Cherokee oral history to elucidate emic understandings of house and townhouse that inform their interpretation of the archaeological record at Coweeta Creek.

## CONCLUSION

This chapter began with a look backward, providing a sketch of the origins of the archaeology of communities and a consideration of how the archaeology of communities has matured, growing more sophisticated and more diverse over the last two decades. Both of these qualities—diversity and sophistication—are exemplified by the contributions to this volume. It seems fitting to conclude with a glimpse into the future of an archaeology of communities. If this volume is any indication, it is a bright future indeed.

As Wilson observes in his foreword, the contributors have built on the rigorous foundations established by household archaeology and settlement survey to demonstrate the productivity of a community approach. Of the many approaches and themes that the authors develop to such great effect, I suspect several will become prominent in future studies. These include: movement beyond individual practices to examine bundles or constellations of related practices; an increasing awareness of the role of nonhuman persons, places, and things in communities; theorization of communities as arenas or social fields for negotiation, contestation, and conflict; increasing consideration of heterarchy and collective action theory; continued fruitful use of multiscalar approaches that examine temporal scales, in addition to spatial scales; and exploration of ties between communities and social memory. The contributors to this volume have sown the seeds for these developments in the theoretically sophisticated and empirically rich case studies they present. I look forward to helping reap the harvest of their efforts.

# REFERENCES CITED

Adair, James A.

1968 [1775] *History of American Indians: Particularly Those Nations Adjoining to the Mississippi, East and West Florida, Georgia, South and North Carolina, and Virginia.* Johnson Reprint, New York.

Adams, Ron L., and Stacie M. King

2011 Residential Burial in Global Perspective. *Archeological Papers of the American Anthropological Association* 20(1):1–16.

Adger, W. Neil

2000 Social and Ecological Resilience: Are They Related? *Progress in Human Geography* 24:347–364.

Alberti, Benjamin, and Tamara L. Bray

2009 Animating Archaeology: Of Subjects, Objects and Alternative Ontologies. *Cambridge Archaeological Journal* 19(3):337–441.

Alberti, Benjamin, and Yvonne Marshall

2009 Animating Archaeology: Local Theories and Conceptually Open-Ended Methodologies. *Cambridge Archaeological Journal* 19(3):344–356.

Alcock, Susan E.

2002 *Archaeologies of the Greek Past: Landscapes, Monuments, and Memories.* Cambridge University Press, Cambridge.

Allison, Penelope M.

1999 Introduction. In *The Archaeology of Household Activities*, edited by Penelope M. Allison, pp. 1–18. Routledge, London.

Alt, Susan M.

1999 Spindle Whorls and Fiber Production at Early Cahokian Settlements. *Southeastern Archaeology* 18:124–133.

2001 Cahokia Change and the Authority of Traditions. In *The Archaeology of Traditions: Agency and History before and after Columbus*, edited by Timothy R. Pauketat, pp. 141–156. University Press of Florida, Gainesville.

2002 Identities, Traditions, and Diversity in Cahokia's Uplands. *Midcontinental Journal of Archaeology* 27:217–235.

2006a The Power of Diversity: The Roles of Migration and Hybridity in Culture Change. In *Leadership and Polity in Mississippian Society*, edited by Brian M. Butler and Paul D. Welch, pp. 289–308. Occasional Paper No. 33. Center for Archaeological Investigations, Southern Illinois University, Carbondale.

2006b Cultural Pluralism and Complexity: Analyzing a Cahokian Ritual Outpost. PhD dissertation, Department of Anthropology, University of Illinois at Urbana-Champaign.

2017 Building Cahokia: Transformation through Tradition. In *Vernacular Architecture in the Pre-Columbian Americas*, edited by Christina T. Halperin and Lauren E. Schwartz, pp. 141–157. Routledge, New York.

2018        *Cahokia's Diverse Farmers*. University of Alabama Press, Tuscaloosa.

2019        From Weeping Hills to Lost Caves: A Search for Vibrant Matter in Greater
            Cahokia. In *New Materialisms Ancient Urbanisms*, edited by Susan M. Alt
            and Timothy R. Pauketat, pp. 1–39. Routledge, London.

Alt, Susan M., Jeffery D. Kruchten, and Timothy R. Pauketat
2010        The Construction and Use of Cahokia's Grand Plaza: A View from the
            Trenches. *Journal of Field Archaeology* 35:131–146.

Alt, Susan M., and Timothy R. Pauketat
2005        Agency in a Postmold? Physicality and the Archaeology of Culture-Making.
            *Journal of Archaeological Method and Theory* 12(3):213–237.
2011        Why Wall Trenches? *Southeastern Archaeology* 30:108–122.

Alt, Susan M., and Timothy R. Pauketat (editors)
2019        *New Materialisms Ancient Urbanisms*. Routledge, London.

Ambrose, Stanley H., Jane E. Buikstra, and Harold W. Krueger
2003        Status and Gender Differences in Diet at Mound 72, Cahokia, Revealed by
            Isotopic Analysis of Bone. *Journal of Anthropological Archaeology* 22:217–226.

Ames, Kenneth M.
2008        The Archaeology of Rank. In *Handbook of Archaeological Theories*, edited by
            R. Alexander Bentley, Herbert D. G. Maschner, and Christopher Chippin-
            dale, pp. 487–513. AltaMira Press, Lanham, Maryland.

Anderson, Benedict
1991        *Imagined Communities: Reflections on the Origin and Spread of Nationalism*.
            Revised edition. Verso Editions, New York.

Anderson, David G.
1994        *The Savannah River Chiefdoms: Political Change in the Late Prehistoric
            Southeast*. University of Alabama Press, Tuscaloosa.
1997        The Role of Cahokia in the Evolution of Southeastern Mississippian Society.
            In *Cahokia: Domination and Ideology in the Mississippian World*, edited by
            Timothy R. Pauketat and Thomas E. Emerson, pp. 248–268. University of
            Nebraska Press, Lincoln.
2018        Foreword: Crafting Community and Identity in the Eastern Woodlands.
            In *The Power of Villages*, edited by Jennifer Birch and Victor Thompson,
            pp. ix–xvii. University Press of Florida, Gainesville.

Anderson, David G., and Robert C. Mainfort Jr.
2002        An Introduction to Woodland Archaeology in the Southeast. In *The Wood-
            land Southeast*, edited by David G. Anderson and Robert C. Mainfort Jr.,
            pp. 1–19. University of Alabama Press, Tuscaloosa.

Anderson, David G., and Kenneth E. Sassaman
2012        *Recent Developments in Southeastern Archaeology: From Colonization to
            Complexity*. Society for American Archaeology Press, Washington, DC.

Anderson, David G., and Joseph Schuldrein (editors)
1985        *Prehistoric Human Ecology along the Upper Savannah River: Excavations at
            Rucker's Bottom, Abbeville and Bullard Site Groups*. Commonwealth Asso-
            ciates. Prepared for US Department of Interior National Park Service, Ar-
            chaeological Services Branch, Atlanta, Georgia.

Anschuetz, Kurt F., Richard H. Wilshusen, and Cherie L. Scheick
2001        An Archaeology of Landscapes: Perspectives and Directions. *Journal of
            Archaeological Research* 9:157–211.

Anthony, David W.
1990        Migration in Archaeology: The Baby and the Bathwater. *American Anthropologist* 92:895–914.

Arkush, Elizabeth
2018        Coalescence and Defensive Communities: Insights from an Andean Hillfort Town. *Cambridge Archaeological Journal* 28(1):1–22.

Armour, Daryl W.
2012        A Comparison of Artifacts and Activities among Mound Area Contexts at Town Creek, A Mississippian Site in Piedmont North Carolina. Master's thesis, Department of Anthropology, East Carolina University, Greenville, North Carolina.

Arnauld, Charlotte, Linda R. Manzanilla, and Michael E. Smith (editors)
2012        *The Neighborhood as a Social and Spatial Unit in Mesoamerican Cities.* University of Arizona Press, Tucson.

Arnold, Dean E.
1998        Ancient Andean Ceramic Technology: An Ethnoarchaeological Perspective. In *Andean Ceramics: Technology, Organization, and Approaches*, edited by Izumi Shimada, pp. 353–367. University of Pennsylvania Museum of Archaeology and Anthropology, Philadelphia.

Ashley, Keith H.
2003        Interaction, Population Movement, and Political Economy: The Changing Social Landscape of Northeastern Florida (A.D. 900–1500). PhD dissertation, Department of Anthropology, University of Florida, Gainesville.
2005a       Introducing Shields Mound (8DU12) and the Mill Cove Complex. *Florida Anthropologist* 58:151–174.
2005b       Toward an Interpretation of Shields Mound (8DU12) and Mill Cove Complex. *Florida Anthropologist* 58:287–301.
2006        Colorinda and Its Place in Northeastern Florida History. *Florida Anthropologist* 59:91–100.
2012        Early St. Johns II Interaction, Exchange, and Politics: A View from Northeastern Florida. In *Late Prehistoric Florida: Archaeology at the Edge of the Mississippian World*, edited by Keith Ashley and Nancy Marie White, pp. 100–125. University Press of Florida, Gainesville.

Ashley, Keith H., and Greg S. Hendryx
2008        Archaeological Site Testing and Data Recovery and Mitigation at the Dolphin Reef Site (8Du276), Duval County, Florida. Report on file, Division of Historical Resources, Tallahassee, Florida.

Ashley, Keith H., and Vicki Rolland
2014        Ritual at the Mill Cove Complex: Realms beyond the River. In *New Histories of Pre-Columbian Florida*, edited Neill J. Wallis and Asa R. Randall, pp. 262–282. University Press of Florida, Gainesville.

Ashley, Keith H., and Neill J. Wallis
2006        Northeastern Florida Swift Creek: Overview and Future Research. *Florida Anthropologist* 59:5–18.

Ashmore, Wendy
2002        "Decisions and Dispositions": Socializing Spatial Archaeology. *American Anthropologist* 104(4):1172–1183.

Ashmore, Wendy, and A. Bernard Knapp (editors)
1999      *Archaeologies of Landscape: Contemporary Perspectives*. Blackwell, Oxford.

Ashmore, Wendy, and Richard R. Wilk
1988      Household and Community in the Mesoamerican Past. In *Household and Community in the Mesoamerican Past*, edited by Richard R. Wilk and Wendy Ashmore, pp. 1–27. University of New Mexico Press, Albuquerque.

Baden, William W.
1983      *Tomotley: An Eighteenth Century Cherokee Village*. Report of Investigations No. 36. Department of Anthropology, University of Tennessee, Knoxville.

Bailey, Garrick (editor)
1995      *The Osage and the Invisible World: From the Works of Francis La Flesche*. University of Oklahoma Press, Norman.

Baires, Sarah E.
2014a     Cahokia's Origins: Religion, Complexity and Ridge-Top Mortuaries in the Mississippi River Valley. PhD dissertation, Department of Anthropology, University of Illinois at Urbana-Champaign.
2014b     Cahokia's Rattlesnake Causeway. *Midcontinental Journal of Archaeology* 39:1–18.
2017      *Land of Water, City of the Dead: Religion and Cahokia's Emergence*. University of Alabama Press, Tuscaloosa.
2018      Introduction: Dynamic Worlds, Shifting Paradigms. In *Relational Engagements of the Indigenous Americas: Alterity, Ontology, and Shifting Paradigms*, edited by Melissa R. Baltus and Sarah E. Baires, pp. vii–xv. Lexington Books, Lanham, Maryland.

Baires, Sarah E., and Melissa R. Baltus
2016      Matter, Places, and Persons in Cahokian Depositional Acts. *Journal of Archaeological Method and Theory* 24(3):974–997.

Baires, Sarah E., Melissa R. Baltus, and Elizabeth Watts Malouchos
2017      Exploring New Cahokian Neighborhoods: Structure Density Estimates from the Spring Lake Tract, Cahokia. *American Antiquity* 82:742–760.

Baires, Sarah E., Amanda J. Butler, B. Jacob Skousen, and Timothy R. Pauketat
2013      Fields of Movement in the Ancient Woodlands of North America. In *Archaeology after Interpretation: Returning Materials to Archaeological Theory*, edited by Benjamin Alberti, Andrew Meirion Jones, and Joshua Pollard, pp. 197–218. Routledge, New York.

Baltus, Melissa R.
2014      Transforming Material Relationships: 13th Century Revitalization of Cahokian Religious-Politics. PhD dissertation, Department of Anthropology, University of Illinois at Urbana-Champaign.
2015      Unraveling Entanglements: Reverberations of Cahokia's Big Bang. In *Tracing the Relational: The Archaeology of Worlds, Spirits, and Temporalities*, edited by Meghan E. Buchanan and B. Jacob Skousen, pp. 146–160. University of Utah Press, Salt Lake City.
2018a     From Caches to Gatherings: The Relationality of Intentionally Deposited Objects in Mississippian Buildings. In *Archaeology and Ancient Religion in the American Midcontinent*, edited by Brad H. Koldehoff and Timothy R. Pauketat, pp. 81–116. University of Alabama Press, Tuscaloosa.
2018b     Vessels of Change: Everyday Relationality in the Rise and Fall of Cahokia. In

Relational Entanglements of the Indigenous Americas: Alterity, Ontology, and Shifting Paradigms, edited by Melissa R. Baltus and Sarah E. Baires, pp. 63–86. Routledge, New York.

Baltus, Melissa R. and Sarah E. Baires
2012    Elements of Ancient Power in the Cahokian World. *Journal of Social Archaeology* 12(2):167–192.
2020    Creating and Abandoning "Homeland": Cahokia as Place of Origin. *Journal of Archaeological Method and Theory* 27:111–127.

Barad, Karen
2003    Posthumanist Performativity: Toward an Understanding of How Matter Comes to Matter. *Signs: Journal of Women in Culture and Society* 28(3):801–831.

Bardolph, Dana N.
2014    Evaluating Cahokian Contact and Mississippian Identity Politics in the Late Prehistoric Central Illinois River Valley. *American Antiquity* 79:69–89.

Bareis, Charles J., and James W. Porter (editors)
1984    *American Bottom Archaeology: A Summary of the FAI-270 Project Contributions to the Culture History of the Mississippi River Valley.* University of Illinois Press, Urbana.

Barker, Alex W.
1999    Chiefdoms and the Economics of Perversity. PhD dissertation, Department of Anthropology, University of Michigan, Ann Arbor.

Barrier, Casey R.
2007    Surplus Storage at Early Moundville: The Distribution of Oversized Jars at Mound W and Other Off-Mound Locations. Master's thesis, Department of Anthropology, University of Alabama, Tuscaloosa.
2011    Storage and Relative Surplus at the Mississippian Site of Moundville. *Journal of Anthropological Archaeology* 30(2):206–219.
2017    Town Aggregation and Abandonment during the Era of Urban Transformations in the Cahokia Region: Bayesian Modeling of the Washausen Mound-Town. *Journal of Archaeological Science: Reports* 11:523–535.

Barrier, Casey R., and Timothy J. Horsley
2014    Shifting Communities: Demographic Profiles of Early Village Population Growth and Decline in the Central American Bottom. *American Antiquity* 79(2):295–313.

Barry, Steven E.
2004    Lithic Raw Material and Chipped Stone Tools: A Comparison of Two Sites in the Moundville Chiefdom. Master's thesis, Department of Anthropology, University of Alabama, Tuscaloosa.

Barth, Fredrik
1969    *Ethnic Groups and Boundaries: The Social Organization of Culture Difference.* Little, Brown, Boston.

Basso, Keith H.
1996    *Wisdom Sits in Places: Landscape and Language among the Western Apache.* University of New Mexico Press, Albuquerque.

Beck, Robin A., Jr.
2003    Consolidation and Hierarchy: Chiefdom Variability in the Mississippian Southeast. *American Antiquity* 68:641–664.
2007    The Durable House: Material, Metaphor, and Structure. In *The Durable*

*House: House Society Models in Archaeology*, edited by Robin A. Beck Jr.,
pp. 3–24. Occasional Paper No. 35. Center for Archaeological Investigations,
Southern Illinois University, Carbondale.

2013       *Chiefdoms, Collapse, and Coalescence in the Early American South*. Cambridge University Press, Cambridge.

Beck, Robin A., Jr. (editor)
2007       *The Durable House: House Society Models in Archaeology*. Occasional Paper
No. 35. Center for Archaeological Investigations, Southern Illinois University, Carbondale.

Bell, Robert E.
1961       Relationships between the Caddoan Area and the Plains. *Bulletin of the
Texas Archeological Society* 31:51–64.

Bender, Barbara
2002       Time and Landscape. *Current Anthropology* 43(S4):S103–S112.

Bengtson, Jennifer D., and Jodie A. O'Gorman
2016       Children, Migration and Mortuary Representation in the Late Prehistoric
Central Illinois River Valley. *Childhood in the Past* 9(1):19–43.

Bennett, Jane
2010       *Vibrant Matter: A Political Ecology of Things*. Duke University Press,
Durham, North Carolina.

Bense, Judith A.
1994       *Archaeology of the Southeastern United States: Paleoindian to World War I*.
Academic Press, New York.

Benyshek, Tasha, Benjamin A. Steere, Paul Webb, Joel Jones, and Hannah Guidry
2010       Finding, Delineating, and Recording Structure Patterns: Recent Excavations
in Western North Carolina. Paper presented at the 67th Annual Meeting of
the Southeastern Archaeological Conference, Lexington, Kentucky.

Betzenhauser, Alleen M.
2011       Creating the Cahokian Community: The Power of Place in Early Mississippian Sociopolitical Dynamics. PhD dissertation, Department of Anthropology, University of Illinois at Urbana-Champaign.

2017       Cahokia's Beginnings: Mobility, Urbanization, and the Cahokian Political
Landscape. In *Mississippian Beginnings*, edited by Gregory D. Wilson,
pp. 71–96. University Press of Florida, Gainesville.

2018       Exploring Measures of Inequality in the Mississippian Heartland. In *Ten
Thousand Years of Inequality*, edited by Timothy A. Kohler and Michael E.
Smith, pp. 180–200. University of Arizona Press, Tucson.

Betzenhauser, Alleen M. (editor)
2019       *East St. Louis Precinct Terminal Late Woodland Features*. Research Report
46. Illinois State Archaeological Survey, Prairie Research Institute, University
of Illinois at Urbana-Champaign.

Betzenhauser, Alleen M., Tamira K. Brennan, M. Brent Lansdell, Sarah E. Harken, and
   Victoria E. Potter
2018       Chronological Implications and External Connections in the East St. Louis
Precinct Ceramic Assemblage. In *Revealing Greater Cahokia: Rediscovery
and Large-Scale Excavations of the East St. Louis Precinct*, edited by Thomas
E. Emerson, Brad H. Koldehoff, and Tamira K. Brennan, pp. 263–332. Studies in Archaeology No. 12. Illinois State Archaeological Survey, Prairie
Research Institute, University of Illinois at Urbana-Champaign.

Betzenhauser, Alleen M., and Timothy R. Pauketat
2019        Elements of Cahokian Neighborhoods. In *Excavating Neighborhoods: A Cross-Cultural Perspective*, edited by David Pacifico and Lise A. Treux. Archeological Paper No. 30, American Anthropological Association, Arlington, Virginia.

Bhabha, Homi K.
1994        *The Location of Culture*. Routledge, New York.

Binford, Lewis R.
1962        Archaeology as Anthropology. *American Antiquity* 28:217–225.
1971        Mortuary Practices: Their Study and Their Potential. In *Approaches to the Social Dimensions of Mortuary Practices*, edited by James A. Brown, pp. 6–29. Memoir No. 25. Society for American Archaeology, Washington, DC.

Birch, Jennifer
2012        Coalescent Communities: Settlement Aggregation and Social Integration in Iroquoian Ontario. *American Antiquity* 77:646–671.
2013        Between Villages and Cities: Settlement Aggregation in Cross-Cultural Perspective. In *From Prehistoric Villages to Cities: Settlement Aggregation and Community Transformation*, edited by Jennifer Birch, pp. 1–22. Routledge, New York.

Birch, Jennifer (editor)
2013        *From Prehistoric Villages to Cities: Settlement Aggregation and Community Transformation*. Routledge, New York.

Birch, Jennifer, Stefan Brannan, Michael Walters, and Michael Lukas
2015        Geophysical Characterization of Terminal Mound Functions at Singer-Moye. Poster presented at the 72nd Annual Meeting of the Southeastern Archaeological Conference, Nashville, Tennessee.

Birch, Jennifer, and Ronald F. Williamson
2018        Initial Iroquoian Coalescence. In *The Archaeology of Villages in Eastern North America*, edited by Jennifer Birch and Victor D. Thompson, pp. 89–105. University Press of Florida, Gainesville.

Bird-David, Nurit
1999        "Animism" Revisited: Personhood, Environment, and Relational Epistemology. *Current Anthropology* 40(S1):S67–S91.

Blank, Andres, Aspen Kemmerlin, Taesoo Jung, Samuel Dilidili, and Gretchen Eggiman
2015        *Studying Space between Mounds and Plazas: Archaeological Investigations at Singer-Moye (9SW2)*. Poster presented at the 72nd Annual Meeting of the Southeastern Archaeological Conference, Nashville, Tennessee.

Blanton, Richard E.
1994        *Houses and Households: A Comparative Study*. Plenum Press, New York.

Blanton, Richard E., and Lane F. Fargher
2008        *Collective Action in the Formation of Pre-Modern States*. Springer, New York.

Blanton, Richard E., Gary M. Feinman, Stephen A. Kowalewski, and Peter N. Peregrine
1996        A Dual-Processual Theory for the Evolution of Mesoamerican Civilization. *Current Anthropology* 37:1–14.

Blitz, John H.
1993        *Ancient Chiefdoms of the Tombigbee*. University of Alabama Press, Tuscaloosa.
1999        Mississippian Chiefdoms and the Fission-Fusion Process. *American Antiquity* 64:577–592.
2008        *Moundville*. University of Alabama Press, Tuscaloosa.

2010        New Perspectives in Mississippian Archaeology. *Journal of Archaeological Research* 18:1–39.

2012        Moundville in the Mississippian World. In *Oxford Handbook of North American Archaeology*, edited by Timothy Pauketat, pp. 534–543. Oxford University Press, New York.

Blitz, John H., and Patrick Livingood

2004        Sociopolitical Implications of Mississippian Mound Volume. *American Antiquity* 69(2):291–301.

Blitz, John H., and Karl G. Lorenz

2002        The Early Mississippian Frontier in the Lower Chattahoochee-Apalachicola River Valley. *Southeastern Archaeology* 21(2):117–135.

2006        *The Chattahoochee Chiefdoms*. University of Alabama Press, Tuscaloosa.

Bohannon, Charles F.

1973        *Excavations at the Mineral Springs Site, Howard County, Arkansas*. Research Series No. 5. Arkansas Archeological Society, Fayetteville.

Bolton, Herbert Eugene

1987        *The Hasinais: Southern Caddoans as Seen by the Earliest Europeans*. University of Oklahoma Press, Norman.

Borremans, Nina Thanz, and Craig D. Shaak

1986        A Preliminary Report on Investigations of Sponge Spicules in Florida "Chalky" Paste Pottery. *Ceramic Notes* 3:125–132. Occasional Publications of the Ceramic Technology Laboratory, Florida State Museum, Gainesville.

Boudreaux, Edmond A., III

2005        The Archaeology of Town Creek: Chronology, Community Patterns, and Leadership at a Mississippian Town. PhD dissertation, Department of Anthropology, University of North Carolina, Chapel Hill.

2007        *The Archaeology of Town Creek*. University of Alabama Press, Tuscaloosa.

2010        Mound Construction and Change in the Mississippian Community at Town Creek. In *Mississippian Mortuary Practices: Beyond Hierarchy and the Representationist Perspective*, edited by Robert C. Mainfort and Lynne P. Sullivan, pp. 195–233. University Press of Florida, Gainesville.

2011        The Current State of Town Creek Research: What Have We Learned after the First 75 Years? In *The Archaeology of North Carolina: Three Archaeological Symposia*, edited by Charles R. Ewen, Thomas R. Whyte, and R. P. Stephen Davis Jr. Publication No. 30. North Carolina Archaeological Council, Raleigh.

2013        Community and Ritual within the Mississippian Center at Town Creek. *American Antiquity* 78:483–501.

2017        Early Mississippian in the North Carolina Piedmont. In *Mississippian Beginnings*, edited by Gregory D. Wilson, pp. 203–233. University Press of Florida, Gainesville.

Boulware, Tyler

2011        *Deconstructing the Cherokee Nation: Town, Region and Nation among Eighteenth-Century Cherokees*. University Press of Florida, Gainesville.

Bourdieu, Pierre

1970        The Berber House or the World Reversed. *Information (International Social Science Council)* 9(2):151–170.

1973        The Berber House. In *Rules and Meanings: The Anthropology of Everyday Knowledge*, edited by Mary Douglas, pp. 98–110. Routledge, New York.

1977     *Outline of a Theory of Practice.* Translated by Richard Nice. Cambridge University Press, Cambridge.

1990     *The Logic of Practice.* Translated by Richard Nice. Stanford University Press, Stanford, California.

Bowen, H. C., and R. D. Wood

1968     Experimental Storage of Corn Underground and Its Implications for Iron Age Settlements. *Bulletin of the Institute of Archaeology* 7:1–14.

Bowser, Brenda J.

2004     Prologue: Toward an Archaeology of Place. *Journal of Archaeological Method and Theory* 11:1–3.

Bradley, Richard

1987     Time Regained: The Creation of Continuity. *Journal of the British Archaeological Association* 140:1–17.

1990     *The Passage of Arms: An Archaeological Analysis of Prehistoric Hoards and Votive Deposits.* Cambridge University Press, Cambridge.

1993     *Altering the Earth: The Origins of Monuments in Britain and Continental Europe.* Society of Antiquaries of Scotland, Edinburgh.

1998     *The Significance of Monuments: On the Shaping of Human Experience in the Neolithic and Bronze Age.* Routledge, London.

2003     The Translation of Time. In *Archaeologies of Memory*, edited by Ruth M. Van Dyke and Susan E. Alcock, pp. 221–227. Blackwell, Malden, Massachusetts.

Brady, James E., and Wendy Ashmore

1999     Mountains, Caves, Water: Ideational Landscapes of the Ancient Maya. In *Archaeologies of Landscapes: Contemporary Perspectives*, edited by Wendy Ashmore and A. Bernard Knapp, pp. 124–148. Blackwell, Oxford.

Brain, Jeffrey P., and Philip Phillips

1996     *Shell Gorgets: Styles of the Late Prehistoric and Protohistoric Southeast.* Peabody Museum Press, Cambridge, Massachusetts.

Brannan, Stefan

2012     A Brief Report on the 2012 UGA Field School Expedition at Singer-Moye (9SW2). Paper presented at the 2012 Symposium on Southeastern Coastal Plain Archaeology, Douglas, Georgia.

2018     The Settlement Archaeology of Singer-Moye, a Large 14th-Century Town in the Chattahoochee Valley, Georgia. PhD dissertation, Department of Anthropology, University of Georgia, Athens.

Brannan, Stefan, and Daniel P. Bigman

2012     Do Mississippian Plazas Represent Open Spaces or Rich Histories? Paper presented at the 69th Annual Meeting of the Southeastern Archaeological Conference, Baton Rouge, Louisiana.

2014     Ground Penetrating Radar and Resistivity Results from Mounds D and F at Singer-Moye (9SW2). *Early Georgia* 42(2):179–192.

Brannan, Stefan, and Jennifer Birch

2017     Settlement Ecology at Singer-Moye: Mississippian History and Demography in the Southeastern United States. In *Settlement Ecology of the Ancient Americas*, edited by Lucas C. Kellett and Eric E. Jones, pp. 57–84. Routledge, New York.

Brannan, Tamira K.

2007     In-Ground Evidence of Above-Ground Architecture at Kincaid Mounds.

In *Architectural Variability in the Southeast*, edited by Cameron H. Lacquement, pp. 73–100. University of Alabama Press, Tuscaloosa.

2014  Mississippian Community-Making through Everyday Items at Kincaid Mounds. PhD dissertation, Department of Anthropology, Southern Illinois University, Carbondale.

2018a  Organization of the East St. Louis Precinct. In *East St. Louis Precinct Mississippian Features*, edited by Tamira K. Brennan, pp. 341–368. Research Report No. 43. Illinois State Archaeological Survey, Prairie Research Institute, University of Illinois at Urbana-Champaign.

2018b  Main Street Mound and the Mississippian Landscape. In *Revealing Greater Cahokia, North America's First Native City: Rediscovery and Large-Scale Excavations of the East St. Louis Precinct*, edited by Thomas E. Emerson, Brad H. Koldehoff, and Tamira K. Brennan, pp. 203–218. Studies in Archaeology No. 12. Illinois State Archaeological Survey, Prairie Research Institute, University of Illinois at Urbana-Champaign.

2018c  Architecture. In *East St. Louis Precinct Mississippian Features*, edited by Tamira K. Brennan, pp. 23–190. Research Report No. 43. Illinois State Archaeological Survey, Prairie Research Institute, University of Illinois at Urbana-Champaign.

2018d  Introduction. In *East St. Louis Precinct Mississippian Features*, edited by Tamira K. Brennan, pp. 1–10. Research Report No. 43. Illinois State Archaeological Survey, Prairie Research Institute, University of Illinois at Urbana-Champaign.

Brennan, Tamira K. (editor)
2016  *Main Street Mound: A Ridgetop Monument at the East St. Louis Mound Complex*. Research Report No. 36. Illinois State Archaeological Survey, Prairie Research Institute, University of Illinois at Urbana-Champaign.

Brennan, Tamira K., Alleen M. Betzenhauser, M. Brent Lansdell, Luke A. Plocher, Victoria E. Potter, and Daniel F. Blodgett
2018  Community Organization of the East St. Louis Precinct. In *Revealing Greater Cahokia: Rediscovery and Large-Scale Excavations of the East St. Louis Precinct*, edited by Thomas E. Emerson, Brad H. Koldehoff, and Tamira K. Brennan, pp. 127–202. Studies in Archaeology No. 12. Illinois State Archaeological Survey, Prairie Research Institute, University of Illinois at Urbana-Champaign.

Brennan, Tamira K., and Eve A. Hargrave
2018  Site Significance and Discussion. In *Mund and Moorehead Phase Occupations at the Russell Site*, edited by Tamira K. Brennan, pp. 237–246. Technical Report No. 128. Illinois State Archaeological Survey, Prairie Research Institute, University of Illinois at Urbana-Champaign.

Brennan, Tamira K., and Lenna M. Nash
2018  Mortuary Features. In *East St. Louis Precinct Mississippian Features*, edited by Tamira K. Brennan, pp. 307–328. Research Report No. 43. Illinois State Archaeological Survey, Prairie Research Institute, University of Illinois at Urbana-Champaign.

Brennan, Tamira K., and Corin C. O. Pursell
2019  Kincaid Mounds and the Cahokian Decline. In *Cahokia in Context: Hegemony and Diaspora*, edited by Charles A. McNutt and Ryan M. Parrish, pp. 87–104. University Press of Florida, Gainsville.

Briggs, Rachel V.
2016     The Civil Cooking Pot: Hominy and the Mississippian Standard Jar in the Black Warrior River Valley. *American Antiquity* 81(2):316–332.
Brightman, Robert A., and Pamela S. Wallace
2004     Chickasaw. In *Southeast*, edited by Raymond D. Fogelson, pp. 478–495. Handbook of North American Indians, Vol. 14, William C. Sturtevant, general editor, Smithsonian Institution, Washington, DC.
Brooks, Robert L.
2012     Decisions in Landscape Setting Selection of the Prehistoric Caddo of Southeastern Oklahoma: A GIS Analysis. In *The Archaeology of the Caddo*, edited by Timothy K. Perttula and Chester P. Walker, pp. 335–362. University of Nebraska Press, Lincoln.
Brown, Ian W.
1981     A Study of Stonebox Graves in Eastern North America. *Tennessee Archaeologist* 6:1–26.
Brown, James A.
1984     Arkansas Valley Caddoan: The Spiro Phase. In *Prehistory of Oklahoma*, edited by Robert E. Bell, pp. 241–263. Academic Press, New York.
1995     On Mortuary Analysis—With Special Reference to the Saxe-Binford Research Program. In *Regional Approaches to Mortuary Analysis*, edited by Lane A. Beck, pp. 3–26. Plenum Press, New York.
1997     The Archaeology of Ancient Religion in the Eastern Woodlands. *Annual Review of Anthropology* 26(1):465–485.
2004     The Cahokian Expression: Creating Court and Cult. In *Hero, Hawk, and Open Hand: American Indian Art of the Ancient Midwest and South*, edited by Robert V. Sharp, pp. 105–123. Yale University Press, New Haven, Connecticut.
2007     The Social House in Southeastern Archaeology. In *The Durable House: House Society Models in Archaeology*, edited by Robin A. Beck Jr., pp. 227–247. Occasional Paper No. 35. Center for Archaeological Investigations, Southern Illinois University, Carbondale.
Brown, James A., Richard A. Kerber, and Howard D. Winters
1990     Trade and the Evolution of Exchange Relations at the Beginning of the Mississippian Period. In *The Mississippian Emergence*, edited by Bruce D. Smith, pp. 251–274. Smithsonian Institution Press, Washington, DC.
Brumfiel, Elizabeth M.
1991     Weaving and Cooking: Women's Production in Aztec Mexico. In *Engendering Archaeology: Women and Prehistory*, edited by Joan M. Gero and Margaret W. Conkey, pp. 224–254. Wiley-Blackwell, Oxford.
1992     Distinguished Lecture in Archaeology: Breaking and Entering the Ecosystem—Gender, Class, and Faction Steal the Show. *American Anthropologist* 94(3):551–567.
Buchanan, Meghan E.
2015a    War-Scapes, Lingering Spirits, and the Mississippian Vacant Quarter. In *Tracing the Relational: The Archaeology of Worlds, Spirits, and Temporalities*, edited by Meghan E. Buchanan and B. Jacob Skousen, pp. 85–99. University of Utah Press, Salt Lake City.
2015b    Warfare and the Materialization of Daily Life at the Mississippian Common

Field Site. PhD dissertation, Department of Anthropology, Indiana University, Bloomington.

2020      Diasporic Longings? Cahokia, Common Field, and Nostalgic Orientations. *Journal of Archaeological Method and Theory* 27:72–89.

Buchanan, Meghan E., and B. Jacob Skousen (editors)

2015      *Tracing the Relational: The Archaeology of Worlds, Spirits, and Temporalities.* University of Utah Press, Salt Lake City.

Buchner, C. Andrew, Karla Oesch, Neal H. Lopinot, Gina S. Powell, Chester P. Walker, J. Rocco DeGregory, Nicholas P. Herrmann, and Susan L. Scott

2012      Archaeological Data Recovery at Foster Place (3LA27) and Site 3LA290 for the Red River Levee Rehabilitation Project (Item 9A-2), Lafayette County, Arkansas. PCI Report 31053. Panamerican Consultants, Memphis, Tennessee.

Butler, Brian M.

1977      The Yearwood Site: A Specialized Middle Woodland Occupation on the Elk River. *Tennessee Anthropologist* 1(2):1–15.

2010      Chert Sources and Hierarchy: Mississippian Chert Usage at Kincaid and Its Surrounding Settlements. Paper presented at the 75th Anniversary Meeting of the Society for American Archaeology, Saint Louis, Missouri.

Butler, Brian M., R. Berle Clay, Michael L. Hargrave, Staffan D. Peterson, John E. Schwegman, John A. Schwegman, and Paul W. Welch

2011      A New Look at Kincaid: Magnetic Survey of a Large Mississippian Town. *Southeastern Archaeology* 30:20–37.

Butzer, Karl W.

2012      Collapse, Environment, and Society. *Proceedings of the National Academy of Sciences* 109:3632–3639.

Butzer, Karl W., and Georgina H. Endfield

2012      Critical Perspectives on Historical Collapse. *Proceedings of the National Academy of Sciences* 109:3628–3631.

Caldwell, Joseph R.

1955      Investigations at Rood's Landing, Stewart County, Georgia. *Early Georgia* 2(1):22–49.

Cameron, Catherine M.

2000      Comment on "Archaeology and Migration: Approaches to an Archaeological Proof of Migration," by Stefan Burmeister. *Current Anthropology* 41:555–556.

Campbell, Meadow

2013      *Report of Excavations on Douglas Mound Kincaid Site 2013.* Manuscript submitted to the Illinois Historic Preservation Agency, Springfield.

Canuto, Marcello A., and Jason Yaeger (editors)

2000      *The Archaeology of Communities: A New World Perspective.* Routledge, New York.

2012      Community. In *Oxford Handbook on Mesoamerican Archaeology*, edited by Deborah L. Nichols and Christopher A. Pool, pp. 697–707. Oxford University Press, Oxford.

Carballo, David M. (editor)

2013      *Cooperation and Collective Action.* University Press of Colorado, Boulder.

Carballo, David M., Paul Roscoe, and Gary M. Feinman

2014      Cooperation and Collective Action in the Cultural Evolution of Complex Societies. *Journal of Archaeological Method and Theory* 21(1):98–133.

Carsten, Janet, and Stephen Hugh-Jones
1995        *About the House: Lévi-Strauss and Beyond.* Cambridge University Press, New York.

Chapman, Carl H.
1980        *The Archaeology of Missouri,* Vol. 2. University of Missouri Press, Columbia.

Chapman, Jefferson
1994        *Tellico Archaeology: 12,000 Years of Native American History.* Report of Investigations No. 43, Department of Anthropology, University of Tennessee. Frank McClung Museum, Occasional Paper No 5. Tennessee Valley Authority Publications in Anthropology No. 41. University of Tennessee Press, Knoxville.

2009        Tellico Archaeology: Tracing Timberlake's Footsteps. In *Culture, Crisis, and Conflict: Cherokee British Relations, 1756–1765,* edited by Anne F. Rogers and Barbara R. Duncan, pp. 45–61. Museum of the Cherokee Indian Press, Cherokee, North Carolina.

Chapman, John
1996        Enchainment, Commodification, and Gender in the Balkan Copper Age. *Journal of European Archaeology* 4:203–242.

Charles, Douglas K., Julieann Van Nest, and Jane E. Buikstra
2004        From the Earth: Minerals and Meaning in the Hopewellian World. In *Soils, Stones, and Symbols: Cultural Perceptions of the Mineral World,* edited by Nicole Boivin and Mary A. Owoc, pp. 43–70. Cavendish, Portland, Oregon.

Cheney, Susan L.
1992        Uncertain Migrations: The History and Archaeology of Victorian Goldfield Community. *Australasian Historical Archaeology* 10:36–42.

Childe, V. Gordon
1940        *Prehistoric Communities of the British Isles.* W. and R. Chambers, London.

Cipolla, Craig N.
2017        *Native American Diaspora and Ethnogenesis.* Oxford Handbooks Online. https://www.oxfordhandbooks.com/, accessed July 12, 2020.

Clark, Jeffery J.
2001        *Tracking Prehistoric Migrations: Pueblo Settlers among the Tonto Basin Hohokam.* Anthropology Papers of the University of Arizona No. 65. University of Arizona Press, Tucson.

Clark, Jeffery J., Jennifer A. Birch, Michelle Hegmon, Barbara J. Mills, Donna M. Glowacki, Scott G. Ortman, Jeffery S. Dean, Rory Gauthier, Patrick D. Lyons, Matthew A. Peeples, Lewis Borck, and John A. Ware
2019        Resolving the Migrant Paradox: Two Pathways to Coalescence in the Late Precontact U.S. Southwest. *Journal of Anthropological Archaeology* 53:262–287.

Clark, Jeffery J., Deborah L. Huntley, J. Brett Hill, and Patrick D. Lyons
2013        The Kayenta Diaspora and Salado Meta-Identity in the Late Pre-Contact Southwest. In *Hybrid Material Culture: The Archaeology of Syncretism and Ethnogenesis,* edited by Jeb Card, pp. 399–424. Occasional Paper No. 39. Center for Archaeological Investigations, Southern Illinois University, Carbondale.

Cobb, Charles R.
1993        Archaeological Approaches to the Political Economy of Nonstratified Societies. *Archaeological Method and Theory* 5:43–99.

2000        *From Quarry to Cornfield: The Political Economy of Mississippian Hoe Pro-
            duction.* University of Alabama Press, Tuscaloosa.
2003        Mississippian Chiefdoms: How Complex? *Annual Review of Anthropology*
            32(1):63–84.
2005        Archaeology and the "Savage Slot": Displacement and Emplacement in the
            Premodern World. *American Anthropologist* 107(4):563–574.

Cobb, Charles R., and Brian M. Butler
2002        The Vacant Quarter Revisited: Late Mississippian Abandonment of the
            Lower Ohio Valley. *American Antiquity* 67:625–642.
2006        Mississippian Migration and Emplacement in the Lower Ohio Valley. In
            *Leadership and Polity in Mississippian Society,* edited by Brian M. Butler and
            Paul D. Welch, pp. 328–347. Occasional Paper No. 33. Center for Archaeo-
            logical Investigations, Southern Illinois University, Carbondale.
2017        Mississippian Plazas, Performances, and Portable Histories. *Journal of Archaeo-
            logical Method and Theory* 24(3):676–702.

Cobb, Charles R., and Patricia H. Garrow
1996        Woodstock Culture and the Question of Mississippian Emergence. *American
            Antiquity* 61:21–38.

Cobb, Charles R., and Adam King
2005        Re-Inventing Mississippian Tradition at Etowah, Georgia. *Journal of Archaeo-
            logical Method and Theory* 12(3):167–192.

Cobb, Charles R., and Michael S. Nassaney
1995        Interaction and Integration in the Late Woodland Southeast. In *Native
            American Interactions: Multiscalar Analyses and Interpretations of the East-
            ern Woodlands,* edited by Michael S. Nassaney and Kenneth E. Sassaman,
            pp. 205–226. University of Tennessee Press, Knoxville.

Coe, Joffre L.
1995        *Town Creek Indian Mound: A Native American Legacy.* University of North
            Carolina Press, Chapel Hill.

Cohen, Anthony P.
1985        *Symbolic Construction of Community.* Routledge, New York.

Cole, Fay-Cooper, Robert Bell, John Bennett, Joseph Caldwell, Norman Emerson,
    Richard MacNeish, Kenneth Orr, and Roger Willis
1951        *Kincaid: A Prehistoric Illinois Metropolis.* University of Chicago Press, Chicago.

Cole, Patricia Ellen
1975        A Synthesis and Interpretation of the Hamilton Mortuary Pattern in East
            Tennessee. Master's thesis. Department of Anthropology, University of Ten-
            nessee, Knoxville.

Collins, James M.
1990        *The Archaeology of the Cahokia Mounds ICT-II: Site Structure.* Illinois Cul-
            tural Resources Study No. 10. Illinois Historic Preservation Agency, Spring-
            field.
1997        Cahokia Settlement and Social Structures as Viewed from the ICT-II. In
            *Cahokia: Domination and Ideology in the Mississippian World,* edited by
            Timothy R. Pauketat and Thomas E. Emerson, pp. 124–140. University of
            Nebraska Press, Lincoln.

Colwell-Chanthaphonh, Chip, and T. J. Ferguson
2006        Memory Pieces and Footprints: Multivocality and the Meanings of Ancient

Times and Ancestral Places among the Zuni and Hopi. *American Anthropologist* 108(1):148–162.

Connaway, John M.

1984a     *The Wilsford Site (22-Co-516) Coahoma County, Mississippi: A Late Mississippi Period Settlement in the Northern Yazoo Basin of Mississippi.* Mississippi Department of Archives and History, Jackson.

1984b     Parchman 4-7-84. Field notes on file, Mississippi Department of Archives and History, Clarksdale, Mississippi.

Connerton, Paul

1989     *How Societies Remember.* Cambridge University Press, Cambridge.

Conrad, Lawrence A.

1991     The Middle Mississippian Cultures of the Central Illinois River Valley. In *Cahokia and the Hinterlands: Middle Mississippian Cultures of the Midwest,* edited by Thomas E. Emerson and R. Barry Lewis, pp. 119–156. University of Illinois Press, Urbana.

Cook, Fred C.

1979     Kelvin: A Late Woodland Phase on the Southern Georgia Coast. *Early Georgia* 7(2):65–86.

2013     *Kelvin: A Late Woodland Culture on the Lower Georgia Coast.* SOGART Special Publication No. 7. Society for Georgia Archaeology, Athens, Georgia.

Cook, Robert A.

2008     *SunWatch: Fort Ancient Development in the Mississippian World.* University of Alabama Press, Tuscaloosa.

2018     The Village Remains the Same: A Fort Ancient Example. In *The Archaeology of Villages in Eastern North America,* edited by Jennifer Birch and Victor D. Thompson, pp. 124–139. University Press of Florida, Gainesville.

Cook, Robert A. and Lane F. Fargher

2008     The Incorporation of Mississippian Traditions into Fort Ancient Societies: A Preliminary View of the Shift to Shell-Tempered Pottery Use in the Middle Ohio Valley. *Southeastern Archaeology* 27:222–237.

Cordell, Ann S.

1984     *Ceramic Technology at a Weeden Island Period Archaeological Site in North America.* Ceramic Note No. 2. Ceramic Technology Laboratory, Florida State Museum, Gainesville.

1992     Technological Investigation of Pottery Variability in Southwest Florida. In *Culture and Environment in the Domain of the Calusa,* edited by William H. Marquardt, pp. 105–189. Monograph No. 1. Institute of Archaeology and Paleoenvironmental Studies, University of Florida, Gainesville.

Cordell, Ann S., and Steven H. Koski

2003     Analysis of a Spiculate Clay from Lake Monroe, Volusia County, Florida. *Florida Anthropologist* 56:113–125.

Corkran, David H. (editor)

1969     A Small Postscript of the Ways and Manners of the Indians Called Cherokees. *Southern Indian Studies* 21:1–49.

Creel, Darrell

1991     Bison Hides in Late Prehistoric Exchange in the Southern Plains. *American Antiquity* 56(1):40–49.

Cresswell, R.
1976        Avant-propos. *Techniques et culture* 1:5–6.
Crusoe, Donald
1971        A Study of Aboriginal Trade: A Petroglyphic Analysis of Certain Ceramic
            Types from Florida and Georgia. *Florida Anthropologist* 24:31–44.
Cunningham, Clark
1973        Order in the Atoni House. Reprinted in *Right & Left*, edited by Rodney
            Needham, pp. 204–237. University of Chicago Press, Chicago.
Currid, John D., and Avi Navon
1989        Iron Age Pits and the Lahav (Tell Halif) Grain Storage Project. *Bulletin of
            the American Schools of Oriental Research* 273:67–78.
Cushman, Horatio Bardwell
1962 [1899] *History of the Choctaw, Chickasaw, and Natchez Indians.* Headlight Printing
            House, Greenville, Texas. Reprinted, Redlands Press, Stillwater, Oklahoma.
Dalan, Rinita A.
1997        The Construction of Mississippian Cahokia. In *Cahokia: Domination and
            Ideology in the Mississippian World*, edited by Timothy R. Pauketat and
            Thomas E. Emerson, pp. 89–102. University of Nebraska Press, Lincoln.
Dalan, Rinita A., George R. Holley, William I. Woods, Harold W. Watters Jr., and
    John A. Koepke
2003        *Envisioning Cahokia: A Landscape Perspective.* Northern Illinois University
            Press, DeKalb.
Davis, Hester A., and E. Mott Davis
2009        An Account of the Birth and Growth of Caddo Archeology, as Seen by Review
            of 50 Caddo Conferences, 1946–2008. *Caddo Archeology Journal* 19:3–72.
Davis, Jera R.
2008        Crafting in the Countryside: A Comparison of Three Late Prehistoric Non-
            mound Sites in the Black Warrior River Valley. Master's thesis, Department
            of Anthropology, University of Alabama, Tuscaloosa.
2016        Crafting Moundville Palettes. In *Rethinking Moundville and Its Hinterland*,
            edited by Vincas P. Steponaitis and C. Margaret Scarry, pp. 234–254. Univer-
            sity Press of Florida, Gainesville.
Davis, Jera R., Chester P. Walker, and John H. Blitz
2015        Remote Sensing as Community Settlement Analysis at Moundville. *Ameri-
            can Antiquity* 80:161–169.
DeBoer, Warren R.
1988        Subterranean Storage and the Organization of Surplus: The View from East-
            ern North America. *Southeastern Archaeology* 7:1–20.
DeJarnette, David L. (editor)
1975        *Archaeological Salvage in the Walter F. George Basin of the Chattahoochee
            River in Alabama.* University of Alabama Press, Tuscaloosa.
DeJarnette, David L., and Steve B. Wimberly
1941        *The Bessemer Site: Excavation of Three Mounds and Surrounding Areas near
            Bessemer, Alabama.* Museum Paper 17, Geological Survey of Alabama, Uni-
            versity of Alabama, Tuscaloosa.
DeLanda, Manuel
2006        *A New Philosophy of Society: Assemblage Theory and Social Complexity.* Con-
            tinuum, New York.

Delcourt, Paul A., and Hazel R. Delcourt
2004    *Prehistoric Native Americans and Ecological Change: Human Ecosystems in Eastern North America since the Pleistocene.* Cambridge University Press, Cambridge.

Deleuze, Gilles, and Felix Guattari
2004    *A Thousand Plateaus: Capitalism and Schizophrenia.* Continuum, London.

Deloria, Vine, Jr.
2003    *God Is Red: A Native View of Religion.* Fulcrum, Golden, Colorado.

DeMarrais, Elizabeth, Luis Jaime Castillo, and Timothy Earle
1996    Ideology, Materialization, and Power Strategies. *Current Anthropology* 37(1):15–31.

Demel, Scott J., and Robert L. Hall
1998    The Mississippian Town Plan and Cultural Landscape of Cahokia, Illinois. In *Mississippian Towns and Sacred Spaces: Searching for an Architectural Grammar,* edited by R. Barry Lewis and Charles Stout, pp. 220–226. University of Alabama Press, Tuscaloosa.

De Montmollin, Olivier
1988    Settlement Scale and Theory in Maya Archaeology. In *Recent Studies in Pre-Columbian Archaeology,* edited by Nicholas J. Saunders and Olivier de Montmollin, pp. 63–104. BAR International Series 431. BAR, Oxford.

Diamond, Jared
2005    *Collapse: How Societies Choose to Fail or Succeed.* Viking Press, New York.

Díaz-Andreu, Margarita, Sam Lucy, Staša Babiæ, and David N. Edwards
2005    *The Archaeology of Identity: Approaches to Gender, Age, Status, Ethnicity and Religion.* Routledge, New York.

Dickens, Roy S., Jr.
1976    *Cherokee Prehistory: The Pisgah Phase in the Appalachian Summit Region.* University of Tennessee Press, Knoxville.
1978    Mississippian Settlement Patterns in the Appalachian Summit Area. In *Mississippian Settlement Patterns,* edited by Bruce D. Smith, pp. 115–139. Academic Press, New York.

Dietler, Michael, and Ingrid Herbich
1998    Habitus, Techniques, Style: An Integrated Approach to the Social Understanding of Material Culture and Boundaries. In *The Archaeology of Social Boundaries,* edited by Miriam Stark, pp. 232–263. Smithsonian Press, Washington, DC.

Dobres, Marcia-Anne
2000    *Technology and Social Agency.* Blackwell, Malden, Massachusetts.

Dobres, Marcia-Anne, and John E. Robb (editors)
2000    *Agency in Archaeology.* Routledge, New York.

Dowd, Elsbeth Linn
2011    Amphibian and Reptilian Imagery in Caddo Art. *Southeastern Archaeology* 30(1):79–95.

Dunning, Nicholas P., Timothy P. Beach, and Sheryl Luzzadder-Beach
2012    Kax and Kol: Collapse and Resilience in Lowland Maya Civilization. *Proceedings of the National Academy of Sciences* 109:3652–3657.

DuPratz, Le Page
1972 [1725] *The History of Louisiana.* Claitor's Publishing Division, Baton Rouge.

Dye, David H.
2009        War Paths, Peace Paths: An Archaeology of Cooperation and Conflict in Na-
            tive Eastern North America. AltaMira Press, Lanham, Maryland.
Dye, David H., and Cheryl Anne Cox (editors)
1990        Towns and Temples along the Mississippi. University of Alabama Press, Tus-
            caloosa.
Early, Ann M.
1988        Standridge: Caddoan Settlement in a Mountain Environment. Research Series
            No. 29. Arkansas Archeological Survey, Fayetteville.
1993        Caddoan Saltmakers in the Ouachita Valley: The Hardman Site. Research Se-
            ries No. 43. Arkansas Archeological Survey, Fayetteville.
Echo-Hawk, Walter R., Jr.
2009        Under Native Skies. George Wright Forum 26(3):58–63.
Eckert, Suzanne L.
2008        Pottery and Practice: The Expression of Identity at Pottery Mound and Hum-
            mingbird Pueblo. University of New Mexico Press, Albuquerque.
Edging, Richard
2007        The Vacant Quarter Hypothesis: A Survivor's Story. Missouri Archaeologist
            68:29–58.
Eisenstadt, Shmuel
1988        Beyond Collapse. In The Collapse of Ancient States and Civilizations, edited
            by Norman Yoffee and George L. Cowgill, pp. 236–243. University of Ari-
            zona Press, Tucson.
Emerson, Thomas E.
1997a       Cahokia and the Archaeology of Power. University of Alabama Press, Tusca-
            loosa.
1997b       Reflections from the Countryside on Cahokian Hegemony. In Cahokia:
            Domination and Ideology in the Mississippian World, edited by Timothy R.
            Pauketat and Thomas E. Emerson, pp. 167–189. University of Nebraska
            Press, Lincoln.
2002        An Introduction to Cahokia 2002: Diversity, Complexity, and History. Mid-
            continental Journal of Archaeology 27:127–148.
2003        Crossing Boundaries between Worlds: Changing Beliefs and Mortuary Prac-
            tices at Cahokia. In A Deep-Time Perspective: Studies in Symbols, Meaning,
            and the Archaeological Record, edited by John Richards and Melvin Fowler.
            Special issue of Wisconsin Archeologist 84(1–2):73–80.
2018a       Creating Greater Cahokia: The Cultural Content and Context of the East
            St. Louis Mound Precinct. In Revealing Greater Cahokia: Rediscovery and
            Large-Scale Excavations of the East St. Louis Precinct, edited by Thomas E.
            Emerson, Brad H. Koldehoff, and Tamira K. Brennan, pp. 25–58. Studies in
            Archaeology No. 12. Illinois State Archaeological Survey, Prairie Research
            Institute, University of Illinois at Urbana-Champaign.
2018b       Greater Cahokia—Chiefdom, State, or City? Urbanism in the North Ameri-
            can Midcontinent, AD 1050–1250. In Revealing Greater Cahokia: Redis-
            covery and Large-Scale Excavations of the East St. Louis Precinct, edited by
            Thomas E. Emerson, Brad H. Koldehoff, and Tamira K. Brennan, pp. 487–
            524. Studies in Archaeology No. 12. Illinois State Archaeological Survey,
            Prairie Research Institute, University of Illinois at Urbana-Champaign.

Emerson, Thomas E., and Eve A. Hargrave
2000    Strangers in Paradise? Recognizing Ethnic Mortuary Diversity on the Fringes of Cahokia. *Southeastern Archaeology* 19:1–23.

Emerson, Thomas E., Eve A. Hargrave, and Kristin Hedman
2003    Death and Ritual in Early Rural Cahokia. In *Theory, Method, and Technique in Modern Archaeology*, edited by Robert J. Jeske and Douglas K. Charles, pp. 163–181. Praeger, Westport, Connecticut.

Emerson, Thomas E., and Kristin M. Hedman
2016    The Dangers of Diversity: The Consolidation and Dissolution of Cahokia, Native North America's First Urban Polity. In *Beyond Collapse: Archaeological Perspectives on Resilience, Revitalization, and Transformation in Complex Societies*, edited by Ronald K. Faulseit, pp. 147–175. Center for Archaeological Investigations, Southern Illinois University, Carbondale.

Emerson, Thomas E., Kristin M. Hedman, Tamira K. Brennan, Alleen Betzenhauser, Susan M. Alt, and Timothy R. Pauketat
2020    Interrogating Diaspora and Movement in the Greater Cahokian World. *Journal of Archaeological Method and Theory* 27:54–71.

Emerson, Thomas E., Kristin M. Hedman, Eve A. Hargrave, Dawn E. Cobb, and Andrew R. Thompson
2016    Paradigms Lost: Reconfiguring Cahokia's Mound 72 Beaded Burial. *American Antiquity* 81:405–425.

Emerson, Thomas E., and Douglas K. Jackson
1984    *The BBB Motor Site (11-Ms-595)*. American Bottom Archaeology FAI-270 Site Report No. 6. University of Illinois Press, Urbana.

Emerson, Thomas E., Brad H. Koldehoff, and Tamira K. Brennan (editors)
2018    *Revealing Greater Cahokia, North America's First Native City: Rediscovery and Large-Scale Excavations of the East St. Louis Precinct*. Illinois State Archaeological Survey, Prairie Research Institute, University of Illinois at Urbana-Champaign.

Emerson, Thomas E., Dale L. McElrath, and Andrew C. Fortier (editors)
2000    *Late Woodland Societies: Tradition and Transformation across the Midcontinent*. University of Nebraska Press, Lincoln.

Emerson, Thomas E., and Timothy R. Pauketat
2002    Embodying Power and Resistance at Cahokia. In *The Dynamics of Power*, edited by Maria O'Donovan, pp. 105–125. Occasional Paper No. 30. Center for Archaeological Investigations, Southern Illinois University, Carbondale.

Ensor, Bradley E.
2013    *The Archaeology of Kinship: Advancing Interpretation and Contributions to Theory*. University of Arizona Press, Tucson.

Ensor, H. Blaine
1991    The Lubbub Creek Microlith Industry. *Southeastern Archaeology* 10(1):18–39.

Espenshade, Christopher
1983    Ceramic Ecology and Aboriginal Household Pottery Production at the Gauthier Site, Florida. Master's thesis, Department of Anthropology, University of Florida, Gainesville.

Ethridge, Robbie
2003    *Creek Country: The Creek Indians and Their World*. University of North Carolina Press, Chapel Hill.

2009    Introduction: Mapping the Mississippian Shatter Zone. In *Mapping the Mississippian Shatter Zone: The Colonial Indian Slave Trade and Regional Instability in the American South*, edited by Robbie Ethridge and Sheri M. Shuck-Hall, pp. 1–62. University of Nebraska Press, Lincoln.

Ethridge, Robbie, and Charles Hudson
2002    *The Transformation of the Southeastern Indians, 1540–1760*. University Press of Mississippi, Jackson.

Eubanks, Paul N.
2014    The Timing and Distribution of Caddo Salt Production in Northwestern Louisiana. *Southeastern Archaeology* 33(1):108–22.

Faulkner, Charles H.
1978    The Origin and Evolution of the Cherokee Winter House. *Journal of Cherokee Studies* 3(2):87–94.
1988    Middle Woodland Community and Settlement Patterns on the Eastern Highland Rim, Tennessee. In *Middle Woodland Settlement and Ceremonialism in the Mid-South and Lower Mississippi Valley*, edited by Robert C. Mainfort Jr., pp. 76–98. Mississippi Department of Archives and History, Jackson.

Faulkner, Charles, and Major C. R. McCollough
1978    *Fifth Report of the Normandy Archaeological Project: 1973 Excavations at the Banks V Site (40CF111)*. Report of Investigations No. 20. Department of Anthropology, University of Tennessee, Knoxville.

Faulseit, Ronald K.
2012    State Collapse and Household Resilience in the Oaxaca Valley of Mexico. *Latin American Antiquity* 23(4):401–425.

Fenton, William N.
1998    *The Great Law and the Longhouse: A Political History of the Iroquois Confederacy*. University of Oklahoma Press, Norman.

Fisher, Christopher T., and Gary M. Feinman
2005    Introduction to "Landscapes over Time." *American Anthropologist* 107:62–69.

Fisher, Christopher T., J. Brett Hill, and Gary M. Feinman (editors)
2009    *The Archaeology of Environmental Change: Socionatural Legacies of Degradation and Resilience*. University of Arizona Press, Tucson.

Flannery, Kent V.
1976    The Early Mesoamerican House. In *The Early Mesoamerican Village*, edited by Kent V. Flannery, pp. 16–24. Academic Press, New York.
2002    The Origins of the Village Revisited: From Nuclear to Extended Households. *American Antiquity* 67(3):417–433.

Fletcher, Alice C., and Francis La Flesche
1992    *The Omaha Tribe*. Vols. 1 and 2. University of Nebraska Press, Lincoln.

Ford, Paige A.
2016    A Spatial Analysis of Bounded Cemeteries at the Town Creek Site (AD 1150–400) in the Southern Piedmont of North Carolina. Master's thesis, Department of Anthropology, East Carolina University, Greenville, North Carolina.

Fortier, Andrew C. (editor)
2007    *The Northside Excavations*. The Archaeology of the East St. Louis Mound Center, Pt. 2. Research Report No. 22. Illinois Transportation Archaeological Research Program, University of Illinois at Urbana-Champaign.

Fortier, Andrew C., Thomas E. Emerson, and Dale L. McElrath
2006        Calibrating and Reassessing American Bottom Culture History. *Southeastern Archaeology* 25:170–211.

Fortier, Andrew C., and Dale L. McElrath
2002        Deconstructing the Emergent Mississippian Concept: The Case for the Terminal Late Woodland in the American Bottom. *Midcontinental Journal of Archaeology* 27:172–215.

Foucault, Michel
1977        *Discipline and Punish: The Birth of the Prison.* Translated by Alan Sheridan. Vintage Books, New York.

Fowler, Chris
2004        *The Archaeology of Personhood.* Routledge, New York.

Fowler, Melvin L.
1997        *The Cahokia Atlas: A Historical Atlas of Cahokia Archaeology.* Revised ed. Studies in Archaeology No. 2. Illinois Transportation Archaeological Research Program, University of Illinois at Urbana-Champaign.

Fowler, Melvin L., Jerome Rose, Barbara Vander Leese, Steven R. Ahler
1999        *The Mound 72 Area: Dedicated and Sacred Space in Early Cahokia.* Illinois State Museum Reports of Investigations No. 54. Illinois State Museum, Springfield.

Fowles, Severin
2009        The Enshrined Pueblo: Villagescape and Cosmos in the Northern Rio Grande. *American Antiquity* 74(3):448–466.

Frankenstein, Susan, and Michael J. Rowlands
1978        The Internal Structure and Regional Context of Early Iron Age Society in Southwest Germany. *University of London Institute of Archaeology Bulletin* 15:73–112.

Friberg, Christina M.
2018        Cosmic Negotiations: Cahokian Religion and Ramey Incised Pottery in the Northern Hinterland. *Southeastern Archaeology* 37(1):39–57.

Gall, Daniel G., and Vincas P. Steponaitis
2001        Composition and Provenance of Greenstone Artifacts from Moundville. *Southeastern Archaeology* 20(2):99–117.

Galloway, Patricia, and Clara Sue Kidwell
2004        Choctaw in the East. In *Southeast*, edited by Raymond D. Fogelson, pp. 499–519. Handbook of North American Indians, Vol. 14, William C. Sturtevant, general editor. Smithsonian Institution, Washington, DC.

Gearing, Fred
1962        *Priests and Warriors: Social Structures for Cherokee Politics in the 18th Century.* Memoir 93. American Anthropological Association, Menasha, Wisconsin.

Georgia Archaeological Site Files (GASF)
2015        Georgia's Natural, Archaeological, and Historic Resources GIS. Online Database, https://www.gnahrgis.org/, accessed May 10, 2015.

Gero, Joan M., and Margaret W. Conkey (editors)
1991        *Engendering Archaeology: Women and Prehistory.* Wiley-Blackwell, Oxford.

Gerritsen, Fokke
2004        Archaeological Perspectives on Local Communities. In *A Companion to Archaeology*, edited by John Bintliff, pp. 141–154. Blackwell, Malden.

Gibson, Jon L.
1974        Aboriginal Warfare in the Protohistoric Southeast: An Alternative Perspec-
            tive. *American Antiquity* 39:130–133.
Giddens, Anthony
1979        *Central Problems in Social Theory: Action, Structure, and Contradiction in
            Social Analysis.* University of California Press, Berkeley.
1984        *The Constitution of Society: Outline of a Theory of Structuration.* University
            of California Press, Berkeley.
Gillespie, Susan D.
2000a       Lévi-Strauss: Maison and Société à Maisons. In *Beyond Kinship: Social and
            Material Reproduction in House Societies*, edited by Rosemary A. Joyce and
            Susan D. Gillespie, pp. 22–52. University of Philadelphia Press, Philadelphia.
2000b       Maya "Nested Houses": The Ritual Construction of Place. In *Beyond Kinship:
            Social and Material Reproduction in House Societies*, edited by Rosemary A.
            Joyce and Susan D. Gillespie, pp. 135–160. University of Pennsylvania Press,
            Philadelphia.
2007        When Is a House? In *The Durable House: House Society Models in Archae-
            ology*, edited by Robin A. Beck Jr., pp. 25–50. Center for Archaeological In-
            vestigations, Southern Illinois University, Carbondale.
2011        Inside and Outside: Residential Burial at Formative Period Chalcatzingo,
            Mexico. *Archeological Papers of the American Anthropological Association*
            20(1):98–120.
Gilmore, Zackary I.
2015        Subterranean Histories: Pit Events and Place-Making in Late Archaic
            Florida. In *The Archaeology of Events: Cultural Change and Continuity in
            the Pre-Columbian Southeast.* Edited by Zackary I. Gilmore and James M.
            O'Donoughue, pp. 119–141. University of Alabama Press, Tuscaloosa.
Girard, Jeffrey S., Timothy K. Perttula, and Mary Beth Trubitt
2014        *Caddo Connections: Cultural Interactions within and beyond the Caddo
            World.* Rowman and Littlefield, Lanham, Maryland.
Goad, Sharon I.
1978        Exchange Networks in the Prehistoric Southeastern United States. PhD dis-
            sertation, Department of Anthropology, University of Georgia, Athens.
Goldstein, Lynne G.
1980        Mississippian Mortuary Practices: A Case Study of Two Cemeteries in the
            Lower Illinois Valley. Scientific Paper No. 4. Northwestern University Arche-
            ological Program, Evanston, Illinois.
1981        One-Dimensional Archaeology and Multi-Dimensional People: Spatial Or-
            ganization and Mortuary Analysis. In *The Archaeology of Death*, edited by
            Robert Chapman, Ian Kinnes, and Klavs Randsborg, pp. 53–69. Cambridge
            University Press, Cambridge.
2002        Exploring Aztalan and Its Role in Mississippian Societies. In *Archaeology:
            Original Readings in Method and Practice*, edited by Peter N. Peregrine,
            Carol R. Ember, and Melvin Ember, pp. 337–359. Prentice Hall, Upper
            Saddle River, New Jersey.
2010        Aztalan Mortuary Practices Revisited. In *Mississippian Mortuary Practices:
            Beyond Hierarchy and the Representationist Perspective*, edited by Lynne P.

Sullivan and Robert C. Mainfort Jr., pp. 90–112. University Press of Florida, Gainesville.

Goldstein, Paul

2000    Communities without Borders: The Vertical Archipelago and Diaspora Communities in the Southern Andes. In *The Archaeology of Communities: A New World Perspective*, edited by Marcello A. Canuto and Jason Yaeger, pp. 182–209. Routledge, London.

Goody, Jack

1958    *The Developmental Cycle in Domestic Groups.* Cambridge University Press, Cambridge.

Gosden, Chris, and Gary Lock

1998    Prehistoric Histories. *World Archaeology* 30(1):2–12.

Gosden, Chris, and Yvonne Marshall

1999    The Cultural Biography of Objects. *World Archaeology* 31(2):169–178.

Gotts, Nicholas M.

2007    Resilience, Panarchy, and World-Systems Analysis. *Ecology and Society* 12(1):24.

Gougeon, Ramie A.

2002    Household Research at the Late Mississippian Little Egypt Site (9MU102). PhD dissertation, Department of Anthropology, University of Georgia, Athens.

2006    Different but the Same: Social Integration of Households in Mississippian Chiefdoms. In *Leadership and Polity in Mississippian Society*, edited by Brian M. Butler and Paul D. Welch, pp. 178–196. Occasional Paper No. 33. Center for Archaeological Investigations, Southern Illinois University, Carbondale.

2007    An Architectural Grammar of Late Mississippian Houses in Northwest Georgia. In *Architectural Variability in the Southeast*, edited by Cameron H. Lacquement, pp. 136–152. University of Alabama Press, Tuscaloosa.

2012    Activity Areas and Households in the Late Mississippian Southeast United States: Who Did What Where. In *Ancient Households of the Americas*, edited by John G. Douglass, pp. 141–162. University Press of Colorado, Boulder.

2015    The King Site: Refining a Pattern Language Model for the Late Mississippian Period in Northwest Georgia. In *Archaeological Perspectives on the Southern Appalachians: A Multiscalar Approach*, edited by Ramie A. Gougeon and Maureen S. Meyers, pp. 85–103. University of Tennessee Press, Knoxville.

2017    Considering Gender Analogies in Southeastern Prehistoric Archaeology. *Southeastern Archaeology* 36(3):183–194.

Gregory, Hiram F.

2009    The Caddo and the Caddo Conference. *Caddo Archeology Journal* 19:1–2.

Griffin, James B. (editor)

1952    *Archaeology of the Eastern United States.* University of Chicago Press, Chicago.

Griffith, Glenn E., James M. Omernik, Jeffrey A. Comstock, Steve Lawrence, George Martin, Art Goddard, Vickie J. Hulcher, and Trish Foster

2001    *Ecoregions of Alabama and Georgia.* Color poster with map (1:1,700,000), descriptive text, summary tables, and photographs. US Geological Survey, Reston, Virginia.

Griffith, William

1954    *The Hasinai Indians of East Texas as Seen by Europeans 1687–1772.* Middle American Research Institute, Tulane University, New Orleans.

Gunderson, Lance H., and C. S. Holling (editors)
2002        *Panarchy: Understanding Transformations in Human and Natural Systems.*
            Island Press, Washington, DC.
Haggis, Donald C.
2013        Social Organization and Aggregated Settlement Structure in an Archaic
            Greek City on Crete. In *From Prehistoric Villages to Cities: Settlement Aggre-*
            *gation and Community Transformation*, edited by Jennifer Birch, pp. 63–86.
            Routledge, New York.
Hall, Robert
1997        *An Archaeology of the Soul: North American Indian Belief and Ritual.* Univer-
            sity of Illinois Press, Urbana.
Hallowell, A. Irving
1960        Ojibwa Ontology, Behavior, and World View. In *Culture in History: Essays in*
            *Honor of Paul Radin*, edited by Stanley Diamond, pp. 19–52. Columbia Uni-
            versity Press, New York.
1975        Ojibwa Ontology, Behavior, and World View. In *Teachings from the Ameri-*
            *can Earth: Indian Religion and Philosophy*, edited by Dennis Tedlock and
            Barbara Tedlock, pp. 141–178. Liveright, New York.
Hally, David J.
1970        *Archaeological Investigations of the Pott's Tract (9Mu103), Carter's Dam, Mur-*
            *ray County, Georgia.* Laboratory of Archaeology Series Report No. 6. De-
            partment of Anthropology, University of Georgia, Athens.
1983        Use Alteration of Pottery Vessel Surfaces: An Important Source of Evidence
            for the Identification of Vessel Function. *North American Archaeologist* 4:3–26.
1996        Platform-Mound Construction and the Instability of Mississippian Chief-
            doms. In *Political Structure and Change in the Prehistoric Southeastern*
            *United States*, edited by John F. Scarry, pp. 92–127. University Press of
            Florida, Gainesville.
2002        "As Caves beneath the Ground": Protohistoric Houses of the Southeastern
            United States. In *Between Contact and Colonies: Archaeological Perspectives*
            *on the Protohistoric Southeast*, edited by Cameron B. Wesson and Mark A.
            Rees, pp. 99–109. University of Alabama Press, Tuscaloosa.
2006        The Nature of Mississippian Regional Systems. In *Light on the Path: The An-*
            *thropology and History of the Southeastern Indians*, edited by Thomas J.
            Pluckhahn and Robbie Ethridge, pp. 26–42. University of Alabama Press,
            Tuscaloosa.
2008        *King: The Social Archaeology of a Late Mississippian Town in Northwestern*
            *Georgia.* University of Alabama Press, Tuscaloosa.
Hally, David J., and John F. Chamblee
2019        The Temporal Distribution and Duration of Mississippian Polities in Alabama,
            Georgia, Mississippi, and Tennessee. *American Antiquity* 84(3):420–437.
Hally, David J., and Hypatia Kelly
1998        The Nature of Mississippian Towns in Georgia: The King Site Example. In
            *Mississippian Towns and Sacred Spaces: Searching for an Architectural Gram-*
            *mar*, edited by R. Barry Lewis and Charles Stout, pp. 49–63. University of
            Alabama Press, Tuscaloosa.
Hally, David J., and James B. Langford
1988        *Mississippi Period Archaeology of the Georgia Valley and Ridge Province.*

Laboratory of Archaeology Series Report No. 25. Department of Anthropology, University of Georgia, Athens.

Hally, David J., and Robert C. Mainfort
2004        Prehistory of the Eastern Interior after 500 B.C. In *Southeast*, edited by
            Raymond D. Fogelson, pp. 265–285. Handbook of North American Indians, Vol. 14, William C. Sturtevant, general editor. Smithsonian Institution,
            Washington, DC.

Hally, David J., and James Rudolph
1986        *Mississippian Period Archaeology of the Georgia Piedmont*. Laboratory of Archaeology Series Report No. 24. Department of Anthropology, University of
            Georgia, Athens.

Halperin, Rhoda H.
1994        *Cultural Economies Past and Present*. Texas Press Sourcebooks in Anthropology No. 18. University of Texas Press, Austin.

Hamilakis, Yanis, and Andrew M. Jones
2017        Archaeology and Assemblage. *Cambridge Archaeological Journal* 27(1):77–84.

Hamlin, Jenna Marie
2004        Sociopolitical Significance of Moorehead Phase Ceramic Assemblage Variation in the Cahokia Area. PhD dissertation, Department of Anthropology,
            Washington University in Saint Louis, Missouri.

Hammel, Eugene A.
1980        Household Structure in Fourteenth-Century Macedonia. *Journal of Family
            History* 5:242–273.

Hammerstedt, Scott W.
2005        Mississippian Status in Western Kentucky: Evidence from the Annis Mound.
            *Southeastern Archaeology* 24:11–27.

Hammerstedt, Scott W., Mintcy D. Maxham, and Jennifer Myer
2016        Rural Settlement in the Black Warrior Valley. In *Rethinking Moundville
            and Its Hinterland*, edited by Vincas P. Steponaitis and C. Margaret Scarry,
            pp. 134–161. University Press of Florida, Gainesville.

Hanenberger, Ned H.
2003        *The Range Site 3: Mississippian and Oneota Occupations (11S47)*. Research
            Report No. 17. Illinois Transportation Archaeological Research Program,
            University of Illinois at Urbana-Champaign.

Hanson, Lee H., Jr.
1970        *The Jewell Site, Bn21 Barren County Kentucky*. Tennessee Archaeological Society Miscellaneous Paper No. 8. University of Tennessee, Knoxville.

Hargrave, Eve A., and Julie Bukowski
2010        Marker Posts, Sacred Space and Mortuary Ritual at the East St. Louis Site.
            Paper presented at the 56th Annual Meeting of the Midwest Archaeological
            Conference, Bloomington, Indiana.

Hargrave, Michael L.
1991        A Selectionist Perspective on Change in Late Prehistoric (A.D. 600–1400)
            Domestic Architecture in the American Bottom Region of Southern Illinois.
            PhD dissertation, Department of Anthropology, Southern Illinois University,
            Carbondale.
1998        *The Yuchi Town Site (1RU63), Russell County, Alabama: An Assessment of the
            Impacts of Looting*. Special Report No. 98/48. US Army Corps of Engineers

Construction Engineering Research Laboratories, Cultural Resources Research Center, Champaign, Illinois.

Harle, Michaelyn S.
2010        Biological Affinities and the Construction of Cultural Identity for the Proposed Coosa Chiefdom. PhD dissertation, Department of Anthropology, University of Tennessee, Knoxville.

Harrington, Mark R.
1920        *Certain Caddo Sites in Arkansas*. Indian Notes and Monographs, Miscellaneous Series No. 10. Museum of the American Indian, Heye Foundation, New York.

Harris, Oliver J. T.
2013        Relational Communities in Prehistoric Britain. In *Relational Archaeologies: Humans, Animals, Things*, edited by Christopher Watts, pp. 173–189. Routledge, London.
2014        (Re)Assembling Communities. *Journal of Archaeological Method and Theory* 21:76–97.
2017        Assemblages and Scale in Archaeology. *Cambridge Archaeological Journal* 27(1):127–139.

Harris, Oliver J. T., and Tim F. Sørensen
2010        Rethinking Emotion and Material Culture. *Archaeological Dialogues* 17(2):145–163.

Harrison-Buck, Eleanor, and Julia A. Hendon (editors)
2018        *Relational Identities and Other-Than-Human Agency in Archaeology*. University Press of Colorado, Louisville.

Harvey, Graham
2006        *Animism: Respecting the Living World*. Columbia University Press, New York.

Hatcher, Mattie Austin
1932        The Expedition of Don Domingo Teran de los Rios into Texas (1691–1692). *Preliminary Studies of the Texas Catholic Historical Society* 2:3–62.

Haviland, William A.
1988        Musical Hammocks at Tikal: Problems with Reconstructing Household Composition. In *Household and Community in the Mesoamerican Past*, edited by Richard R. Wilk and Wendy Ashmore, pp. 121–134. University of New Mexico Press, Albuquerque.

Hawsey, Kareen L.
2015        Morphology and Function in the West Jefferson Phase of the Black Warrior Valley, Alabama. Master's thesis, Department of Anthropology, University of Alabama, Tuscaloosa.

Hegmon, Michelle
2002        Concepts of Community in Archaeological Research. In *Seeking the Center Place: Archaeology and Ancient Communities in the Mesa Verde Region*, edited by Mark D. Varien and Richard H. Wilshusen, pp. 263–279. University of Utah Press, Salt Lake City.

Hemmings, E. Thomas
1982        Spirit Lake (3LA83): Test Excavations in a Late Caddo Site on the Red River. In *Contributions to the Archeology of the Great Bend Region*, edited by Frank F. Schambach and Frank Rackerby, pp. 55–89. Research Series No. 22. Arkansas Archeological Survey, Fayetteville.

Hendon, Julia A.
1996      Archaeological Approaches to the Organization of Domestic Labor: House-hold Practice and Domestic Relations. *Annual Review of Anthropology* 25:45–61.
2000a     Round Structures, Household Identity, and Public Performance in Preclassic Maya Society. *Latin American Antiquity* 11(3):299–301.
2000b     Having and Holding: Storage, Memory, Knowledge, and Social Relations. *American Anthropologist* 102(1):42–53.
2004      Living and Working at Home: The Social Archaeology of Household Pro-duction and Social Relations. In *A Companion to Social Archaeology*, edited by Lynn Meskell and Robert W. Preucel, pp. 272–286. Blackwell, Oxford.
2010      *Houses in a Landscape: Memory and Everyday Life in Mesoamerica.* Duke University Press, Durham, North Carolina.

Herbich, Ingrid
1987      Learning Patterns, Potter Interaction and Ceramic Style among the Luo of Kenya. *African Archaeological Review* 5:193–204.

Hilgeman, Sherri L.
2000      *Pottery and Chronology at Angel.* University of Alabama Press, Tuscaloosa.

Hirth, Kenneth
1993a     The Household as an Analytical Unit: Problems in Method and Theory. In *Prehispanic Domestic Units in Western Mesoamerica: Studies of the House-hold, Compound, and Residence*, edited by Robert S. Santley and Kenneth Hirth, pp. 21–36. CRC Press, Boca Raton, Florida.
1993b     Identifying Rank and Socioeconomic Status in Domestic Contexts: An Ex-ample from Central Mexico. In *Prehispanic Domestic Units in Western Meso-america: Studies of the Household, Compound, and Residence*, edited by Robert S. Santley and Kenneth Hirth, pp. 121–146. CRC Press, Boca Raton, Florida.

Hitchcock, Louise, and Aren M. Maeir
2013      Beyond Creolization and Hybridity: Entangled and Transcultural Identities in Philistia. *Archaeological Review of Cambridge* 28:51–73.

Hodder, Ian
2011      Human-Thing Entanglement: Towards an Integrated Archaeological Per-spective. *Journal of the Royal Anthropological Institute* 17:154–177.
2012      *Entangled: An Archaeology of the Relationships between Humans and Things.* Wiley and Blackwell, London.

Hodder, Ian (editor)
1982      *Symbolic and Structural Archaeology.* New Directions in Archaeology. Cam-bridge: Cambridge University Press.

Hodder, Ian, and Craig Cessford
2004      Daily Practice and Social Memory at Catalhoyuk. *American Antiquity* 69(1):17–40.

Hoffman, Michael
1970      Archaeological and Historical Assessment of the Red River Basin in Arkan-sas. In *Archeological and Historical Resources of the Red River Basin*, edited by Hester A. Davis, pp. 137–194. Research Series No. 1. Arkansas Archeo-logical Survey, Fayetteville.

Holland, Dorothy, William Lachicotte, Debra Skinner, and Carole Cain
1998        *Identity and Agency in Cultural Worlds.* Harvard University Press, Cambridge, Massachusetts.

Holley, George R.
1989        *The Archaeology of Cahokia Mounds ICT-II: Ceramics.* Illinois Cultural Resources Study No. 11. Illinois Historic Preservation Agency, Springfield.
2000        Late Woodland on the Edge of Looking Glass Prairie: A Scott Joint-Use Archaeological Project Perspective. In *Late Woodland Societies: Tradition and Transformation across the Midcontinent*, edited by Thomas E. Emerson, Dale L. McElrath, and Andrew C. Fortier, pp. 149–162. University of Nebraska Press, Lincoln.

Holley, George R., Rinita A. Dalan, and Philip A. Smith
1993        Investigations in the Cahokia Site Grand Plaza. *American Antiquity* 58:306–319.

Holling, Crawford S.
1973        Resilience and Stability of Ecological Systems. *Annual Review of Ecology and Systematics* 4:1–23.
2001        Understanding the Complexity of Economic, Ecological, and Social Systems. *Ecosystems* 4(5):390–405.

Holt, Julie Z.
2009        Rethinking the Ramey State: Was Cahokia the Center of a Theater State? *American Antiquity* 74(2):231–254.

Homsey-Messer, Lara, and Kayce Humkey
2016        Microartifact Analysis and Site Formation of a Mississippian House Floor at Wickliffe Mounds, Kentucky. *Southeastern Archaeology* 35(1):8–24.

Horne, Lee
1994        *Village Spaces: Settlement and Society in Northeastern Iran.* Smithsonian Institution Press, Washington, DC.

Horning, Audrey J.
2000        Community-Based Archaeology in the Blue Ridge Mountains. In *The Archaeology of Communities: A New World Perspective*, edited by Marcello A. Canuto and Jason Yaeger, pp. 210–230. Routledge, New York.

Hudson, Charles
1976        *The Southeastern Indians.* University of Tennessee Press, Knoxville.

Huscher, Harold H.
1959        *Appraisal of the Archaeological Resources of the Walter F. George Reservoir, Chattahoochee River, Alabama and Georgia.* Smithsonian Institution, River Basin Surveys, Washington, DC.
1971        Two Mississippian Mound Sites in Quitman County, Georgia. *Southeastern Archaeological Conference Newsletter* 10(2):35–36.

Hutson, Scott R.
2010        *Dwelling, Identity, and the Maya: Relational Archaeology at Chunchucmil.* AltaMira Press, Plymouth, United Kingdom.

Ingmanson, J. Earl
1964        Archaeology of the South Plateau, Ocmulgee National Monument. US Department of the Interior, National Park Service Southeast Region. Richmond, Virginia. Manuscript on file at the Georgia Archaeological Site File, Athens.

Ingold, Tim

1993      The Temporality of the Landscape. *World Archaeology* 25:152–174.

2011      *Being Alive: Essays on Movement, Knowledge and Description.* Routledge, London.

Isbell, William H.

2000      What We Should Be Studying: The "Imagined Community" and the "Natural Community." In *The Archaeology of Communities: A New World Perspective,* edited by Marcello A. Canuto and Jason Yaeger, pp. 243–266. Routledge, New York.

Iseminger, William R., Timothy R. Pauketat, Brad H. Koldehoff, Lucretia S. Kelly, and Leonard Blake

1990      *The Archaeology of the Cahokia Palisade: East Palisade Investigations.* Illinois Cultural Resources Study No. 14. Illinois Historic Preservation Agency, Springfield.

Jackson, H. Edwin, C. Margaret Scarry, and Susan Scott

2016      Domestic and Ritual Meals in the Moundville Chiefdom. In *Rethinking Moundville and Its Hinterland,* edited by Vincas P. Steponaitis and C. Margaret Scarry, pp. 187–233. University Press of Florida, Gainesville.

Jackson, H. Edwin, and Susan L. Scott

1995      The Faunal Record of the Southeastern Elite: The Implications of Economy, Social Relations, and Ideology. *Southeastern Archaeology* 14(2):103–119.

2003      Patterns of Elite Faunal Utilization at Moundville, Alabama. *American Antiquity* 68(3):552–572.

Jackson, H. Edwin, Susan L. Scott, and Frank F. Schambach

2012      At the House of the Priest: Faunal Remains from the Crenshaw Site (3MI6), Southwest Arkansas. In *The Archaeology of the Caddo,* edited by Timothy K. Perttula and Chester P. Walker, pp. 47–85. University of Nebraska Press, Lincoln.

Jackson, Jason Baird

2003      *Yuchi Ceremonial Life: Performance, Meaning, and Tradition in a Contemporary American Indian Community.* University of Nebraska Press, Lincoln.

Jacobi, Keith P.

1999      Rock of Ages: Sandstone, a Mortuary Legacy. Manuscript on file, Department of Anthropology, University of Alabama, Tuscaloosa.

2003      The Malevolent "Undead": Cross-Cultural Perspectives. In *Handbook of Death and Dying,* Vol 1, edited by Clifton D. Bryant, pp. 96–109. Sage, Thousand Oaks, California.

James, Jenna

2010      Modeling Mortuary Behavior Based on Secondary Burial Data from Carson Mound Group, Coahoma County, Mississippi. Master's thesis, Department of Anthropology, University of Mississippi, Oxford.

2015      Social Houses at Carson Mounds, 22-CO-518, as Evidenced by Dental Morphological Analysis. PhD dissertation, Department of Anthropology, University of Alabama, Tuscaloosa.

Jefferies, Richard W.

2018      Population Aggregation and the Emergence of Circular Villages in Southwest Virginia. In *The Archaeology of Villages in Eastern North America,* ed-

          ited by Jennifer Birch and Victor D. Thompson, pp. 140–159. University
          Press of Florida, Gainesville.

Jenkins, Ned J.
1976      Terminal Woodland-Mississippian Interaction in Northern Alabama: The
          West Jefferson Phase. *Southeastern Archaeological Conference Special Publica-
          tion* 5:21–27.

Jenkins, Ned J., and H. Blaine Ensor
1981      *The Gainesville Lake Area Excavations.* Archaeological Investigations in the
          Gainesville Lake Area of the Tennessee-Tombigbee Waterway, Vol. 1. Report
          of Investigations No. 11. Office of Archaeological Research, University of
          Alabama, Tuscaloosa.

Johnson, Jay K., and John M. Connaway
2020      Carson and Cahokia. In *Cahokia in Context: Hegemony and Diaspora*, edited
          by Charles H. McNutt and Ryan M. Parish, pp. 276–300. University Press of
          Florida, Gainesville.

Johnson, Jay K., and Bryan S. Haley
2006      A Cost-Benefit Analysis of Remote Sensing Applications in Cultural Resource
          Management Archaeology. In *Remote Sensing in Archaeology: An Explicitly
          North American Perspective*, edited Jay K. Johnson, pp. 33–46. University of
          Alabama Press, Tuscaloosa.

Johnson, Jay K., Bryan S. Haley, Stephen Harris, Erika Carpenter, and Travis Cureton
2016      *Mississippi Mound Trail, Northern Region: Phase II Investigations.* Report
          prepared for Mississippi Department of Archives and History, Jackson.

Jones, B. Calvin, and Louis Tesar
2001      *1983–1995 Survey, Salvage and Mitigation of Archaeological Resources within
          the Mount Royal Site (8PU35) Village Area, Putnam County, Florida.* Bureau
          of Archaeological Research, Division of Historical Resources, Florida De-
          partment of State.

Jones, Eric E.
2018      When Villages Do Not Form: A Case Study from the Piedmont Village
          Tradition-Mississippian Borderlands, AD 1200–1600. In *The Archaeology
          of Villages in Eastern North America*, edited by Jennifer Birch and Victor D.
          Thompson, pp. 73–88. University Press of Florida, Gainesville.

Joyce, Arthur A.
2019      Assembling the City: Monte Albán as a Mountain of Creation and Suste-
          nance. In *New Materialisms Ancient Urbanisms*, edited by Susan M. Alt and
          Timothy R. Pauketat, pp. 105–159. Routledge, London.

Joyce, Rosemary A.
2000a     Girling the Girl and Boying the Boy: The Production of Adulthood in An-
          cient Mesoamerica. *World Archaeology* 31:473–483.
2000b     Heirlooms and Houses: Materiality and Social Memory. In *Beyond Kinship:
          Social and Material Reproduction in House Societies*, edited by Rosemary A.
          Joyce and Susan D. Gillespie, pp. 189–212. University of Pennsylvania Press,
          Philadelphia.

Joyce, Rosemary A., and Susan D. Gillespie
2000      Beyond Kinship. In *Beyond Kinship: Social and Material Reproduction in
          House Societies*, edited by Rosemary Joyce and Susan D. Gillespie, pp. 1–21.
          University of Pennsylvania Press, Philadelphia.

Joyce, Rosemary A., and Julia A. Hendon
2000        Heterarchy, History, and Material Reality: "Communities" in Late Classic
            Honduras. In *The Archaeology of Communities: A New World Perspective*,
            edited by Marcello A. Canuto and Jason Yaeger, pp. 143–160. Routledge,
            New York.
Jurney, David H., and William Young
1995        Southwestern Pottery and Turquoise in Northeastern Texas. *Caddo Arche-
            ology Journal* 6:15–28.
Kay, Marvin
1984        Late Caddo Subtractive Technology in the Red River Basin. In *Cedar Grove:
            An Interdisciplinary Investigation of a Late Caddo Farmstead in the Red River
            Valley*, edited by Neal L. Trubowitz, pp. 174–206. Research Series No. 23.
            Arkansas Archeological Survey, Fayetteville.
Kay, Marvin, and George Sabo III
2006        Mortuary Ritual and Winter Solstice Imagery of the Harlan-Style Charnel
            House. *Southeastern Archaeology* 25(1):29–47.
Keel, Bennie C.
1976        *Cherokee Archaeology: A Study of the Appalachian Summit.* University of
            Tennessee Press, Knoxville.
2007        *The Ravensford Tract Archaeological Project.* Southeast Archaeological
            Center, Tallahassee, Florida.
Kellar, James H., A. R. Kelly, and Edward V. McMichael
1962        The Mandeville Site in Southwest Georgia. *American Antiquity* 27(3):336–355.
Kelley, David B. (editor)
1997        *Two Caddoan Farmsteads in the Red River Valley.* Research Series No. 51.
            Arkansas Archeological Survey, Fayetteville.
Kelly, Arthur R., Frank T. Schnell, Donald F. Smith, and Ann L. Schlosser
1965        Explorations in Sixtoe Field, Carter's Dam, Murray County, Georgia: Sea-
            sons of 1962, 1963, 1964. Report submitted to the US National Park Service,
            Atlanta. University of Georgia Library of Archeology, Manuscript No. 160.
Kelly, John E.
1980        *Formative Developments at Cahokia and the Adjacent American Bottom: A
            Merrell Tract Perspective.* PhD dissertation, Department of Anthropology,
            University of Wisconsin, Madison.
1984        Wells Incised or O'Byam Incised, *variety Wells*, and Its Context in the
            American Bottom. Paper presented at the Paducah Ceramic Conference,
            Paducah, Kentucky.
1990a       The Emergence of Mississippian Culture in the American Bottom Region. In
            *The Mississippian Emergence*, edited by Bruce D. Smith, pp. 113–152. Smith-
            sonian Institution Press, Washington, DC.
1990b       Range Site Community Patterns and the Mississippian Emergence. In *The
            Mississippian Emergence*, edited by Bruce D. Smith, pp. 67–112. Smithsonian
            Institution Press, Washington, DC.
2006        The Ritualization of Cahokia: The Structure and Organization of Early Ca-
            hokia Crafts. In *Leadership and Polity in Mississippian Society*, edited by
            Brian M. Butler and Paul D. Welch, pp. 236–263. Occasional Paper No. 23.
            Center for Archaeological Investigations, Southern Illinois University, Car-
            bondale.

2012        The Mississippi Period in Florida: A View from the Mississippian World of
            Cahokia. In *Late Prehistoric Florida: Archaeology at the Edge of the Mississip-
            pian World*, edited by Keith Ashley and Nancy Marie White, pp. 296–309.
            University Press of Florida, Gainesville.

Kelly, John E., James A. Brown, and Lucretia S. Kelly
2008        The Context of Religion at Cahokia: The Mound 34 Case. In *Religion, Ar-
            chaeology, and the Material World*, edited by Lars Fogelin, pp. 297–318. Oc-
            casional Paper No. 36. Center for Archaeological Investigations, Southern
            Illinois University, Carbondale.

Kelly, John E., Andrew C. Fortier, Steven J. Ozuk, and Joyce A. Williams
1987        *The Range Site: Archaic through Late Woodland Occupations.* American Bot-
            tom Archaeology FAI-270 Site Report No. 16. University of Illinois Press,
            Urbana.

Kelly, John E., Steven J. Ozuk, and Joyce A. Williams
1990        *The Range Site 2: The Emergent Mississippian Dohack and Range Phase Occu-
            pations.* American Bottom Archaeology FAI-270 Site Report No. 20. Univer-
            sity of Illinois Press, Urbana.

2007        *The Range Site 4: Emergent Mississippian George Reeves and Lindeman Phase
            Occupation.* Research Report No. 18. Illinois Transportation Archaeological
            Research Program, University of Illinois at Urbana-Champaign.

Kelly, Lucretia
1997        Patterns of Faunal Exploitation at Cahokia. In *Cahokia: Domination and
            Ideology in the Mississippian World*, edited by Timothy R. Pauketat and
            Thomas E. Emerson, pp. 103–123. University of Nebraska Press, Lincoln.

Kelly, Robert L., Lin Poyer, and Bram Tucker
2005        An Ethnoarchaeological Study of Mobility, Architectural Investment,
            and Food Sharing among Madagascar's Mikea. *American Anthropologist*
            107:403–416.

Kent, Susan
1984        *Analyzing Activity Areas: An Ethnoarchaeological Study of the Use of Space.*
            University of New Mexico Press, Albuquerque.

Kent, Susan (editor)
1990        *Domestic Architecture and the Use of Space.* Cambridge University Press,
            New York.

Khan, Sammyh S., Nick Hopkins, Stephen Reicher, Shruti Tewari, Narayanan Srinivasan,
    and Clifford Stevenson
2015        How Collective Participation Impacts Social Identity: A Longitudinal Study
            from India. *Political Psychology* (37):309–325.

Kidder, Tristam R.
2004        Plazas as Architecture: An Example from the Raffman Site, Northeast Loui-
            siana. *American Antiquity* 69:514–532.

Kidder, Tristam R., and Sarah C. Sherwood
2016        Look to the Earth: The Search for Ritual in the Context of Mound Con-
            struction. *Archaeological and Anthropological Sciences* 9:1077–1099.
            DOI:10.1007/s12520-016-0369-1.

Kilgore, Eli, Emily E. Lew, Justin N. Lynch, Adam C. S. Kazmi, and Jennifer Birch
2015        Palisades and the Segmentation of Space at Singer-Moye. Poster presented at

the 72nd Annual Meeting of the Southeastern Archaeological Conference, Nashville, Tennessee.

King, Adam

2001a     Long-Term Histories of Mississippian Centers: The Developmental Sequence of Etowah and Its Comparison to Moundville and Cahokia. *Southeastern Archaeology* 20(1):1–17.

2001b     *Excavations at Mound B, Etowah: 1954–1958.* Laboratory of Archaeology Series, Report No. 37. Department of Anthropology, University of Georgia, Athens.

2003     *Etowah: The Political History of a Chiefdom Capital.* University of Alabama Press, Tuscaloosa.

2007     Mound C and the Southeastern Ceremonial Complex in the History of the Etowah Site. In *Southeastern Ceremonial Complex: Chronology, Content, Context,* edited by Adam King, pp. 107–133. University of Alabama Press, Tuscaloosa.

2010     Multiple Groups, Overlapping Symbols, and the Creation of a Sacred Space at Etowah's Mound C. In *Mississippian Mortuary Practices: Beyond Hierarchy and the Representationist Perspective,* edited by Lynne P. Sullivan and Robert C. Mainfort Jr., pp. 54–73. University Press of Florida, Gainesville.

King, Adam, and Jennifer A. Freer

1995     The Mississippian Southeast: A World-Systems Perspective. In *Native American Interactions: Multiscalar Analyses and Interpretations in the Eastern Woodlands,* edited by Michael S. Nassaney and Kenneth E. Sassaman, pp. 266–288. University of Tennessee Press, Knoxville.

King, Adam, and Maureen S. Meyers

2002     Exploring the Edges of the Mississippian World. *Southeastern Archaeology* 21(2):113–116.

King, Adam, Chester P. Walker, Robert V. Sharp, F. Kent Reilly III, and Duncan P. McKinnon

2011     Remote Sensing from Etowah's Mound A: Architecture and the Re-Creation of Mississippian Tradition. *American Antiquity* 75(2):355–371.

King, Duane H. (editor)

2007     *The Memoirs of Lieutenant Henry Timberlake: The Story of a Soldier, Adventurer, and Emissary to the Cherokees, 1756–1765.* Museum of the Cherokee Indian Press, Cherokee, North Carolina.

King, Mary Elizabeth, and Joan S. Gardner

1981     The Analysis of Textiles from Spiro Mound, Oklahoma. In *The Research Potential of Anthropological Museum Collections,* edited by Anne-Marie E. Cantwell, James B. Griffin, and Nan A. Rothschild, pp. 123–139. New York Academy of Sciences, New York.

King, Stacie M.

2011     Remembering One and All: Early Postclassic Residential Burial in Coastal Oaxaca, Mexico. *Archeological Papers of the American Anthropological Association* 20(1):44–58.

Kline, Gerald W., Gary D. Crites, and Charles H. Faulkner

1982     *The McFarland Project: Early Middle Woodland Settlement and Subsistence in the Upper Duck River Valley in Tennessee.* Miscellaneous Paper Number 8. Tennessee Anthropological Association, Knoxville.

Knapp, A. Bernard
2003      The Archaeology of Community in Bronze Age Cyprus: Politiko Phorades in
          Context. *American Journal of Archaeology* 107:559–580.
Knight, Vernon J., Jr.
1981      Mississippian Ritual. PhD dissertation, Department of Anthropology, Uni-
          versity of Florida, Gainesville.
1985      *Tukabatchee: Archaeological Investigations at an Historic Creek Town, Elmore
          County, Alabama.* Office of Archaeological Research, Alabama State Mu-
          seum of Natural History, University of Alabama, Tuscaloosa.
1986      The Institutional Organization of Mississippian Religion. *American Antiquity*
          51:675–687.
1990      Social Organization and the Evolution of Hierarchy in Southeastern Chief-
          doms. *Journal of Anthropological Research* 46(1):1–22.
1994      The Formation of the Creeks. In *The Forgotten Centuries: Indians and Eu-
          ropeans in the American South, 1521–1704*, edited by Charles Hudson and
          Carmen Chaves Tessar, pp. 373–392. University of Georgia Press, Athens.
1997      Some Developmental Parallels between Cahokia and Moundville. In *Ca-
          hokia: Domination and Ideology in the Mississippian World*, edited by
          Timothy R. Pauketat and Thomas E. Emerson, pp. 229–247. University of
          Nebraska Press, Lincoln.
1998      Moundville as a Diagrammatic Ceremonial Center. In *Archaeology of the
          Moundville Chiefdom*, edited by Vernon J. Knight Jr. and Vincas P. Stepo-
          naitis, pp. 44–62. Smithsonian Institution Press, Washington, DC.
2001      Feasting and the Emergence of Platform Mound Ceremonialism. In *Feasts:
          Archaeological and Ethnographic Perspectives on Food, Politics, and Power*,
          edited by Michael Dietler and Brian Hayden, pp. 311–333. University of Ala-
          bama Press, Tuscaloosa.
2006      Symbolism of Mississippian Mounds. In *Powhatan's Mantle: Indians in the
          Colonial Southeast*, rev. ed., edited by Gregory A. Waselkov, Peter H. Wood,
          and Tom Hatley, pp. 421–434. University of Nebraska Press, Lincoln.
2010      *Mound Excavations at Moundville: Architecture, Elites, and Social Order.*
          University of Alabama Press, Tuscaloosa.
2016      Social Archaeology of Monumental Spaces at Moundville. In *Rethinking
          Moundville and Its Hinterland*, edited by Vincas P. Steponiatis and C. Margaret
          Scarry, pp. 23–43. University Press of Florida, Gainesville.
Knight, Vernon J., Jr., James A. Brown, and George E. Lankford
2001      On the Subject Matter of Southeastern Ceremonial Complex Art. *Southeast-
          ern Archaeology* 20(2):129–141.
Knight, Vernon J., Jr., and Tim S. Mistovich
1984      *Walter F. George Lake Archaeological Survey of Free Owned Lands Alabama
          and Georgia.* Office of Archaeological Research, University of Alabama. Sub-
          mitted to US Army Corps of Engineers, Contract No. DACW01-83-C-0173.
Knight, Vernon J., Jr., and Vincas P. Steponaitis (editors)
1998      *Archaeology of the Moundville Chiefdom.* Smithsonian Institution Press,
          Washington, DC.
2007      *Archaeology of the Moundville Chiefdom.* New ed. University of Alabama
          Press, Tuscaloosa.

Kohler, Timothy A., and Michael E. Smith (editors)
2018    *Ten Thousand Years of Inequality: The Archaeology of Wealth Differences.* University of Arizona Press, Tucson.

Kohring, Sheila
2011    Social Complexity as a Multi-Scalar Concept: Pottery Technologies, "Communities of Practice" and the Bell Beaker Phenomenon. *Norwegian Archaeological Review* 44(2):145–163.

Kolb, Michael F.
2007    Site Setting and Prehistoric Landscape Practice. In *The Northside Excavations*, edited by Andrew C. Fortier, pp. 477–504. The Archaeology of the East St. Louis Mound Center, Pt. 2. Research Report No. 22. Illinois Transportation Archaeological Research Program, University of Illinois at Urbana-Champaign.

2018    Riverine and Anthropogenic Landscapes of the East St. Louis Area. In *Revealing Greater Cahokia, North America's First Native City: Rediscovery and Large-Scale Excavations of the East St. Louis Precinct*, edited by Thomas E. Emerson, Brad H. Koldehoff, and Tamira K. Brennan, pp. 95–126. Studies in Archaeology, No. 12. Illinois State Archaeological Survey, Prairie Research Institute, University of Illinois at Urbana-Champaign.

Kolb, Michael J., and James E. Snead
1997    It's a Small World After All: Comparative Analyses of Community Organization in Archaeology. *American Antiquity* 62:609–628.

Koldehoff, Brad H., and Tamira K. Brennan
2010    Exploring Mississippian Polity Interaction and Craft Specialization with Ozarks Chipped-Stone Resources. *Missouri Archaeologist* 71:131–164.

Kornfeld, Marcel, and Alan J. Osborn (editors)
2003    *Islands on the Plains: Ecological, Social, and Ritual Use of Landscapes.* University of Utah Press, Salt Lake City.

Kowalewski, Stephen A.
2006    Coalescent Societies. In *Light on the Path: The Anthropology and History of the Southeastern Indians*, edited by Thomas J. Pluckhahn and Robbie Etheridge, pp. 94–122. University of Alabama Press, Tuscaloosa.

2013    The Work of Making Community. In *From Prehistoric Villages to Cities: Settlement Aggregation and Community Transformation*, edited by Jennifer Birch, pp. 201–218. Routledge, New York.

Kozuch, Laura
2002    Olivella Beads from Spiro and the Plains. *American Antiquity* 67(4):697–709.

Kramer, Carol
1982    *Village Ethnoarchaeology: Rural Iran in Archaeological Perspective.* Academic Press, New York.

Krech, Shepard, III
1999    *The Ecological Indian: Myth and History.* Norton, New York.

Krus, Anthony M.
2016    The Timing of Precolumbian Militarization in the U.S. Midwest and Southeast. *American Antiquity* 81:375–388.

Lacquement, Cameron H.
2007    Typology, Chronology, and Technological Changes of Mississippian Domestic Architecture in West-Central Alabama. In *Architectural Variability in the*

*Southeast*, edited by Cameron H. Lacquement, pp. 49–72. University of Alabama Press, Tuscaloosa.

Lankford, George E.
1998        *Native American Legends: Southeastern Legends; Tales from the Natchez, Caddo, Biloxi, Chickasaw, and Other Nations.* August House, Atlanta.
2004        World on a String: Some Cosmological Components of the Southeastern Ceremonial Complex. In *Hero, Hawk, and Open Hand: American Indian Art of the Midwest and South*, edited by Richard F. Townsend and Robert V. Sharp, pp. 207–218. Yale University Press, New Haven, Connecticut.
2006        Some Southwestern Influences in the Southeastern Ceremonial Complex. *Arkansas Archeologist* 45:1–25.
2007        Some Cosmological Motifs in the Southeastern Ceremonial Complex. In *Ancient Objects and Sacred Realms: Interpretations of Mississippian Iconography*, edited by F. Kent Riley III and James Garber, pp. 8–38. University of Texas Press, Austin.
2012        Weeding Out the Noded. *Arkansas Archeologist* 50:50–68.

Lansdell, Michael Brent, Alleen Betzenhauser, and Tamira K. Brennan
2017        Wings, Warriors, and Weeping Eyes: Spatial and Temporal Distribution of Ramey Incised Motifs at the East St. Louis Mound Precinct. *Illinois Archaeology* 29:165–190.

Larson, Lewis H., Jr.
1971        Archaeological Implications of Social Stratification at the Etowah Site, Georgia. In *Approaches to the Social Dimensions of Mortuary Practices*, edited by James A. Brown, pp. 58–67. Memoir No. 25. Society for American Archaeology, Washington, DC.
1972        Functional Considerations of Warfare in the Southeast during the Mississippi Period. *American Antiquity* 37:383–392.
2004        The Submound and Mound Architecture and Features of Mound C, Etowah, Bartow County, Georgia. *Southeastern Archaeology* 23(2):127–141.

Latour, Bruno
1993        *We Have Never Been Modern.* Translated by Catherine Porter. Harvard University Press, Cambridge, Massachusetts.
2005        *Reassembling the Social: An Introduction to Actor Network Theory.* Oxford University Press, Oxford.

Lave, Jean
1993        *The Practice of Learning.* In *Understanding Practice: Perspectives on Activity and Context*, edited by Seth Chaiklin and Jean Lave, pp. 3–32. Cambridge University Press, Cambridge.

Lave, Jean, and Etienne Wenger
1991        *Situated Learning: Legitimate Peripheral Participation.* Cambridge University Press, Cambridge.

Lawson, John
1709        *A New Voyage to Carolina; Containing the Exact Description and Natural History of That Country: Together with the Present State Thereof. And a Journal of a Thousand Miles, Travel'd Thro' Several Nations of Indians. Giving a Particular Account of Their Customs, Manners, &c.* London.

Layton, Robert
1991        *The Anthropology of Art.* Cambridge University Press, Cambridge.

Layton, Robert, and Peter Ucko (editors)
1999    *The Archaeology and Anthropology of Landscape*. Routledge, London.
Leach, Edmund R.
1954    *Political Systems of Highland Burma: A Study of Kachin Social Structure*. Harvard University Press, Cambridge, Massachusetts.
Ledbetter, Jerald
1997    *The Bull Creek Site, 9ME1, Muscogee County, Georgia*. Occasional papers in Cultural Resource Management, No. 9. Georgia Department of Transportation, Office of Environment and Location, Atlanta.
2007    Summary of Lamar Farmstead Data Recovery Projects on Reynolds Plantation. Manuscript on File, University of Georgia Laboratory of Archaeology, Athens.
Ledbetter, Jerald R., Lisa D. O'Steen, and Scott Jones
2009    *The Late Archaic to Early Woodland Transition in Northwest Georgia: Evidence for Terminal Archaic (ca. 1100–600 B.C.) Period Occupation in the Region*. Occasional papers in Cultural Resource Management, No. 14. Georgia Department of Transportation Office of Environment and Location, Atlanta.
Lemonnier, Pierre
1986    The Study of Material Culture Today: Toward an Anthropology of Technical Systems. *Journal of Anthropological Archaeology* 5:147–186.
1992    *Elements for an Anthropology of Technology*. Anthropological Paper No. 88. Museum of Anthropology, University of Michigan, Ann Arbor.
Lepper, Bradley T.
2004    The Newark Earthworks: Monumental Geometry and Astronomy at a Hopewellian Pilgrimage Center. In *Hero, Hawk, and Open Hand: American Indian Art of the Ancient Midwest and South*, edited by Richard F. Townsend, pp. 73–82. Yale University Press, New Haven, Connecticut.
Lesure, Richard
1999    On the Genesis of Value in Early Hierarchical Societies. In *Material Symbols: Culture and Economy in Prehistory*, edited by John E. Robb, pp. 23–55. Center for Archaeological Investigations, Southern Illinois University, Carbondale.
Lévi-Strauss, Claude
1982    *The Way of the Mask*. University of Washington Press, Seattle.
1987    *Anthropology and Myth: Lectures, 1951–1982*. Translated by Roy G. Willis. Blackwell, Oxford.
Lewis, R. Barry
1990    The Late Prehistory of the Ohio-Mississippi Rivers Confluence Region, Kentucky and Missouri. In *Towns and Temples along the Mississippi*, edited by David H. Dye and Cheryl A. Cox, pp. 38–59. University of Alabama Press, Tuscaloosa.
Lewis, R. Barry, and Charles Stout (editors)
1998    *Mississippian Towns and Sacred Spaces: Searching for an Architectural Grammar*. University of Alabama Press, Tuscaloosa.
Lewis, R. Barry, Charles Stout, and Cameron B. Wesson
1998    The Design of Mississippian Towns. In *Mississippian Towns and Sacred Spaces: Searching for an Architectural Grammar*, edited R. Barry Lewis and Charles B. Stout, pp. 1–21. University of Alabama Press, Tuscaloosa.

Lewis, Thomas M. N., and Madeline D. Kneberg
1946    *Hiwassee Island: An Archaeological Account of Four Tennessee Indian Peoples.* University of Tennessee Press, Knoxville.

Lewis, Thomas M. N., and Madeline D. Kneberg Lewis (editors)
1995    *The Prehistory of the Chickamauga Basin in Tennessee.* University of Tennessee Press, Knoxville.

Lightfoot, Kent. G., Antoinette Martinez, and Ann M. Schiff
1998    Daily Practice and Material Culture in Pluralistic Social Settings: An Archaeological Study of Culture Change and Persistence from Fort Ross, California. *American Antiquity* 63(2):199–222.

Lindauer, Owen, and John H. Blitz
1997    Higher Ground: The Archaeology of North American Platform Mounds. *Journal of Archeological Research* 5:169–207.

Lipe, William D.
1989    Social Scale of Mesa Verde Anasazi Kivas. In *The Architecture of Social Integration in Prehistoric Pueblos*, edited by William D. Lipe and Michelle Hegmon, pp. 53–71. Occasional Paper No. 1, Crow Canyon Archaeological Center, Cortez, Colorado.

Lipe, William D., and Michelle Hegmon (editors)
1989    *The Architecture of Social Integration in Prehistoric Pueblos.* Occasional Paper No. 1. Crow Canyon Archaeological Center, Cortez, Colorado.

Little, Keith J.
1999    The Role of Late Woodland Interactions in the Emergence of Etowah. *Southeastern Archaeology* 18(1):45–56.

Little, Maran
2013    Unpublished Field Notes on the Faunal Analysis of the 2013 Field Season at Singer-Moye. Manuscript on file, Laboratory of Archaeology, University of Georgia, Athens.

Lollis, Charly, Neill J. Wallis, and Ann S. Cordell
2015    Was St. Johns Pottery Made with Swamp Muck as Temper? An Experimental Assessment. *Florida Anthropologist* 68:97–112.

Lopinot, Neal H.
1997    Subsistence Practices at Cahokia. In *Cahokia: Domination and Ideology in the Mississippian World*, edited by Timothy R. Pauketat and Thomas E. Emerson, pp. 103–123. University of Nebraska Press, Lincoln.

Lovell, Nadia
1998    Belonging in Need of Emplacement. In *Locality and Belonging*, edited by Nadia Lovell, pp. 1–24. Routledge, London.

Lu, Houyuan, Jianping Zhang, Kam-biu Liu, Naiqin Wu, Yumei Li, Kunshu Zhou, Maolin Ye, Tianyu Zhang, Haijiang Zhang, Xiaoyan Yang, Licheng Shen, Deke Xu, and Quan Li
2009    Earliest Domestication of Common Millet (*Panicum miliaceum*) in East Asia Extended to 10,000 Years Ago. *Proceedings of the National Academy of Sciences of the United States of America* 106:7367–7372.

Lulewicz, Jacob
2019a   A Bayesian Approach to Regional Ceramic Seriation and Political History in the Southern Appalachian (Northern Georgia) Region of the Southeastern United States. *Journal of Archaeological Science* 105:1–10.

2019b        The Social Networks and Structural Variation of Mississippian Sociopolitics in the Southeastern United States. *Proceedings of the National Academy of Sciences* 116(14):6707–6712.

MacEachern, Scott

1998        Scale, Style, and Cultural Variation: Technological Traditions in the Northern Mandara Mountains. In *The Archaeology of Social Boundaries*, edited by Miriam T. Stark, pp. 107–131. Smithsonian Institution Press, Washington, DC.

MacSweeney, Naoise

2011        *Community Identity and Archaeology: Dynamic Communities at Aphrodisias and Beycesultan.* University of Michigan Press, Ann Arbor.

Marcoux, Jon B.

2000        Display Goods Production and Circulation in the Moundville Chiefdom: A Mississippian Dilemma. Master's thesis, Department of Anthropology, University of Alabama, Tuscaloosa.

2007        On Reconsidering Display Goods Production and Circulation in the Moundville Chiefdom. *Southeastern Archaeology* 26(2):232–245.

2008        Cherokee Household and Communities in the English Contact Period, A.D. 1670–1740. PhD dissertation, Department of Anthropology, University of North Carolina, Chapel Hill.

2010a        The Materialization of Status and Social Structure at Koger's Island Cemetery, Alabama. In *Mississippian Mortuary Practices: Beyond Hierarchy and the Representationist Perspective*, edited by Lynne P. Sullivan and Robert C. Mainfort Jr., pp. 145–173. University Press of Florida, Gainesville.

2010b        *Pox, Empire, Shackles, and Hides: The Townsend Site, 1670–1715.* University of Alabama Press, Tuscaloosa.

2012        Glass Trade Beads from the English Colonial Period in the Southeast, ca. A.D. 1607–1783. *Southeastern Archaeology* 31:157–184.

Marcoux, Jon B., and Gregory D. Wilson

2010        Categories of Complexity and the Preclusion of Practice. In *Ancient Complexities: New Perspectives in Precolumbian North America*, edited by Susan M. Alt, pp. 138–152. University of Utah Press, Salt Lake City.

Markin, Julie Gayle

2007        Woodstock: The Rise of Political Complexity in Northern Georgia. PhD dissertation, Department of Anthropology, University of Georgia, Athens.

Marrinan, Rochelle A., and Nancy Marie White

2007        Modeling Fort Walton Culture in Northwest Florida. *Southeastern Archaeology* 26(2):292–318.

Maxham, Mintcy D.

2000        Rural Communities in the Black Warrior Valley, Alabama: The Role of Commoners in the Creation of the Moundville I Landscape. *American Antiquity* 65(2):337–354.

2004        Native Constructions of Landscapes in the Black Warrior Valley, Alabama, A.D. 1020–1520. PhD dissertation, Department of Anthropology, University of North Carolina, Chapel Hill.

McAnany, Patricia A.

1995        *Living with the Ancestors: Kinship and Kingship in Ancient Maya Society.* University of Texas Press, Austin.

2011        Practices of Place-Making, Ancestralizing, and Re-Animation within Memory
            Communities. *Archeological Papers of the American Anthropological Associa-*
            *tion* 20(1):136–142.

McAnany, Patricia A., and Norman Yoffee (editors)
2010        *Questioning Collapse: Human Resilience, Ecological Vulnerability, and the*
            *Aftermath of Empire.* Cambridge University Press, Cambridge.

McElrath, Dale L., Thomas E. Emerson, Andrew C. Fortier, and James L. Phillips
1984        Late Archaic Period. In *American Bottom Archaeology: A Summary of the*
            *FAI-270 Project Contributions to the Culture History of the Mississippi River*
            *Valley,* edited by Charles J. Bareis and James W. Porter, pp. 34–58. University
            of Illinois Press, Urbana.

McElrath, Dale L., and Andrew C. Fortier
1983        *The Missouri Pacific #2 Site.* American Bottom Archaeology FAI-270 Site Re-
            port No. 3. University of Illinois Press, Urbana.

McGill, Dru E.
2013        Social Organization and Pottery Production at Angel Mounds, a Mississip-
            pian Archaeological Site. PhD dissertation, Department of Anthropology,
            Indiana University, Bloomington.

McGimsey, Charles R., and Michael D. Wiant
1986        Middle Woodland Features. In *Woodland Period Occupations of the Na-*
            *poleon Hollow Site in the Lower Illinois Valley,* edited by Michael D. Wiant
            and Charles R. McGimsey, pp. 114–170. Center for American Archaeology,
            Kampsville, Illinois.

McGuire, Randall, and Michael Schiffer
1983        A Theory of Architectural Design. *Journal of Anthropological Archaeology*
            2:277–303.

McKinnon, Duncan P.
2009        Exploring Settlement Patterning at a Premier Caddo Mound Site in the Red
            River Great Bend Region. *Southeastern Archaeology* 28(2):248–258.
2010        Continuing the Research: Archaeogeophysical Investigations at the Battle
            Mound Site (3LA1) in Lafayette County, Arkansas. *Southeastern Archaeology*
            29(2):250–260.
2011        Foster Trailed-Incised: A GIS-Based Analysis of Caddo Ceramic Distribu-
            tion. *Caddo Archeology Journal* 21:71–88.
2015        Zoomorphic Effigy Pendants: An Examination of Style, Medium, and Distri-
            bution in the Caddo Area. *Southeastern Archaeology* 34(2):116–135.
2016        Distribution of Design: The Rayed Circle. *Caddo Archeology Journal* 26:29–42.
2017        *The Battle Mound Landscape: Exploring Space, Place, and History of a Red*
            *River Caddo Community in Southwest Arkansas.* Research Series No. 68. Ar-
            kansas Archeological Survey, Fayetteville.

McKinnon, Duncan P., and Bryan S. Haley
2017        Evaluating the Use of Community Space at Two Southeastern Mound Cen-
            ters Using Magnetic Gradient and Surface Collection Data. In *Archaeological*
            *Remote Sensing in North America: Innovative Techniques for Anthropological*
            *Applications,* edited by Duncan P. McKinnon and Bryan S. Haley, pp. 46–64.
            University of Alabama Press, Tuscaloosa.

McKinnon, Duncan P., Ryan Nguyen, Tyler Yeager, and Leslie L. Bush
2017        Salvage along the Red Cox Site: The Red Cox (3LA18) Site and Its Place on
            the Caddo Landscape. *Caddo Archeology Journal* 27:36–50.

McNutt, Charles H., and Ryan M. Parish (editors)
2020        *Cahokia in Context: Hegemony and Diaspora*. University Press of Florida, Gainesville.

McNutt, Charles H., and Guy G. Weaver
1983        *The Duncan Tract Site (40TR27), Trousdale County, Tennessee*. Tennessee Valley Authority Publication in Anthropology No. 33. University of Tennessee Press, Knoxville.

Means, Bernard K.
2007        *Circular Villages of the Monongahela Tradition*. University of Alabama Press, Tuscaloosa.

Meeks, Scott C., and David G. Anderson
2013        Drought, Subsistence Stress, and Population Dynamics: Assessing Mississippian Abandonment of the Vacant Quarter. In *Soils, Climate & Society*, edited by John D. Wingard and Sue E. Hayes, pp. 61–84. University Press of Colorado, Boulder.

Mehrer, Mark W.
1988        The Settlement Patterns and Social Power of Cahokia's Hinterland Households. PhD dissertation, Department of Anthropology, University of Illinois at Urbana-Champaign.
1995        *Cahokia's Countryside: Household Archaeology, Settlement Patterns, and Social Power*. Northern Illinois University Press, Dekalb.
2000        Heterarchy and Hierarchy: The Community Plan as Institution in Cahokia's Polity. In *The Archaeology of Communities: A New World Perspective*, edited by Marcello A. Canuto and Jason Yaeger, pp. 44–57. Routledge, New York.

Mehrer, Mark W., and James M. Collins
1995        Household Archaeology at Cahokia and Its Hinterlands. In *Mississippian Communities and Households*, edited by J. Daniel Rogers and Bruce D. Smith, pp. 32–57. University of Alabama Press, Tuscaloosa.

Mehta, Jayur M.
2015        Native American Monuments and Landscape in the Lower Mississippi Valley. PhD dissertation, Department of Anthropology, Tulane University.

Mehta, Jayur M., David Abbott, and Charlotte D. Pevny
2016        Mississippian Craft Production in the Yazoo Basin: Thin-Section Analysis of a Mississippian Structure Floor on the Summit of Mound D at the Carson Site. *Journal of Archaeological Science: Reports* 5:471–484.

Melton, Mallory A.
2013        Analysis, Contextualization, and Conceptualization of Macrobotanical Remains Recovered from Parchman Place (22CO511). Unpublished manuscript on file at Research Laboratories of Archaeology, University of North Carolina, Chapel Hill.

Milanich, Jerald T.
1994        *Archaeology of Precolumbian Florida*. University Press of Florida, Gainesville.
2004        Timucua. In *Southeast*, edited by Raymond D. Fogelson, pp. 219–228. Handbook of North American Indians, Vol. 14, William C. Sturtevant, general editor, Smithsonian Institution Press, Washington, DC.

Millhouse, Philip G.
2012        The John Chapman Site and Creolization on the Northern Frontier of the Mississippian World. PhD dissertation, Department of Anthropology, University of Illinois at Urbana-Champaign.

Mills, Barbara J.
2008        Remembering while Forgetting: Depositional Practices and Social Memory
            at Chaco. In *Memory Work: Archaeologies of Material Practice*, edited by
            Barbara J. Mills and William H. Walker, pp. 88–108. School for Advanced
            Research Press, Santa Fe, New Mexico.
Mills, Barbara J., and William H. Walker (editors)
2008        *Memory Work: Archaeologies of Material Practices*. School for Advanced Re-
            search Press, Santa Fe, New Mexico.
Milner, George R.
1986        Mississippian Period Population Density in a Segment of the Central Missis-
            sippi River Valley. *American Antiquity* 51:468–488.
1990        The Late Prehistoric Cahokia Cultural System of the Mississippi River Val-
            ley: Foundations, Florescence, and Fragmentation. *Journal of World Pre-
            history* 4:1–43.
1998        *The Cahokia Chiefdom: The Archaeology of a Mississippian Society*. Smithson-
            ian Institution Press, Washington, DC.
1999        Warfare in Prehistoric and Early Historic Eastern North America. *Journal of
            Archaeological Research* 7:105–151.
Milner, George R., Eve Anderson, and Virginia G. Smith
1991        Warfare in Late Prehistoric West-Central Illinois. *American Antiquity*
            56(4):581–603.
Milner, George R., Thomas E. Emerson, Mark W. Mehrer, Joyce A. Williams, and Duane
    Esarey
1984        Mississippian and Oneota Periods. In *American Bottom Archaeology: A
            Summary of the FAI-270 Project Contributions to the Culture History of the
            Mississippi River Valley*, edited by Charles J. Bareis and James. W. Porter,
            pp. 158–186. University of Illinois Press, Urbana.
Minar, C. Jill, and Patricia Crown
2001        Learning and Craft Production: An Introduction. *Journal of Anthropological
            Research* 57:369–380.
Minnis, Paul E.
2003        *People and Plants in Ancient Eastern North America*. Smithsonian Institution
            Scholarly Press, Washington, DC.
Mooney, James
1900        *Myths of the Cherokee*. Smithsonian Institution, Bureau of American Eth-
            nology Annual Report 19:3–576, Washington, DC.
Moore, Clarence B.
1895        Certain River Mounds of Duval County, Florida. *Journal of the Academy of
            Natural Sciences of Philadelphia*, 2nd ser. 10:448–502.
1912        Some Aboriginal Sites on the Red River. *Journal of Academy of Natural Sci-
            ences of Philadelphia*, 2nd ser. 14:481–638.
Moore, David G.
2002a       *Catawba Valley Mississippian: Ceramics, Chronology, and Catawba Indians*.
            University of Alabama Press, Tuscaloosa.
2002b       Pisgah Phase Village Evolution at the Warren Wilson Site. In *The Ar-
            chaeology of Native North Carolina: Papers in Honor of H. Trawick Ward*,
            edited by Jane M. Eastman, Christopher D. Rodning, and Edmond A. Bou-
            dreaux III, pp. 76–83. Southeastern Archaeological Conference, Biloxi, Mis-
            sissippi.

Moran, Emilio F.
2008        *Human Adaptability: An Introduction to Ecological Anthropology.* Westview
            Press, Boulder, Colorado.
Morse, Dan F., and Phyllis A. Morse
1983        *Archaeology of the Central Mississippi Valley.* Academic Press, New York.
Muller, Jon
1978a       The Southeast. In *Ancient Native Americans,* edited by Jesse D. Jennings,
            pp. 281–327. W. H. Freeman, San Francisco.
1978b       The Kincaid System: Mississippian Settlement in the Environs of a Large
            Site. In *Mississippian Settlement Patterns,* edited by Bruce D. Smith, pp. 269–
            292. Academic Press, New York.
1984        Mississippian Specialization and Salt. *American Antiquity* 49:489–507.
1986        *Archaeology of the Lower Ohio River Valley.* Academic Press, New York.
1997        *Mississippian Political Economy.* Plenum Press, New York.
2007        Prolegomena for the Analysis of the Southeastern Ceremonial Complex. In
            *Southeastern Ceremonial Complex: Chronology, Content, Context,* edited by
            Adam King, pp. 15–37. University of Alabama Press, Tuscaloosa.
Murdock, George P.
1949        *Social Structure.* Macmillan, New York.
Murray, Wendi Field, and Barbara J. Mills
2013        Identity Communities and Memory Practices: Relational Logics in the US
            Southwest. In *Relational Archaeologies: Humans, Animals, Things,* edited by
            Christopher Watts, pp. 135–53. Routledge, London.
Myer, Jennifer L.
2003        Archaeological Testing at Three Non-Mound Mississippian Sites in the
            Black Warrior Valley, Alabama: Final Report of Season IV of the Black War-
            rior Valley Survey. Unpublished report submitted to the Alabama Historical
            Commission, Montgomery.
Nash, Lenna M., Tamira K. Brennan, and Kristin M. Hedman
2016        Burials and Human Remains. In *Main Street Mound: A Ridgetop Monument
            at the East St. Louis Mound Complex,* edited by Tamira K. Brennan, pp. 57–
            88. Research Report No. 36. Illinois State Archaeological Survey, Prairie Re-
            search Institute, University of Illinois at Urbana-Champaign.
Nelson, Erin Stevens
2014        Intimate Landscapes: The Social Nature of the Spaces Between. *Archaeo-
            logical Prospection* 21(1):49–57.
2020        *Authority, Autonomy, and the Archaeology of a Mississippian Community.*
            University Press of Florida, Gainesville.
Nelson, Erin Stevens, Ashley Peles, and Mallory A. Melton
2020        Foodways and Community at the Late Mississippian Site of Parchman Place.
            *Southeastern Archaeology* 39(1):29–50.
Netting, Robert M.
1982        Some Home Truths on Household Size and Wealth. *Archaeology of the
            Household: Building a Prehistory of Domestic Life* 25(6):641–662.
Netting, Robert M., Richard Wilk, and Eric Arnould
1984        Introduction. In *Households: Comparative and Historical Studies of the Do-
            mestic Group,* edited by Robert M. Netting, Richard Wilk, and Eric Arnould.
            pp. xiii–xxxviii. University of California Press, Berkeley.

O'Brien, Michael J.
1996      *Paradigms of the Past: The Story of Missouri Archaeology.* University of Missouri Press, Columbia.

O'Brien, Michael J. (editor)
2001      *Mississippian Community Organization: The Powers Phase in Southeastern Missouri.* Kluwer Academic/Plenum, New York.

O'Brien, Michael J., John L. Beets, Robert E. Warren, Tachpong Hotrabhavananda, Terry W. Barney, and Eric E. Voigt
1982      Digital Enhancement and Grey-Level Slicing of Aerial Photographs: Techniques for Archaeological Analysis of Intrasite Variability. *World Archaeology* 14(2):173–190.

Oetelaar, Gerald A.
1987      The Archaeological Study of Settlement Structure: An Illinois Mississippian Example. PhD dissertation, Department of Anthropology, Southern Illinois University.

Oliver, Billy L.
1992      Settlements of the Pee Dee Culture. PhD dissertation, Department of Anthropology, University of North Carolina, Chapel Hill.

Olsen, Bjørnar
2007      Keeping Things at Arm's Length: A Genealogy of Symmetry. *World Archaeology* 39:579–588.

Olwig, Kenneth R.
2001      Landscape as a Contested Topos of Place, Community, and Self. In *Textures of Place: Exploring Humanist Geographies,* edited by Paul C. Adams, Steven Hoelscher, and Karen E. Till, pp. 93–117. University of Minnesota Press, Minneapolis.

Ortner, Sherry B.
1984      Theory in Anthropology since the Sixties. *Comparative Studies in Society and History* 26:126–166.

Parker, Kathryn E.
2013      A Mississippian House on Avery Lake, Kincaid Mounds. Paper presented at the 70th Annual Southeastern Archaeological Conference, Greenville, South Carolina.

Pauketat, Timothy R.
1987      A Burned Domestic Dwelling at Cahokia. *Wisconsin Archeologist* 68: 212–237.
1994      *The Ascent of Chiefs: Cahokia and Mississippian Politics in Native North America.* University of Alabama Press, Tuscaloosa.
1997      Specialization, Political Symbols and the Crafty Elite of Cahokia. *Southeastern Archaeology* 16:1–15.
1998      *The Archaeology of Downtown Cahokia: The Tract 15A and Dunham Tract Excavations.* Studies in Archaeology No. 1. Illinois Transportation Archaeological Research Program, University of Illinois at Urbana-Champaign.
2000a     Politicization and Community in the Pre-Columbian Mississippi Valley. In *The Archaeology of Communities: A New World Perspective,* edited by Marcello A. Canuto and Jason Yaeger, pp. 16–43. Routledge, New York.
2000b     The Tragedy of the Commoners. In *Agency in Archaeology,* edited by Marcia-Anne Dobres and John E. Robb, pp. 113–129. Routledge, London.

2003    Resettled Farmers and the Making of a Mississippian Polity. *American Antiquity* 68:39–66.

2004    *Ancient Cahokia and the Mississippians.* Cambridge University Press, Cambridge.

2005a   The Forgotten History of the Mississippians. In *North American Archaeology*, edited by Timothy R. Pauketat and Diana DiPaolo Loren, pp. 187–211. Blackwell, Malden, Massachusetts.

2005b   Mounds, Buildings, Posts, Palisades, and Compounds. In *The Southside Excavations*, edited by Timothy R. Pauketat, pp. 113–193. The Archaeology of the East St. Louis Mound Center, Pt. 1. Research Report No. 21. Illinois Transportation Archaeological Research Program, University of Illinois at Urbana-Champaign.

2007    *Chiefdoms and Other Archaeological Delusions.* AltaMira Press, New York.

2008a   The Grounds for Agency in Southwestern Archaeology. In *The Social Construction of Communities: Agency, Structure, and Identity in the Prehispanic Southwest*, edited by Mark D. Varien and James M. Potter, pp. 233–250. AltaMira Press, New York.

2008b   Founders' Cults and the Archaeology of *Wa-kan-da.* In *Memory Work: Archaeologies of Material Practices*, edited by Barbara J. Mills and William H. Walker, pp. 61–79. School for Advanced Research Press, Santa Fe, New Mexico.

2009    Wars, Rumors of Wars, and the Production of Violence. In *Warfare in Cultural Conflict: Practice, Agency, and the Archaeology of Violence*, edited by Axel E. Nielsen and William H. Walker, pp. 244–261. University of Arizona Press, Tucson.

2010    The Missing Persons in Mississippian Mortuaries. In *Mississippian Mortuary Practices*, edited by Lynne P. Sullivan and Robert C. Mainfort Jr., pp. 14–29. University Press of Florida, Gainesville.

2013a   *Archaeology of the Cosmos: Rethinking Agency and Religion in Ancient America.* Routledge, New York.

2013b   *The Archaeology of Downtown Cahokia II: The 1960 Excavation of Tract 15B.* Studies in Archaeology No. 8. Illinois State Archaeological Survey, University of Illinois at Urbana-Champaign.

Pauketat, Timothy R. (editor)

2001    *The Archaeology of Traditions: Agency and History before and after Columbus.* University Press of Florida, Gainesville.

Pauketat, Timothy R., and Susan M. Alt

2003    Mounds, Memory, and Contested Mississippian History. In *Archaeologies of Memory*, edited by Ruth M. Van Dyke and Susan E. Alcock, pp. 151–179. Blackwell Press, Oxford.

2004    The Making and Meaning of a Mississippian Axe Head Cache. *Antiquity* 78:779–797.

2005    Agency in a Postmold? Physicality and the Archaeology of Culture-Making. *Journal of Archaeological Method and Theory* 12:213–236.

2007    Sex and the Southern Cult. In *Southeastern Ceremonial Complex: Chronology, Content, Context*, edited by Adam King, pp. 232–250. University of Alabama Press, Tuscaloosa.

2018    Water and Shells in Bodies and Pots: Mississippian Rhizome, Cahokian

Poiesis. In *Relational Personhood and Other-Than-Human Agency in Archaeology*, edited by Eleanor Harrison-Buck and Julia Hendon, pp. 72–99. University of Colorado Press, Boulder.

Pauketat, Timothy R., Susan M. Alt, and Jeffrey D. Kruchten
2015    City of Earth and Wood: New Cahokia and Its Material-Historical Implications. In *Early Cities in Comparative Perspective, 4000 BCE–1200 CE*, edited by Norman Yoffee, pp. 437–454. The Cambridge World History, Vol. 3, Merry E. Wiesner-Hanks, editor in chief, Cambridge University Press, Cambridge.
2017    The Emerald Acropolis: Elevating the Moon and Water in the Rise of Cahokia. *Antiquity* 91:207–222.

Pauketat, Timothy R., and Thomas E. Emerson
1991    The Ideology of Authority and the Power of the Pot. *American Anthropologist* 93:919–941.
1997    Conclusion: Cahokia and the Four Winds. In *Cahokia: Domination and Ideology in the Mississippian World*, edited by Timothy R. Pauketat and Thomas E. Emerson, pp. 269–278. University of Nebraska Press, Lincoln.
1999    Representation of Hegemony as Community at Cahokia. In *Material Symbols: Culture and Economy in Prehistory*, edited by John E. Robb, pp. 302–317. Occasional Paper No. 26. Center for Archaeological Investigations, Southern Illinois University, Carbondale.

Pauketat, Timothy R., and Thomas E. Emerson (editors)
1997    *Cahokia: Domination and Ideology in the Mississippian World*. University of Nebraska Press, Lincoln.

Pauketat, Timothy R., Andrew C. Fortier, Susan M. Alt, and Thomas E. Emerson
2013    A Mississippian Conflagration at East St. Louis and Its Political-Historical Implications. *Journal of Field Archaeology* 38:210–226.

Pauketat, Timothy R., Lucretia S. Kelly, Gayle J. Fritz, Neal H. Lopinot, Scott Elias, and Eve A. Hargrave
2002    The Residues of Feasting and Public Ritual at Early Cahokia. *American Antiquity* 67:257–279.

Pauketat, Timothy R., and Neal H. Lopinot
1997    Cahokian Population Dynamics. In *Cahokia: Domination and Ideology in the Mississippian World*, edited by Timothy R. Pauketat and Thomas E. Emerson, pp. 103–123. University of Nebraska Press, Lincoln.

Pauketat, Timothy R., Mark A. Rees, Amber M. VanDerwarker, and Kathryn E. Parker
2010    Excavations into Cahokia's Mound 49. *Illinois Archaeology* 22:397–436.

Pauketat, Timothy R., and William I. Woods
1986    Middle Mississippian Structure Analysis: The Lawrence Primas Site (11-MS-895) in the American Bottom. *Wisconsin Archeologist* 67:104–127.

Payne, Claudine
2002    Architectural Reflections of Power and Authority in Mississippian Towns. In *The Dynamics of Power*, edited by Maria O'Donovan, pp. 188–213. Occasional Paper No. 30. Center for Archaeological Investigations, Southern Illinois University, Carbondale.

Peebles, Christopher S.
1971    Moundville and Surrounding Sites: Some Structural Considerations of Mortuary Practices II. In *Approaches to the Social Dimensions of Mortuary Prac-*

*tices*, edited by James A. Brown, pp. 68–91. Memoir No. 25. Society for American Archaeology, Washington, DC.

Peebles, Christopher S., and Susan M. Kus
1977    Some Archaeological Correlates of Ranked Societies. *American Antiquity* 42(3):421–448.

Penney, David W.
2004    The Archaeology of Aesthetics. In *Hero, Hawk, and Open Hand: American Indian Art of the Ancient Midwest and South*, edited by Richard F. Townsend, pp. 43–56. Yale University Press, New Haven, Connecticut.

Peregrine, Peter N.
1992    Social Change in the Woodland-Mississippian Transition: A Case Study of Household and Community Patterns in the American Bottom. *North American Archaeologist* 13:131–147.
1993    An Archaeological Correlate of War. *North American Archaeologist* 14:139–151.
2017    Political Participation and Long-Term Resilience in Pre-Columbian Societies. *Disaster Prevention and Management: An International Journal* 26(3):314–329.

Perttula, Timothy K.
1992    *"The Caddo Nation": Archaeological and Ethnohistoric Perspectives*. University of Texas Press, Austin.
2002    Archaeological Evidence for the Long-Distance Exchange of Caddo Indian Ceramics in the Southern Plains, Midwest, and Southeastern United States. In *Geochemical Evidence for Long-Distance Exchange*, edited by Michael D. Glascock, pp. 89–107. Bergin and Garvey, Westport, Connecticut.
2005    1938–1939 WPA Excavations at the Hatchel Site (41BW3) on the Red River in Bowie, County, Texas. *Southeastern Archaeology* 24:180–198.
2008    The Archeology of the Roitsch Site (41RR16), an Early to Historic Caddo Period Village on the Red River in Northeast Texas. In *Collected Papers from Past Texas Archeological Society Summer Field Schools*, edited by Timothy K. Perttula, pp. 313–628. Special Publication No. 5. Texas Archeological Society, San Antonio.
2009    Extended Entranceway Structures in the Caddo Archaeological Area. *Southeastern Archaeology* 28(1):27–42.
2012    The Archaeology of the Caddo in Southwest Arkansas, Northwest Louisiana, Eastern Oklahoma, and East Texas: An Introduction to the Volume. In *The Archaeology of the Caddo*, edited by Timothy K. Perttula and Chester P. Walker, pp. 1–25. University of Nebraska Press, Lincoln.
2017    *Caddo Landscapes in the East Texas Forests*. Oxbow Books, Oxford.

Perttula, Timothy K., James E. Bruseth, Nancy Adele Kenmotsu, and William A. Martin
1995    *Archeological Testing at the Cabe Mounds (41BW14), Bowie County, Texas*. Cultural Resource Management Report No. 8. Department of Antiquities Protection, Texas Historical Commission.

Perttula, Timothy K., Bo Nelson, Robert L. Cast, and Bobby Gonzalez
2010    *The Clements Site (41CS25): A Late 17th- to Early 18th-Century Nasoni Caddo Settlement and Cemetery*. Anthropological Paper No. 92. American Museum of Natural History, New York.

Perttula, Timothy K., and Robert Rogers
2007    The Evolution of a Caddo Community in Northeastern Texas: The Oak Hill Village Site (41RK214), Rusk County, Texas. *American Antiquity* 72(1):71–94.

2012    The Evolution of a Caddo Community in Northeastern Texas. In *The Archaeology of the Caddo*, edited by Timothy K. Perttula and Chester P. Walker, pp. 209–238. University of Nebraska Press, Lincoln.

Perttula, Timothy K., and Chester P. Walker (editors)
2012    *The Archaeology of the Caddo*. University of Nebraska Press, Lincoln.

Perttula, Timothy K., Chester P. Walker, and T. Clay Shultz
2008    A Revolution in Caddo Archaeology: The Remote Sensing and Archaeological View from the Hill Farm Site (41BW169) in Bowie County, Texas. *Southeastern Archaeology* 27(1):93–107.

Peterson, Staffan
2010    Townscape Archaeology at Angel Mounds, Indiana: Mississippian Spatiality and Community. PhD dissertation, Department of Anthropology, Indiana University, Bloomington.

Phillips, Erin E.
2006    Social Status as Seen through the Distribution of Paint Palettes, Stone Pendants, and Copper Gorgets in Moundville Burials. Master's thesis, Department of Anthropology, University of Alabama, Tuscaloosa.

Phillips, Philip
1970    *Archaeological Survey in the Lower Yazoo Basin, Mississippi, 1949–1955*. Papers of the Peabody Museum of American Archaeology and Ethnology No. 60. Harvard University, Cambridge, Massachusetts.

Phillips, Philip, and James A. Brown
1978    *Pre-Columbian Shell Engravings from the Craig Mound at Spiro, Oklahoma*. Pt. 1. Peabody Museum Press, Cambridge, Massachusetts.

Phillips, Philip, James A. Ford, and James B. Griffin
2003 [1951] *Archaeological Survey in the Lower Mississippi Alluvial Valley, 1940–1947*. Classics in Southeastern Archaeology. University of Alabama Press, Tuscaloosa.

Phillips, Philip, and Gordon R. Willey
1953    Method and Theory in American Archeology: An Operational Basis for Culture-Historical Integration. *American Anthropologist* 55(5):615–633.

Pluckhahn, Thomas J.
1996    Joseph Caldwell's Summerour Mound (9F016) and Woodland Platform Mounds in the Southeastern United States. *Southeastern Archaeology* 15(2):191–211.
2010    Household Archaeology in the Southeastern United States: History, Trends, and Challenges. *Journal of Archaeological Research* 18(4):331–385.

Pluckhahn, Thomas J., and Robbie Ethridge, editors
2006    *Light on the Path: The Anthropology and History of the Southeastern Indians*. University of Alabama Press, Tuscaloosa.

Pluckhahn, Thomas J., and Neil Wallis
2018    Swift Creek at a Human Scale. *Southeastern Archaeology* 37(3):1–9.

Polhemus, Richard R.
1987    *The Toqua Site: A Late Mississippian Dallas Phase Town*. University of Tennessee Department of Anthropology Report of Investigations No. 41, Tennessee Valley Authority Publications in Anthropology No. 44. Tennessee Valley Authority, Knoxville.

1998    Activity Organization in Mississippian Households: A Case Study from the Loy Site in East Tennessee. PhD dissertation, Department of Anthropology, University of Tennessee, Knoxville.

1990    Dallas Phase Architecture and Sociopolitical Structure. In *Lamar Archaeology: Mississippian Chiefdoms in the Deep South*, edited by Mark Williams and Gary Shapiro, pp. 125–138. University of Alabama Press, Tuscaloosa.

Pollack, David

2004    *Caborn-Welborn: Construction a New Society after the Angel Chiefdom Collapse*. University of Alabama Press, Tuscaloosa.

Pollard, Joshua

2008    Deposition and Material Agency in the Early Neolithic of Southern Britain. In *Memory Work: Archaeologies of Material Practices*, edited by Barbara J. Mills and William H. Walker, pp. 41–59. School for Advanced Research Press, Santa Fe, New Mexico.

Pope, Melody

1989    Microdrills from the Black Warrior River Valley: Technology, Use, and Context. Master's thesis, Department of Anthropology, State University of New York, Binghamton.

Poplin, Eric C.

1990    *Prehistoric Settlement in the Dog River Valley: Archaeological Data Recovery at 9D034, 9D039, and 9D045, Douglas County, Georgia*. Brockington and Associates Technical Report. Athens, Georgia.

Porth, Erik D.

2017    Reconsidering Institutional Collapse and Social Transformation at Moundville during the Fifteenth Century. PhD dissertation, Department of Anthropology, University of Alabama, Tuscaloosa.

Prentice, Guy

1983    Cottage Industries: Concepts and Implications. *Midcontinental Journal of Archaeology* 8(1):1–16.

1985    Economic Differentiation among Mississippian Farmsteads. *Midcontinental Journal of Archaeology* 10(1):77–122.

Preucel, Robert W.

2000    Making Pueblo Communities: Architectural Discourse at Kotyiti, New Mexico. In *The Archaeology of Communities: A New World Perspective*, edited by Marcello A. Canuto and Jason Yaeger, pp. 58–77. Routledge, New York.

Price, James E., and James B. Griffin

1979    *The Snodgrass Site of the Powers Phase of Southeast Missouri*. Anthropological Paper No. 66. University of Michigan, Ann Arbor.

Prokopetz, A. Wayne

1974    An Analysis of Post Houses, Site 1Bi4, Macon, Georgia. Unpublished manuscript on file, Laboratory of Archaeology, University of Georgia, Athens.

Pursell, Corin C. O.

2004    Geographic Distribution and Symbolism of Colored Mound Architecture in the Mississippian Southeast. Master's thesis, Department of Anthropology, Southern Illinois University, Carbondale.

2013    Colored Monuments and Sensory Theater among the Mississippians. In *Making Senses of the Past: Toward a Sensory Archaeology*, edited by Jo Day, pp. 69–89. Occasional Paper No. 40. Center for Archaeological Investigations, Southern Illinois University, Carbondale.

2016        Afterimages of Kincaid Mounds. PhD dissertation, Department of Anthropology, Southern Illinois University, Carbondale.

Quinn, David B.
1979        The Expedition of Hernando de Soto and His Successor, Luís de Moscoso, 1539–1543. In *New American World: Major Spanish Searches in Eastern North America*, Vol. 2, edited by David B. Quinn, pp. 90–188. Arno Press, New York.

Randall, Asa
2013        (Not) Another Paper about Archaic Shell Mounds on the St. Johns River in Northeast Florida. Expanded version of paper presented at the 70th Annual Meeting of the Southeastern Archaeological Conference, Tampa, Florida.

Randolph, J. Ralph
1973        *British Travelers among the Southern Indians, 1600–1763*. University of Oklahoma Press, Norman.

Rapoport, Amos
1969        *House Form and Culture*. Prentice-Hall, Engelwood Cliffs, New Jersey.
1976        Sociocultural Aspects of Man-Environment Studies. In *The Mutual Interaction of People and Their Built Environment*, edited by Amos Rapoport, pp. 7–36. Mouton, Paris.
1989        On the Attributes of "Tradition." In *Dwellings, Settlements and Tradition: Cross-Cultural Perspectives*, edited by Jean-Paul Bourdier and Nexar Alsayyad, pp. 77–105. University Press of America, New York.

Rautman, Allison E.
2013        Social Integration and the Built Environment of Aggregated Communities in the North American Puebloan Southwest. In *From Prehistoric Villages to Cities: Settlement Aggregation and Community Transformation*, edited by Jennifer Birch, pp. 111–133. Routledge, New York.
2014        *The Archaeology of Early Villages in Central New Mexico*. University of Arizona Press, Tucson.

Redfield, Robert
1989        *The Little Community and Peasant Society and Culture*. University of Chicago Press, Chicago.

Redman, Charles
1999        *Human Impacts on Ancient Environments*. University of Arizona Press, Tucson.
2005        Resilience Theory in Archaeology. *American Anthropologist* 107(1):70–77.

Redman, Charles L., and Ann P. Kinzig
2003        Resilience of Past Landscapes: Resilience Theory, Society, and the *Longue Dureé*. *Ecology and Society* 7(1). http://www.consecol.org/vol7/iss1/art14.

Reilly, F. Kent, III
2004        People of Earth, People of Sky: Visualizing the Sacred in Native American Art of the Mississippian Period. In *Hero, Hawk, and Open Hand: American Indian Art of the Ancient Midwest and South*, edited by Richard F. Townsend, pp. 125–139. Yale University Press, New Haven, Connecticut.

Renfrew, Colin
2001        Production and Consumption in a Sacred Economy: The Material Corre-

lates of High Devotional Expression at Chaco Canyon. *American Antiquity* 66(1):14–25.

Renfrew, Colin, and John F. Cherry

1986    *Peer Polity Interaction and Socio-Political Change.* Cambridge University Press, Cambridge.

Reynolds, Peter J.

1977    Experimental Iron Age Storage Pits: An Interim Report. *Proceedings of the Prehistoric Society* 40:118–131.

1979    *Iron Age Farm: The Butser Experiment.* British Museum, London.

Rice, Prudence M.

1987    *Pottery Analysis: A Sourcebook.* University of Chicago Press, Chicago.

Richter, Bob

1993    Surface Collections from 8DU66, the McCormack Site. Manuscript on file, Archaeology Lab, University of North Florida, Jacksonville.

Riggs, Brett H.

2008    *A Synthesis of Documentary and Archaeological Evidence for Early 18th Century Cherokee Villages and Structures: Data for the Reconstruction of the Tsa-La-Gi Ancient Village, Cherokee Heritage Center, Park Hill, Oklahoma.* Research Laboratories of Archaeology, University of North Carolina, Chapel Hill.

Riggs, Brett H., Norman D. Jefferson, and George M. Crothers

1998    *Hiwassee Old Town.* Tennessee Department of Conservation, Division of Archaeology, Knoxville.

Riggs, Brett H., and M. Scott Shumate

2003    *Archaeological Testing at Kituhwa: 2001 Investigations at 31SW1, 31SW2, 31SW287, 31SW316, 31SW317, 31SW318, and 31SW320.* Report submitted to the Office of Cultural Resources, Eastern Band of Cherokee Indians, Cherokee, North Carolina.

Riordan, Robert V.

1975    Ceramics and Chronology: Mississippian Settlement in the Black Bottom, Southern Illinois. PhD dissertation, Department of Anthropology, Southern Illinois University, Carbondale.

Robb, John, and Timothy R. Pauketat

2013    From Moments to Millennia: Theorizing Scale and Change in Human History. In *Big Histories, Human Lives*, edited by John Robb and Timothy R. Pauketat, pp. 3–34. School for Advanced Research Press, Santa Fe, New Mexico.

Robin, Cynthia

2002    Outside of Houses: The Practices of Everyday Life at Chan Noòhol, Belize. *Journal of Social Archaeology* 2:245–268.

2003    New Directions in Classic Maya Household Archaeology. *Journal of Archaeological Research* 11:307–356.

Rodning, Christopher B.

2001a    Mortuary Ritual and Gender Ideology in Protohistoric Southwestern North Carolina. In *Archaeological Studies of Gender in the Southeastern United States*, edited by Jane M. Eastman and Christopher B. Rodning, pp. 77–100. University Press of Florida, Gainesville.

2001b       Architecture and Landscape in Late Prehistoric and Protohistoric West-
            ern North Carolina. In *Archaeology of the Appalachian Highlands*, edited by
            Lynne P. Sullivan and Susan C. Prezzano, pp. 238–249. University of Tennes-
            see Press, Knoxville.
2002a       The Townhouse at Coweeta Creek. *Southeastern Archaeology* 21:10–20.
2002b       William Bartram and the Archaeology of the Appalachian Summit. In *Be-
            tween Contacts and Colonies: Archaeological Perspectives on the Protohistoric
            Southeast*, edited by Cameron B. Wesson and Mark A. Rees, pp. 67–89. Uni-
            versity of Alabama Press, Tuscaloosa.
2004        The Cherokee Town at Coweeta Creek. PhD dissertation, Department of
            Anthropology, University of North Carolina, Chapel Hill.
2007        Building and Rebuilding Cherokee Houses and Townhouses in Southwest-
            ern North Carolina. In *The Durable House: House Society Models in Archae-
            ology*, edited by Robin A. Beck Jr., pp. 464–484. Occasional Paper No. 35.
            Center for Archaeological Investigations, Southern Illinois University, Car-
            bondale.
2008        Temporal Variation in Qualla Pottery at Coweeta Creek. *North Carolina
            Archaeology* 57:1–49.
2009a       Mounds, Myths, and Cherokee Townhouses in Southwestern North Caro-
            lina. *American Antiquity* 74:627–663.
2009b       Domestic Houses at Coweeta Creek. *Southeastern Archaeology* 28:1–26.
2010a       Architectural Symbolism and Cherokee Townhouses. *Southeastern Archae-
            ology* 29:59–79.
2010b       European Trade Goods at Cherokee Settlements in Southwestern North
            Carolina. *North Carolina Archaeology* 59:1–84.
2011        Mortuary Practices, Gender Ideology, and the Cherokee Town at the
            Coweeta Creek Site. *Journal of Anthropological Archaeology* 30:145–173.
2013        Architecture of Aggregation in the Southern Appalachians: Cherokee Town-
            houses. In *From Prehistoric Villages to Cities: Settlement Aggregation and
            Community Transformation*, edited by Jennifer Birch, pp. 179–200. Rout-
            ledge, London.
2015a       *Center Places and Cherokee Towns: Archaeological Perspectives on Native
            American Architecture and Landscape in the Southern Appalachians.* Univer-
            sity of Alabama Press, Tuscaloosa.
2015b       Native American Public Architecture in the Southern Appalachians. In
            *Archaeological Perspectives on the Southern Appalachians: A Multiscalar Ap-
            proach*, edited by Ramie A. Gougeon and Maureen S. Meyers, pp. 105–140.
            University of Tennessee Press, Knoxville.
Rodning, Christopher B., and Amber M. VanDerwarker
2002        Revisiting Coweeta Creek: Reconstructing Ancient Cherokee Lifeways in
            Southwestern North Carolina. *Southeastern Archaeology* 21:1–9.
Rogers, Anne F.
2009        Archaeology at Cherokee Town Sites Visited by the Montgomery and Grant
            Expeditions. In *Culture, Crisis, and Conflict: Cherokee British Relations,
            1756–1765*, edited by Anne F. Rogers and Barbara R. Duncan, pp. 34–44.
            Museum of the Cherokee Indian Press, Cherokee, North Carolina.
Rogers, J. Daniel
1995a       Introduction. In *Mississippian Communities and Households*, edited by

J. Daniel Rogers and Bruce D. Smith, pp. 1–6. University of Alabama Press, Tuscaloosa.

1995b      The Archaeological Analysis of Domestic Organization. In *Mississippian Communities and Households*, edited by J. Daniel Rogers and Bruce D. Smith, pp. 7–31. University of Alabama Press, Tuscaloosa.

Rogers, J. Daniel, and Bruce D. Smith (editors)

1995      *Mississippian Communities and Households*. University of Alabama Press, Tuscaloosa.

Rolingson, Martha Ann, and Douglas W. Schwartz

1966      *Late Paleo-Indian and Early Archaic Manifestations in Western Kentucky*. Studies in Anthropology No. 3. University of Kentucky Press, Lexington.

Rolland, Vicki L.

2004      Measuring Tradition and Variation: A St. Johns II Pottery Assemblage from the Shields Site (8DU12). Master's thesis, Department of Anthropology, Florida State University, Tallahassee.

Rolland, Vicki L., and Paulette Bond

2003      The Search for Spiculate Clays near Aboriginal Sites in the Lower St. Johns River Region, Florida. *Florida Anthropologist* 56:91–112.

Romain, William

2015      Moonwatchers of Cahokia. In *Medieval Mississippians: The Cahokian World*, edited by Timothy R. Pauketat and Susan M. Alt, pp. 33–41. School for Advanced Research Press, Santa Fe, New Mexico.

Rosen, Arlene M., and Isabel Rivera-Collazo

2012      Climate Change, Adaptive Cycles, and the Persistence of Foraging Economies during the Late Pleistocene/Holocene Transition in the Levant. *Proceedings of the National Academy of Sciences* 109:3640–3645.

Rosenwinkel, Heidi A.

2013      A Mortuary Analysis of the Structure 7 Cemetery at Town Creek, a Mississippian Site in the Piedmont of North Carolina. Master's thesis, Department of Anthropology, East Carolina University, Greenville, North Carolina.

Rouse, Irving

1939      Prehistory in Haiti: A Study in Method. Yale University Publications in Anthropology, No. 21. Yale University Press, New Haven, Connecticut.

Russ, Kurt C., and Jefferson Chapman

1983      *Archaeological Investigations at the Eighteenth Century Overhill Cherokee Town of Mialoquo*. University of Tennessee, Department of Anthropology, Report of Investigations No. 37. Tennessee Valley Authority Publication in Anthropology No. 36. University of Tennessee Press, Knoxville.

Russell, Margaret C., and R. Donald Gordy

2012      The Archaeology of Mound H, Singer-Moye Mound Center, Stewart County, Georgia. *Early Georgia* 40(2):127–154.

Sabo, George, III

1987      *Contributions to Ozark Prehistory*. Research Series No. 27. Arkansas Archeological Survey, Fayetteville.

1995      Encounters and Images: European Contact and the Caddo Indians. *Historical Reflections/Reflexions Historiques* 21:217–242.

2012      The Terán Map and Caddo Cosmology. In *The Archaeology of the Caddo*, edited by Timothy K. Perttula and Chester P. Walker, pp. 431–448. University of Nebraska Press, Lincoln.

Sabo, George, III, Ann M. Early, Jerome C. Rose, Barbara A. Burnett, Louis Vogele Jr., and James P. Harcourt
1988        *Human Adaptation in the Ozark-Ouachita Mountains*. Research Series No. 31. Arkansas Archeological Survey, Fayetteville.

Saitta, Dean J.
1994        Agency, Class, and Archaeological Interpretation. *Journal of Anthropological Archaeology* 13(3):201–227.

Salberg, Daniel J.
2013        Ceramics and the Political Economy of Moundville: A Compositional Study Using Neutron Activation Analysis. Master's thesis, Department of Anthropology, University of Alabama, Tuscaloosa.

Sampson, Kelvin W., and Duane Esarey
1993        A Survey of Elaborate Mississippian Copper Artifacts from Illinois. *Illinois Archaeology* 5:452–480.

Sanger, Matthew C.
2017        Coils, Slabs, and Molds: Examining Community Affiliation between Late Archaic Shell Ring Communities Using Radiographic Imagery of Pottery. *Southeastern Archaeology* 36(2):95–109.

Santley, Robert S., and Kenneth G. Hirth (editors)
1993        *Prehispanic Domestic Units in Western Mesoamerica: Studies of the Household, Compound, and Residence*. CRC Press, Boca Raton, Florida.

Sassaman, Kenneth E.
2010        *The Eastern Archaic, Historicized*. AltaMira Press, Lanham, Maryland.

Sassaman, Kenneth E., Meggan E. Blessing, and Asa R. Randall
2006        Stallings Island Revisited: New Evidence for Occupational History, Community Pattern, and Subsistence Technology. *American Antiquity* 71(3):539–565.

Sassaman, Kenneth E., and Wictoria Rudolphi
2001        Communities of Practice in the Early Pottery Traditions of the American Southeast. *Journal of Anthropological Research* 57(4):408–425.

Sattler, Richard A.
1995        Women's Status among the Muskogee and Cherokee. In *Women and Power in Native North America*, edited by Laura F. Klein and Lillian A. Ackerman, pp. 214–229. University of Oklahoma Press, Norman.

Saxe, Arthur A.
1970        Social Dimensions of Mortuary Practices in a Mesolithic Population from Wadi Halfa, Sudan. PhD dissertation, Department of Anthropology, University of Michigan, Ann Arbor.

Scarry, C. Margaret
1993        Agricultural Risk and the Development of the Moundville Chiefdom. In *Foraging and Farming in the Eastern Woodlands*, edited by C. Margaret Scarry, pp. 157–181. University Press of Florida, Gainesville.

Scarry, C. Margaret, and Vincas P. Steponaitis
2016        Moundville as a Ceremonial Ground. In *Rethinking Moundville and Its Hinterland*, edited by Vincas P. Steponaitis and C. Margaret Scarry, pp. 255–268. University Press of Florida, Gainesville.

Scarry, John F.
1992        Political Offices and Political Structure: Ethnohistoric and Archaeological
            Perspectives on the Native Lords of Apalachee. In *Lords of the Southeast:
            Social Inequality and the Native Elites of Southeastern North America*, edited
            by Alex W. Barker and Timothy R. Pauketat, pp. 163–179. Archeological
            Paper No. 3. American Anthropological Association, Washington, DC.
1995        Apalachee Homesteads: The Basal Social and Economic Units of a Missis-
            sippian Chiefdom. In *Mississippian Communities and Households*, edited
            by J. Daniel Rogers and Bruce D. Smith, pp. 32–57. University of Alabama
            Press, Tuscaloosa.
2001        Resistance and Accommodation in Apalachee Province. In *The Archae-
            ology of Traditions: Agency and History before and after Columbus*, edited by
            Timothy R. Pauketat, pp. 34–57. University Press of Florida, Gainesville.
Scarry, John F., H. Edwin Jackson, and Mintcy D. Maxham
2016        Late Prehistoric Social Practice in the Rural Black Warrior River Valley. In
            *Rethinking Moundville and Its Hinterland*, edited by Vincas P. Steponaitis
            and C. Margaret Scarry, pp. 162–186. University Press of Florida, Gaines-
            ville.
Scarry, John F., and Bonnie G. McEwan
1995        Domestic Architecture in Apalachee Province: Apalachee and Spanish Resi-
            dential Styles in the Late Prehistoric and Early Historic Period Southeast.
            *American Antiquity* 60:482–495.
Schachner, Gregson
2012        *Population Circulation and the Transformation of Ancient Zuni Communities.*
            University of Arizona Press, Tucson.
Schambach, Frank F.
1982a       An Outline of Fourche Maline Culture in Southwest Arkansas. In *Arkan-
            sas Archeology in Review*, edited by W. Fredrick Limp, pp. 132–197. Research
            Series 14, Arkansas Archeological Survey, Fayetteville.
1982b       The Archeology of the Great Bend Region in Arkansas. In *Contributions to
            the Archeology of the Great Bend Region*, edited by Frank F. Schambach and
            Frank Rackerby, pp. 1–11. Research Series No. 22. Arkansas Archeological
            Survey, Fayetteville.
1990        The "Northern Caddoan Area" Was Not Caddoan. *Caddoan Archeology
            Newsletter* 1(4):2–6.
1993        The End of the Trail: Reconstruction of the Route of Hernando de Soto's
            Army through Southwest Arkansas and East Texas. In *The Expedition of
            Hernando de Soto West of the Mississippi, 1541–1543. Proceedings of the de
            Soto Symposia, 1988 and 1990*, edited by Gloria A. Young and Michael P.
            Hoffman, pp. 78–105. University of Arkansas Press, Fayetteville.
1996        Mounds, Embankments, and Ceremonialism in the Trans-Mississippi South.
            In *Mounds, Embankments, and Ceremonialism in the Midsouth*, edited by
            Robert C. Mainfort and Richard Walling, pp. 36–43. Research Series No. 46.
            Arkansas Archeological Survey, Fayetteville.
1998        *Pre-Caddoan Cultures in the Trans-Mississippi South: A Beginning Sequence.*
            Research Series No. 53. Arkansas Archeological Survey, Fayetteville, Arkansas.
2000        Spiroan Traders, the Sanders Site, and the Plains Interaction Sphere: A Reply
            to Bruseth, Wilson, and Perttula. *Plains Anthropologist* 45(171):17–33.

2003          Osage Orange Bows, Indian Horses, and the Blackland Prairie of Northeast-
             ern Texas. In *Blackland Prairies of the Gulf Coastal Plain: Nature, Culture,
             and Sustainability*, edited by Evan Peacock and Timothy Schauwecker,
             pp. 212–236. University of Alabama Press, Tuscaloosa.

Schatzki, Theodore R.
2002          *The Site of the Social: A Philosophical Account of the Constitution of Social
             Life and Change.* Pennsylvania State University Press, University Park.

Schilling, Timothy
2013          Chronology of Monks Mound. *Southeastern Archaeology* 32(1):14–28.

Schnell, Frank T., Vernon J. Knight Jr., and Gail S. Schnell
1981          *Cemochechobee: Archaeology of a Mississippian Ceremonial Center on the
             Chattahoochee River.* University Press of Florida, Gainesville.

Schnell, Frank T., and Newell O. Wright Jr.
1993          *Mississippi Period Archaeology of the Georgia Coastal Plain.* Laboratory of
             Archaeology Series No. 26. University of Georgia, Athens.

Schroedl, Gerald F.
1989          Overhill Cherokee Household and Village Patterns in the Eighteenth Cen-
             tury. In *Households and Communities*, edited by Scott MacEachern, David
             J. W. Archer, and Richard D. Garvin, pp. 350–60. Archaeological Association
             of the University of Calgary, Alberta, Canada.
1998          Mississippian Towns in the Eastern Tennessee Valley. In *Mississippian
             Towns and Sacred Spaces: Searching for an Architectural Grammar*, edited by
             R. Barry Lewis and Charles Stout, pp. 64–92. University of Alabama Press,
             Tuscaloosa.
2000          Cherokee Ethnohistory and Archaeology from 1540 to 1838. In *Indians of
             the Greater Southeast: Historical Archaeology and Ethnohistory*, edited by
             Bonnie G. McEwan, pp. 64–92. University Press of Florida, Gainesville.
2001          Cherokee Archaeology since the 1970s. In *Archaeology of the Appalachian
             Highlands*, edited by Lynne P. Sullivan and Susan C. Prezzano, pp. 278–297.
             University of Tennessee Press, Knoxville.
2009          Overhill Cherokee Architecture and Village Organization. In *Culture, Crisis,
             and Conflict: Cherokee British Relations, 1756–1765*, edited by Anne F.
             Rogers and Barbara R. Duncan, pp. 62–82. Museum of the Cherokee Indian
             Press, Cherokee, North Carolina.

Schroedl, Gerald F. (editor)
1986          *Overhill Cherokee Archaeology at Chota-Tanasee.* Report of Investigations
             No. 38. Department of Anthropology, University of Tennessee, Knoxville.

Schroedl, Gerald F., and C. Clifford Boyd Jr.
1991          Late Woodland Period Culture in East Tennessee. In *Stability, Transforma-
             tion, and Variation: The Late Woodland Southeast*, edited by Michael S.
             Nassaney and Charles R. Cobb, pp. 69–90. Plenum Press, New York.

Schroedl, Gerald F., C. Clifford Boyd Jr., and R. P. Stephen Davis Jr.
1990          Explaining Mississippian Origins in East Tennessee. In *The Mississippian
             Emergence*, edited by Bruce D. Smith, pp. 175–196. Smithsonian Institution
             Press, Washington, DC.

Schroedl, Gerald F., R. P. Stephen Davis Jr., and C. Clifford Boyd Jr.
1985          *Archaeological Contexts and Assemblages at Martin Farm.* University of Ten-
             nessee, Department of Anthropology, Report of Investigations No. 39. Ten-

nessee Valley Authority Publication in Anthropology No. 37. University of Tennessee Press, Knoxville.

Schwandes, Lawrence P., and Mary Ellen Collins
1994    Distribution and Significance of Freshwater Sponge Spicules in Selected Florida Soils. *Transactions of the American Microscopical Society* 113:242–257.

Sears, William H.
1957    *Excavations on Lower St. Johns River, Florida*. Contributions of the Florida State Museum No. 2. Florida State Museum, Gainesville.

Shapiro, Gary
1984    Ceramic Vessels, Site Permanence, and Group Size: A Mississippian Example. *American Antiquity* 49(4):696–712.

Sherwood, Sarah C., and Tristram R. Kidder
2011    The DaVincis of Dirt: Geoarchaeological Perspectives on Native American Mound Building in the Mississippi River. *Journal of Anthropological Archaeology* 30:69–87.

Shumate, M. Scott, Brett H. Riggs, and Larry P. Kimball
2005    *The Alarka Farmstead Site: Archaeological Investigations at a Mid-Seventeenth-Century Cherokee Winter House/Summer House Complex, Swain County, North Carolina*. Appalachian State University Laboratories of Archaeological Science and Research Laboratories of Archaeology, Boone and Chapel Hill, North Carolina. Submitted to Rodney J. Snedeker, Forest Archaeologist, National Forests in North Carolina.

Simon, Mary L.
2014    Reevaluating the Introduction of Maize into the American Bottom and Western Illinois. In *Reassessing the Timing, Rate, and Adoption Trajectories of Domesticate Use in the Midwest and Great Lakes*, edited by Maria E. Raviele and William A. Lovis, pp. 97–134. Occasional Paper No. 1. Midwest Archaeological Conference.

2017    Reevaluating the Evidence for Middle Woodland Maize from the Holding Site. *American Antiquity* 82:140–150.

Simon, Mary L., and Kathryn E. Parker
2006    Prehistoric Plant Use in the American Bottom: New Thoughts and Interpretations. *Southeastern Archaeology* 25(2):170–211.

Skousen, B. Jacob
2012    Posts, Places, Ancestors, and Worlds: Dividual Personhood in the American Bottom Region. *Southeastern Archaeology* 31(1):57–69.

2015    Moonbeams, Water, and Smoke: Tracing Otherwordly Relationships at the Emerald Site. In *Tracing the Relational: The Archaeology of Worlds, Spirits, and Temporalities*, edited by Meghan E. Buchanan and B. Jacob Skousen, pp. 38–53. University of Utah Press, Salt Lake City.

Skousen, B. Jacob, and Meghan E. Buchanan
2015    Introduction: Advancing and Archaeology of Movements and Relationships. In *Tracing the Relational: The Archaeology of Worlds, Spirits, and Temporalities*, edited by B. Jacob Skousen and Meghan E. Buchanan, pp. 1–20. University of Utah Press, Salt Lake City.

Slater, Philip A., Kristin M. Hedman, and Thomas E. Emerson
2014    Immigrants at the Mississippian Polity of Cahokia: Strontium Isotope Evidence for Population Movement. *Journal of Archaeological Science* 44:117–127.

Smith, Adam T.
2003        *The Political Landscape: Constellations of Authority in Early Complex Polities.*
            University of California Press, Berkeley.

Smith, Alexandre Livingstone
2000        Processing Clay for Pottery in Northern Cameroon: Social and Technical
            Requirements. *Archaeometry* 42:21–42.

Smith, Bruce D.
1978        Variation in Mississippian Settlement Patterns. In *Mississippian Settlement
            Patterns*, edited by Bruce D. Smith, pp. 479–503. Academic Press, New York.
1995        The Analysis of Single-Household Mississippian Settlements. In *Mississip-
            pian Communities and Households*, edited by J. Daniel Rogers and Bruce D.
            Smith, pp. 224–250. University of Alabama Press, Tuscaloosa.

Smith, Bruce D. (editor)
1978a       *Prehistoric Patterns of Human Behavior: A Case Study in the Mississippi Val-
            ley.* Academic Press, New York.
1978b       *Mississippian Settlement Patterns.* Academic Press, New York.
1990        *The Mississippian Emergence.* Smithsonian Institution Press, Washington, DC.

Smith, F. Todd
1995        *The Caddo Indians: Tribes at the Convergence of Empires, 1542–1854.* Texas
            A&M University Press, College Station.

Smith, Karen Y., and Vernon J. Knight Jr.
2012        Style in Swift Creek Paddle Art. *Southeastern Archaeology* 31(2):143–156.

Smith, Marvin T.
1994        *Archaeological Investigations at the Dyar Site, 9GE5.* Laboratory of Archae-
            ology Series Report No. 32. Department of Anthropology, University of
            Georgia, Athens.

Smith, Michael E.
2010        The Archaeological Study of Neighborhoods and Districts in Ancient Cities.
            *Journal of Anthropological Archaeology* 29:137–154.

Smith, Michael E., Gary M. Feinman, Robert D. Drennan, Timothy Earle, and Ian Morris
2012        Archaeology as a Social Science. *Proceedings of the National Academy of
            Sciences* 109(20):7617–7621.

Smyth, Michael P.
1991        *Modern Maya Storage Behavior: Ethnoarchaeological Case Examples from the
            Puuc Region of Yucatan.* Latin American Archaeology Publications, Univer-
            sity of Pittsburgh, Pittsburgh, Pennsylvania.

Snead, James E.
2004        Ancestral Pueblo Settlement Dynamics: Landscape, Scale, and Context in
            the Burnt Corn Community. *Kiva* 69(3):243–269.

Sørensen, Tim F.
2015        More Than a Feeling: Towards an Archaeology of Atmosphere. *Emotion,
            Space and Society* 15:64–73.

South, Stanley
2002        *Archaeological Pathways to Historic Site Development.* Kluwer Academic/
            Plenum, New York.

Speck, Frank G.
1907        Notes on Chickasaw Ethnology and Folk-Lore. *Journal of American Folk-
            Lore* 20(76):50–58.

1909      *Ethnology of the Yuchi Indians.* Anthropological Paper No. 1. University of Pennsylvania Museum, Philadelphia.

Stanish, Charles, and Kevin J. Haley

2005      Power, Fairness, and Architecture: Modeling Early Chiefdom Development in the Central Andes. In *Foundations of Power in the Prehispanic Andes,* edited by Kevin J. Vaughn, Dennis Ogburn, and Christina A. Conlee, pp. 53–70. Archaeological Paper No. 14. American Anthropological Association, Arlington, Virginia.

Stark, Miriam T.

2006      Glaze Ware Technology, the Social Lives of Pots, and Communities of Practice in the Late Prehistoric Southwest. In *The Social Life of Pots: Glaze Wares and Cultural Dynamics in the Southwest, AD 1250–1680,* edited by Judith A. Habicht-Mauche, Suzanne L. Eckert, and Deborah L. Huntley, pp. 17–33. University of Arizona Press, Tucson.

Steadman, Dawnie Wolfe

2008      Warfare Related Trauma at Orendorf, a Middle Mississippian Site in West-Central Illinois. *American Journal of Physical Anthropology* 136:51–64.

Steere, Benjamin A.

2017      *The Archaeology of Houses and Households in the Native Southeast.* University of Alabama Press, Tuscaloosa.

Steere, Benjamin A., and Aaron Deter-Wolf

2013      Postholes and Structures. In *The Fernvale Site (40WM51): Late Archaic and Multicomponent Occupations along the South Harpeth River in Williamson County, Tennessee,* edited by Aaron Deter-Wolf and Michael C. Moore, pp. 49–66. Tennessee Department of Environment and Conservation, Division of Archaeology, Nashville.

Steponaitis, Vincas P.

1986      Prehistoric Archaeology in the Southeastern United States, 1970–1985. *Annual Review of Anthropology* 15:363–404.

1992      Excavations at 1Tu50, an Early Mississippian Center near Moundville. *Southeastern Archaeology* 11:1–13.

2016      Moundville Palettes—Prestige Goods of Inalienable Possessions? In *Rethinking Moundville and Its Hinterland,* edited by Vincas P. Steponaitis and C. Margaret Scarry, pp. 121–133. University Press of Florida, Gainesville.

Story, Dee Ann

1990      Culture History of the Native Americans. In *The Archeology and Bioarcheology of the Gulf Coastal Plain,* Vol. 1, by Dee Ann Story, Janice A. Guy, Barbara A. Burnett, Martha Doty Freeman, Jerome C. Rose, D. Gentry Steele, Ben W. Olive, and Karl J. Reinhard, pp. 163–366. Research Series No. 38. Arkansas Archeological Survey, Fayetteville.

Stout, Charles B.

1989      The Spatial Patterning of the Adams Site, a Mississippian Town in Western Kentucky. PhD dissertation, Department of Anthropology, University of Illinois at Urbana-Champaign.

Stout, Charles, and R. Barry Lewis

1998      Mississippian Towns in Kentucky. In *Mississippian Towns and Sacred Spaces: Searching for an Architectural Grammar,* edited by R. Barry Lewis and Charles Stout, 151–178. University of Alabama Press, Tuscaloosa.

Streeter, Richard, Andrew J. Dugmore, and Orri Vesteinsson
2012        Plague and Landscape Resilience in Premodern Iceland. *Proceedings of the National Academy of Sciences* 109:3658–3663.

Sullivan, Lynne P.
1986        The Late Mississippian Village: Community and Society of the Mouse Creek Phase in Southeastern Tennessee. PhD dissertation, Department of Anthropology, University of Wisconsin-Milwaukee.
1987        The Mouse Creek Phase Household. *Southeastern Archaeology* 6:16–29.
1989        Household, Community, and Society: An Analysis of Mouse Creek Settlements. In *Households and Communities*, edited by Scott MacEachern, David J. W. Archer, and Richard D. Garvin, pp. 15–21. Archaeological Association of the University of Calgary, Alberta, Canada.
1995        Mississippian Household and Community Organization in Eastern Tennessee. In *Mississippian Communities and Households*, edited by J. Daniel Rogers and Bruce D. Smith, pp. 99–123. University of Alabama Press, Tuscaloosa.
2001a       Gendered Contexts of Mississippian Leadership in Southern Appalachia. In *Leadership and Polity in Mississippian Society*, edited by Paul Welch and Brian Butler, pp. 264–285. Southern Illinois University Press, Carbondale.
2001b       "Those Men in the Mounds": Gender, Politics, and Mortuary Practices in Late Prehistoric Eastern Tennessee. In *Archaeological Studies of Gender in the Southeastern United States*, edited by Jane M. Eastman and Christopher B. Rodning, pp. 101–126. University Press of Florida, Gainesville.
2016        Reconfiguring the Chickamauga Basin. In *New Deal Archaeology in Tennessee: Intellectual, Methodological, and Theoretical Contributions*, edited by David H. Dye, pp. 138–170. University of Alabama Press, Tuscaloosa.
2018        The Path to the Council House: The Development of Mississippian Communities in Southeast Tennessee. In *The Archaeology of Villages in Eastern North America*, edited by Jennifer Birch and Victor D. Thompson, pp. 106–123. University Press of Florida, Gainesville.

Sullivan, Lynne P., and Shannon D. Koerner
2010        New Perspectives on Late Woodland Architecture and Settlement in Eastern Tennessee: Evidence from the DeArmond Site (40RE12). *Tennessee Archaeology* 5(1):31–50.

Sullivan, Lynne P., and Robert C. Mainfort Jr.
2010        Mississippian Mortuary Practices and the Quest for Interpretation. In *Mississippian Mortuary Practices: Beyond Hierarchy and the Representationist Perspective*, edited by Lynne P. Sullivan and Robert C. Mainfort Jr., pp. 1–13. University Press of Florida, Gainesville.

Sullivan, Lynne P., and Christopher B. Rodning
2011        Residential Burial, Gender Roles, and Political Development in Late Prehistoric and Early Cherokee Cultures of the Southern Appalachians. In *Residential Burial: A Multi-Regional Exploration*, edited by Ron Adams and Stacie King, pp. 79–97. AP3A Series. American Anthropological Association, Washington, DC.

Sullivan, Stephanie M., and Duncan P. McKinnon
2013        The Collins Site (3WA1): Exploring Architectural Variation in the Western Ozark Highlands. *Southeastern Archaeology* 32(1):70–84.

Sundberg, Juanita
2013        Decolonizing Posthumanist Geographies. *Cultural Geographies* 21(1):33–47.
Swanton, John R.
1928        Social Organization and Social Usages of the Indians of the Creek Confederacy. In *Forty-Second Annual Report of the Bureau of American Ethnology*, 23–472. Government Printing Office, Washington, DC.
1931        *Source Material for the Social and Ceremonial Life of the Choctaw Indians.* Bulletin No. 103. Bureau of American Ethnology, Smithsonian Institution, Washington, DC.
1942        *Source Material on the History and Ethnology of the Caddo Indians.* Bulletin No. 132. Bureau of American Ethnology, Smithsonian Institution, Washington, DC.
1946        *The Indians of the Southeastern United States.* Smithsonian Institution Press, Washington, DC.
2001 [1931] *Source Material for the Social and Ceremonial Life of the Choctaw Indians.* Smithsonian Institution, Washington, DC. Reprinted, University of Alabama Press, Tuscaloosa.
2006 [1928] *Chickasaw Society and Religion.* Smithsonian Institution, Washington, DC. Reprinted, University of Oklahoma Press, Norman.
Tainter, Joseph A.
1988        *The Collapse of Complex Societies.* Cambridge University Press, Cambridge.
2006        Archaeology of Overshoot and Collapse. *Annual Review of Anthropology* 35:59–74.
Tarlow, Sarah
2012        The Archaeology of Emotion and Affect. *Annual Review of Anthropology* 41:169–185.
Tehrani, Jamshid J., and Felix Riede
2008        Towards an Archaeology of Pedagogy: Learning, Teaching and the Generation of Material Culture Traditions. *World Archaeology* 40:316–331.
Thomas, Julian
2001        Archaeologies of Place and Landscape. In *Archaeological Theory Today*, edited by Ian Hodder, pp. 165–186. Blackwell, Malden, Massachusetts.
Thomas, Larissa A.
2001        The Gender Division of Labor in Mississippian Households: Its Role in Shaping Production for Exchange. *Archaeological Studies of Gender in the Southeastern United States*, edited by Jane M. Eastman and Christopher B. Rodning, pp. 27–56. University Press of Florida, Gainesville.
Thompson, Claire E.
2011        Ritual and Power: Examining the Economy of Moundville's Residential Population. PhD dissertation, Department of Anthropology, University of Alabama, Tuscaloosa.
Thompson, Victor D.
2017        Conceptualizing the Anthropogenic Islands of Southern Florida with LiDAR. In *Archaeological Remote Sensing in North America: Innovative Techniques for Anthropological Applications*, edited by Duncan P. McKinnon and Bryan S. Haley, pp. 127–140. University of Alabama Press, Tuscaloosa.
Thompson, Victor D., and Jennifer Birch
2018        The Power of Villages. In *The Archaeology of Village Societies in Eastern*

*North America*, edited by Jennifer Birch and Victor D. Thompson, pp. 1–19. University Press of Florida, Gainesville.

Thunen, Robert L.
2005          Grant Mound: Past and Present. *Florida Anthropologist* 58:253–261.

Tilley, Christopher
1994          *A Phenomenology of Landscape: Places, Paths and Monuments.* Berg, Oxford.

Todd, Zoe
2016          An Indigenous Feminist's Take on the Ontological Turn: "Ontology" Is Just Another Word for Colonialism. *Journal of Historical Sociology* 29(1):4–22.

Townsend, Richard F., and Chester P. Walker
2004          The Ancient Art of Caddo Ceramics. In *Hero, Hawk, and Open Hand: American Indian Art of the Ancient Midwest and South*, edited by Richard F. Townsend, pp. 231–246. Yale University Press, New Haven, Connecticut.

Tringham, Ruth E.
1991          Households with Faces: The Challenge of Gender in Prehistoric Architectural Remains. In *Engendering Archaeology: Women and Prehistory*, edited by Joan M. Gero and Margaret W. Conkey, pp. 93–132. Blackwell, Oxford.
1995          Archaeological Houses, Households, Housework and the Home. In *The Home: Words, Interpretations, Meanings, and Environments*, edited by David N. Benjamin and David Stea, pp. 79–107. Avebury Press, Aldershot.

Trubitt, Mary B.
1996          Household Status, Marine Shell Bead Production, and the Development of Cahokia in the Mississippian Period. PhD dissertation, Department of Anthropology, Northwestern University, Evanston, Illinois.
2000          Mound Building and Prestige Goods Exchange: Changing Strategies in the Cahokia Chiefdom. *American Antiquity* 65(4):669–690.
2009          Burning and Burying Buildings: Exploring Variation in Caddo Architecture in Southwest Arkansas. *Southeastern Archaeology* 28(2):233–247.

Trubowitz, Neal L. (editor)
1984          *Cedar Grove.* Research Series No. 23. Arkansas Archeological Survey, Fayetteville.

Tuchman, Barbara
1978          *A Distant Mirror: The Calamitous 14th Century.* Ballantine Books, New York.

Turner, Victor
1969          *The Ritual Process: Structure and Anti-Structure.* Penguin, London.

Urban, Greg, and Jason Baird Jackson
2004          Social Organization. In *Southeast*, edited by Raymond Fogelson, pp. 697–706. Handbook of North American Indians, Vol. 14, William C. Sturtevant, general editor, Smithsonian Institution, Washington, DC.

VanDerwarker, Amber M., Dana N. Bardolph, and C. Margaret Scarry
2017          Maize and Mississippian Beginnings. In *Mississippian Beginnings*, edited by Gregory D. Wilson, pp. 29–70. University Press of Florida, Gainesville.

Van Dyke, Ruth M., and Susan E. Alcock (editors)
2003          *Archaeologies of Memory.* Blackwell, Malden, Massachusetts.

Varien, Mark D., and James M. Potter
2008          The Social Production of Communities: Structure, Agency, Identity. In *The Social Construction of Communities: Agency, Structure, and Identity in the Prehispanic Southwest*, edited by Mark D. Varien and James M. Potter, pp. 1–20. AltaMira Press, New York.

Varien, Mark D., and James M. Potter (editors)
2008    *The Social Construction of Communities: Agency, Structure, and Identity in the Prehispanic Southwest.* AltaMira Press, Lanham, Maryland.

Vehik, Susan C.
1990    Late Prehistoric Exchange on the Southern Plains and Its Periphery. *Midcontinental Journal of Archaeology* 13(1):41–68.

Vehik, Susan C., and Timothy G. Baugh
1994    Prehistoric Plains Trade. In *Prehistoric Exchange Systems in North America*, edited by Timothy G. Baugh and Jonathon E. Ericson, pp. 249–274. Plenum Press, New York.

Vogel, Gregory
2012    Viewshed Characteristics of Caddo Mounds in the Arkansas Basin. In *The Archaeology of the Caddo*, edited by Timothy K. Perttula and Chester P. Walker, pp. 139–176. University of Nebraska Press, Lincoln.

Walker, Chester P.
2009    Landscape Archaeo-Geophysics: A Study of Magnetometer Surveys from Etowah (9BR1), the George C. Davis Site (41CE14), and the Hill Farm Site (41BW169). PhD dissertation, Department of Anthropology, University of Texas, Austin.

Walker, Chester P., and Duncan P. McKinnon
2012    Exploring Prehistoric Caddo Communities through Archaeogeophysics. In *The Archaeology of the Caddo*, edited by Timothy K. Perttula and Chester P. Walker, pp. 177–208. University of Nebraska Press, Lincoln.

Walker, Chester P., and Timothy K. Perttula
2008    Geophysical Investigations on Caddo Sites in East Texas and Surrounding States. *Bulletin of the Texas Archeological Society* 79:159–176.

Walker, Leslie
2014    Liminal River: Art, Agency, and Cultural Transformation along the Protohistoric Arkansas River. PhD dissertation, Department of Anthropology, University of Arkansas, Fayetteville.

Wallis, Neill J.
2011    *The Swift Creek Gift: Vessel Exchange on the Atlantic Coast.* University of Alabama Press, Tuscaloosa.

Ward, H. Trawick, and R. P. Stephen Davis Jr.
1993    *Indian Communities on the North Carolina Piedmont, A.D. 1000 to 1700.* Monograph No. 2. Research Laboratories of Anthropology, University of North Carolina, Chapel Hill.
1999    *Time before History: The Archaeology of North Carolina.* University of North Carolina Press, Chapel Hill.

Waring, Antonio J., Jr.
1968    The Southern Cult and Muskhogean Ceremonial. In *The Waring Papers: The Collected Works of Antonio J. Waring, Jr.*, edited by Stephen Williams, pp. 30–69. Papers of the Peabody Museum of Archaeology and Ethnology No. 58. Harvard University, Cambridge, Massachusetts.

Waring, Antonio J., Jr., and Preston Holder
1945    A Prehistoric Ceremonial Complex in the Southeastern United States. *American Anthropologist* 47(1):1–34.

Warrick, Gary A.
1988    Estimating Ontario Iroquoian Village Duration. *Man in the Northeast* 36:21–60.

Waselkov, Gregory A., and Kathryn E. Holland Braund (editors)
1995        *William Bartram on the Southeastern Indians*. University of Nebraska Press,
            Lincoln.

Waselkov, Gregory A., and Marvin T. Smith
2017        *Forging Southeastern Identities: Social Archaeology, Ethnohistory, and Folk-*
            *lore of the Mississippian to Early Historic South*. University of Alabama Press,
            Tuscaloosa.

Watanabe, John M.
1992        *Maya Saints and Souls in a Changing World*. University of Texas Press,
            Austin.

Watts, Christopher (editor)
2013        *Relational Archaeologies: Humans, Animals, Things*. Routledge, New York.

Watts, Vanessa
2013        Indigenous Place-Thought and Agency amongst Humans and Non-Humans
            (Woman and Sky Woman Go on a European World Tour!). *Decolonization:*
            *Indigeneity, Education and Society* 2(1):20–34.

Watts Malouchos, Elizabeth
2020a       Angel Ethnogenesis and the Cahokian Diaspora. *Journal of Archaeological*
            *Method and Theory* 27:128–156.
2020b       Assembling Mississippian Communities: Integration, Identities, and
            Everyday Practices in the Angel Hinterlands. PhD dissertation, Department
            of Anthropology, Indiana University, Bloomington.

Wauchope, Robert
1966        *Archaeological Survey of Northern Georgia with a Test of Some Cultural*
            *Hypotheses*. Memoir No. 25. Society for American Archaeology, Salt Lake
            City, Utah.

Webb, Clarence H.
1959        *The Belcher Mound, a Stratified Caddoan Site in Caddo Parish, Louisiana*.
            Memoir No. 16. Society for American Archaeology, Salt Lake City, Utah.

Weber, J. Cynthia
1971        The Hays Mound: A Very Preliminary Report. *Field Notes: Newsletter of the*
            *Arkansas Archeological Society* 76:3–6.
1972        "Lizard" Effigy Pendants. *Field Notes: Newsletter of the Arkansas Archeologi-*
            *cal Society* 90:4–5.

Webmoor, Timothy
2007        What about "One More Turn after the Social" in Archaeological Reasoning?
            Taking Things Seriously. *World Archaeology* 39:563–578.

Wedel, Mildred Mott
1978        *La Harpe's 1719 Post on Red River and Nearby Caddo Settlements*. Bulletin
            No. 30. Texas Memorial Museum, University of Texas, Austin.

Welch, Paul D.
1991        *Moundville's Economy*. University of Alabama Press, Tuscaloosa.
1994        The Occupational History of the Bessemer Site. *Southeastern Archaeology*
            13(1):1–26.
1996        Control over Goods and the Political Stability of the Moundville Chiefdom.
            In *Political Structure and Change in the Prehistoric Southeastern United*
            *States*, edited by John. F. Scarry, pp. 69–91. University Press of Florida,
            Gainesville.
1998        Outlying Sites within the Moundville Chiefdom. In *Archaeology of the*

> *Moundville Chiefdom*, edited by Vernon J. Knight Jr. and Vincas P. Stepo-
> naitis, pp. 133–166. Smithsonian Institution Press, Washington, DC.

2013     *Excavations at Kincaid, 2013*. Paper presented at the 2013 Mississippian Conference, Crisp Museum, Southeast Missouri State University, Cape Girardeau.

Welch, Paul D., Brian M. Butler, and Corin C. O. Pursell

2008     *Report of 2007 Fieldwork at Kincaid Mounds State Historic Site*. Report submitted to the Illinois Historic Preservation Agency. Center for Archaeological Investigations, Southern Illinois University, Carbondale.

Wenger, Etienne

1998     *Communities of Practice: Learning, Meaning, and Identity*. Cambridge University Press, New York.

Wernke, Steven A.

2007     Negotiating Community and Landscape in the Peruvian Andes: A Trans-Conquest View. *American Anthropologist* 109(1):130–152.

2015     *Negotiated Settlements: Andean Communities and Landscapes under Inka and Spanish Colonialism*. University Press of Florida, Gainesville.

Wesson, Cameron B.

1999     Chiefly Power and Food Storage in Southeastern North America. *World Archaeology* 31(1):145–164.

2001     Creek and Pre-Creek Revisited. In *The Archaeology of Traditions: Agency and History before and after Columbus*, edited by Timothy R. Pauketat, pp. 94–106. University Press of Florida, Gainesville.

2008     *Households and Hegemony: Early Creek Prestige Goods, Symbolic Capital, and Social Power*. University of Nebraska Press, Lincoln.

2016     From Households to Communities and Back Again: Bridging Analytical Scales in Search of Conflict, Coalescence, and Communitas. Paper presented at the 81st Annual Meeting of the Society for American Archaeology, Orlando, Florida.

Wetmore, Ruth Y.

1990     *The Ela Site (31SW5): Archaeological Data Recovery of Connestee and Qualla Phase Occupations at the East Elementary School Site, Swain County, North Carolina*. Western Carolina Archaeology Laboratory, Cullowhee, North Carolina.

Wharton, Charles H.

1978     *The Natural Environments of Georgia*. Georgia Department of Natural Resources, Atlanta.

Whittaker, John

1994     *Flintknapping: Making and Understanding Stone Tools*. University of Texas Press, Austin.

Whittle, Alastair

2003     *The Archaeology of People: Dimensions of Neolithic Life*. Routledge, London.

Wiewel, Rebecca

2014     Constructing Community in the Central Arkansas River Valley: Ceramic Compositional Analysis and Collaborative Archaeology. PhD dissertation, Department of Anthropology, University of Arkansas, Fayetteville.

Wilk, Richard R.

1983     Little House in the Jungle: The Causes of Variation in House Size among Modern Kekchi Maya. *Journal of Anthropological Archaeology* 2(2):99–116.

1988        Maya Household Organization: Evidence and Analogies. In *Household and Community in the Mesoamerican Past*, edited by Richard R. Wilk and Wendy Ashmore, pp. 135–151. University of New Mexico Press, Albuquerque.

Wilk, Richard R., and Wendy Ashmore (editors)
1988        *Household and Community in the Mesoamerican Past.* University of New Mexico Press, Albuquerque.

Wilk, Richard R., and Robert Netting
1984        Households: Changing Forms and Functions. In *Households: Comparative and Historical Studies of the Domestic Group*, edited by Robert Netting, Richard R. Wilk, and Eric Arnould, pp. 1–28. University of California Press, Berkeley.

Wilk, Richard R., and William L. Rathje
1982        Archaeology of the Household: Building a Prehistory of Domestic Life. *American Behavioral Scientist* 25(6):617–640.

Willey, Gordon R.
1953        *Prehistoric Settlement Patterns in the Viru Valley, Peru.* Bulletin No. 155. Bureau of American Ethnology, Washington, DC.

Williams, J. Raymond
1974        The Baytown Phases in the Cairo Lowland of Southeast Missouri. *Missouri Archaeologist* 36:1–109.

Williams, Samuel Cole (editor)
1927        *Lieutenant Henry Timberlake's Memoirs.* Watauga Press, Johnson City, Tennessee.
1928        *Early Travels in the Tennessee Country, 1540–1800.* Watauga Press, Johnson City, Tennessee.
1930        *James Adair's History of the North American Indians.* Watauga Press, Johnson City, Tennessee.

Williams, Stephen
1990        The Vacant Quarter and Other Late Events in the Lower Ohio Valley. In *Towns and Temples along the Mississippi*, edited by David H. Dye and Cheryl Anne Cox, pp. 170–180. University of Alabama Press, Tuscaloosa.

Wills, W. H., and Robert D. Leonard (editors)
1994        *The Ancient Southwestern Community: Models and Methods for the Study of Prehistoric Social Organization.* University of New Mexico Press, Albuquerque.

Wilson, Gilbert L.
1917        *Agriculture of the Hidatsa Indians: An Indian Interpretation.* Studies in the Social Sciences No. 9. University of Minnesota, Minneapolis.

Wilson, Gregory D.
2001        Crafting Control and the Control of Crafts: Rethinking the Moundville Greenstone Industry. *Southeastern Archaeology* 20(2):118–128.
2005        Between Plaza and Palisade: Household and Community Organization at Early Moundville. PhD dissertation, Department of Anthropology, University of North Carolina, Chapel Hill.
2008        *The Archaeology of Everyday Life at Moundville.* University of Alabama Press, Tuscaloosa.
2010        Community, Identity, and Social Memory at Moundville. *American Antiquity* 75:3–18.
2012        Living with War: The Impact of Chronic Violence in the Mississippian-

Period Central Illinois River Valley. In *The Oxford Handbook of North American Archaeology*, edited by Timothy R. Pauketat, pp. 523–533. Oxford University Press, New York.

2016 Long-Term Trends in the Making and Materialization of Social Groups. In *Rethinking Moundville and Its Hinterland*, edited by Vincas P. Steponaitis and C. Margaret Scarry, pp. 44–53. University Press of Florida, Gainesville.

Wilson, Gregory D. (editor)

2017 *Mississippian Beginnings*. University Press of Florida, Gainesville.

Wilson, Gregory D., Jon B. Marcoux, and Brad H. Koldehoff

2006 Square Pegs in Round Holes: Organizational Diversity between Early Moundville and Cahokia. In *Leadership and Polity in Mississippian Society*, edited by Brian M. Butler and Paul D. Welch, 43–72. Occasional Paper No. 33. Center for Archaeological Investigations, Southern Illinois University, Carbondale.

Wilson, Gregory D., Vincas P. Steponaitis, and Keith P. Jacobi

2010 Social and Spatial Dimensions of Moundville Mortuary Practices. In *Mississippian Mortuary Practices: Beyond Hierarchy and the Representationist Perspective*, edited by Lynne P. Sullivan and Robert C. Mainfort Jr., pp. 74–89. University Press of Florida, Gainesville.

Wilson, Gregory D., and Lynne P. Sullivan

2017 Mississippian Origins: From Emergence to Beginnings. In *Mississippian Beginnings*, edited by Gregory D. Wilson, pp. 1–28. University Press of Florida, Gainesville.

Winter, Marcus C.

1972 Tierras Largas: A Formative Community in the Valley of Oaxaca, Mexico. PhD dissertation, Department of Anthropology, University of Arizona, Tucson.

1976a The Archaeological Household Cluster in the Valley of Oaxaca. In *The Early Mesoamerican Village*, edited by Kent V. Flannery, pp. 25–31. Academic Press, New York.

Witmore, Christopher L.

2007 Symmetrical Archaeology: Excerpts of a Manifesto. *World Archaeology* 39:546–562.

Witthoft, John

1949 *Green Corn Ceremonialism in the Eastern Woodlands*. University of Michigan Press, Ann Arbor.

Woods, William I., and George R. Holley

2000 Upland Mississippian Settlement in the American Bottom Region. In *Cahokia and the Hinterlands: Middle Mississippian Cultures of the Midwest*, edited by Thomas E. Emerson and R. Barry Lewis, pp. 35–45. University of Illinois Press, Urbana.

Worth, John E.

1998 *Assimilation*. The Timucuan Chiefdoms of Spanish Florida, Vol. 1. University Press of Florida, Gainesville.

2017 What's in a Phase? Disentangling Communities of Practice from Communities of Identity in Southeastern North America. In *Forging Southeastern Identities: Social Archaeology, Ethnohistory, and Folklore of the Mississippian to Early Historic South*, edited by Gregory A. Waselkov and Marvin T. Smith, pp. 117–156. University of Alabama Press, Tuscaloosa.

Yaeger, Jason
2000      The Social Construction of Communities in the Classic Maya Countryside:
          Strategies of Affiliation in Western Belize. In *The Archaeology of Communi-
          ties: A New World Perspective*, edited by Marcello A. Canuto and Jason Yae-
          ger, pp. 123–142. Routledge, New York.
2003      Untangling the Ties That Bind: The City, the Countryside, and the Nature of
          Maya Urbanism at Xunantunich, Belize. In *The Social Construction of An-
          cient Cities*, edited by Monica L. Smith, pp. 121–155. Smithsonian Books,
          Washington, DC.
Yaeger, Jason, and Marcello A. Canuto
2000      Introducing an Archaeology of Communities. In *The Archaeology of Com-
          munities: A New World Perspective*, edited by Marcello A. Canuto and Jason
          Yaeger, pp. 1–15. Routledge, New York.
Yanagisako, Sylvia J.
1979      Family and Household: The Analysis of Domestic Groups. *Annual Review of
          Anthropology* 8:161–205.
Yerkes, Richard W.
1983      Microwear, Microdrills, and Mississippian Craft Specialization. *American
          Antiquity* 48:499–518.
1989      Mississippian Craft Specialization in the American Bottom. *Southeastern
          Archaeology* 8:93–106.
2005      Bone Chemistry, Body Parts, and Growth Marks: Evaluating Ohio Hopewell
          and Cahokia Mississippian Seasonality, Subsistence, Ritual, and Feasting.
          *American Antiquity* 70(2):241–265.
Zedeño, María Nieves
2008      Bundled Worlds: The Roles and Interactions of Complex Objects from
          the North American Plains. *Journal of Archaeological Method and Theory*
          15:362–378.
Zimmermann Holt, Julie
2009      Rethinking the Ramey State: Was Cahokia the Center of a Theater State?
          *American Antiquity* 74(2):231–254.

# CONTRIBUTORS

**Keith Ashley** is assistant professor of anthropology in the Department of Sociology, Anthropology, and Social Work at the University of North Florida. His current research focuses on the histories and cultures of Native Americans in Florida and beyond, before and after European arrival.

**Melissa R. Baltus** is an assistant professor in the Department of Sociology and Anthropology at the University of Toledo, Ohio. Her research focuses on processes of urbanization and de-urbanization in the context of the Native North American city of Cahokia. She studies how sociopolitical change and community identity transformations are embedded within the practices and choices of daily life. Additionally, she studies the broader impacts of coalescence at and abandonment of Cahokia on social practices and population movements within the Midwest and Great Lakes regions.

**Alleen Betzenhauser** is the coordinator of the Illinois State Archaeological Survey's American Bottom Field Station within the University of Illinois Prairie Research Institute. Her research interests include the Terminal Late Woodland–Mississippian transition in the American Bottom, ceramic analysis, and the relationships between spatiality and community formation and dissolution.

**Jennifer Birch** is an associate professor in the Department of Anthropology at the University of Georgia. Her research interests are in the development of organizational complexity and diversity, particularly among the Native societies of eastern North America. She approaches these topics through multiscalar research designs focused on reconstructing the archaeological histories of communities and regions. She is the coauthor of *The Mantle Site: An Archaeological History of an Ancestral Wendat Community*, editor of *From Prehistoric Villages to Cities: Settlement Aggregation and Community Transformation*, and coeditor of *The Archaeology of Villages in Eastern North America*.

**Edmond A. Boudreaux III** is director of the Center for Archaeological Research at the University of Mississippi and an associate professor in the Department of Sociology and Anthropology. His research has focused on late precontact through contact period Native American communities across the southeastern United States. He is the author of *The Archaeology of Town Creek* and coeditor of *Contact, Colonialism, and Native Communities in the Southeastern United States*.

**Stefan Brannan** is a principal investigator and archaeologist with New South Associates. His interests include the development and historical trajectories of large precontact period settlements in the southeastern United States and the ways that the communities that lived there formed and maintained society. His more recent work includes research into late precontact through early Historic period Indigenous farmsteads in north Georgia, ongoing repatriation efforts associated with the Carlisle Indian Industrial School, and continued research into settlements found in the Lower Chattahoo-chee River Valley.

**Tamira K. Brennan** is the curator for the Center for Archaeological Investigations at Southern Illinois University. Her research focus is the late pre-Columbian peoples of the Midwest and mid-South. She specializes in ceramic and architectural analyses and collections management and is interested in how communities are made and maintained through human interaction with material items and the built environment. Her current research involves tracking changes in the late Mississippian communities in southern Illinois and southeastern Missouri as they pertain to the decline of Greater Cahokia.

**Meghan E. Buchanan** is an assistant professor in the Department of Sociology, Anthropology, and Social Work at Auburn University, Alabama. Her research explores the historically contingent relationships between political fragmentation, warfare, and daily practices (ceramic and faunal analysis) as well as the political and social impacts of violence among Mississippian peoples in the Midwest and Southeast, particularly at the Common Field site in Missouri. Her current research focuses on the Mississippian period occupation of the lower Tallapoosa River Valley in Alabama as the region experienced periods of population expansion, violence, coalescence, and abandonment.

**Jera R. Davis** is an anthropological archaeologist primarily interested in early complex societies, institutionalized inequality, built environments, and political economy in the eastern woodlands. She works at New South Associates.

**Heidi A. de Gregory** is an archaeologist and editor with Tennessee Valley Archaeological Research in Huntsville, Alabama. Her main research interests include the Mississippian period in the Southeast, mortuary analysis, and the management and care of archaeological collections.

**Paige A. Ford** is a PhD candidate in the Department of Anthropology at the University of Oklahoma. Her primary research interests include late precontact southeastern United States and great plains, borderlands, frontiers, social network analysis, communities of practice, learning networks, ceramics, and public archaeology.

**Adam King** is research associate professor in the South Carolina Institute of Archaeology and Anthropology at the University of South Carolina. His research interests focus on the early history of Native Americans, particularly during the Mississippian period. He has ongoing research projects exploring the development of Mississippian communities in the Etowah River Valley of northwestern Georgia and the middle Savannah River Valley on the Georgia–South Carolina border. His research attempts to understand how Mississippian societies in these areas came into being and changed over the course of their individual histories, using traditional archaeological excavation coupled with remote sensing, the exploration of ancient imagery, and absorbed residue studies. He is the editor of *Archaeology in South Carolina: Exploring the Hidden Heritage of the Palmetto State.*

**Duncan P. McKinnon** is assistant professor of anthropology at the University of Central Arkansas, director of the Jamie C. Brandon Center for Archaeological Research, and research associate at the Center for American Archeology. He is the coeditor of *Archaeological Remote Sensing in North America: Innovative Techniques for Anthropological Applications* and *Ancestral Caddo Ceramic Traditions*. Current research includes distributional analyses of Caddo art and ceramics to evaluate social exchange and interaction throughout Caddo and neighboring regions and an examination of the constructed landscape of Woodland period communities in the Lower Illinois River Valley.

**Erin S. Nelson** is assistant professor of anthropology in the Department of Sociology, Anthropology, and Social Work at the University of South Alabama. Her research examines the material remains of foodways, monumental and domestic architecture, and the organization of space to understand how past people negotiated issues of kinship, group identity, leadership, and worldview in the context of their communities. Nelson is the author of *Authority, Autonomy, and the Archaeology of a Mississippian Community*.

**Christopher B. Rodning** is professor of anthropology in the Department of Anthropology at Tulane University, Louisiana. His interests include the archaeology of contact and colonialism, architecture and landscape, and mortuary practices. He is the author of *Center Places and Cherokee Towns: Archaeological Perspectives on Native American Architecture and Landscape in the Southern Appalachians* and coeditor of *Fort San Juan and the Limits of Empire: Colonialism and Household Practice at the Berry Site* and *Archaeological Studies of Gender in the Southeastern United States*. He is the current editor of the *SAA Archaeological Record*.

**Benjamin A. Steere** is an associate professor in the Department of Anthropology and Sociology at Western Carolina University, North Carolina. He has worked on collaborative archaeological research projects with the Tribal Historic Preservation Office of the Eastern Band of Cherokee Indians since 2011. Some of his areas of interest include the archaeology of domestic and monumental architecture, indigenous archaeology, and public archaeology. His book *The Archaeology of Houses and Households in the Native Southeast* offers a broadscale, comparative perspective on the archaeology of Woodland, Mississippian, and Historic period Native American communities through the lens of domestic architecture.

**Amber R. Thorpe** is a paralegal for two interconnected nonprofit criminal defense organizations in New Orleans, the Capital Appeals Project and the Promise of Justice Initiative.

**Elizabeth Watts Malouchos** is a research archaeologist at the Illinois State Archaeological Survey's American Bottom Field Station within the University of Illinois Prairie Research Institute. Her current research focuses on the relationships between communal identity formation and the built environment, specifically the intersections between everyday practices, household and community architecture, and socioreligious integration in the Mississippian Midwest and Southeast. Her interests include the construction of social landscapes, Mississippian communities, frontier interactions, identity politics, ceramic analysis, geophysics, and spatial analysis.

**Gregory D. Wilson** is an associate professor in the Department of Anthropology, University of California, Santa Barbara. His research interests include identity politics, social inequality, and violence in pre-Columbian eastern North America. He is the author of *The Archaeology of Everyday Life at Early Moundville*, editor of *Mississippian Beginnings*, and coeditor of *The Archaeology of Food and Warfare: Food Insecurity in Prehistory*.

**Jason Yaeger** is the President's Endowed Professor of Anthropology at the University of Texas at San Antonio. Since 1990, he has conducted archaeological fieldwork in Belize, Bolivia, the United States, and India. His primary research interests are the archaeology and ethnohistory of Mesoamerica and the Andes, with a focus on the organization of ancient households and communities, ancient urbanism, and material culture and identity. He is coeditor of *Classic Maya Provincial Politics: Xunantunich and Its Hinterlands* and *The Archaeology of Communities: A New World Perspective*.

# INDEX

abandonment: of neighborhoods, 45; regional, 34, 36, 42; and reoccupation, 28, 96; of structures, 67, 93, 125. *See also* site abandonment
actor-network theory, 31, 229
affect, central to community, 122
agency theory, 11, 16–17
aggregation, at Singer-Moye, 213, 218–23
Alabama Museum of Natural History, 205
alliances, between Historic period towns, 64
Alt, Susan M., 16–18, 26, 28–30, 142
alterity, shift to, 28–29
American Bottom, ix, 24, 32–35, 74, 123–24, 127, 130, 146, 148, 151, 190; storage practices, 146–47, 151–61. *See also* Greater Cahokia; *and individual site names*
ancestral grounds, at Moundville, 197, 202
ancestral spirits, marker posts and, 161
ancestral ties, 119
*Ancient Southwestern Community* (Wills & Leonard 1994), 227
Anderson, Benedict, 20–22
Angel Mounds site (SW Indiana), 23
animals, in Cherokee oral traditions, 167
anthropocentrism, 29, 122, 147–48, 229
Apple River Valley (NW Illinois), 27
archaeological units of analysis, 227–28
archaeology of communities, 9, 228–29; overview, 18–31
*Archaeology of Communities* (Canuto & Yaeger 2000), 228–29
archaeology of social organization, 227
Archaic artifacts, heirloom/salvaged, 190, 192–93, 233, 238
architectural database, for identifying variation patterns, 83–86
architectural forms, at Etowah, 142–43
architectural investment, 93, 95
architectural variation, patterns of, 81–98
architecture, active role of, 165, 176
Arnold, Dean E., 188

artifacts: at Etowah, 135; at Town Creek, 108–9. *See also* ceramic assemblages; lithic objects; *and specific types of objects*
ash: cosmological associations of, 73; ritual deposit of, 78
assemblages: Battle Mound community as, 56; Caddo landscapes as, 61–62; and community-making, 231–32; created through storage practices, 162; Powers, 208. *See also* ceramic assemblages
assemblage theory, 31
authority, 16–17
axis, organizational: at Cahokia, 27, 123–24, 154; at Common Field, 126–27
axis mundi, 53, 57, 117–18, 161

Baires, Sarah E., 30, 47, 161–62
Baltus, Melissa R., 30, 160–62
Bardolph, Dana N., 18
Barrier, Casey R., 22
Barth, Fredrik, 231
Bartram, William, 171
Battle Mound site/community (SW Arkansas), 50–62, 238; Cedar Grove farmstead, 54, 56; Field Bayou Mound, 56; Hensley Mound, 55–56; Red Cox farmstead, 54, 56; Red Hill Mound, 56; Spirit Lake Farm Mound, 56; Spirit Lake farmstead, 55–56
Beneath World (Underworld), 57
Bengtson, Jennifer D., 25
Bennett, Jane, 148
bent-pole construction, 142, 160
Betzenhauser, Alleen, 2, 14–15
Bhabha, Homi K., 28
Birch, Jennifer, 23–25, 35, 75, 121, 234
Birdman imagery, 201
Black Bottoms, 39–43
Black Warrior River, 197
Black Warrior Valley sites, 13, 203
Black Warrior Valley Survey, 206
Blitz, John H., 218, 225

Boudreaux, Edmond A., III, 16, 23
Bourdieu, Pierre, 11, 81, 181
Brazos Reservation (Texas), 51
Brennan, Tamira K., 14
Briggs, Rachel V., 149
Brown, James A., 12, 57
Browne site, 196n2
Brumfiel, Elizabeth M., 228
Buchanan, Meghan E., 31, 126
building-block approach, 11, 19–20, 81
building programs, at Singer-Moye, 221
built environment: and collective identity,
    147–48; creation of, 137; as reflection of
    cosmology, 167; social construction of,
    161; at Town Creek site, 106. See also
    landscape
bundled practices, 129, 231–32
bundling, 29–30
burial, as clan obligation, 76–77
burial demographics, at Town Creek site,
    109–12
burials, 123, 237; with artifacts, 109, 115–17;
    at Coweeta Creek, 174–75; in domestic
    vs. public spaces, 109–12; floor burials,
    105, 234; intergenerational, 65; at Mill
    Cove Complex, 190; pit burials, 159; at
    Powers site, 208; prone burials, 186, 195;
    stone box burials, 205; at Town Creek
    site, 103, 109–15, 117–18; and townhouse
    construction, 169
burning: at Common Field site, 126; at East
    St. Louis site, 39; pre-abandonment, 67;
    ritual, 124; of storage compound at East
    St. Louis, 124. See also site burning
burning-burial-rebuilding sequence, 44,
    72–73, 78
Burnt Corn, Ancestral Pueblo community
    of, 238
Butler, Brian M., 31

caching, 29, 169
Caddo Archaeology Conference, 62
Caddo homeland, 51–52
Caddo peoples, 50–62, 238
Cahokia, ix, 17–18, 24, 117, 122–24, 127, 129,
    140, 142, 148, 191, 195, 231, 235, 239;
    abandonment, 30–31; Downtown Ca-
    hokia, 152, 154, 156; Dunham Tract, 152–
    56; Mound 49, 74; Mound 72, 123; politi-
cal economy, 10–11, 14–15; Rattlesnake
    Causeway, 196n6; storage practices, 147,
    151–56, 159–60; Tract 15A, 152–56; Tract
    15B, 152–56. See also Greater Cahokia
Cahokian culture, construction of, 25
"Cahokian Mississippian," as coalescent so-
    ciety, 35
Cane Creek phase, 138
Canuto, Marcello A., 21–22, 81, 121
Caracasi/Atosi site, 185
cardinal points, 16, 53, 117, 154, 168
Carson site, 76–77
case studies, 234, 236; of communities of
    conflict, 123–27. See also individual site
    names
causeways, 196n6
"caves above the ground," 167
celt preform, 208, 210–11
celts, 190, 208, 210; greenstone, 197–99,
    210–11
cemeteries, 237; Battle Mound, 56; Caddo
    community, 56; East St. Louis, 39; en-
    closed, 105, 108, 117–18; houses reused
    as, 105, 117, 234; McCormack, 186; Mill
    Cove Complex, 189–91; Moundville, 202;
    Town Creek, 102–3, 105–6, 108–15. See
    also burials
Cemochechobee site, 218, 222
Center for Archaeological Investigations, 41
Central Illinois River Valley, 18
ceramic assemblages, 223, 225; Colorinda,
    182–89, 191; Common Field, 127; Kelvin,
    186; St. Johns II, 183–84, 186–89, 191
ceramic chronology, 182; Battle Mound, 55
ceramic decoration, at Etowah, 141–42
ceramic diversity, at Singer-Moye, 219
ceramic technology, 187–88; limestone tem-
    pering, 138, 140; sand tempering, 140,
    182; shell tempering, 140, 232
ceremonial activity, 78; East St. Louis, 39;
    Town Creek, 103
chaîne opératoire, 182, 187, 229
Chattahoochee River, 214–16, 218
Cherokee oral tradition, 166–72, 240; "Bear
    Man," 167; "Bear Songs," 167; "How the
    World Was Made," 168; "Mounds and the
    Constant Fire: The Old Sacred Things,"
    168–69; "Removed Townhouses," 169–70;
    "Spirit Defenders of Nĭkwăsĭ'," 170–71

Chickasaw people, 63–64, 66, 75, 79–80

Choctaw people, 63, 66, 75, 80

circular village, Town Creek as, 103

civilizational collapse, 199

clan affiliation, 76

clan obligations, 76

clan system, 63–64; and social competition, 79–80

clans, matrilineal, 102

Clark, Jeffery J., 188

class, as social category, 228

coalescence, 24–25, 35, 121, 137, 192–95, 232–36

coalescent societies, 64, 96, 121

Cobb, Charles R., 13, 28, 31, 65, 95, 225

Coker Ford phase, 138

Collins, James M., 17

Colorinda (phase and culture), 182–86, 195

Columbus Museum, 214, 221

commensality, 122, 129, 235; at Common Field, 127; at Olin, 125–26. *See also* feasting

Common Field site (SE Missouri), 31, 122, 126–27, 130; destruction, 238; evidence of violence, 127; excavations, 126–27; palisade, 128

communion with the past, 238

communitas, 25–26

communities, 19, 120–22, 179–80, 227–32; as active fields, 213; as assemblages, 29, 82, 97, 147–49, 229–30; as coresidential unit, 18–20; and cosmology, 26–27; as emergent phenomena, 236; functionalist theory of, 228; Historic period, 101–2; imagined, 20–22, 38, 43, 49, 233; longitudinal, 238; multiethnic, 27–28; as multiple connected interest groups, 101; as networks, 81; and ontological turn, 28–31; physical and social aspects, 135, 137; reinscriptions of, 238; as relational assemblages, 29, 81; as site, 3, 20, 81, 121, 227, 229–30, 232–36; social construction of, 20–28, 229; structured through daily practice, 121; as universal building block, 19–20; variability within, 101–19

communities of conflict, 120–31

communities of practice, 21, 23, 97, 128–29, 137, 179–82, 195, 229, 231; at Etowah, 140–44; multiple, 180–81

community, at Town Creek, 102–6

community, regional, Greater Cahokia as, 34

community activities, at Kincaid Mounds, 42

community histories, multiscale approach to, 213–26

community-making, 22–24, 26–28, 43, 77–78, 128, 130–31, 137, 221; Cahokian, 30; East St. Louis, 47–48; and storage practices, 162–63

community members, 179–80

community organization: Central Caddo, 52–53; Upper Nasoni, 53

community pattern, 19

community plan, 19

comparative studies, 98, 228

competition, 79–80, 201, 222–23, 230, 239–40

conflict, 24, 120–31, 222–23, 230–31, 235–36

conservatism, in pottery-making, 188

constellations of practice, 182, 231

construction projects, large-scale, 221–22

cooking pot forms, 201

Cool Branch site, 217

co-option, of multiple monuments, 45–46

copper artifacts, 190; axes, 116–17; fragments, from grave goods, 109, 115; pendants, 202

copresence, 21

corporate groups, 101–2, 105, 119; Cahokia and Moundville, 117; Town Creek, 102–3, 115–19

cosmogonic creation, 232

cosmograms, 165, 171, 176

cosmology, 15–16, 26–27, 73, 141–43, 232, 235; Battle Mound, 56–57; Caddo, 53; Cherokee, 168, 175–76; Town Creek, 109

council house, at Range, 158

courtyards and courtyard groupings, 36–37, 68–69, 152, 156, 160

Coweeta Creek site (SW North Carolina), 12, 16, 165, 172–75

craft production, at Cahokia and Moundville, 117, 210–11

creation, mound building as, 143–44

creation stories, 140

Creek people, 64, 94, 143

creolization, 27

cross-cultural comparisons, 13, 228

cross-cultural examples, of food storage practices, 150

cross-cultural features, at Mill Cove, 194–95
cuisine, shifts in, 129. *See also* foodways
cultural resource management projects, 3
culture contact, 17–18, 27
culture-historical approach, 19
culture history, household and, 9–10
Currid, John D., 150

Davis site, 144
DeBoer, Warren R., 146
decentralization, 199; at Singer-Moye, 223–25
decommissioning, of large pits, 160
DeJarnette, David L., 205, 207
demographic shifts, 25
demography, 11
Denny, Sidney, 124
depopulation, at Cahokia, 129
design creation, for stamped design, 141
design motifs: avian, 129; centering, 141–
   42, 232; at Common Field, 127; cross-in-
   circle, 109; martial, 130; rayed circle, 57–
   59; Swift Creek designs, 141
de Soto, Hernando, 52
destruction and renewal, cycle of, 118
diasporic communities, 233
diet, elite vs. nonelite, 149
Dillow's Ridge site (S Illinois), 15
dispersed populations, 224–25
division of labor, changes in, inferred from
   segmentation, 91
Dolphin Reef site, 184–85
domestic activities, in household archaeology, 10
domestic architecture, 1–2, 12, 14–16, 95,
   98, 143; Creek, 94; East St. Louis, 47–48;
   Greater Cahokia, 35; patterns of variation in, 81–98; and public architecture,
   164–66
domestic areas, at Town Creek, 103–5
domestic cycle, and repair/rebuilding, 93
domestic structures. *See* houses
duration of occupation, and repair/
   rebuilding, 93
duration of structure use, variability in, 108, 116

earth island, Cherokee, 168, 171, 175–76
earth moving and deposition, and
   community-making, 161–62
East St. Louis site (S Illinois), 32–33, 123–

24; excavations, 36–39, 46–48; Exchange
   Avenue corridor, 39; Main Street Mound,
   38, 47, 74, 233
economy, at Moundville, 197–212
elite domination, opposition to, 146
elite residence, at Singer-Moye, 224
elites, 16, 146, 149, 199–200, 202
Emerald Mounds site, 16, 30, 48, 123
Emerson, Thomas E., 17, 158
entanglement, 135–37, 147, 230–33; at
   Etowah, 140–44
environmental adaptation, 10
epistemology, in archaeology of communities, 238–39
erasures, from landscape, 237–38
ethnogenesis, 231
ethnographic analogy, 239–40
ethnographic data, 239–40; from Historic
   period Mississippian descendants, 63–64;
   on pottery-making, 181–82, 188; "travel
   data," 188
ethnography, cross-cultural, 10
ethnohistorical record, 83, 239–40
Etowah Archaeo-Geophysical Survey, 138
Etowah River, 135
Etowah site (NW Georgia), 12, 25, 28, 65,
   239; early history, 135–45; Mound A,
   143; multicultural origins, 137–40; and
   regional context, 144–45
exchange, 192; interregional, 52, 179
exotic assemblages, 235
exotic materials: access to, 102, 115–17; acquisition of, 195
expansion, at East St. Louis site, 36
experimental studies, 150
extended families, and courtyard groupings,
   36–37

factionalism, at Moundville, 202
FAI-270 project, 34
familiarity, as factor in resettlement, 192–93
farmsteads, 54–55, 148, 158, 160, 203
feasting, 26, 77, 118, 123, 145, 158, 193, 233;
   elite, 70, 72; at Etowah, 143; potluck-
   style, 70, 77–78, 234; at Town Creek, 103.
   *See also* commensality
fire: constant, 169, 171, 175–76; sacred, 53,
   70–72, 78, 109, 169; shared, 64. *See also*
   burning

fire ceremonies, 234, 236
Fitts site (along Black Warrior River), 203, 206–7, 211
Flannery, Kent V., 10
Flint River, 216
floor area, 92, 151, 154, 156, 158–59
foodways, 146, 201
Ford, James A., 19
forgetting, process of, 237
fortification, 123, 127. *See also* palisades
fortified sites, 124–27
Fort Walton, 218–19, 223
founders and founding, 44, 77, 80, 118, 220, 232–36; Parchman Place, 69–72

Gary's Fish Pond site, 217, 225
gateways, physical/symbolic, 56
Gearing, Fred, 65
gender, as social category, 228
genealogical time, 65
generational continuity, at Coweeta Creek, 175
geophysical remote sensing, 238–39
George Reeves/Merrell phase, 151
Giddens, Anthony, 11
Goad, Sharon I., 190
Gougeon, Ramie A., 14–15
GPR (ground-penetrating radar), 214
gradiometry, 138–39, 239
Grand site, 185
grave goods, 109, 189, 194
Greater Cahokia, 33–40, 48
Great League (Iroquois), 144
Great Salt Springs site (S Illinois), 15
"great tradition," of elites, 199
Great Tree of Peace, 144
Green Corn ceremonies, 158, 234
greenstone index, 208–9
Griffin, James B., 19
Gypsy Joint site (SE Missouri), 10

habitus, 81, 121, 128, 181
Hally, David J., 14, 16, 97, 143
Halperin, Rhoda H., 149
Hamilton tradition (SE Tennessee), 138
Hanenberger, Ned H., 156
Harris, Oliver J. T., 29, 82, 97, 121–22, 148, 229–30, 235
Harvey, Graham, 29
hearth, in Cherokee dwelling, 171

Hendon, Julia A., 160
hipped-roof construction, 160
historical processual approach, x
Hiwassee Island site, 144
Hodder, Ian, 230
house construction, 82, 95. *See also* single-set post construction; wall-trench construction
household: defining, 3, 75, 166, 228; nodal, 17; in post-processual paradigm, 11–18; symbolic construction of, 12
household archaeology, ix, 1–3, 9–18, 227, 240
household demographics, at Town Creek, 102
houses, 81, 83, 86, 166; Cherokee, 164–76; Coweeta Creek, 174–75; as dwellings of animals, 166–67; floor area, 92, 151, 154, 156, 158–59; reused as cemeteries, 102–3, 105, 117, 234; shape, 82, 86–88, 105; size, 82–83, 106
house society model, 12
human sacrifice, 123
hybridity, 28
hypercentralization, 24

identities, crosscutting, 64–65
identity: clan, 66, 76; collective, 22–24, 147; community, 233; emblems of, 59–61; group, 20–21, 26, 43; households and, 17–18, 76; and matrilineal membership, 102; shared, 77
identity-making, and place-making, 22
Illinois State Archaeological Survey, 36; American Bottom Field Station, 1
imagined communities, 20–22, 38, 43, 49, 233
immigration, 191, 195, 234–35. *See also* migration
integration, political, 17, 35, 62, 228
integration, social, 23–25, 28, 31, 37, 45, 48, 77, 94–97, 158–59, 234–35; Battle Mound, 54–55, 61–62; Little Egypt, 14; Mill Cove, 192, 194; Parchman Place, 77; Singer-Moye, 213, 216, 225
integrative activities, 26, 103, 144, 162, 213, 221
interactional approaches, 20–21
intercommunity conflict, 120–31, 144
interregional interaction, 191–92, 219, 224; Battle Mound, 50, 57–61
intersectionality, x

intraregional interaction, at Battle Mound,
    50, 53–57
Iroquois, 144
Isbell, William H., 21

Jackson, Jason Baird, 64
James, Jenna, 76
John Chapman site (Apple River Valley, NW
    Illinois), 27
joint enterprise, in communities of prac-
    tice, 181
Jones, Walter B., 205, 207
Juniper Spring Run Dune site, 193

Kelly, Arthur R., 143
Kelly, John E., 117, 156, 160
Kelly, Lucretia, 149
Kelvin culture, 186, 195
Kidder, Tristram R., 73
Kincaid Mounds site (Lower Ohio River),
    32–33, 39–46, 237; Douglas Mound, 46;
    palisades, 42, 44–45
King, Adam, 25, 28, 65, 95
King site (NW Georgia), 14
kinship, and household archaeology, 9
kinship-based groups, 66, 109
kinship relations, 23, 62–65, 72, 77, 80,
    191, 199
Knight, Vernon J., Jr., 64, 115, 117, 143, 203,
    206, 208–9
Kolb, Michael J., 228
Koldehoff, Brad H., 14
Kowalewski, Stephen A., 24, 96, 121, 137, 221
Krause, Richard, 207
Kruchten, Jeff, 2
Kruckeberg #1 site, 124
Kus, Susan M., 200

labor, gendered division of, 15, 140–41,
    181, 232
Lamb site, 18
landscape: and built environment, 137, 142,
    147, 160–62; of Caddo homeland, 51–56,
    61–62; Cahokian, 24, 26–27, 30; Chero-
    kee, 165–68, 175–76; and community,
    12, 16, 21–23, 64, 230, 233, 238; dispersal
    across, 105, 118, 235; Mississippianized,
    25–26; modification of, 24, 32–33, 38, 44,
    50; monumental, 15, 26–27, 31, 45–46,

197, 214, 216, 224–26; movement across,
    66, 80, 95, 179, 191–95; obliteration of,
    33, 35, 237–38; of settlement, 16, 203, 213
landscape archaeology, 50
Latour, Bruno, 31
Lave, Jean, 21, 181, 229
Lemonnier, Pierre, 181
Lévi-Strauss, Claude, 12
Lightning, as deity, 166
limestone tempering, 140; used at Etowah, 138
Lindeman/Edelhardt phase, 151
lithic assemblages, 203
lithic objects, 203–12
Little, Keith J., 138, 144
Little Community and Peasant Society and
    Culture (Redfield 1989), 199
Little Egypt site (NW Georgia), 14–15
Little Tennessee Valley (SW North Caro-
    lina), 165
"little tradition," and societal restructur-
    ing, 199
locally available materials, used in house
    construction, 82
Lohmann phase, 151
Lollis, Charly, 196n3
Longe, Alexander, 167, 172
longevity: of Coweeta Creek community,
    175; of households at Town Creek site,
    102; of structures, 108
longitudinal community, 238
Lorenz, Karl G., 218, 225
Louisiana, northwestern, 51
Lower Chattahoochee River Valley, 213–26
Lower St. Johns, archaeological record,
    182–86
Lunsford Pulcher site, 156

Macon Plateau, 195
magnetometry, 41, 67, 214, 216, 224, 239
maize agriculture, 146, 149–51, 191, 201
maize consumption, 149
Mandeville site, 217
Marcoux, Jon B., 13, 18, 31
material culture, 17, 35, 48, 122, 182, 231–
    32; change in, 33, 35, 45, 95, 148; within
    Greater Cahokia, 35–36; shared, 19, 57; at
    Singer-Moye, 219, 223
Maxham, Mintcy D., 23
Maya, modern, storage practices of, 150

McCormack site, 184–85
Mehrer, Mark W., 11, 17
memory-making, as community-making, 26–27
men, as woodworkers, 141, 232
Mesoamerican archaeology, 10
methods, in archaeology of communities, 238–39
microdrill index, 208–9
microdrills, 201, 206–7, 209–10
Middle World, 53, 57, 109, 117–18, 141, 143
migration, 94, 148, 188, 196n1; East St. Louis, 48; Kincaid Mounds, 45; Mill Cove, 179, 188, 191–95; Moundville, 202; Singer-Moye, 202, 213, 216–18
Mill Cove Complex site, 179–96, 233, 238–39; Grant Mound, 185, 189–91, 193–95, 196n6, 235; Kinzey's Knoll, 189; Shields Mound, 185, 189–95, 196n6, 233, 235, 238
Millhouse, Philip G., 27
*Mississippian Communities and Households* (Rogers & Smith 1995), ix, 1–3, 5, 11, 20, 81, 97, 101, 120, 227, 230
Mississippianization, 30
Mississippi River Valley, 140
moieties, 194
monumental post circles, 159
Mooney, James, 167
Moore, Clarence B., 190, 196n6
Moorehead phase, 36
Morton Village (Central Illinois River Valley), 25
mortuary mound, at Etowah, 135
mortuary practices, 15, 103, 119, 130, 162, 186
mound building, 25–26, 49, 72–74, 79, 118, 122–23, 130, 131n2, 162, 168–69; and community building, 32–49, 72–74, 78; East St. Louis, 39; Etowah, 143–44; Kincaid Mounds, 45; Parchman Place, 63, 65–66, 72–74, 76–80; Town Creek, 103, 118
mound centers, 25, 95–96, 148, 160, 162, 191
mounds, 26, 143, 197; dome-shaped, 214; paired, 194; physical incorporation of one by another, 72–74, 79; platform, 26–27, 63, 103, 118, 135, 190, 201, 214, 216–18, 221; ridgetop, 47; single, in Moundville hinterland, 203

mound-top residence, at Kincaid Mounds, 45
Moundville site (west-central Alabama), 13–14, 16, 23, 31, 65, 115, 117, 197, 218, 236; abandonment, 236, 238; early, 75, 140, 200–203; hinterlands, 23, 197–212, 239; houses, 89–90, 96–97; as sociogram, 201–2, 236
mountain summits, in Cherokee oral traditions, 166, 175
Mount Royal site, 182, 189, 191–93, 195, 196n6
Mount Taylor groups, 196n5
Mouse Creek phase (Lower Hiwassee Valley, SE Tennessee), 11
multiscalar approach, 22–24, 32, 43, 50, 61–62, 74–75, 101–2, 128, 147–48, 162, 179, 213–26, 230, 239
Murdock, George P., 18
Myer, Jennifer L., 206

Nassaney, Michael S., 95
naturalization, of new ideologies, 48–49
neighborhoods, 23, 66, 68, 75; new, 154–56; preplanned, 48
new archaeology, 10–11, 19–20. *See also* processual approach
New Mississippi River Bridge project, 34, 36
nondomestic structures, 86
nonelites, and craft production, 210–11
Nûñně'hï, 169–71

object agency, 137, 229
occupational history, for Singer-Moye, 213–26
occupation sequence, at Etowah, 135
"octagonal" structures, 88
Office of Archaeological Research (Moundville), 203, 205
O'Gorman, Jodie A., 25
Oklahoma, eastern, 51
Olin site (Bethalto, IL), 122, 124–26
Omussee Creek site, 223
ontological alterity, 4
ontological turn, 147–48; communities and, 28–31
oral tradition, Cherokee, 166–72, 240
Orange groups, 196n5

paddle, used for ceramic decoration, 141–42
"paint palettes," sandstone, 197–99, 205–6, 211

palisade construction, 120–23, 128, 231
palisaded sites, 120–31
palisades, 232; Cahokia, 123–24; Common
    Field, 126–28; Cool Branch, 217; Etowah,
    135; Kincaid Mounds, 42, 44–45; Mound-
    ville, 197, 202; Olin, 124–25, 127; Singer-
    Moye, 220, 234; Town Creek, 103
Parchman Place site (N Yazoo Basin, NW
    Mississippi), 63–80, 234; Mound E, 237
Pauketat, Timothy R., 17–18, 24–27, 29–30,
    74, 89–90, 122, 137, 142, 148–49, 152, 225
pax Cahokiana, 25, 122–23
Peebles, Christopher S., 200
peer-polity interaction, 222–23
pendants, 59–61, 197–99, 202, 211
Peregrine, Peter N., 121
Peterson, Staffan, 23
Pfeffer site (SW Illinois), 1–2
Phillips, Philip, 19, 57
Piedmont Village Tradition, 103
pipes, deposition of, 161
pit-to-structure ratios, 151–52, 154, 156, 159
place, in defining community, 232–36. See
    also landscape
place-making, 22, 221–22. See also
    community-making
plaza construction, 35, 220
plazas, 26, 31, 66, 75, 102, 154; Cahokia, 154,
    159; Etowah site, 135; Moundville, 197;
    Olin, 125; Singer-Moye, 214, 219–20, 234;
    Town Creek, 102–3, 119
Pluckhahn, Thomas J., 3, 13, 16, 141
political complexity, and segmentation, 91
political consolidation, at Cahokia, 149
political economy, of Moundville, 13, 200–201
politicization, of Common Field, 128
population, East St. Louis, 36
population decline, 34; Cahokia, 124; Town
    Creek, 105
population density, 34
population growth, 154; Mill Cove, 195
population movement, 75, 191–95, 220–21.
    See also migration
Porth, Erik D., 209
posthole density, and rebuilding ratio, 108
post-in-ground construction, 82
post-processual paradigm, households in,
    11–18
post setting, 18, 90–91, 103

pottery, 125, 129, 142. See also ceramic as-
    semblages; ceramic technology
pottery-making, 42, 140–41, 181–82, 188, 231
pottery styles: Etowah phase, 138; Lamar,
    219, 223; Ramey Incised, 35, 123; St.
    Johns, 180, 182, 187–88, 195, 231; Wood-
    stock phase, 138
Powers site (Millians Creek near Moundville),
    203, 207–8; Class III structure, 207–8
practice theory, 11–12, 65, 230. See also com-
    munities of practice
prestige economy models, 13–14
Pride Place site (on Black Warrior River),
    203, 205–6, 211
processual approach, ix, 3, 10
public architecture, and domestic architec-
    ture, 164–66
Purcell's Landing site, 217

quadripartite organization of space, 16, 26,
    152, 156, 158, 162
Qualla phase, 172

radiocarbon dating, 138, 145, 186, 218, 220
radiometric dating, 182, 184–86, 195
Randall, Asa, 192
Range site, storage practices at, 147, 151,
    156–60
rank/social status, at Town Creek, 102, 106,
    108–9, 119
rebuilding: of domestic structures, 16, 93–94,
    97, 108, 116, 237; of palisades, 237
reciprocity, 117, 202–3, 211, 236
redistributive networks, 146
Red River, 52, 55, 57
redundancy, iconic, at Moundville, 202, 211
refuge groups, 96
refuse pits, 188–89; at Range, 158
reinscriptions, of communities, 238
relational approach, x, 4, 29, 31, 101, 122, 148
relocation, of towns, 75, 78, 80
renewal of the world, 144
repair of houses, patterns of variation in,
    93–94
repurposing, of storage pits for refuse dis-
    posal, 150
resilience, 197–212
resistance, 16–17
Riggs, Brett, 66

Rodning, Christopher B., 12, 15–16
Rogers, J. Daniel, 1–3, 5, 20, 101
Rolland, Vicki L., 187
Rood's Landing site, 217, 222, 225
rotundas, 138, 159

Sabo, George, III, 53, 55–56
sacred geography, of Mill Cove and Mount
    Royal, 195
Sale Creek site, 144
Salomon site, 75
sand tempering, 140, 182
Sassaman, Kenneth E., 196n5
saws, sandstone, 206–9, 211
Schnell, Frank, 221
Sears, William H., 182
sedentism, inferred from segmentation, 91
segmentation, 91–93
settlement archaeology, 227
settlement hierarchies, 19, 200–201
settlement patterns, 19–20, 34, 39, 47, 63,
    148, 213, 223
settlement surveys, 9, 240
shape of structures, 86–88; circular, 87, 105;
    oval, 87; rectangular, 88; square, 88 (see
    also square grounds); T-shaped, 88
shared practices, 96, 128, 181
shared space, 21
shell, cosmological associations of, 73
shell beads, 197–99, 210
shell gorgets (Pine Island), 109, 116–17
shell mounds, Archaic, co-option of, 192–93
shell tempering, 140, 232
Sherwood, Sarah C., 73
Singer-Moye site (SW Georgia), 213–26,
    234–35, 239; aggregation at, 218–23; and
    environment, 214–16; initial occupation,
    216–18; Mound A, 214, 216–17, 220–
    21, 223, 235; Mound B, 220; Mound C,
    214, 216–17, 220–21; Mound D, 214, 221;
    Mound F, 214, 220
single-set post construction, 82, 90–91, 95,
    138, 142, 156
site, 19; as community, 3, 20, 81, 121, 227,
    229–30, 232–36. See also individual site
    names
site abandonment, 30–31, 120, 122, 124, 130,
    148, 223, 235; Moundville, 202–3, 211;
    Town Creek, 103

site burning, 123; Common Field, 126
site comparisons, 120–31
site maps, in study of architectural variation
    patterns, 83
Sixtoe Field site, 145
size: of East St. Louis site, 36; of Kincaid
    Mounds site, 41. See also structure size
Skousen, B. Jacob, 30
Smith, Bruce D., 10, 20
Snead, James E., 238
social construction: of built environment,
    161; of communities, 5, 20–28, 137, 229–
    30; of households, 12; of space, 4
social division, at Mill Cove, 193–94
social groups, in household archaeology, 9–10
social hierarchy, 72, 200–203
social houses, 76
social interaction theories, 65
social learning theory, 229
social memory, 26, 222, 237–38
social order, at Moundville, 200–203
social organization, 2–3, 9, 20, 74; and ar-
    chitectural variation, 95, 97. See also clan
    system
social unit, as analytical unit, 228
Society for American Archaeology (SAA)
    Annual Meeting, 3–4
sociogram, Moundville as, 201–2, 236
socio-spatial practices, at Cahokia, 148–49
sources, of Cherokee oral traditions, 167
Southern Illinois University Carbondale, 41
Southern Illinois University Edwardsville, ar-
    chaeological field schools, 124
space: gendered division of, 15; status-
    creating, 128
spatial analysis, 11
specialized work areas, at Kincaid Mounds, 42
special-use architecture, 38–39
sponge spicules, in ceramic paste, 187–88,
    196n3, 196n4
square: as cosmogram, 117–18; used at mul-
    tiple scales, 117
square grounds, 117–18, 143
standardization: at East St. Louis, 46–47; at
    Greater Cahokia, 48
Steere, Benjamin A., 1, 16
Steponaitis, Vincas P., 65
Stirling phase, 151
St. Johns I, 182

St. Johns II, 182, 185–86, 191–95

St. Johns ceramic technology, 187–88, 195

St. Johns River Basin, 179

St. Louis (city), ix

stone pendants, 197–99, 211

storage, 91, 146, 150, 160; house-level, 39; overhead, 160; subterranean, 146–47, 150–51, 161

storage buildings, 86

storage pits, 150–51

storage practices, 146–63, 235

structural poses, 65

structured autonomy, 66

structure drawings, in study of architectural variation patterns, 83

structures, of unknown function, 86

structure size: patterns of variation in, 88–90; at Town Creek, 106, 115

style zones, regional, 182

subclan groups, 64

subcommunities, 139

subsistence, 11, 149

succession of leaders, 72, 78

Sullivan, Lynne P., 11, 15–16, 25

Summerour site (N Georgia), 143

Sun, as deity, 166

surplus crops, storage for, 146. See also storage practices

surveys, large-scale regional, 19

Swanton, John R., 78

sweat lodges: at Cahokia, 159; at Olin, 125

symmetrical archaeology, 229

temples, at Cahokia, 159

Tennessee, southeastern, 25

Terán de los Ríos, Domingo, expedition, 52–53

Terán map, 55

Texas, eastern, 51

third spaces, 28

Thomas, Larissa A., 15

Thompson, Claire E., 209, 211

Thompson, Victor D., 23

Thunder, as deity, 166

Tillie Fowler site, 184–85

Timberlake, Lt. Henry, 171–72

Timucua people (N Florida), 194

Town Creek site (North Carolina piedmont), 16, 23, 101–19, 233–34, 240; cemeteries, 105–6, 108–15, 117–18; palisade, 103;

platform mound, 103, 118; plaza, 102–3, 119; Structure 1, 118; Structure 2, 118; Structure 5a, 115; Structure 7, 112, 115–16, 118

townhouses, Cherokee, 164–76, 235

town membership, 66

town plan, at Singer-Moye, 221

towns, 23, 64, 66, 75, 77, 80

Townsend site (North Carolina), 18

trade-based relationships, 72, 77

traditions, and community-making, 27–28

transformation, 232–36

Trans-Mississippi South, 51

transportation data recovery projects, large-scale, 3, 34

TR Preserve site, 185

Tuchman, Barbara, 212

Turner, Victor, 25–26

type-variety typologies, used for culture groups, 19

unification, at Kincaid Mounds, 46

University of Alabama, 203; field schools, 205, 207

University of Chicago graduate field schools, 41

Upper Nasoni, 53, 55–56

Urban, Greg, 64

urbanization, at Cahokia, 24, 154

vacant centers, 53, 225

Vacant Quarter, 129–31

VanDerwarker, Amber M., 146

variability, intracommunity, at Town Creek, 119

vernacular architecture, 15–16, 48

village-communities, 23–24

village-mound settlements, 185, 195

villages, 23

violence, archaeological evidence for, 120–31

Walker Point site, 196n2

walled compounds, at Cahokia, 159

Wallis, Neil, 141

walls, patterns of variation in, 90–91

wall-trench construction, 82, 90–91, 95–96, 138–40, 142–43, 154, 158–60, 231–32

warfare, 120–31, 231–32; bundled practices of, 129; endemic, 120

Waring, Antonio J., Jr., 143

Warrick, Gary A., 108

water, associated with Beneath World, 140
watery spaces, at Cahokia, 30
Watts Malouchos, Elizabeth, 2
Welch, Paul D., 200–201
Wenger, Etienne, 21, 182, 229
Wesson, Cameron B., 16–17, 143, 146, 228
West Jefferson phase, 201
white (color), symbolic associations of, 73
width-to-length ratio, for structures, 151–52,
    154, 156, 158–59
Wilson, Gregory D., 13–14, 16, 22–23, 31,
    90, 211
Winter, Marcus C., 10
winter house, 92–93
Wittry, Warren L., 152

women: and creation stories, 140; as potters,
    140, 181, 232
Wood River, 124
Woodstock phase (NW Georgia), 138
woodworking, 141
Works Progress Administration, 41
work teams, for wall-trench construction,
    142–43
world system, Indigenous, 192
Worth, John E., 182

Yaeger, Jason, 21–22, 81, 121
Yazoo Basin, northern, 63, 66, 76–77, 80

zoomorphic effigy pendants, 59–61